An Outstanding Haitian, Maurice Dartigue

An Outstanding Haitian, Maurice Dartigue

The Contribution of Maurice Dartigue in the Field of Education in Haiti, the United Nations, and UNESCO

Esther Dartigue

VANTAGE PRESS
New York

Published by Vantage Press, Inc.
516 West 34th Street, New York, New York 10001

Manufactured in the United States of America
ISBN: 0-533-10704-0

Library of Congress Catalog Card No.: 93-93972

0 9 8 7 6 5 4 3 2 1

To our son, John.

Contents

Foreword

Maurice Dartigue was the most enlightened minister of education Haiti has ever had. He was the only one with training and experience in the field, first as student, then as teacher, and later as director of rural education for ten years, before being appointed to the high office of minister of education by the president-elect, Elie Lescot, in May 1941. It is for these reasons Dartigue was able to carry out the extensive reforms that he thought essential for the social amelioration and national and racial rehabilitation of his disadvantaged compatriots.

In reference to these reforms, Charles Tardieu Dehoux in his book *L'Education en Haiti* states: "He was an upright and efficient administrator as well as an outstanding manager of human and material resources."

As minister, Dartigue held two other portfolios, that of agriculture and that of labor. Although education was his specialty, he had had training and experience in agriculture while a student and a graduate of the School of Agriculture and the Normal School at Damien. He was minister during the war years 1941–46. As such he was one of the three Haitian board members (the three others being Americans) of the Société Haitiano-Americaine pour le Developpement Agricole (SHADA), which was created to promote the welfare of the peasants in agriculture. However, due to the war, SHADA concentrated on putting thousands of acres of land into growing rubber for the war effort. This was not successful but devastated the lands and homes of the peasants. Dartigue defended the interests of his country when the American Rubber Corporation denied proper compensation for the lands destroyed.

The Lescot government fell in January 1946. Dartigue left the country. He was fortunate in finding a modest opening for the first UN General Assembly in New York in the fall of 1946. He rose to become senior specialist in education in the Trusteeship Department, which dealt with information and studies concerning trusteeships and non-self-governing territories.

Seconded to UNESCO (United Nations Educational, Scientific, and Cultural Organization) he distinguished himself in the manner in which he carried out missions and assignments as well as administering the division with its four units. It was the Congo crisis in July 1960 that was Dartigue's greatest challenge since he left Haiti. Here, as the first chief of the UNESCO Emergency Program, he showed his mettle. Amid insecurity and warring factions, surmounting difficulties of various kinds, he, with a very small team, not only kept the educational system afloat, but laid down the basis upon which the action of UNESCO would be built by those who followed him. He also was part of the consultative group set up to advise the chief of the Civil Operations in the Congo (ONUC). It was later considered that this activity was of more importance than the actual carrying out of the program.

On his return from this unusual mission, Dartigue's status was put into question as power politics came into play. When that was settled, he was given the task of creating the African Division, which came into being to come to the aid of the newly independent nations. He was its first chief. It was under his leadership that the first professionals from the freed African states made their entry into UNESCO.

During his whole career, in his quiet way, Dartigue tried to oppose racial discrimination and power politics where and when he could. He inspired and motivated those who worked with him or under his guidance to give the best of themselves in the common endeavor.

This book came about because, on looking through his private files after his death, and on doing research in Haiti at the UN and UNESCO archives, it became apparent that Dartigue's contribution should be recorded to give courage, determination, and inspiration to those who try to ameliorate the lives of the disadvantaged through education, with whatever means they have and wherever they can.

I wish to express my gratitude to the friends and others who, in various ways, helped me with this study. Special thanks go to our son, John, M. Jarvinen, chief of the UNESCO archives, and Carlos Pereira in Haiti.

Introduction

Before going on, it may be necessary to give a brief glimpse of the history and geography of Haiti. It is situated in the western third of the island of Hispaniola, bordered on the east by the Dominican Republic, between the Atlantic Ocean and the Caribbean Sea. Haiti's surface is 10,714 square miles or 27,750 square kilometers, and its population, which in the early twentieth century was about 3 million, is today more than 6 million. There are thus twice as many people living on the same amount of land, which has become poorer by constant use and lack of proper upkeep. Many Haitians live far below the poverty level.

The capital, Port-au-Prince, is built on the shores of the Gulf of La Gonâve, sheltered from the east by surrounding hills and protected from the west by the island of La Gonâve. Creole is the language of the people. French is the official language, taught in the schools and used by the bourgeoisie. The country, made up of coastal plains and mountains, was heavily wooded early in the century. Now, due to deforestation to make charcoal and objects for household use and exports, it is denuded, with its precious surface soil being washed down by the rains into the bay.

The climate is tropical except in the high hills, where frost can occur in the winter months. Although many peasants have drifted into the cities, agriculture still occupies more than 70 percent of the population, with coffee, sugarcane, corn, sisal, cotton, cocoa, tobacco, and rice being those most produced. There are no mineral resources except for some bauxite now almost exhausted. Actually, Haiti has become an importer of sugar and rice.

Discovered in 1492 by Christopher Columbus, the island of Hispaniola became one of Spain's important colonies. The efforts of Bartholomé Las Casas, a Spanish Dominican priest, to save the native Arawak Indians, decimated by forced labor, by replacing them with slaves imported from Africa did not succeed. The Arawaks died off, but the colony thrived on slave labor.

By the Treaty of Ryswick, signed in 1697, the island was divided between France and Spain. The French built Haiti into a prosperous colony, with products such as tobacco, ebony, and sugarcane. There arose an aristocracy of French and Creole planters. There also came about a special society of mulattoes and freed slaves, and a vast slave population. Relations with France deteriorated. Agitation of the colonists for autonomy broke out. In 1790 the slaves revolted against the colonists, with Toussaint L'Ouverture as their leader. By order of Napoléon, L'Ouverture was tricked and captured. He was sent to France, where he was imprisoned in the fort of Joux in the cold Jura Mountains. Here he died a few months later of chagrin and utter neglect. Jean-Jacques Dessalines, a black general, took up the cause. He chased away the French or had them murdered, tore the white out of the tricolored French flag, and proclaimed the independence of Haiti in 1804. Two years later, he was ambushed and killed. Another black general, Henri Cristophe, made himself king and later emperor in the north and ruled from 1811–20. Suffering from increasing paralysis and realizing that the people were coming to overthrow him, he took his life using a silver bullet (so it was said). His family dragged his body up to the Citadel La Ferrière to keep him from being torn to pieces by a populace tired of his excessive demands.

A republic was formed in the south under the presidency of Alexandre Petion (a mulatto educated in France), who stayed in office from 1807 until his death in 1818. Then General Jean Pierre Boyer became president, uniting the two parts of the island until 1843, when the eastern part (which was Spanish) broke away to become the Dominican Republic. Haiti, after becoming for a second time a so-called empire under Faustin Soulouque, finally chose to become a republic, troubled by civil wars and agricultural problems as well as a heavy debt imposed upon it by succeeding French governments as indemnities for losses incurred by the French colonists during the revolt for independence.

The lynching of President Guillaume Sam in July 1915 by the mob, after he had had massacred over 150 young political prisoners, provoked the intervention of the United States to protect its nationals and its investments. The United States occupied Haiti until July 1934, when the marines were withdrawn, leaving a few advisers for the army and the financial ministries.

An Outstanding Haitian, Maurice Dartigue

The Formative Years

Jean Joseph Maurice Dartigue was born in Cayes, Haiti, on March 14, 1903. The Dartigue family was mulatto and fairly well off. This permitted Maurice to carry on his studies at a private Catholic school and live the life of an adolescent without problems as a member of the bourgeoisie and later to enter the law in the footsteps of his father. Maurice's father, Jean Baptiste, better known as "Manto," was a lawyer as well as a proprietor of lands planted in sugarcane which, transformed into syrup, was then sold to the makers of rum and *tafia,* a strong, cheap alcohol drunk by the populace. From his union with Regina Duperval there were born four children: Thérèse; Renée; Jean Joseph, called Maurice; and Jehan-Sebastian.

In 1902 Manto was elected by popular vote as deputy for three years to represent the district of Cayes in the national legislature. He refused a second mandate. It may be that it is after this that he went to Panama to work on the building of the Panama Canal, as he stayed out of politics until 1912, when he accepted the post of governor for the south of Haiti (except Jeremie), which the president, Tancrede Auguste, proposed to him. This post Manto kept also under President Michel Oreste, who succeeded Auguste, who died in May 1913. Michel Oreste resigned in January 1914, and in February Oreste Zamor became president, to be destituted at the end of eight months. He asked Manto to replace him. Manto refused, saying he would not take office without being properly elected. It is then that he took his family to Curaçao, where he stayed for several months. Another president, Davelmar Théodore, was in power from November 1914 to March 1915, then Vilbrun Guillaume Sam from March 1915 to July 1915. In less than three years there had been five presidents. A historian wrote: "Permanent generalized anarchy is increasing each day. It is leading the country imperceptibly to the border of the abyss."

Manto returned with his family in August 1915 after the lynching of Guillaume Sam. The U.S. Army officer in charge of finding a president had Manto approached for this post. Manto, indignant, refused, saying, "I do not wish to be a puppet president."

Sudre Dartiguenave finally accepted the offer and stayed as president from August 1915 to June 1922. Under him Manto did accept the Ministry

1

of Agriculture and Public Works. However, he soon had misunderstandings with the president and returned to private practice as a lawyer in Cayes. His family remained in Port-au-Prince to permit the children to continue their studies. Manto came to stay with them two or three times a year but wrote every week giving recommendations for the children. (There were no telephones.) The trip on horseback took several days.

Manto gained a reputation as an orator and jurist. He was known for his honesty and integrity. Money was not everything for him; he never hesitated to help those of merit temporarily in need. Maurice also had these qualities.

Thérèse and Renée, like all young ladies of good families at that time, did not work; but when their father died in March 1924, six months after a stroke, their situation became precarious and they had to work. Manto had not had the time or the thought to provide for his family, even though he had a good practice. He did not always send bills, expecting his clients to honor their debts as he did. Unfortunately for the family, several of his clients never paid.

After the settlement of the estate there was a sum of $2,000, which Maurice, thinking of making a good investment, changed into German marks, which in a few months was lost in the succeeding devaluations of this money. Perhaps this hard lesson was the reason why for the rest of his life Maurice was wary of investing in stocks. He became an excellent administrator of his private funds and the public funds entrusted to him. The youngest of the four children, Jehan-Sebastian, was still a law student in 1930 when I became acquainted with Maurice.

Thérèse found a job as a clerk in a bank, and Renée gave lessons to children at home. Maurice, who was in his third year of law school, applied to enter the Central School of Agriculture, opened by the Americans in 1924 at Damien, a large domain several miles north of Port-au-Prince, offered by the Haitian government. While studying, he held a part-time job in the office of the American director, Carl Colvin, which helped to support the family.

A few words about myself. I was born on December 30, 1908, in Vizakna, Hungary, in the Transylvanian Alps, which became a part of Romania under the name of Sibelieu after the war of 1914–1918. I was the third of nine children. My father, Janos Reithoffer, having done his military service in the Balkans, which in 1913 were part of the Austro-Hungarian Empire, sensed the unrest of the people and on his return to Vizakna decided, in consultation with my mother, born Katalina Hassler, to immigrate to the

United States. According to local standards we were "well off," having two houses. One was sold to pay for our passage in "steerage." The other, two-storied, was to provide us a modest income in America. However, it became a refuge for the entire Hassler family during World War I, as the property was enclosed by a high wall. It was never rented and provided no income. We left in April 1914 via Trieste to join my father's brother and family in Cleveland, Ohio. The war broke out in August.

My father was one of the immigrants who did not succeed very well in the new world, and our growing-up years were quite difficult. To go on to high school and college, I worked for room and board in several homes but managed to stay in the same high school of Glenville, at that time mostly frequented by the surrounding middle-class Jewish families. It was at Wooster College in Wooster, Ohio, that I earned my B.A. degree in June 1930, in English literature and education. Besides working for my room and board by taking care of a young child afternoons, I also waited on tables in private homes, corrected papers for professors, worked in the library, etc. At Wooster it was obligatory to have a B average to be permitted to work.

After Wooster, though I had obtained a teaching position in a secondary school in Bowling Green, Ohio, I had also received a scholarship for Hartford Seminary in Connecticut, so I decided to continue my studies there. Between buses from Cleveland to Hartford, I had time to stop at Columbia University in New York City. Before the morning was over, I was registered at Teachers' College in the Department of Rural Education. My intention was to go to Lahore, India, as a teacher in a mission. Wooster College was Presbyterian and was connected with a mission in that part of India. I obtained a loan scholarship and a job for my room and board. It was in the rural education classes that I saw and came to know the young Haitian, Maurice Dartigue.

Back to him. After obtaining his degree in 1926, Dartigue continued his now full-time job as assistant to the American director of the Technical Service for Agriculture at Damien. This service included a school for training teachers for rural schools and a school to prepare agricultural agents, as well as experimental laboratories for plants and animals, a plantation, and distribution of cuttings, seeds, plants. There was also animal husbandry, etc. In 1931 its name was changed to the National Service for Agricultural Production and Rural Education, SNPA and ER.

The director recognized rapidly that Maurice was a man of value and was able to obtain a grant for him in 1927 and let him go for six months to

3

Teachers' College, Columbia University, for further training. Dartigue was fortunate enough to secure a room at the International House, which had opened in 1924 to receive American students, but also those of other countries—especially non-whites—because of the color problem at that time in the United States. Not all students would be as lucky and some had great difficulty in finding decent quarters at reasonable prices. As one of those, the son of a Ugandan chief, remarked bitterly, "To think that I am obliged because of my color to live in Harlem." Race prejudice and consideration of skin color were very strong even in New York City.

After six months Dartigue returned to Haiti and as a teacher gave courses at the Normal School for teachers of rural schools at Damien. In 1929 for eight months he took charge and directed Chatard, the only rural postprimary boarding school in Haiti, located near the town of Plaisance in the Puilboro Mountains on the road to the cape. This school was created by Allan Hulsizer, the American director of rural education in 1928; Maurice was its first director. The school was composed of a dormitory, classrooms, workshop, and plantation, where farm animals were raised. Thirty young boys followed the program in order to go on to study at Damien.

Dartigue's sense of responsibility revealed him to the Americans as a possible leader. He was given a second grant to return to finish his M.A. degree in rural education in the fall of 1930 at Teachers' College. It was then that we met.

Dartigue acquired his M.A. degree in February 1931. Before he returned to Haiti in late March to work, we decided to marry. Although the marriage was performed in strict privacy, somehow a Harlem newspaper learned of it and published an item stating that a Haitian had married a white student. At that time such an event was extremely rare. In the southern states it was forbidden by law. Cohabitation between whites and blacks could happen, marriages never. In the North such marriages were permitted but were the exception.

*   *   *

Maurice left for Haiti. I was to follow when I had obtained my M.A. degree, which I did in June of that year. However, having no money, I could not go to Haiti without earning some to pay for a few clothes and passage on a ship. I decided that the best and easiest way to build a nest egg was to find a job as a cook. This is what I had been doing to earn my room and board in a Union Seminary professor's home while studying. I do not remember how I found the job, but I did find one in the home of the dean of the Cathedral of Saint John the Divine in New York. The couple had an apartment in New York, a summer home in Massachusetts, and a property on the Hudson River. I enjoyed the experience. A student from Tallahassee cleaned and waited on the table, so I was not alone.

By November I had put aside enough money to pay my passage to Haiti. There I was cordially welcomed by Maurice's family and friends. Having had French in high school, I remembered enough to carry on a conversation. I was quickly accepted.

Because of the American occupation the Haitian upper class spoke only in French and refused to speak English. Moreover, there was little social intercourse between the Haitian and American families, except at the official level. The Haitians are a proud and dignified people and resented the American occupation.

*　　*　　*

When Maurice and I looked for a house in the hills surrounding Port-au-Prince to be out of the heat of the center of the town, which I could not bear, we found one in Pacot recently vacated by Americans. It had a living-dining area, two bedrooms, and a bathroom in which we installed an electric water heater, a great luxury on the salary Maurice received. A young maid helped with the household chores. I gave lessons in English to augment our income. The view from the front porch was unusual. We overlooked, at a distance, the Cul de Sac plain and the mountains beyond. The sunsets were superb.

Very quickly we became part of a group of Maurice's friends and their wives, several of whom, like myself, were foreigners from various countries of Europe. In Haiti such couples were not unusual, as monied families sent their sons to Europe for their higher studies and some returned home with brides. We went on picnics, walks, and excursions and to dances. I must say, although Maurice worked very hard and took his responsibilities seriously, he could relax; later, even as minister, he danced and chatted as if he had not a care in the world.

The death of his father and his studies at Damien completely changed Maurice's outlook on life and his future. His law studies would permit him to be knowledgeable about law matters. This would help him throughout

5

his career, especially when he became a functionary of UNESCO. The studies at Damien led him to a life of service for others in the realm of education not only in Haiti, but far beyond. However, in 1931 he was only interested in doing well in his job.

Director of Rural Education, 1931–41

The year 1931, in which Maurice returned to Haiti with his M.A. degree, saw the election of a new president, Stenio Vincent, a journalist. He would hold the presidency until May 1941. Maurice and I had a good relationship with the Vincents, especially with Stenio's sister, Resia, who became his hostess after she returned to Haiti from the United States, where she had taught French in private schools in New Jersey.

Maurice's office was in the building of the SNPA and ER at Damien. Maurice was named director of rural education. He was given the responsibility of managing not only the 72 farm schools created by the Americans, but also 224 rural schools, of which 43 were coeducational, transferred from the Ministry of Education to the Ministry of Agriculture, for better control. There were also the parochial schools but these were independent, linked only by the subsidies given by the rural education service. These schools were created by French priests in certain areas in virtue of an accord signed in 1913 with the Haitian government.

Maurice and one of his friends, André Liautaud, also trained at Teachers' College, directed the Department of Rural Education together for a time. They intended to introduce reforms to make education in the rural schools more practical by giving instruction in basic agriculture and simple practice in animal husbandry besides manual arts. They felt that the rural school programs were too theoretical and could not help to ameliorate the lives of the peasantry. More practical subjects were needed.

Before the American occupation there had been urban and some rural schools. Some existed in name only. The Americans were permitted to create the farm schools with their workshops and gardens. But they were not permitted to take on the rural schools, which were neglected in some areas, if they even existed, and over which there seemed little if any control by the Ministry of Public Instruction under which they had operated before the transfer.

The first thing Maurice and his very small team did was to make a survey to find out where the schools were, the kind of teachers they had, the number of children attending, and the material condition of the schools.

They called upon teachers of farm schools and others to aid in collecting the data.

They found very few rural schools in good condition. Some were used by the directors or teachers as their homes while the children were taught outdoors under a tree or an arbor. In a few schools the teacher had not come for months, the children being taught, if one can use the word, by an almost illiterate substitute. It was found that some teachers in these mostly one-room schools could hardly read or write. How could they teach when they themselves needed to be taught? There were supposed to be inspectors to control the schools, but often they did not know where the schools were or if they had ever existed. These "inspectors" drew their salaries, such as they were, and let it go at that.

The situation was really lamentable. Maurice himself took trips to the interior to ascertain the conditions. Until I had my own school I often went with him. We started out usually at 5:00 A.M. armed with sandwiches, drinking water, and extra gasoline, for there were no service stations in the interior. The roads were often bumpy.

Up to that time many teachers had been appointed through favoritism. Maurice instituted a simple examination that all those who did not have diplomas and those who were candidates for teaching posts had to take and pass. One day President Vincent telephoned my husband to tell him that he would like to recommend a man for a teaching post. Maurice replied, "No problem, Mr. President; all he has to do is come to Damien and take the test. If he passes he will have a job." The president had to accept this response, whether he liked it or not.

Maurice wanted above all to professionalize education, which meant hiring through competitive exams or proper credentials, thus moralizing the system and keeping politicians out. At the first examination, of the 500 candidates, mostly employed teachers, 229 men and 89 women did not pass and had to be dismissed, although there were not enough teachers to go around. There were very few coeducational schools. It was under Maurice's initiative, as he believed strongly in the education of women, that more classes for girls in either existing schools for boys or new ones were opened. Little by little the better-prepared teachers replaced the least competent, the irresponsible or undisciplined.

A year after the changes were made, when some renovations had taken place to turn the rural schools into the semblance of real schools, with as good teachers as could be had, regular hours, more appropriate programs, and a minimum of materials, one was impressed to see the whitewashed schoolrooms, some plants growing out in front, see the flagpole with the Haitian flag hoisted to the top, and hear a busy sound as one entered. Once we arrived at a school as the children were saluting the flag. We listened while they sang the national hymn. It made the heart glad. No uniforms were demanded. The burden would have been too great for peasant families. The important thing was to have the children come to school, shoes or no shoes.

Maurice and André put together a more efficient administration. They shut down schools that were not serving the population and united others to make for better materials and teaching. A census was taken. All the schools were pinpointed on a map, indicating the location of everyone. This was done by a statistician who had learned his job through experience and would go for four summer sessions to Teachers' College to earn a degree in statistics. Through the help of questionnaires sent to the rural schoolteachers as to pupil presence, grading, etc., he was able to put together a body of statistics for planning and finances as well as distribution of materials.

Certain schools had very little, if any, furniture. What there was, was in poor condition. In one school the children brought their own stools from home. One of the first things Maurice did was to have repaired or made school benches and desks, teachers' desks, cupboards, blackboards, and other necessary furnishings. The schoolhouses were repaired and repainted. Three schools were built by the peasants of the different localities using mud bricks or mud plaster.

Lessons concerning agriculture were introduced and shovels, rakes, hoes, hatchets, and machetes sent to those schools where there was enough land to have a school garden. Seeds and plants brought from Damien were also distributed in the various areas according to what could be grown.

The seventy-two farm schools created by the Americans were comparatively well equipped with proper furnishings, materials, workshop, and gardens. They also had the best teachers, graduates of the Normal School at Damien or the Normal School of Port-au-Prince.

To ameliorate the teaching, Maurice instituted summer courses centralized at the Normal School at Damien, the program of which had been reorganized to better prepare teachers and agricultural agents. These courses of fifteen days or a month were intensive. They dealt with questions of pedagogy, the utilization of manuals, administrative procedures, hygiene, sports, basic knowledge of agriculture, and social action in the community.

All these innovations Maurice carried on with perseverance. He was

9

determined to bring the changes about to show what the rural schools could be and do. He lightened the theoretical studies to include new subjects. Like his friend André Liautaud, Maurice knew that to have a good system one needed good teachers, good conditions, good programs, as well as good administrators and specialists to advise, encourage, and show the way.

Maurice spoke out against political interference and wrote articles in the newspapers to explain the necessity for the changes and innovations and what he was going to do with his collaborators. The politicians were obliged to accept the reforms and conditions, although with reluctance. Maurice did not hesitate to criticize the educated townspeople, some of the bourgeoisie, of which he was a part, reproaching them for their indifference toward the uneducated.

(I myself gave a conference in 1932 that was reported in the newspapers. I criticized the poor education being offered to the young ladies of the bourgeoisie and their total ignorance of the problems of their country. "Madame, Put on Your Gloves" was the heading of one of the newspapers reporting. I repeated my admiration for the women of the people, who very often carried alone the responsibility of raising a family. They had no ill will, for the most part, toward the fathers of their children. These Haitian women were and are people of great courage, fighting with and against misery and penury.)

One of my English friends, seeing a postcard representing a group of peasant women washing clothes by and in the river, was astonished that they seemed to be happy and merry. She asked, "How can they smile so with the kind of life they lead?" Because they take life as it is and make the best of it.

Maurice with his collaborators wanted to give his country schools that would better respond to the needs of its people. He first strove to assess the problems and understand them and then tried to resolve them.

From 1931 on Maurice and his staff produced a yearly report appearing as a bulletin under the aegis of the SNPA and ER to show what had been undertaken and what had been accomplished each year, letting be known also the disappointments and the difficulties. The bulletins were drawn up with data sent in from the schools, the supervisors, and the statisticians and Maurice's own observations and research. He discussed the projects, the finances, in fact, all areas of his administration. The reports were made public so that those who wished to do so could know what was being done in rural education and how the allotted budget was spent.

The bulletin contained several chapters: "Farm Schools," "Rural Schools," "In-Service Training," "Supervision," "The Post-Primary School at Chatard," "Housing and Land Services," "Finances," and "Recommendations." Later "The Normal School" and "The Agricultural School at Damien" were included.

Of course the bulletins differed from year to year, and if in 1931 and 1932 the bulletins announced projects successfully carried out, other years progress was slower. Maurice began the regular compiling of statistics in Haiti, believing them to be a very important part of school administration to ascertain present and future needs. Later in Congo-Zaire he would insist on setting up a bureau, as in Haiti, for the same reasons. In fact, how to conceive what must be done for the coming year if there are no statistics for guidance? Standardized testing was also introduced.

In the first bulletin appearing at the end of the 1931 school year Maurice wrote:

This is the first time that an organization has proceeded in an orderly, methodical, concise, honest fashion for the education of Haitians by Haitians.

He continued:

It is the first time that teachers are appointed through competitive examinations. It is the first time a president has taken a firm position in spite of attacks, to uphold the work of the education service. It is the first time there is a system based on a philosophy of education, on a science which takes into consideration the needs of the Haitian people. It is the first time young people are willing to spend their own money to study abroad to return better trained to help in the reforms . . .

For the first time, too, the state became a publisher of school manuals and published a number of classics destined for schools. In 1930 Maurice had published by the state a book he wrote titled *Problems of the Community*. As a preface to this book Maurice wrote:

The formation of useful citizens is one of the most important aims of education. For this the schools must develop in the child certain

11

essential qualities such as interest in the well-being of the community, civic ideals, practical knowledge of social institutions and the capacity to appreciate the means and proper methods to promote common well-being. In consequence, what we wish is not that the pupils learn well the lessons in civics, but that the pupils become capable of observing and thinking civically so as to be able to fill their role as members of a nation. . . .

In 1931, in collaboration with André Liautaud, Maurice wrote *Local Geography,* the first time that Haitian schoolchildren would learn about the geography of their own country before that of France.

Parent associations began to be created by the teachers with the rural school as the center. Maurice was convinced that the child could not be separated from his milieu and the school must come to the aid of the adults and the community, as they must come to the aid of the schools. He was of the opinion that the amelioration in the lives of the peasants would come about through the interaction of the school, the parents, and the community. He asked for a bigger budget to be able not only to raise the teachers' salaries and to build more schools, but also because he believed firmly in the education of girls, to augment the number of girls' sections and the recruitment of women teachers for these classes.

Maurice stated: "Progress, particularly social progress, is closely connected with the education of women." Thirteen sections for girls were added to the farm schools.

In 1932–33 the name of L'Ecole Centrale de l'Agriculture was changed to L'Ecole Pratique d'Agriculture. Maurice introduced the graduation ceremony with the giving of the diploma and the occasion to give a talk to send the graduates on their way. He emphasized that graduation was not so much an end as a beginning of a career in service of their country. Twenty-two of the thirty-two graduates that year were immediately given positions in the Department of Rural Education.

As to the budget, it was 793,786.50 gourdes (or $157,357.30), of which 54,144 gourdes went to the parochial schools. Almost 68 percent went for teachers' salaries. Supervision was about 6 percent, administration about 6 percent, surveillance, construction, repairs, and maintenance 4.74 percent, materials and furniture 4.05 percent, rentals 3.2 percent, the survey of the situation of the schools 0.69 percent, and summer courses 0.45 percent. Whatever was left Maurice put in a reserve fund for emergencies, grants, and future projects. As with his private budget, he put aside part of the allocated funds for unforeseen expenses.

In spite of a diminishing budget that necessitated the lowering of all salaries, including his own, due to the economic problems of the country, the Department of Rural Education was able to open six new rural schools, and attach eighteen sections for girls in the boys' rural schools. Two farm schools, one built by the Ministry of Public Works and the other offered by a priest, were created, making a total of seventy-four. Examinations were held for the recruitment of teachers. Each year there occurred vacancies due to illness, job changes, and sometimes death. During the year, circulars were sent to the schools containing information, suggestions for better ways of teaching, lists of parent associations, explanations of new laws, etc. Inspectors, appointed through competitive exams or chosen from among the best teachers, made the rounds in the schools in the region to which they had been assigned. They also came to Damien for consultations and meetings.

One of Maurice's preoccupations was the health of the teaching and administrative personnel, especially some of the teachers living in outlying regions in quite primitive conditions (in rare cases in real discomfort, with no electricity, no running water, and only a privy) and without easy access to provisions. Very often they felt completely cut off if they were the only professionals in the area. In some localities there was a church or a chapel with a priest in occasional or permanent residence and a worker in a field dispensary open on the same basis. With these people the teacher could exchange ideas. The roads in the interior, at that time, were of dirt, sometimes difficult to manage during the rainy season, as were the rivers. One teacher to have his pupils attend school set up a sort of dormitory in the workshop of his school in case rivers became too high for the children to cross. He set up a rudimentary kitchen to provide at least a meal of boiled sweet potatoes for those unable to go home. The visits of the inspector or the agricultural agent were special events. It must be remembered that very few people had cars and it was on foot or horseback or in trucks that people outside the cities went from one area to another. Very few teachers asked for time off, and if they did it was for malaria or dysentery. At this time, a rural school teacher was a missionary and evoked admiration for the sacrifices and privations faced. The teachers became very important in the surrounding country and the schools often the center of activities.

Little by little Maurice's idea that a good system of education for the masses could not be organized without technicians and specialists in the different branches of education and without a corps of teachers graduating from an adequately organized normal school was beginning to be accepted by a limited number of his class. He kept repeating that the teacher was the key to a good school, and for this training was essential.

It was a little later that mobile teams were composed and sent out to the various districts to stimulate and encourage the teachers, but the summer courses began as early as 1932. It was indispensable to ameliorate teaching. The best teachers after examinations were employed; they were far from well prepared, and in-service training was the only way open to improve methods and philosophy. Classes were held for women teachers, too.

In 1934, encouraged and aided by Maurice and André Liautaud, I opened a school with classes for three-year-olds and up through the elementary grades. We named it L'Ecole Moderne, hoping to attract parents ready to give up the rigid, set ways in which children were taught. This was the first nursery school as we know it today, with dollhouse, blocks, water play, dough, and clay, children choosing their activities, stories and rest times.

It was most difficult to find teachers with our ideas capable of teaching through centers of interest, not insisting on memorization, recitation, and dictation. Few parents were ready for this type of school, and some were poor payers. Moreover, it was hard to convince parents that their children were better off in our kind of school than in the others or staying at home with often ignorant maids. I did find one good teacher who made up in enthusiasm and initiative what she lacked in formal training. But I cannot say that the school was a big success. Nevertheless, it kept me very busy.

A little later the sister of the president of the republic, Resia Vincent, with whom I had formed a friendship, created a school for very poor girls and orphans of the peasantry or the city poor in a poor section of the city to prepare them to become maids, cooks, housekeepers, or seamstresses. Up to that time there was no such school. Young girls, usually from the country, were hired as domestics and for the most part not well treated. Some were not even given a room and had to sleep on mats under the staircase. Resia Vincent hoped to prepare girls for their future occupations, give them a trousseau on leaving, and have them placed in families that would provide properly for them. For this school she was able to obtain a group of five nuns of the Order of the Auxiliary of Jean Bosco, known as the Salesian Sisters. One of the original group is still living in Haiti. The school had a chapel, a dormitory of a hundred beds, a simple dining area used for many purposes, a large, simple kitchen, and a large laundry area. (I machine-hemmed dozens of sheets and nightgowns cut from bolts of muslin begged from dry goods stores.)

To supply a basic stable income Resia Vincent created a sports club on the far outskirts of Port-au-Prince in the area of Thor on the bay, on land offered by the government. She organized, with the help of friends, balls, dinners, and lotteries, to raise money to fit up the club with four tennis courts, a swimming pool, Ping-Pong or table tennis, a restaurant, a ballroom, and an enclosed (to be safe from sharks) bathing space in the bay. She searched for someone to manage the club of some three hundred members. Finally she asked me to take it on. For a time I carried on with my school and the club, but I decided for the latter, as my school gave less satisfaction than I had hoped. I also had to admit that there were not enough parents ready for my kind of school.

The club was at times very animated. We organized swimming competitions and tennis and Ping-Pong matches, as well as catering dinners and lunches. We even gave a lunch for over one thousand people—doctors and their wives from other countries who had been at a conference in Cuba invited by the Haitian doctors. It was quite a feat, but we brought it off. A fixed sum was sent to the school run by the Salesian Sisters. Maurice on weekends oversaw the gardeners' work as well as my accounts. He was a severe taskmaster, and I had to take care to have the books properly done. The fact that he managed the distance (as Thor was some miles south of Port-au-Prince and Damien about the same distance to the north), having to drive through the heart of the city in the heat and fumes in an open car, showed his stamina and endurance.

But back to Maurice's work as director of rural education, and the annual bulletins. In that of 1933–34 he invoked the important accomplishments, especially the increasing professionalism of his growing staff due to his obtaining grants for some of them each year for study abroad, mostly in the United States, from where most of the grants came, the summer courses at Damien for the teachers in service, the work of the inspectors, and the exams for the recruitment of new or more teachers.

It was that year that Maurice introduced the study of social sciences in the curriculum of the Normal School for rural schoolteachers and the Practical School of Agriculture, which had been transferred to his department. He wished to make the students more aware of the needs of the populace and the institutions at work in their behalf. The students were taken to visit in Port-au-Prince the police station, the hospital, the medical school, the barracks, the fire department, the prison, the courts of justice, the town hall, and the sugar factory. For agriculture, the experimental station at Damien was used. Each student was given a plot on which to plant his own garden. In the final semester they were sent to the best farm schools for practice teaching.

At Chatard, the students visited various institutions in Cape Haitian and paid their expenses to go to see the citadel. They also formed committees to keep the premises clean and a committee for student discipline. On Flag Day they joined the local parade at Plaisance with the flag at the head of the group.

Another contribution was the introduction of the study of education as a science. In Haiti a new conception of education was given birth. Maurice insisted that it be considered a mental development process and should take into consideration the child in its milieu: "Haitians must recognize that they do not have to accept the existing conditions but should become capable of changing them for the better." He also had installed a system of analytic accounting for the classification of expenditures to have a precise idea of the cost of the various activities of the rural education system he had put into being.

A most important event occurred in that year, 1934, just before the end of the American occupation. President Franklin Roosevelt came by ship to Cape Haitian on the north coast of the country to announce the departure of the occupying forces as a gesture of the "Good-Neighbor Policy." Maurice, as part of the government, was there. He went by car. Of course the president of Haiti, Stenio Vincent, hosted the reception in Roosevelt's honor. Fortunately for me, I was also present, due to the kindness of Resia Vincent, for whom a military plane had been offered so that she would not be tired from a twelve-hour hot and dusty road journey. She; Mme. Leon Laleau, the wife of the minister of foreign affairs; and I had the plane to ourselves and were in the cape within an hour.

Roosevelt came by car from the port. A ramp had been placed over the entrance steps of the reception hall to permit the president, who had had polio, to be wheeled up. With difficulty he was helped out of the car. Flanked by his two sons, one on either side, and wearing heavy leg braces, Roosevelt managed with great dignity to mount the ramp on foot. He filled us with great admiration. I can still picture him refusing his handicap, determined to enter the hall with all the solemnness of his role as president of the United States. It was most moving and impressive.

In 1943, Maurice, then minister of public instruction, agriculture and labor, had the honor and the pleasure of dining at the White House, when he accompanied President Lescot on an official visit to Canada, the United States, and Cuba. (Of this trip I will report further on.)

The American occupation ceased in July 1934, and most of the American functionaries and their families left. On this occasion Maurice wrote:

The Americans in departing have given over to us an efficient army, and admirable public services such as the Health and Hygiene Service, the Public Works, the Agricultural Service and the Farm schools as well as the Revenue and Financial Services. Now it is up to us to protect these services from political intervention, favoritism and anti-administrative and anti-governmental measures. So that discipline can be implanted in Haiti it should come from "above." On the other hand, the masses must be educated so that they can watch over to see that the services are run properly. If the masses are educated they will no longer accept seeing the roads they use deteriorate through lack of upkeep. They will no longer accept that hospitals and clinics cease to function, nor accept untrained doctors or nurses, nor illiterate teachers. They will see the difference between good and bad schools and will not tolerate the latter anymore. They no longer will permit their representatives to vote laws contrary to their interests. [Alas, these words did not have a lasting effect.]

But we are not there. The year 1934 was encouraging. The teachers through the various courses and the help of the inspectors understood their work better. They became more competent in the various aspects and subjects as well as in their activities in the communities.

It is of interest to note that the mean attendance in the rural schools was 14,727 pupils (11,073 boys and 3,654 girls) with a minimum of 12,761 in October and a maximum of 15,644 in June. However, this made for only 10 percent of the possible rural school population, which saddened Maurice, but the budget just did not permit the opening of more schools, nor were there enough teachers. There was also the problem of distances and/or rivers to cross or no roads, although in some areas with only narrow footpaths winding over the hills the peasants managed to go from place to place, although not in the rainy season. Maurice once on an inspection tour was determined to cross a swollen river to reach another school. For this he found a horse, which, led by a peasant who carried Maurice's clothes in a bundle on top of his head, was guided to the opposite side.

Testing became a yearly function. Maurice stated that without objective controls it is difficult to assess the effectiveness of teaching. The Bureau of Statistics and Research created by him prepared, administered and interpreted the tests. In the farm schools the advanced group went from 3.13 percent in 1931 to 15.58 percent in obtaining test scores of 70 out of 100 and those who made more than 50 came to 36.36 percent of the group. This was encouraging.

It was about this time that Maurice's brother, Jehan, obtained a grant from Cornell University, where he spent a year for training in agriculture. He returned to Damien later to become chief of one of the services. Maurice never favored his family in any way. Each had to make out for himself. Maurice shared with me some of his problems, and I did help him with the chapter on education in Haiti for the yearbook put out by the International Institute of Teachers' College. The book's title was *Education in Latin American Countries;* it was edited by I. L. Kandel and published in French, English, and Spanish. We put it together in early 1940. As it was on urban education, it presented a dark picture. It was published in 1942, when, through the reforms begun in the fall of 1941, the picture had already changed. (I never held a position in Maurice's service or any other government service. The Thorland Club, which I managed, was private.)

In *Bulletin no. 11* for 1935–36, Maurice notes that in general, progress was not as spectacular as back in 1931–32, but he was able to find grants to send eighteen supervisors and other employees to the United States to Teachers' College, Columbia University, where they were received for two months during the summer. These young people had not had the training to be accepted or registered as the usual Teachers' College students, mostly there to earn a master's degree or their doctorates in education. The Department of Rural Education at Teachers' College went out of its way to respond to the needs of this special group. It hired for the occasion such people as Allan Hulsizer, who had directed rural education in Haiti at Damien from 1927 to 1929 and spoke French. He was given leave from the U.S. Department of Indian Affairs to come to the aid of this group. Back of all this was Mabel Carney, director of the department, who had been so impressed with Maurice when he studied there and, through corresponding with him and me, was "au courant" with what he was trying to do in Haiti now that he had been given the opportunity to make changes and put into practice what he had seen, heard, and adapted to advance rural education. A few went at their own expense. With the knowledge acquired, these young people returned with renewed enthusiasm and desire to help in the educational endeavor.

The summer courses given in Haiti were varied and aroused interest. Among the subjects were theories of agriculture, singing, drawing, physical culture, methods of teaching, principles of education, manual arts such as weaving and basket making, and hygiene. Also discussed was how to teach reading. At this time the "global" method was introduced, that is, learning words as a whole rather than by phonetics, letters or syllables. (Not all children could learn by this method, but to Maurice it appeared a better method than the others.) Included also was how to administer the class, write monthly reports, and keep a register. Quite intensive, the courses helped to unify the system and professionalize the teachers. Moreover, they gave those attending the feeling that the administration cared about them and what they were trying to do. Perhaps these are the reasons why many gave of their best to encourage the education of the children in rural areas.

Despite the scarcity of funds, Maurice sent two women teachers to Puerto Rico. When they returned, they put together a domestic science program. In July, intensive courses for women teachers were organized. Supervisors had chosen these women. In the fall a written course in simple sewing was sent to the feminine sections of rural and farm schools. This was done for cooking, too, and in a few schools for child care. In one school a contest for the healthiest baby took place. Six women teachers were invited to gain practical experience in the maternity ward of the general hospital on Saturdays, as were the last-year pupils in one school. These were steps forward in the education of girls in the nonurban areas of Haiti.

But the most important event was the transfer of sixty-three small market town schools to the Department of Rural Education. So after the seventy-four farm schools and the more than 200 rural schools put under Maurice's direction, the sixty-three market town schools were added. As stated in the report,

There has been progress in the work of education undertaken by the government through the intermediary of the SNPA and ER, in its entrusting us with these schools. Not all are in accord with the reorganization because it deprives them of favoritism or nepotism. Teachers are appointed through competitive exams, outside of political interference, and they will no longer have the right to leave their schools to substitutes and use their time for political activities. School locales will be rented because of what they can offer to accommodate the work of the schools and not to accommodate the proprietor, whoever he may be. And yet it is just such things, that are very important aspects of the reforms, that attract approbation. The populations concerned have given their consent. The proof is that attendance has doubled since the reorganization. Another proof is that notables of certain small market towns where the schools have not been handed over to our department have tried to have the schools of their towns come under our control.

Maurice was reproached for trying to "ruralize" the schools of the small market towns. Here is the answer he gave to one of his critics:

One talks of "ruralization." But there is no question of that as the programs are not the same. Education must be adapted to the conditions of the milieu and to the needs of the children of the community. It is not "ruralization" but "haitianization" of these schools, that is, to give in these schools such education as to make the children feel their Haitianness. A Haitian program must be elaborated with books on Haiti written by Haitians and Haitian teachers (not foreign educators) so that the pupils can become conscious of who they are and where they belong individually, nationally and racially, and can develop confidence in the capacities and possibilities of our race, acquire necessary attitudes and proper methods to promote advancement and bring about a really national Haitian culture.

Maurice would also try to make Haitians understand that it was not a dishonor to work with one's hands, that book learning did not exclude manual arts:

This prejudice that exists among us against manual work in the country-side must be severely fought if we mean to come out definitely from the rut in which we have sunk for more than a century and enter in a serious fashion in the path of progress and of national independence under the political, economic and intellectual aspects of our national life.

At the same time, the teachers, in the rural areas where polygamy and concubinage were the way of life, tried to help the priests to persuade the people to adopt Christian marriages and monogamy. Several marriages were brought about and celebrated in church. In the same order of ideas, 2,887 children took First Communion from among those of the rural schools and 1,989 from among those of the schools of the small market towns.

In 1936, Maurice was able to send Haitian young people to the United States, among them a young lady of the bourgeoisie, Laura Nadal, her departure provoking an outcry. In effect it was the first time that a young female was to travel without a chaperone and in a group of young men! This young lady, perhaps twenty-eight or twenty-nine years old, had musical abilities and had studied music. At Teachers' College she trained in the teaching of music and allied subjects. On her return she became music supervisor for the rural schools and did very well. She helped the teachers enlarge their repertoires and demonstrated teaching methods, how to organize singing, etc. (The devotion to their work of all the returnees was remarkable. They were so grateful for having had the opportunity of studying abroad that they really worked hard to prove that the confidence placed in them had been justified. Only twice in the fifteen years that Maurice obtained grants was he disappointed. One of those grantees decided to stay in the United States and the other did not live up to the hope placed in him.)

As stated, Maurice introduced, besides music, manual arts and gardening, when possible, in the rural schools and those of the small market towns. Physical culture had been introduced in urban schools earlier, but not with a trained specialist. Maurice believed that physical culture should have a definite place in the program, carried out by someone who knew the procedure. For this he found a grant for a young man to study for a year in the States to come back to set up a good program, give demonstrations, and supervise. Later one of the women employees at Damien was able to go to Bryn Mawr College for Women. She went as far as the doctorate in social service and returned to be of great help to Maurice and the department in organizing programs and get-togethers for mothers to discuss child care, simple hygiene, domestic science, etc.

Little by little the number of parent associations grew. Maurice hoped they would link the school, the parents, and the community closer together. There were evening meetings during which new laws concerning the peasantry and people of small towns were explained, agricultural problems, problems of animal husbandry, and the sale of produce discussed, but also counseling on health problems offered. More and more teachers with the pupils and sometimes some parents worked together to clean up swamps, clean and extend irrigation canals or roadside ditches, and/or ameliorate and beautify the public grounds or parents' homes. They renovated chapels (163) and built privies (63), as well as repaired parts of the main road after the rains. They also prepared for and took part in the national holiday activities. They even put on amateur theatricals—and, so important, they distributed plants, seedlings, and cuttings sent from Damien such as banana, coconut, cotton, and vegetable seeds. The school became more and more the center of the area. Volleyball was introduced. Other sports, begun by the teachers, were carried on as leisure activities among the villagers.

Here is part of an article concerning the teachers written by Maurice Lubin for a newspaper in 1972 or 1973, when we returned to Haiti after an absence of fifteen years (for Maurice):

> These young educators did not stay inside the walls of their schools. They drained ponds, repaired the roads, built culverts, made coffins and furniture, took up local cottage industries, gave first aid to the victims of accidents if there was no dispensary. They tried to teach the principles of the rational culture of the land and organized healthy leisure-time activities. Basketball and volleyball, both newly introduced in the country, were played. They put on simple plays, short comedies, or readings.

Homage was paid to this ardent generation in this article, which went on to say:

> One saw them everywhere, these young educators, in the mountains, on the plains and in the valleys, braving the inclement weather, organizing rural gatherings, sensitizing the populations so that they could understand and take part in a way of living that was better than the old way.

It was really remarkable, all that Maurice with his growing team was able to accomplish, for it was very important to give birth to cooperative living. The cultural web of the countryside was enriched in this way. People got to know each other better and began to feel that they belonged to a developing group and were on the move from the static, do-nothing, narrow ways of before. The primary school, with its devoted, energetic teachers, showed the way.

But as Maurice wrote in one of his reports, "Just at the moment when because of the amelioration of the training of the personnel, our capacities for realizing further projects have augmented, our budget has been seriously amputated. We could paraphrase the words of the Gospel. The workers are here and ready but there are no instruments for the harvesting." Anyone else would have been completely discouraged. Maurice refused to be discouraged and fought on.

It was in 1936 that Maurice wrote a short bulletin titled *The Work of Rural Education Accomplished by the Government of President Vincent 1931–36*. It gave Maurice the occasion to summarize what he had tried to do and perhaps plead his cause for more funds. He discussed the takeover of the rural schools, the training of technical executive personnel, the reorganization of the Central School of Agriculture, the amelioration of the farm schools, the new philosophy in action, and the transfer of the small market town schools.

A foreign educator wrote: "Your service should be highly congratulated for the beginning of practical education in Haiti. Having been able to organize primary public schools in the interest of the country has been, I know, a formidable effort. I think you have an extraordinary institution at Damien. Your work in research at the institute and the supervision in the schools are, I believe, things of the first importance for a republic such as Haiti."

In spite of the financial difficulties, he and his staff did not spare themselves. He explained:

We have been able to keep the schools functioning because of the ingenuity of more than one, and the adhering to strict economy. We were also able to make better arrangements in certain schools, but the compression of the budget has been difficult to bear. Our service was given 63 more schools to manage and yet our budget has been cut. We were to have more inspectors but the same number as before must now supervise the new schools too. And the furniture, the school materials, without mentioning salaries—how to raise those of the teachers who have so merited raises?

Maurice also noted in one of his reports: "If important realizations have come about much remains to be done." And this is what he proposed:

(1) absolute necessity to augment funds to supply farm tools, school materials, furniture as well as money for more inspectors so that more constant supervision can be carried out; (2) the creation of two professional schools of Agriculture for those finishing their studies in the Farm schools; (3) the creation of a Normal School for women to teach in rural schools; (4) the obtaining of a grant for someone to be trained abroad in rural cottage industries; (5) the sending abroad of two women now in rural education for further study; (6) the sending of two technicians of the personnel of the department of supervision; (7) augmentation of the budget to raise salaries all along the line. It goes without saying that the cut of 5 percent taken out of salaries should be restored; (8) studies should be made of school construction without neglecting the repairs to be made on existing premises. [He was determined to persist even against the odds.]

Moreover, there were crippling droughts in some areas in 1936–37 so that school gardens died. One teacher was able to build an irrigation canal and revive his school garden. The surrounding peasants, seeing the results, begged the teacher to help them build canals. From 1936 Maurice, with the help of the agricultural agents, put emphasis on reforestation and the planting of trees on the plains. A yearly Tree Day ceremony was instituted. Due to the economic difficulties and the drought, school attendance fell temporarily. Due to absences throughout the school years some pupils as old as fourteen were no further than the third year.

After special study of almost a year, an agronomist became inspector-instructor for the teaching of principles of agriculture in the schools. He was to go from school to school to help the teachers to improve educational methods. Trials were made in some schools to grow new plants. Maurice hoped that this would be a beginning of improving the basic methods of farming. However, no sooner had the agronomist been named than he was transferred to one of the newly created agricultural colonies established in various parts of the country.

By going begging to the Ministry of Public Works, Maurice was able to obtain 10,000 gourdes for repairing certain school buildings.

In 1938, bang, the government handed over thirty-nine communal schools to the rural education service. These were reorganized, as had been the rural schools and the sixty-three schools in the small market towns. Maurice took this in his stride. The reason behind the government's move could be taken either as a compliment for the way Maurice managed the rural education service or as a provocation to see just how much he could take and succeed. Maurice still had to keep on giving subsidies to the parochial schools over which he had no control and in which he could not take a hand at reorganizing and it was a burden to give this money from his meager funds.

It was only in January 1939 that the reorganization of the thirty-nine communal schools could take place, as the money promised was not given until then. Even that money was too little to pay all the expenses necessitated for teacher salaries, furniture, repairs, material, and administration. Personnel had to be hired to handle this new task. After exams for the hiring of teachers, those selected were given an intensive course of fifteen days of training to initiate them to ways of keeping records and guides to the program. The supervisor worked hard to prepare them for their responsibilities, etc. Therefore, 1938–39 did not see certain projects undertaken or carried out in those activities which Maurice most encouraged—agriculture and manual arts—for lack of money.

Maurice's work was a battle every minute. Among other things, it was imperative that he find better-trained women teachers so that such subjects as hygiene, first aid, domestic science, weaving, and basket making could be better taught. The school could not be improved if the personnel was not better prepared. Even basic classical instruction suffered from lack of books and materials. Maurice was afraid that the pupils, once they left school, would return to illiteracy if they were not well taught and did not have access to a library. He also wanted to preserve the national folklore and develop a culture starting from the indigenous culture through the publishing of folktales, the gathering of songs, choreography, etc., but he found himself frustrated from the lack of personnel and funds. Even the instruction in the Practical School of Agriculture necessitated more financial means, which it did not have, for work in the laboratories and the library and on the plantation.

The most vexing circumstance was that the rural education service budget was reduced in February 1938 by 35,410 gourdes[1] while, at the same time, the budget of the Ministry of Public Instruction, which controlled the urban schools, was raised by 200,000 gourdes, although 90 percent of the population at that time was rural. Maurice, determined to carry on, declared, "However, in spite of the lack of money, in spite of difficulties of every kind, we will not let ourselves be discouraged. We are continuing to progress in what we have undertaken. We have been able to obtain some results and some improvements."

He pointed out that there were far more rural than urban schools and the fact that because the rural schools were dispersed and some quite far away they engendered far more expense to supervise and provide materials for, too. Just the price for the transport of both men and provisions took a great deal from the budget. Yet these distant schools had to be considered and provided for. Besides, the teaching of principles of agriculture, manual arts, and domestic science cost more than the teaching of the usual subjects. He added:

> And 56,120 gourdes of the budget goes to the parochial schools leaving 992,372 gourdes for all the other schools outside the Farm schools. Of the 85,402 gourdes foreseen for the communal schools only 59,480 gourdes were put at the disposal of the service. The cost per capita in the Farm schools is about 57 gourdes, in the small market town schools it is 38 gourdes and in the rural schools only 33 gourdes. Anyone with an idea of school finance and school administration can judge the situation with which we are confronted.

Only two employees could be sent abroad.

What is so extraordinary is that Maurice was able to do as much as he did with the small budget he had. It is for this reason that foreigners who visited the various types of schools, learning about the small amount of money earmarked for his service, were astonished, not to say filled with admiration, at what he was able to get done. One such was Charles Loram of Yale University, who visited the schools with a group of twenty-five students from Yale. He said, "With that amount we could not have done a tenth of what you have done." And to Mabel Carney, director of the Department of Rural Education at Teachers' College, Loram wrote, "Maurice is one of the ablest educators today. You may be proud to have helped in his training."

During that year Maurice carried out a study with the help of volunteers, teachers, older students, and supervisors on 884 rural families titled *Conditions Rurales en Haiti,* published by the State Press as *Bulletin no. 13* of the SNPA and ER. It was the first such study ever done in Haiti. He admitted that it was not the most scientific study, but it did take into account all the realities of the rural areas: finances, agriculture, economy, animal husbandry, customs, and *plaçage,* a special custom of concubinage that may be of interest to outsiders.

Although it was rare, a man could have up to eight common-law wives who took care of the various bits of farmland he had in several localities. It was not a question of being a profligate but a way to manage the properties: the women were "placed" on the different lands for which they had the entire responsibility. This made for a sort of matriarchy. The "placed" woman had all the rights and duties of a wife, especially as concerns fidelity. The woman was the head of the hut in a particular locality, and it was she who brought up their children. There was one man named Ti-Joe who had nine common law wives who among them gave him fifty-four children. Most men were monogamous even when not married.

This system of *plaçage* was accepted, and the demand for the woman was as formal as for a marriage. It is a custom that in 1992 is still carried on in some parts of the country.

In the *Bulletin no. 27,* brought out for the year 1939–40, it is stated that the work done that year was not as impressive as the years before, but that through experience and counseling the technical value of the personnel had increased and that the methods to help resolve the Haitian rural education problems had been pursued with vigor and perseverance.

To find grants to send students abroad was a veritable fight, but finally three were able to go to work for the master's degree, so that the number of the team having that degree rose to eight. Most of the others had earned B.A. or B.S. degrees.

It must be kept in mind that these were the first college-trained personnel in educational matters, as there was no higher-training institution of education in Haiti. There existed a school of engineering, a medical school, a school for dentistry, and a law school. These will be referred to later.

For the first time the giving of diplomas was introduced at Chatard, the postprimary boarding school. Maurice felt that those finishing and not going on to Damien to either the Practical School of Agriculture or the Normal School for rural schoolteachers should at least obtain a degree of knowledge in the three R's and in the other subjects that Chatard offered such as agriculture, animal husbandry, maintenance of tools, ideas of

27

construction, weaving, and basketry. He hoped they would go back to pass on their know-how in the areas from which they had come.

Of course the ever-present problem of money took up much of Maurice's time. How could he do all that needed to be done, all that he wanted so much to do and have done, if the money that was essential was not allocated? In 1936 there had been 19,036 pupils in the schools. Now in 1939–40 there were 22,369, yet the budget, which should have been augmented, was, on the contrary, diminished. Maurice became a juggler of the budget, not always knowing from where to take how much to put into something else.

He was determined, wisely or not, to put up a farm school for girls with domestic science in all its phases, the raising of livestock, gardening, and manual arts being taught along with the three R's. It was to be a boarding school, and 100 girls from all over the country were selected from among the best in the girls' sections of the rural and farm schools to attend. He was enthusiastic about this venture. He was fortunate to have found enough good teachers and a directress to manage it. The establishment functioned somewhat like Chatard with its dormitory, classrooms, workshop, plantation, and animals.

In the same year President Vincent created a special school in Cape Haitian. It was called La Maison Populaire de l'Education and was a sort of primary technical school for less privileged boys. It had its own budget. The control and responsibility of managing it was given to the Department of Rural Education, which meant more work for Maurice and his staff. Did the answer Maurice gave to President Vincent back in 1931 concerning a protégé the president wanted hired and the management of the schools of the rural areas and the small market towns convince the president that here was a man of integrity, honest, capable, and responsible, for whom each new task was a challenge that he would meet to the best of his ability? At all events, the two new schools were not long in showing their importance and producing results.

Maurice learned of the growing demands for cordage and baskets of all sorts as well as coconut braids in the United States, due to the disturbances in the production of these caused by the oncoming war in Poland, Czechoslovakia, and Romania. He established projects in certain schools for the fabrication of these necessities, also made from bamboo, sisal and other grasses, and leaves. By teaching the art of producing these, Maurice hoped to increase the income of the peasants. He searched for local plants that could be used in this way, all this through the schools.

One of the possible difficulties for the export of the products was that those producing the handmade objects were not used to standardization. There always had been basketry, but it is doubtful if any two baskets were exactly alike. Now whimsy and irregularities could not be accepted. Maurice pressed for standardization. Orders began to come from the United States. Exports of these products began in August 1940. Maurice wrote: "Certain measures must be taken to protect the workers and the standardization as well as the regulation of prices, the control of the raw materials and the rhythm of production and especially the advantageous sale of the products for the benefit of the workers."

From 1932 on, the parent associations did not cease to multiply, and many functioned quite well considering how and with whom they were formed. It was the first experience of working together for the betterment of all for most of those taking part. Never before had they been called upon to give of themselves for the school and the community. In 1939 there were 458 schools (mostly one-room schools) functioning throughout the rural areas in all categories.

A constant concern was the amelioration of the facilities and offerings of the Practical School of Agriculture and the Normal School for rural schoolteachers. Each year there were repairs, of course, and the small planting areas for the students' own gardens were increased and a rural school was created for observation and demonstration. As elsewhere, the teaching of manual arts was part of the program (work with the hands as well as the head), but the head, too, was not neglected. There was an excellent group of Haitian professors teaching in these two schools. Most had degrees from universities in the United States or Europe. They also did research on soil, plants, and animals. They were a stimulating team. Damien at that time was a busy place.

Maurice tried hard to better the library at Damien and to increase attendance. He felt there were not enough books, pamphlets, reviews, and newspapers, so he set up the mechanism for the exchange of information with various schools in the United States. He also encouraged Haitian authors to donate their works, as well as books written about Haiti. In this way the library grew in the number of written works it had to offer. Naturally all the research and studies in the various laboratories and activities of the

SNPA and ER were placed in the library, too, as the depositary. He hoped more and more students would use it.

In 1939 Maurice himself added to the library with his short study *L'Enseignement en Haiti* (Education in Haiti), a book on the history of education since Haiti's independence. He also wrote articles to defend his program and explain it. Among others he wrote "Why Our Methods Are Good," "The Concept of Education," "Education and General Intelligence," and "Some Aspects of the Haitian Educational Problem." He also wrote a few articles concerning why modern languages were more important than Greek or Latin and stating that Greek and Latin should be optional and not obligatory in the secondary school program. He also insisted that the teaching of the sciences was indispensable in today's world.

Incidentally, it was planned that I take a trip to Paris in the summer of 1939. I had learned so much about the literature of France that I was eager to see and be in this capital where so many of the Haitians I had come to know had steeped themselves in French culture. In fact, some of the Haitian upper-class women were far more interested in what was going on in France than in Haiti. They ordered the latest French books, magazines, and newspapers. Few paid attention to the problems at hand. I criticized them for this but did appreciate the French culture they had acquired. However, Maurice sensed that war would soon erupt. Instead I went to the summer courses held at Laval University in Quebec, Canada.

The school year 1940–41 would be Maurice's last as director of rural education. He had fought for ten years to have accepted the idea that professional training was essential if one wanted to direct and occupy oneself in the different branches of such a service as education. He also fought for better-trained teachers and appointments through competitive exams, without political influence or pressure. He fought for a school program that contained not only the classic studies, but the more practical subjects such as those he had introduced. He had put together the mobile teams to go to the various districts to give demonstrations and help the teachers arrange their programs. He tried to inculcate the feeling of belonging to a nation, pride in being a Haitian, and the idea that one could ameliorate one's milieu and one's own lot through education. It was said he was authoritarian, but he had to be; otherwise he could not have accomplished that which he had decided to undertake. Knowing the character weaknesses of some of his countrymen, he succeeded through his demands and requirements in having them give the best of themselves. He also appreciated their efforts and their devotion. In the 1941 bulletin he wrote: "The enthusiasm, the goodwill of the administrative and teaching personnel of the Department of Rural Education during this decade especially that of 1940–41 have made up for the insufficiency of allocated funds. But there is a limit beyond which these factors can no longer be counted upon. They can only do so much." He was always conscious that only 10 percent of the possible school population was in school. He said that this number was not great enough to bring change to rural life.

A few words about the three establishments created, two by Maurice and one by President Vincent—the farm school for girls at Martissant, the Center of Apprenticeship for Trades at Saint Martin, also near Port-au-Prince, and La Maison Populaire de l'Education. All three recruited their pupils from the poorest sections of the population and prepared them, with mostly practical courses, to be able to go out and gain a livelihood on finishing school.

It was in 1940 that an exposition of manual arts of the rural, farm, and small market town schools, as well as Martissant, Saint Martin, La Maison Populaire de l'Education, the Practical School of Agriculture, and the Normal School for rural schoolteachers was organized by the Department of Rural Education. For the first time the general public was given the opportunity to see what had been achieved in this area of endeavor. The minister of agriculture, Luc Fouché, was surprised at the many different objects of wood, clay, cloth, metal, and grasses, some quite simple, some having taken time and reflection to create, that were exposed.

This minister accepted Maurice's ideas. Not all did. For whatever reason, one minister, Dumarsais Estimé, was not helpful. In fact, he seemed to try to discourage Maurice by questioning his actions constantly. Maurice spent precious time going to see him to explain, because of rumors and newspaper criticism. Another was the Belgian director of SNPA and ER brought in by the government after the departure of the Americans. This agronomist made verbal promises he did not keep. Here Maurice had to take the time to confirm by writing what had been consented to, although the men were in the same building at Damien. Each project and demand was questioned. After the Belgian's departure it was a friend, at the same time a rival, a Haitian agronomist, who headed the SNPA and ER. A friend since youth, Georges Heraux, would create problems when Maurice became his minister.

Of course each time one tries to innovate there is criticism. Maurice

31

did not escape this rule. The criticism came from politicians of all ranks and a few of the bourgeoisie. Apart from the articles, Maurice did not waste his time answering these. He said, "The work should speak for itself. If the critics took the time to understand what I am trying to do and come and see for themselves, they would change their minds." He developed his ideas and prepared for the future. His constructive spirit appeared wherever he was able to express his views. In such dailies as the *Haiti Journal, Le Matin,* and *Les Echos,* he discussed such things as the mobilization of the youth in service for the country and the use of Creole in the first two years of primary school. Articles did appear by others in favor of his books and what he was trying to do. But as some of these were job seekers, Maurice was wary of the compliments. There was one newspaper, *Le Nouvelliste,* that criticized most of what he did, especially after he became minister.

A few of the activities that went on in the period 1939–40 need mentioning. Maurice reported that he had not been able to raise salaries of some rural schoolteachers. This bothered him. Moreover, because the rural families were so poor the schools supplied pencils and paper and some books, but he did not know how long he could keep this up. Basketmaking was catching on. He hoped that someday a demonstration school could be set up in each of the fifteen rural school districts with a national program of home economics and teachers would come to them for further training.

By 1939–40, 127 parent groups had been formed. Teachers also formed youth groups for activities in school and out. There were 144 of these, including the Boy Scouts. Social and civil activities were carried on.

In 1940 Maurice organized the third conference on education of the Caribbean countries. He had been in Puerto Rico as a delegate in 1939. The conference was cordial, and as we were living at Thorland, I invited the delegates to the club, although they had little time to relax.

It was also at this time that Maurice and I searched to buy a house in the hills of Port-au-Prince. The hills rose on two sides back of Port-au-Prince away from the center where the bourgeoisie had lived before. Land became available on the hills above the center of the city, which had taken root during the time of the early French colony. We found a property in the area called Turgeau, near one of the sources of the water that was piped into the city. On it we had built a simple two-storey house that had a living/dining room, terrace, carport, and kitchen on the ground floor and three bedrooms of different sizes and one bath upstairs. There was a magnificent view of the bay and the mountains. In the spring of 1940 we moved in, and it was there our son, Joseph Maurice Jean Frederik, was born on September 12, 1940. He Americanized his name to John and is now an American citizen living in Los Angeles, California.

A few years before Maurice and I had bought two hectares (about 5 acres) of land in the mountains, several hours by car and horse (at that time) from town in an unspoiled area called Furcy, where peasants lived and a few city people had built small, simple houses as summer homes. We were fortunate in that the Americans were selling a very simple structure made of sheet iron and mosquito wiring, with a wooden floor. This we bought for seventy-five dollars and had it dismantled and carried over the hills on the heads of peasants to the property where it was rebuilt. The mosquito wiring was replaced by more sheet iron, and windows were inserted. There was no running water. Both the shower and the toilet were outdoors. The cottage consisted of two rooms and a primitive kitchenette, with most cooking being done outdoors. The view in the mornings toward the mountains higher up called Morne La Selle was breathtaking. Not able to stand the heat of town, I went up as often as possible. The primitiveness of the small house and the surrounding area of woods and hills was a restorative from the heat and demands of life in the city.

Before leaving this period of ten years, 1931–41, I would like to evoke a few souvenirs. Maurice took me to see historic sights in the north of Haiti such as the Citadel La Ferrière, built by the self-proclaimed king and later emperor Christophe, who also created a nobility, with an etiquette based on the French royal court. This disappeared at his death in 1820. That period was portrayed in the play called *La Tragedie du Roi Christophe* (The Tragedy of King Christophe), written by Aimé Cesaire from the French Antilles, an eminent poet, playwright, and professor. (More about him later.) We also visited the "baths" built for Pauline Bonaparte, who spent some time in Cape Haitian when her husband, the general Leclerc, was sent by Napoléon to Haiti to put down the rebellion of the slaves.

We also were able to go to the Dominican Republic in 1933 through the kindness of a dear friend, André Chevalier—later ambassador to that country—when a military plane was put at his disposal by the president of the Dominican Republic, Rafael Trujillo Molina. There we visited various sights, most impressive of which was the metal or wooden trunk of Christopher Columbus kept in the main cathedral in Ciudad Trujillo.

From February through April 1941, Maurice was invited by the United States government, certainly by the Department of Latin American Affairs,

33

through Richard Pattee, who was attached to that service and had met Maurice in Puerto Rico. Maurice visited the Indian reservations in Minnesota and South Dakota to observe the activities carried on that might be of interest for schools in Haiti.

In *Bulletin no. 31* (1940–41), Maurice made a resumé in a few lines of the work he and his group undertook and carried out for rural education. He recalled that he had found, on his return in 1931, the seventy-two farm schools created by the Americans. Immediately were added the more than two hundred rural schools. From the very beginning it demanded a constant effort. It was the first time that a man of his caliber, with his kind of training and experience, headed the service. One must add that he had deep convictions for which he was willing to go to battle. He fought inertia, lack of discipline, irresponsibility, political recommendations and incompetence. He worked ceaselessly to eradicate these. He tried to base promotion on merit. He showed that it was necessary to try to do something, even if it was not always successful. He strove to motivate his colleagues and staff to greater efforts to help the population without a veritable structure to improve its condition through education, which, he thought, was the only way to do it.

Maurice severely condemned negligence and mediocrity. He fired several hundred so-called teachers who were supposedly teaching in nonexistent schools or who had hired substitutes to teach while they did something else, as well as the constantly absent ones. Of course those who were then deprived of their sinecures hated Maurice, and he acquired many enemies. He was menaced several times. Once when we stopped in our car he said, "Duck your head." He then slowly restarted the car and calmly drove on. I asked him why he had told me to duck. He answered, "A man on the opposite corner was aiming this way, and I did not want you to be hurt." Did the man not shoot because I was with Maurice?

Faced with someone higher in the ranks than he was (director of SNPA and ER, ministers, or the president of Haiti) Maurice showed his force of character and defended his belief that only through reforms in education such as he was introducing could there be a process of development.

Maurice knew what had to be done and how it could be done. He had acquired a philosophy and had learned the principles and the methodology of education. He knew his country and how far he could go, which is why he used basically the same strategy from the beginning as each new group of schools was handed over to his department—survey analyses, plans, and reforms begun. He quickly understood the needs of the schools not only as to personnel, but also as to furnishings, furniture, teaching materials, etc. He could not obtain all he needed but did the best he could and far more than anyone had done before him. He also made the best of the teaching personnel who, even of those chosen through examination, were not highly qualified.

That was one of the reasons for Maurice's creating the mobile teams mentioned earlier. Moreover, he insisted on the summer courses, when a group of teachers was brought together in a certain town of a district for fifteen days or more. I visited one such group with Maurice. It was held in Fort Liberté, near the Dominican border in the north. Living under primitive conditions, this group was still enthusiastic and willing to participate.

In the last bulletin appearing while he was still the director of rural education, Maurice was not afraid to judge his own actions. He stated:

It has not been possible to extend, which everyone would have wanted, and which without a doubt is necessary, the work undertaken since 1931 and carried on since with obstinacy. The educational problem is badly posed because the benefits of an education have not been extended beyond a minority of the population. This struggle against ignorance cannot suffice to launch the country on the road to development and progress. The highest number of attendance was in May 1941. It was 35,508 pupils when there should have been 400,000 corresponding to the school population of the several districts of Haiti.

However, one can measure the progress accomplished in a year compared with the year before.

Some interesting statistics: All rural schools put together had 32,824 pupils in 444 schools, with 13,519 pupils in the rural schools, 9,375 pupils in the farm schools, 6,404 pupils in the small market town schools, 2,496 pupils in the communal schools, and 1,030 pupils in the schools put up in the *colonies agricoles* (agricultural colonies) created for the refugees of the massacre of the cane cutters committed in the Dominican Republic, of which I shall speak later.

To this total must be added the 150 children of the Maison Populaire of Cape Haitian, 130 pupils at the Center of Apprenticeship for Trades at Saint Martin, 100 girls at the special farm school at Martissant, 20 students at the Practical School of Agriculture, 20 in the normal school section, and

22 at the boarding school of Chatard, the total being 33,266 pupils, excluding students of private and parochial schools.

The number of inspector-supervisors increased from 8 in 1931 to 15 in 1941, some being supervisors of special subjects. The number of teachers went from 408 to 667. However, the budget was not significantly augmented. In 1940 it was brought back to 830,794 gourdes, which was approximately the budget back in 1932–33, instead of the 1,038,798 foreseen.

Charles Tardieu Dehoux wrote in the dissertation he prepared for his doctorate in 1986:

> Maurice Dartigue accomplished in the course of ten years as director of education for the non-urban schools much more than any other for Haitian education. Dartigue's performance contains a mixture of three points from which emerge the educational policy. Dartigue thought out a coherent philosophy of education in general, a philosophy that guided his actions. He was a competent technician, who had a scientific approach to reality, and no action was envisioned, let alone initiated, without a preliminary survey or investigation. Finally Dartigue showed himself a tested administrator of high integrity, a manager without peer as concerns human and material resources.

I have taken the time to evoke Maurice's philosophy and his interest in promoting the cooperative life of the rural areas. I also wish to recall the School of the Agricultural Colonies set up quickly to accommodate the children of the refugees fleeing from the massacre of the Haitian sugarcane cutters in the Dominican Republic.

General Trujillo, president of the Dominican Republic, had an obsession concerning color. At least, this was the rumor. The Dominican population was on the whole a lighter shade than the Haitian population. Trujillo objected that the Haitian cane cutters, all black, wished to stay on in his country once the sugarcane had been cut. In 1937, a great number of these people resided in the republic, ignoring the accords signed by the governments. A similar accord had been made with Cuba, but Cuba was much farther away and with a sea in between. Haiti and the Dominican Republic were land neighbors with some unguarded frontiers. Infiltration was much easier. Too many Haitians, besides the cane cutters, chose to settle there. Instead of negotiating with the government of Haiti, Trujillo in a sudden raid had many killed, more than three thousand at the minimum. Some put it as high as fifteen thousand. To keep from being killed, hundreds fled across the border into Haiti. Confronted with this sudden influx, the Haitian government quickly set up agricultural colonies to organize the repatriation and open schools for the children. André Liautaud was appointed director of the colonies. I think there were five. Several specialists in the Department of Rural Education were also transferred without Maurice's being informed or consulted. These transfers provoked disorder in his services and in his allocated budget. In a letter to the director of SNPA and ER he made a formal protest.

When Maurice returned from his trip to the Indian reservations in the United States in the spring of 1941 he little thought that in a few weeks' time he would be asked to serve in the ministerial cabinet of the newly elected president, Elie Lescot.

Note

1. One gourde at the time was worth twenty cents; five gourdes equaled a dollar and was exchanged without difficulty.

Minister of Public Instruction

Public Instruction—The Educational Reforms

Whether it was the Americans who convinced Stenio Vincent not to run for another term, since he had already held the presidential office for almost ten years, or whether President Vincent decided it was time to give up the post, he let it be known that he would not run again. I still can recall the suspense in which we all were until he made up his mind definitely.

Several candidates appeared, among them Elie Lescot, ambassador of Haiti to the United States. He had also been ambassador to the Dominican Republic, so he had the backing of the two governments. On one of his visits to Haiti during the campaign, Lescot toured the interior of the country. He was much impressed by the farm schools, whitewashed, ornamental plants in front, a flagpole and a garden on both sides of the paths leading to the entrances of the schools. He asked, "Who is responsible?" The answer: "Maurice Dartigue." Lescot received the same impression on visiting the rural schools and even, on a much simpler scale, the small market town schools. When told each time that it was Dartigue's service that was behind all this, he said, "If I become president it is this man I will choose to be the minister of public instruction." He kept his word.

Just three months or so before the elections, the post of the undersecretary for agriculture became vacant. Georges Heraux, of whom I have already spoken, came to ask my husband if he was going to try for the job. (The incident occurred at a charity ball at Thorland. We were seated at a table, so I took part in the conversation.) Maurice answered, "I will not ask for the job. If I am needed, it is known where I can be reached." George Heraux presented himself and became the undersecretary for the short time until the elections. Had he then hoped to become the minister for agriculture?

At the National Archives of the United States, where I did research in the spring of 1991, I found a confidential note sent by the chargé d'affaires stationed in Haiti to the State Department concerning the makeup of the newly elected (May 15, 1941) president's cabinet. For the other ministers mention was made of whether they were married or not, had children or not, but for Maurice, the following statement was made: "A young intelligent man married to a *white* woman. He would probably cooperate." (author's emphasis) A mixed marriage was so unusual for Americans at that time that the chargé d'affaires felt it necessary to mention this fact. As to the cooperation, there would be limits as to how far Maurice would be willing to cooperate.

So Maurice became minister of the three portfolios: public instruction, agriculture, and labor. He would be the only minister who would remain in the cabinet from the beginning to the end of Lescot's presidency, but after November 1945 Maurice would give up the ministry of public instruction and keep agriculture and labor. As minister of public instruction, he became responsible for the urban schools, but as minister of agriculture he kept under his control not only rural education, but the entire SNPA and ER, of which Georges Heraux became director.

Considering rural education first, the fact that Maurice vacated the directorship of the service caused changes all along the line. André Liautaud succeeded him but in a short time was named to the post of undersecretary for finance, and a year later posted to Washington as ambassador. Then Oscar Boisgris was installed as director for the time that Maurice held the office of minister of public instruction. He did his best.

Due to the possible effects of the war in Europe on Haiti and to offset shortages of one kind or another, special projects were undertaken in the two schools, that of Saint Martin and Martissant for the fabrication of soap and bricks, vegetable oil production, workshops for spinning cotton, etc. The 4-H clubs (Head, Hand, Heart, and Health), so well known in the rural areas of the United States, were adopted and adapted for Haiti. These, too, did useful work between the school and the community.

Due to the expanding war and the extension of SHADA, which involved the destruction of a large number of farms and plantations and of which more later, importance was given to the planting in the school and village gardens of corn, sorghum, sweet potatoes, manioc, and beans, all mainstays of the rural population.

From 1941 on through the war, difficulties of several kinds arose for the teachers and inspectors, including transportation problems and galloping prices. For the inspectors there was an added burden, the hiring of new teachers because SHADA siphoned off some of the old teachers by offering them better salaries. The new teachers did not have the experience, the philosophy, or the methods that the rural education service, especially the inspectors, had succeeded in inculcating. They worked hard to initiate those newly recruited. Even among them there were transfers, job changes permitting the better-experienced teachers to accede to inspectorship, but they in turn needed help.

Unfortunately, not everyone responded with pleasure to all the demands. A few complained of the extra work and time put into planning, preparation, and the schedule. That is why Maurice wrote an article in one of the newspapers, *The Septentrion,* in which he stated: " . . . One cannot work on a farm only from 8 A.M. to 1 P.M. One cannot do research working only from 8 A.M. to 1 P.M. One cannot develop an educational system working from 8 A.M. to 1 P.M. One cannot seriously organize or ameliorate an administration working just from 8 A.M. to 1 P.M. We should banish laziness. The keyword of the day should be work, stubborn work, intelligent and efficient work."

The many changes severely disturbed the smooth running of the rural education service. It was for this reason perhaps, among others, that Maurice called upon his mentor and friend of his early career, Allan Hulsizer, now in the Department of Indian Affairs, to come to Haiti for two years as a senior adviser at Damien, where he had been from 1927 to 1929, to overlook, suggest, advise, smooth misunderstandings, and show a good way out of a difficult situation. He was objective, devoted, and interested. He brought modifications to the program and methods at the Practical School of Agriculture and the Normal School. But some in the service resented his presence.

The national holiday of May 1 in 1943 was exceptional for the schools. It was celebrated at Damien in the presence of the president of the republic. The celebration took on the aspect of a fair. Prizes were given for the best animals (peasants had brought sheep, cows, pigs, fowl, and goats from far and near), the best farm products, and the best in carving, embroidery, basketry, pottery, and even furniture. Prizes were also given to the winners of school sports events. A number of schools were represented, as were the upper schools at Damien and the schools at Chatard, Saint Martin, and Martissant. The public had been invited, and many visitors showed up. The director of a private secondary school in Port-au-Prince was so enthusiastic that he offered a grant to a student who on finishing his studies would go back to work in the community from which he came.

Because of all the changes, as stated, the inspector-instructors had much more to do. At times they were called upon to work with their hands to help repair school furniture and make blackboards, small ovens for clay work, molds for the making of bricks, simple bake ovens, etc. They also visited the notables of the area in order to obtain playing fields and possible permits to put up schools.

In spite of these various changes and upsets, the administrative services managed. The central bureau sent out circulars and leaflets especially to help the new teachers. The more experienced inspectors gave help to the recently hired ones. A magazine called *The Rural Teacher* was founded. In it appeared articles on aids in methods, school programs, suggestions, extracts, original contributions, news, etc. The number of school canteens, the plant nurseries, and the raising of chickens, rabbits, and goats progressed.

In 1943 Maurice offered the police the school at Saint Martin so that courses could be given to rural chiefs of sections to give them a basic training for greater knowledge of their duties and responsibilities. The instructors were from the army or the police.

Under Maurice's guidance even greater effort was put into growing food products, as well as encouraging basketry and weaving of different grasses. He looked for new markets for the sale of these products.

Students from Damien were sent to SHADA for apprenticeship in basketry. Eleven pupils from rural schools were sent to Saint Martin for six months to learn the manual art so as to return to their communities to help the school to diffuse the technique. That year Saint Martin housed 100 students but also held classes for 65 externs. At Saint Martin there were built by its students 43 looms and 100 spinning wheels. In the feminine sections of the rural schools, domestic science and principles of child care were important parts of the program.

The specialists in the various fields of the central bureau of rural education made their rounds, being more often in the field than at the bureau, to second the mobile teams, the inspector-instructors, and often the teachers, since so many at each level had less experience than those who had left.

After four years of summer courses forty-three male teachers and seven female teachers of rural schools received diplomas. The determination and perseverance of these teachers, especially the women, were exemplary. Special courses were organized for all the inspector-instructors of primary education.

It was in January 1944 that the reorganized Normal School for women to teach in primary schools was opened in Martissant. The former Normal School had been closed soon after Maurice became minister. He felt that the program was outdated. (It had not changed since 1915.) Moreover, most of the young ladies attending did not go on to teach. It was more like a finishing school, for up to that time, until Maurice opened the first one, there was no secondary school for girls. There were no manual arts except embroidery, no observation nor any practice teaching. Teachers were needed. A more useful normal school was needed. By putting the school on the outskirts and making it into a boarding school, it would respond to the real needs and have as its students young women who would go into teaching as a career. Until a Haitian woman was trained to direct it, an American woman of experience offered by the U.S. government was called in. This was loudly criticized. There was such a fear of Americanization, it was almost a phobia.

Maurice had the former locale of the Normal School transformed into the first "lycée," or secondary school, for girls ever in Haiti, thus permitting its graduates to go on to higher studies after obtaining the baccalaureate. Very few young women had it, and the very few who did acquired it through private tutoring and permission to take the examinations or through study abroad (very, very rare). Ambitious young women would now have the chance to be on a par with the young men of Haiti.

Who would have thought during the years 1941–46 that several of the staff trained under Maurice in rural education and the ministry would be called upon in 1961 by him to go to the Congo (Zaire) as professors and/or administrators to help in the reorganization of education in that country? The first twenty-nine of them included Oscar Boisgris, the statistician and later director already cited, and Abelard Desenclos, as well as Ludovic Bourand, who with great conscientiousness and honesty handled the budget and finances. Recruited by UNESCO, they proved what trained Haitians could do. The team formed by Maurice showed they could meet the exigencies of an international organization such as UNESCO and demonstrated that training can be a trump card for all the developing countries.

In 1943 thirty-two teachers took the weaving and basketry courses at SHADA. Others (ten men and eight women teachers) took the summer courses at Damien. In September fifty-seven teachers of secular and parochial schools took courses in clay work, drawing, and bookbinding to introduce these manual arts in their schools. This was a feather in Maurice's cap, as parochial schools were not obliged to do this.

Salaries were raised. Money had to be found to continue in-service training. Change was noted. In effect, here and there it was ascertained that efforts were being made by teachers to further themselves from old methods of "book learning" to vary and ameliorate the program by making room for arts and crafts. The classroom became more informal, with groups doing different things and the teachers busy with one or the other, rather than the teacher in front with the children staring at him or her or all bent over their desks with pencil and paper or sharing the few books. It is necessary to say "here and there," for not all teachers were willing or able to change. Sometimes conditions did not lend themselves to change. Moreover, as stated earlier, this kind of teaching took much more planning, preparation, and exertion. However, change did come about.

The Reforms in the Urban Schools

The rural schools and the rural education service have been discussed first because of the changes caused by Maurice's being named minister and leaving this service. As he became not only minister of public instruction, but also minister of agriculture, under whose control the rural education service functioned, it seemed appropriate to continue to discuss this area of endeavor. But as will be recognized, it would be the urban schools that would take up much of his time. The urban schools needed reforms, which he would carry out, and urban schools would cause the greatest and constant criticism by some of those who had been to school, had acquired a certain status, were articulate, and felt satisfied with the status quo, that is, the classical, so-called humanist studies that met the needs of fewer than 10 percent of the population.

When Maurice was appointed minister of public instruction, a pharmacist friend said, "Tell him to leave things as they are; have him keep the status quo." My reply was: "Not if I know my husband! That is, I am sure just what he is *not* going to do. There are too many things that need changing."

Very little is known about public schools in Haiti before 1848, but in that year, when Honoré Féry became the first minister of public instruction, three town and three rural schools, all nonpaying, were created. The number of public primary schools grew. In 1941 there was a certain structure of administration of these schools. There were 499 teachers in 134 schools functioning in various numbers in 39 cities and towns throughout the country.

Two months after his being named, Maurice sent the president-elect a plan. It consisted of four steps.

The *first step* included the following points:

(1) The elimination of the service of general inspection, as it in no way contributed to the improvement of education and cost the state 28,000 gourdes.

(2) The fusion of the Normal School for Men with the one at Damien to become one good school, since that normal school had been built on a solid basis and had good professors and a well-adapted program.

(3) The schools in the small market towns still under the control of the urban education service (which made possible direct political interference) being placed under another service (more outcries of ruralization).

(4) Suppression of two lycées (which had been created for friends of politicians) and the giving of grants for the best students who would be admitted to the lycée of either Gonaives or Port-au-Prince.

The *second step* included:

(1) The nomination and training of competent personnel.

(2) Sending the best inspectors and teachers to the United States for summer courses in July and August.

(3) The establishment of a budget for the training of teachers and specialists in the different educational and administrative branches so that the Normal School, especially its teachers, would be of a higher level.

The *third step* concerned itself with:

(1) School construction.

(2) The buying and providing of adequate school supplies.

(3) The making of proper school furniture, repairs, etc.

The *fourth step* involved:

(1) The reform of programs and methods of teaching in the urban public schools.
(2) The teaching of manual arts and civic and moral instruction not only in theory, but also in practice. Maurice urged the change from "brain cramming" to the encouragement of reflection and real understanding.
(3) The modification of the program of the Normal School for young women situated in Port-au-Prince. (This has been referred to earlier.)

President Elie Lescot accepted these proposals, and Maurice started to carry out the plan. He had the support of the president throughout.

The Primary Schools

First, as he had proceeded in rural education, Maurice had a survey made. For this important task he formed a directional committee consisting of himself, André Liautaud, M. Latortue, Oscar Boisgris, R. Dreyfus, and Mme. Comhaire Sylvaim, all of them personnel of the rural education service. In pairs or alone, they took charge of an area, in some cases with added members. The investigation took into consideration the physical condition of the schools, the attendance and administration, and, even more important, a simple test for aspiring candidates, the same sort of test as that of the first certificate test given at the end of primary grades. Information was also needed as to how the teachers were distributed and their competence. Maurice said, "The teacher makes the school. If the teachers are incapable, have little culture and no training, if they have no enthusiasm or professional ethics and are not guided by an educational philosophy to which they adhere, there will not be real schools, and the money provided for them will be a total loss."

The survey showed that almost half the schools were in a poor state. Moreover, most belonged to private proprietors. The best rooms were usually taken by the directress or teacher. (Most of the urban schools were taught and directed by women.) Half the school benches were for one or two and at most for three pupils, yet often occupied by five children. Most of the benches, like all the other school furniture, were old, if they existed

45

at all. Walls were empty and classrooms unattractive. Most of the black-boards needed blackening.

As to the school materials, most of the children attending the 134 public primary schools were from needy families, so they could not buy the minimum necessary for school work. "It," Maurice said, "was up to the state to provide this." Yet according to the direction and teaching staffs of these schools, first, the little given by the authorities was unequally distributed and if the material were divided among the 134 schools having over 13,000 children it meant 2 boxes of chalk, 5 pencils, 24 notebooks, 3 pens, and less than two small bottles of ink for each school. As to books, 4 arithmetic texts and 2 geographies had been received. The few books used were imported mostly from France and not meaningful to young Haitians. Those were the sad facts.

As to the teachers, of the 499 teachers only 138 women and men teachers had normal school diplomas. Five had certificates of pedagogic aptitude of secondary school level and 72 did come from the post-primary Catholic School of Elie Dubois, where they had taken courses in pedagogy. Altogether 306 teachers had studied—the equivalent of a certificate of the sixth-grade level through the last year of high school—but no one had courses in teaching.

Those teachers not among the 306 mentioned were given a very simple test. One hundred and fifty-eight took the exam. (Eighty-one refused or pleaded illness.) Of those, 126, or 78 percent, obtained 50 or less out of a possible 100. Only 6 had a higher score than 70. There were 24 who understood nothing. What picture would the 81 not taking the test give? The survey stated: "This is the ransom of politics and administrative negligence. It explains many things. If there were no other teachers, it is half an excuse. But there are teachers trained at the State's expense who are anxious to be employed." There were more serious charges mentioned that proved how necessary the survey was.

Another anomaly revealed was the unequal distribution of teachers. In one school there were fourteen teachers for about sixty pupils; in another, ten teachers for the same number. "If one estimates that it is usual that a teacher have a class of 21 pupils one can judge the situation. The department of public instruction has become the department of social service or assistance," wrote Maurice. The incompetent and least-prepared needed dismissal; then for those who remained salaries could be raised, and thus better teachers would be attracted. Not only that; in the schools with such teacher-pupil ratios one would think that the results at the certificate exams would be brilliant. Not in the least, because the so-called teachers were so ill prepared to teach.

On the results of the survey measures were taken immediately. Maurice, as he had done with the cleaning up of the rural school situation, instituted hiring through examination. He insisted on the taking of attendance, the enforcement of a regular schedule, discipline, and teacher self-discipline. School buildings and furniture were repaired. School materials were sent, as were explanatory pamphlets, to help initiate the teachers as to how the new system worked. Useless posts were eliminated, some personnel transferred. There was apprehension, confusion, and problems with these last measures. Meetings were held to explain the change and answer questions.

In the summer of 1942 a certain number of teachers took the summer courses organized for them. These included Psychology, Methodology, Principles of Education, Manual Arts, Principles of Home Economy, Child Care, Physical Culture, and Ethnology. The teachers were taken to visit Damien, Martissant, and the Museum of Ethnology. Of course this one month of intensive courses was far from enough, as Maurice himself admitted, but he hoped that the courses could give the teachers a certain idea of what teaching involved and open their eyes to the seriousness, the complexity, and the importance of their chosen profession. Ten apprentice teachers in their last year at the School of Elie Dubois also attended.

Maurice reasoned that it was essential to put the public primary schools on a solid and serious basis. He insisted that the primary school constituted the foundation of the educational system; not only because for children going on to further studies primary studies were a requirement, but also, he noted, because for the majority it was all the schooling they would have. Therefore, it was imperative to give the pupils a minimum of knowledge: "Moreover, it is in the primary school that a common culture is engendered, and a social and national solidarity is inculcated." His aim was not only to have the three R's taught and learned, but also to have developed in all citizens a common base of habits, ideas, and ideals.

At the same time Maurice and his collaborators proposed to reorganize the whole administrative structure of the general direction of urban education. At the head of the different services would be placed as qualified a specialist as could be found at that time in Haiti. A corps of inspectors, serious and as familiar as possible with the principles and methods of modern education, would be chosen, but the number reduced to be able to pay better salaries and expenses. The division of the large towns into zones and the fusion of the very small schools into a larger one in the same zone were carried out. Among other changes, a new program was to be created to better respond to the children's needs, a better way of teaching promoted. Other points have already been discussed, and through the annual reports that he had made for urban education as he had for rural education Maurice noted what had been accomplished.

Time was taken to discuss the survey and the steps initiated to ameliorate the situation. What the survey also showed was what the education ministers before Maurice had not done. In some measure this must have upset these men, who, although they had had the opportunity to do so, either dared not or didn't possess the know-how to attack the problems.

So in October 1941 changes took place. Repairs were begun; materials were sent to the schools. Flags were hoisted, with the same salute and hymn as in the rural schools. The teachers were gratified to receive so much material. Some exclaimed that they had never seen so much.

One of the most important realizations was the raising of salaries. The lowest were raised from fifty to sixty gourdes a month. Maurice meant to raise them every year if he could, to encourage and motivate the teachers. He also put in a research and statistic service in the various sections of the department.

Maurice probably hurt feelings when he reorganized the service of inspection. Up to that time the inspectors for the most part had been given the posts through favoritism. It is true that some were educated men, even doctors and lawyers, but they knew little of the work the post implied and had no pedagogical competence. From July 1941 on, inspectors were selected after examination of their curricula vitae and their experience and without political recommendation, a decision that honored the president. In this service, too, Maurice insisted on a schedule, regular visits, and reports. He held a meeting in January 1942 to give the new inspectors directives and in July 1942 gathered them together for a month's course at Damien. At the head of the urban primary school department he appointed a specialist, Morriseau Leroy, trained at Teachers' College, Columbia University.

Some physical education had been introduced by a former minister, but a program had not been systematically organized. A specialist was put in charge. The teachers came together in groups to be initiated in means and methods. In the summer courses begun in 1942, physical culture had its place in the program. The teachers were asked to carry out a simple program of exercises and games.

Some of what has been written above concerning the program put in action was gleaned from the first annual report put out by Maurice and his services. The title of the report was *The Results of the First Year of the Reform 1941–1942*. In it is discussed activities of the various sections of the Department of Urban Education.

The Trade Schools

Noting that the primary schools were showing signs of revival and progress, Maurice and his collaborators attacked the schools where trades were taught. Of course a survey and investigation were first made. There were two such schools in Port-au-Prince: L'Ecole Central des Arts et des Metiers (Central School of Arts and Trades) and the school of J. B. Damier. There was a trade school in each of the following cities: Cape Haitian, Cayes, Jeremie, Gonaive, and Jacmel. It was found that even in these schools there was no fixed program and that the machines donated and placed by the Americans before 1934 were unusable. They had been left to rust. They were neglected and even ignored. Most lessons had been in theory. The teachers who were supposed to teach and handle the machines were incompetent. Some had no manual capacities and yet they had been employed. As to tools for woodworking, leather and metal work, there were almost none.

The Central School housed 110 boarding students. Although the food was adequate and good, the students slept on straw mats spread on the floor. The showers and toilets were in very poor condition. Immediately beds and bedding were bought and repairs made to the showers and toilets.

In a certain sense the trade schools were more difficult to reorganize than the primary urban schools, as the teachers here had to know how to man the machines and show they had mastered the art of the trades they taught, as well as have a well-planned program of development. Moreover, the materials, the tools, and the machines were much more expensive and were difficult to obtain, as more and more shipping was disturbed due to the war (with the sinking of ships by enemy U-boats), which pushed prices up. Only a very small group could be taught at one time at any machine.

The schools were closed temporarily except the Central School (because of boarders) in order to reorganize, repair what could be repaired, and replace what had to be replaced if a real program was to go on. The incompetent teachers were dismissed; the others were sent to the Salesian Brothers School of Trades to take their trade courses for six months. The directors who were serious and capable of being trained were sent to Hampton and Tuskegee, higher-training schools in the United States. Because of the cost of the machines for teaching, not all trades were to be taught in all the schools. A study was made to learn what trades were the most needed so as to provide for them.

Five young men were chosen (one from each geographical department of Haiti) to take courses in the United States in carpentry and woodwork, masonry, electricity, plumbing, and electrical installations. In Haiti most of these trades had been taught through apprenticeship—learning by doing only. A young sculptor in wood also was sent to Hampton, then to an art school in New York City.

The same procedure was carried out for the school of J. B. Damier and those in the other towns. It is certain that with all the fervor of change around them the teachers must have been worried that their daily routines would be completely disturbed. They understood that if they wanted to keep their posts they would have to work much harder, really know their subjects, and keep learning and perfecting themselves; otherwise they would have to look for another job. Perhaps this was one of the reasons that there were negative reactions in some quarters.

The schools were reopened on the return of the four directors of the trade schools and the teachers from the courses they had taken with the Salesian Brothers and as soon as the necessary equipment was ready in the schools. Before the schools were opened, a meeting took place in Port-au-Prince with the directors to study measures to guarantee the proper functioning of these establishments. Here are some of the measures: Only students having a certificate of having finished primary studies would be accepted. (Formerly boys with almost no schooling, if any, were entered. With no background and no education it was difficult for them to follow the program.) Only properly equipped workshops would be used; schedules would be adhered to; administrative controls would be regularly made, as well as the taking of an inventory at regular intervals. From now on the schools were to give a seriously thought-out training.

Secondary Education

As the reforms in the primary schools were encouraging, Maurice looked into conditions in the secondary schools. It was at this level in these schools that the "elite" was formed, through classical studies of French origin, with Latin and Greek as essential parts of the studies.

In March 1942 a survey was launched (as for all the other types of schools that had come under Maurice's control) to learn how and with what kind of teachers they functioned, how the teachers were recruited, their competence, the state of the premises, the pedagogical methods employed, and the way the schools worked in general.

The first measures recommended in July 1942 were the following:

(1) The dismissal of all teachers who had not finished their secondary school studies, except those who through personal study and recognized efforts had acquired a high degree of culture.
(2) The dismissal of the incompetent teachers and those who were notoriously undisciplined.
(3) Suppression of certain posts, such as that of tutor, to be replaced by substitutes with certain duties who could step in during absences of the titulary instructors and eventually be named to a permanent post when a vacancy occurred.
(4) The appointment of an assistant director to second the director.
(5) The appointment of teachers through competitive examinations or curricula vitae.
(6) The sending abroad of the lycée directors for more training for at least six months.
(7) Special courses to be given to the teachers and grants for study abroad for specialization.
(8) The organization of the schedule and work of the teachers for more efficiency.

Program and Methods Where possible, the subjects were to be grouped in sections or departments for more efficiency. A committee of specialists for the elaboration of a new program and a better-structured organization of secondary education would be formed not later than November 1942. Only the "B" sections (Latin and sciences) in the lycées in the provinces would be maintained and better teaching methods for the learning of English

51

and later of Spanish would be introduced. A special place in the new program was to be accorded for the study of civics, the study of the geography and history of Haiti, then the study of North and South America. The buildings and grounds were to be repaired and enough materials acquired for teaching, including laboratories for physical and natural sciences.

The Realization of the Objectives All that was recommended as concerns the personnel was carried out except for those teachers who were near retirement and were kept so that they would receive their pensions. Those tutoring were replaced by substitutes. The recruitment for these posts was done through competition. Promotions were given based on merit and seniority and not automatically nor through favoritism or political influence. That is why those who had sinecures and were articulate began to write against the reforms.

All salaries at all levels were raised. One of the important objectives was to have a one-month course of in-service training during the summer for all teachers in the public secondary schools, with foreign professors and Haitian specialists (more on this later).

In the provinces, Section "A" (literature, Greek and Latin), judged too literary, was replaced by Section "B" and by Section "C" in Jacmel and Cape Haitian. The students who desired Section "A" were to be sent to Port-au-Prince to study. The subjects' being regrouped permitted the teachers to specialize in one of the subjects, such as natural or social sciences, mathematics, etc. The study of natural sciences was encouraged by the setting up of simple laboratories in the lycées of Cape Haitian, Gonaive, Jacmel, and Jeremie. The ones in Port-au-Prince were refitted. It was in 1943 that a businessman, Oswald Brandt, donated $10,000 to build and equip a new laboratory for the Lycée Petion. It was the first time that such a gesture had been made for the amelioration of education in Haiti. At its opening he was thanked by Maurice in the name of the government at an official ceremony.

The study of English was made obligatory by a decree issued on March 30, 1942. Maurice hoped that the study of Spanish would become more common. It seemed reasonable to include these languages in the curriculum with the United States and Canada (bilingual) to the north and Latin America (apart from Brazil) to the south and west, not to speak of the next-door neighbor the Dominican Republic and Cuba across the Windward Passage. True, French was and is the official language and the language of the educated class, but this fact did not need to exclude the other two languages. Even in the forties there were already sufficient contacts, especially with the United States, to warrant the teaching of these languages.

Thanks to the Office of Coordination of Inter-American Affairs of the United States, an accord was signed between the Haitian and American governments through a department of this branch of the U.S. State Department, the Inter-American Educational Foundation, to have a mission of American teachers come for from one to three years to help train Haitian teachers to better teach English. The head of this mission was Mercer Cook. He became a life-long friend, as did his wife, Vashti. Later he would become the first Afro-American to head the Voice of America in Paris and one of the first such to represent the United States as ambassador to Mali and then to Senegal after the independence of those countries. We renewed contacts with them in Paris and Senegal.

One of the American teachers taking part in this mission was Dewitt Peters. He may have been a teacher of English in this circumstance, but his real profession was that of a painter, a watercolorist. It is he who discovered the unrecognized natural artistic talents of the Haitian people. He resigned from the mission and put all his efforts into creating an art center. He interested a group of young, educated Haitians, artists and others, to work for this project. This is the origin of Haitian naive or primitive art. The group either was sent or came on its own to ask Maurice for financial aid. From his budget he took funds to pay the rental of a large house in the center of town for the Centre d'Art. It opened in 1944. Dewitt Peters headed it for many years. The center is still active and has encouraged and nurtured not only primitive but modern painting, as well as sculpture in wood, stone, and metal. It was only in 1989, with the second edition of the book *Haitian Arts (La Peinture Haitienne)* published by Nathan in Paris and put together by Marie José Nadal and Gerald Bloncourt, that Maurice's gesture was acknowledged.

Back to the American mission. It carried out its program. At its termination it produced booklets consisting of excerpts of American literature, which were distributed to the Haitian teachers of English for use in their classes. Some of the Haitian teachers went to the United States for study for short periods. (With the growth of tourism, use of American English progressed among the populace and later the increasing exodus of Haitians to the United States accelerated the learning of English, often without benefit of school studies.)

It was at this time that two accords were signed, one with the French government for the creation of the French Institute of Haiti (for cultural purposes) and one with the American government for the opening of the American Institute to promote relations between Haiti and the United States. These are still functioning. Through the years they have been, especially the French Institute, a great addition to the cultural life of the country.

The reform of the secondary school program was retarded by more urgent problems. However, in the summer courses a better way of teaching both the geography and history of Haiti was demonstrated and the introduction of the study of South America was welcomed. Another change in the program would be to have workshops for woodwork, electricity, and book-binding.

The Results of the Second Year of Reform, 1942–43

It was felt that the results of the second year of the three-year plan were positive: "One of the conditions sine qua non for the success of the plan resided in the choice of personnel, honest, competent, devoted individuals, interested in their profession, who had brought their integrity, their knowledge and their zeal to the work undertaken." President Lescot showed great merit in encouraging that the appointments be made on the basis of university diplomas and/or competitive examinations. "If this practice is maintained in the future it will have considerable repercussion on the development and progress in education in Haiti," said Maurice. Alas! After his departure and the change in government in January 1946, the old habits and old ways eventually reappeared.

During this school year a look was taken into the private vocational schools preparing the young for the commercial world. It was quickly realized that the preparation was quite inadequate for the jobs open in business. Since these schools were important for the economy of the country, it was decided that they should be better controlled. To this end a decree was taken in 1943 that permitted the section of urban professional education to collaborate closely with the directors of these commercial schools to bring what they offered up-to-date and make it more effective. This governmental initiative was applauded by a good number of the directors of these schools, happy for the technical aid from which they could benefit at present.

It was in 1942–43 that the teaching in Creole in the first two years of public primary schools began. Creole had always been used orally by teachers to facilitate the comprehension of many children who on coming to school encountered French for the first time or had had only simple, imperfect French, as Creole was the language of the people. The educated class knew it from birth, too, and used it in all contacts with the uneducated. The ambition of the uneducated parents was to have their children learn French, which was the gateway to upward mobility.

On the other hand, it was argued that before the children could learn French they had to understand what they were learning. In using Creole, which was the only language of 90 percent of the population, the teacher could better initiate the children into school life before introducing French as the school language.

The Creole language was constituted during the seventeenth century, built from the vocabulary of the filibusters, the buccaneers, the inhabitants, and the slaves. According to J. B. Romain, it is a mixture of Africanisms, French, and a few Marcorix terms (the language of the Arawak Indians), as well as some English and Spanish. Very early teachers tried to formulate a program starting with Creole. One of the first was the grammar put together by F. Doret in French and Creole, another by the preacher Holly published in 1931 with a phonetics orthography, and another by Suzanne C. Sylvain for her doctoral dissertation, *Haitian Creole—Morphology and Syntax* (Waterson, Belgium, 1936). However, each had his own way of writing Creole. It was only a few years before that a vocabulary was finally written based on the ideas of the preacher Frank Lauback in concurrence with Dr. Charles Pressoir. Lauback used phonetics, Pressoir an approach to the French language. (Personally, I am for the latter, as the Creole as now written is far removed from French and makes for a completely different language, which does not help children to learn French.)

The teaching in Creole was a pilot project in the schools. It also became a project to teach adults to read and write. Maurice had a committee formed including those who advocated Creole, those who had written the grammars, and those who would go about putting the project into action. A bureau was created, meetings held, booklets on how to teach put out. Large teaching posters were put up in the evening schools, volunteers were found to teach. Five thousand copies of a newspaper in Creole were published. Near Port-au-Prince, where the population had had contacts with pictures in magazines and on billboards, the posters were understood. In the mountains, far from the city, the comprehension was less evident as the peasants had little, if any, contact with the written word or printed images. Many could not translate reality to that which was on a piece of paper. However, some volunteer teachers were successful and in the area of Croix des Bouquets near Damien about four hundred illiterates were taught to read or at least sign their names that year.

The various reforms and innovations seemed to be assimilated by the directors of the schools. They understood that it was important to encourage student initiative, to promote a sense of social service, and that it was time to gradually abandon old methods of recitation, including excessive memorization, for discussion and investigation and the adoption of a project method. These could be applied even in primary schools. It was also important to help the students to auto-discipline, cooperation and participation in certain tasks of interest to the whole school.

All the reforms were not to the liking of everyone, especially those who lost their posts and those who had been happy as things had been and those of the "humanist" group who thought that classical studies were the only ones that could form an "educated" person. Beginning in 1942 some of the articulate individuals launched a veritable tempest through the press. Although only a few articles are preserved, a list was found in the correspondence as to the number and dates. The debate was so heated that in one month there appeared twenty-eight articles in the various newspapers for and against "Dartigue and his reforms!," the most violent being that in the *Nouvelliste,* which referred to Maurice as "The Master of Masters" because of his M.A. degree. Its proprietor had been disappointed in not having a proposition concerning a soya bean project accepted by the minister of agriculture, Maurice. From then on there was a constant barrage of misinformation and deliberate misinterpretation of the various phases of the reforms. Maurice refused to be intimidated and was backed by President Lescot, who must be congratulated for his steadfastness.

Already in 1930 the Moton Commission sent by the United States Department of Education had pointed out this lack of adaptation of the secondary schools in Haiti to the needs of the country, especially, it was noted, as they were deficient in the teaching of natural sciences.

While Maurice was director of rural education there was some opposition to the reforms in rural schools but not the incessant attacks. Of course at that time he dealt with the education of the peasants, far away. Those in the city did not feel threatened. Now he was in the heart of town, interfering with their own treasured education. For some it was too much.

As stated earlier, it was decided by Maurice and the president to open the first secondary school for girls. This was a momentous event. Never before had it been thought that girls could and should go on to higher studies. Now the secondary school would permit them to do this. Maurice stated, "The secondary school for girls responds to the actual social climate and is necessary." It opened in the fall of 1943. Since then hundreds of young women have become professionals, especially in the fields of medicine, education, law and even architecture and engineering, thanks to Maurice, who opened the way.

The first forty young ladies were admitted at the *troisième* in the French system and tenth grade in the American system or senior high school. A Haitian woman was appointed to be its directress. It had the same curriculum as the young men's school, but with domestic science and child care added.

It may be interesting to give the results of the baccalaureate examinations for the year 1942–43. There were 365 candidates for the first part, of whom 128 succeeded. Of the 165 candidates for the "philosophy" (the final year), 108 were admitted. It must be noted that only 1,353 students were registered in the whole of the national public lycées. This meant that most candidates came from the private parochial or secular schools.

Either in 1943 or 1944 the questions for the baccalaureate in Cape Haitian were leaked or sold to a certain group. Notified of the possibility, Maurice carried out an investigation. The culprits were found. Very severe sanctions were taken, and the examinations were held a second time. It angered and upset Maurice that he could no longer have full confidence in all the personnel of his services. Whether this action was carried out to discredit the reforms or for venal purposes was not divulged. Maurice could not tolerate what he felt was a betrayal of the principles and aims of honesty, integrity, and self-discipline that he had been trying all these years to inculcate in his fellow workers and his compatriots.

As with the reforms in the other categories of schools, one of the first tasks was to organize the administration and create different sections for more efficiency and control. Those who did not have the baccalaureate were dismissed, as well as those who were beyond retirement age. Maurice sent some of the personnel abroad for training in the different branches of administration and sciences. He raised the salaries of the substitutes to 150 gourdes and those of the regular teachers to 220 gourdes. By a better partition of the work and hours and the reduction of the number of teachers he was able to do this. Competition for jobs was obligatory and a vice principal appointed to aid the director for a better control of studies, attendance, and discipline.

Inventory of the furniture and material was taken and a surveillance instituted. Monthly reports were demanded, which indicated attendance of both the students and their teachers. Programs were changed inasmuch as the local geography and Haitian history were to be studied before the French. This should have been done long before.

These measures seem autocratic and authoritarian, but there was such disorder, such negligence, such laxity, that they were deemed necessary to overcome these failings.

To have better, more competent guidance personnel Maurice sent three young men to study at Hampton Institute and to Teachers' College. Maurice said, "They won't be experts, but at least they will have learned how to proceed."

By a law decree voted September 25, 1944, the government decided to affect 20 percent of the surplus of the communal receipts for the execution of a plan of public primary school construction in all the communes of the republic and 10 percent for the creation of a university center.

Maurice defended his reforms with tenacity. In one of his reports he wrote:

Was it necessary or not to extirpate politics from public instruction? Was it necessary or not to entrust the directional posts to specialists, taken from the higher echelon of personnel having received special training in recognized universities? Was it necessary or not to put together a corps of inspectors in the same way? Was it necessary or not to establish order, discipline, hierarchy and regularity in all schools and at all levels? Was it necessary or not to reform the Normal Schools? Was it not necessary to introduce seriousness and honesty in public examinations? Was it not necessary to house the schools better and aim for a program of school construction? Was it not necessary to furnish the schools with adequate furniture and necessary teaching materials as the budget permits? Was it necessary or not to introduce honesty, economy and control in the administration of public funds allocated to the Ministry of Public Instruction? Was it not necessary to have a system of Statistics and card files of the personnel so that the Department would not be in ignorance of elementary information of its own Administration? Was it necessary or not to dismiss the incompetent and try to ameliorate the personnel in service so as to have a more efficient professional corps imbued with the problems of education, a corps which Haiti needs to resolve to get out of the social, economic and cultural stagnation in which it has allowed more than 75% of the population to stay? Was it necessary or not to try to organize a system of National Education taking into consideration the aspirations of the Haitian people? Should a technical elite have been formed or should we have resigned ourselves indefinitely to having to call in foreigners? Those who have worked courageously for the reforms may wait for the judgement of history with confidence. [The only possible answer to all these questions could be "Of course it was necessary."]

Secondary Education, 1943–44

The reorganization was carried out quite well during 1942–43 in spite of the attacks and discontent of some. This permitted the section of secondary school education of the department to consolidate in 1943–44 the measures taken:

(1) Control of teacher and student attendance.
(2) The professional amelioration of the teachers in service since 1942 and those hired through competitive exams.
(3) Distribution of class materials.
(4) Upkeep of the school premises.
(5) The added activities without which the lycées would have continued to be no more than institutions of academic learning instead of centers of education for youth and the community, which they are becoming. ("The effect of the effort to vitalize secondary education will be shown in the social and civic behavior of the new generation of graduates," said Maurice.)
(6) The reorganization and the reform of the program by the committee constituted.

In October 1943 a series of circulars were sent to directors and teachers of lycées with the following directives:

(1) To organize committees to discuss the program: languages and literature, social sciences, physical and natural sciences, art and plastic arts,
hygiene, physical education, and recreation at the different class
levels. (It is likely that Maurice was trying to have the teachers
participate actively in the workings of the school, to learn to work in
and as a team rather than just give their courses in isolation, without
contact and without interest in the welfare of the school.)

(2) To make a survey to determine the professions and trades that students
desire to enter on graduating.

(3) To try to learn the number of dropouts and the reasons for their leaving
without finishing their studies.

(4) To prepare teaching material in the social sciences.

(5) To collaborate with the teachers having tenure in putting together a
plan of studies and a distribution of a schedule for the different school
hours.

It was hoped that these directives would encourage the teachers to meet
and do research in education to accept the necessity of certain modifications
in the programs (organization of the work in the laboratory, the repartition
of the courses, the amelioration of methods, etc.). The groups of teachers in
social sciences in the different schools sent lists to the section of the
administration concerned with the subject, of what they needed for better
teaching of social sciences. These included books, manuals, large sheets of
cardboard, and boxes of crayons for the preparation of diagrams to better
illustrate their courses.

It could not but be evident that the life of the schools was changing
from the former inertia. It became much more diversified for the students
with the installation of laboratories, the introduction of manual arts, the
preparation of expositions of all kinds, music, physical education, art, etc.
The teachers gave the students opportunities to show their talents and
initiative and be appreciated by their peers.

That year there were several special activities in the secondary schools,
which demonstrated the awakening of the students to their abilities and
sense of responsibility. In different towns they assumed the direction of
different activities. In Jeremie and Cape Haitian they took on the responsibility for the celebration of the anniversary of the consecration of Notre
Dame de Perpétuel Secours (Our Lady of Perpetual Succor), the patron saint

of Haiti, on December 8. A public concert led by the brass band of the students of the Jacmel lycée on the public square Toussaint L'Ouverture was held on the same day. An assembly of students and teachers was held on the closing day of the first trimester. A Christmas tree was set up at the Lycée Petion in Port-au-Prince with a distribution of clothing, shoes, candies, and refreshments. A medical service was set up at the Jeremie lycée with the effective collaboration of the head of the hygiene service of the town. (The lycée club donated money to buy medicines for their comrades in need.) A weekly get-together (Friday afternoons) of the members of the English clubs of these lycées took place to put on programs of music, literature, and games. There also were organized conferences, receptions, sport events, and amateur theater.

At the Cape Haitian lycée the students worked to fix up the school. They also repaired the streets surrounding it. In all the lycées Tree Day was celebrated with talks on the dangers of erosion, with the planting of trees taking place. Finally the ceremony marking the one hundredth year of the Lycée Philippe Guerrier of Cape Haitian took place with imposing manifestations. Never before had the students taken such an active part, working together, in the school and for the school.

As has been stated several times and cannot be stated enough, politics were totally banished from school appointments. Little by little the competitive exams made for a healthier disciplinary climate. No longer were posts sinecures. They were gained and kept by hard work and dependability. Moreover, through the reorganization of the administration into responsible branches the teachers were better controlled, but they too benefited, as they now had more direct contact with the branch of the Department of Education in which they were concerned.

As soon as the young people sent abroad for training returned they were integrated into the personnel, permitting others to go abroad for a year or at least to attend summer school in various universities in Canada, the United States, Puerto Rico, or Mexico.

- 81 grants in 1941–42
- 68 grants in 1942–43 (11 students would remain a second year)
- 61 grants in 1943–44 (the figures for 1944–45 are unavailable)

These figures are very important when one considers how small the number of graduates of secondary school was, how low the budget was, and what the situation was in the United States. It must be said that some grantees paid most of their expenses, but in some cases salaries were paid and the grantees had the backing of the government, which facilitated their departure and their standing in the training schools to which they were sent. Moreover of the 61 grants obtained in 1943–44 the Haitian government offered 31 and the others were given by the American government or private institutions in the United States and Canada.

Not all who could have profited from study abroad could be sent. To offset this, Maurice instituted summer courses for secondary school teachers in Port-au-Prince, an outstanding innovation. For these courses he was able to bring to Haiti professors from abroad through contacts and use Haitian professors with European degrees. A special one was Auguste Viatte, a French Swiss, with degrees from the University of Fribourg and the Sorbonne in French literature. Maurice had met him at International House in New York City in 1927, when Viatte was teaching at City College. He admitted that Maurice was the first educated nonwhite he had met. He was so impressed that he became interested in the French-speaking peoples outside of Europe, those of the Caribbean, the other French possessions, and Canada. He came to Haiti with his bride in 1934 or 1935 and from that time on made repeated trips there. He developed a real passion for collaboration and cooperation between French-speaking peoples. He made a name for himself in this matter. (At the time he came for the summer courses he was teaching at the University of Laval in Quebec.) He wrote books on the subject as well as on the literature of French-speaking countries beyond or outside of France. He included Haiti in these studies, making its literature known to the rest of the French-speaking world. His first books were *Histoire Litteraire de l'Amérique Française des Origines à 1950* (Paris: Presses de l'Université de Laval, Quebec, and PUF, 1954) and *L'Anthologie Litteraire de l'Amérique Francophone* (Sherbrooke, Canada: CELEF, 1971). Viatte took part in or helped create French clubs. Such a one was the Association France-Haiti, which he set up in 1954 with the collaboration of the Haitian ambassador at that time, Gen. Frank Lavaud, former chief of the Haitian army and interim head of the Haitian government after the fall of the government of Elie Lescot in January 1946.

Back to the summer courses in 1943. Here is a testimonial that appeared after the death of my husband in July 1983 (forty years later). It appeared in the *Septentrion,* a Cape Haitian newspaper, in October 1983. Its title was, "The Maurice Dartigue I Knew," and it was written by Eric F.

Etienne. It starts with the reforms Maurice undertook to "establish a more realistic program and more propitious for inculcating a culture more appropriate to the needs and mentality of our fellow citizens and extend the programs to the immense majority of backward Haitians and in this fashion lay down on a firm foundation the eventual development of Haiti."

The author of this article then recounts under what circumstances he met Maurice for the first time, which gave him "once and for all, the just measure, never modified nor tarnished since, of the real stature of the man." Having learned that there would be summer courses held for public secondary school teachers, although he was a teacher in a private school, Etienne wanted very much, after having consulted the program, to participate. Only forty-eight hours remained to register. Taking the time to pack a few belongings and find transportation in a primitive, overcrowded, overloaded bus that took from fifteen to twenty-four hours and even more to travel from Cape Haitian to Port-au-Prince, he was on his way. When he arrived one hour before the closing of the registry he was told that the courses were open only for teachers of the national public secondary schools. Etienne explained the circumstances to the section head, who answered that only the minister could make an exception.

Having been told of my situation, Maurice Dartigue received me immediately and looking at me intensely said these words: "Do you know that what you are doing at this moment is something unheard of as well as encouraging for the initiative of my Department? While some of the teachers of the national lycées invent all sorts of excuses to escape the obligation to come for the four weeks at the expense of the government, you, a teacher in a private school, invited only but not obligated to participate, you show a wonderful spirit in wanting to be with us." At the same moment he gave instructions to have me registered, which was done at the expense of the government.

Etienne was reimbursed for the transportation costs and was lodged and nourished as were the others.

This anecdote reveals that not all teachers were in favor of the summer courses. Perhaps they thought they didn't need them or had other things planned or simply wanted to forget school, classes, and programs. It also reveals the narrow horizons they had to let pass by opportunities to encounter others and to partake of the activities and especially the offerings of the professors from abroad.

The courses were a success and were the first step toward the continued training of teachers of secondary schools. The students of the other college-level schools were invited to the conferences.

During the summer courses of 1944, Dr. W. E. B. Du Bois, an eminent black American, historian, professor of sociology, and one of the founders of NAACP (the National Association for the Advancement of Colored People, the spearhead for the fight for equality in the American economic and social system), gave a talk: "The Conception of Education." He was not afraid to say, "The truth is that your cultural elite with all its realizations does not in any way approach the grandeur which it could have known had it helped the masses to education, health and the richness of your culture."

Perhaps Maurice should have given more information to the public concerning some of the reforms. He had the national library closed, as it was in disrepair. Water seepage and lack of care for the few books made it look abandoned. Fortunately, in a few months it was opened again, the building having been repaired, repainted in and out, new shelving made, a new card filing system put in, and a new director installed. Compared to libraries in the United States it was very small, with a limited number of books, magazines, and newspapers. There was some criticism but no great outcry during the time it was closed.

However, after a survey of the municipal libraries in other towns that revealed the very poor conditions as to the physical plant, the state of the books, their number, and the kind of person who was in charge, Maurice decided to close them, but he had the books transferred to the libraries of the lycées in each town. Whether he meant to repair the municipal libraries and return the books is not clear. The outcry was violent: "Dartigue has closed the libraries!" "Dartigue is depriving the people." This was deliberate misinformation, as the libraries were open in their new locations.

The life of the schools became more animated with the multiplication of social activities in the sense of service, public manifestations, recreational gatherings, and interschool sports. Flag Day was celebrated by all schools so that the population could become aware of this symbol of the unity of the nation. This manifestation was the occasion for a town parade and interschool sports competitions.

Tree Day also became very important. Maurice carried out with the Service National de la Production Agricole at Damien a program of tree planting. Damien provided the young trees; the schools, with the help of the agricultural agents, did the planting in chosen areas. Even the president took part on that special day. Trees were planted and had the program gone on perhaps the mountains and the plains would not be as denuded as they are today. Deforestation was already a problem in Haiti. It was necessary to insist on and demonstrate the replacement of trees. Moreover, terracing also was undertaken. The peasants had the habit of planting in rows, beginning at the top of the hillside and moving straight down. This way of planting made for topsoil depletion, with the rains carrying it away. It was hard work convincing the peasants used to traditional ways, but was hoped that through the school and the agents the peasants would adopt better soil-retaining methods.

The annual inter-American competition for the best essay on a subject of interest to Latin America must be included in the activities. Thirteen secondary schools partook in this event. The two best essays from each school were sent to a jury of notables that met at the School of Law in Port-au-Prince between May 10 and May 15 that year to read and judge the twenty-six essays. The theme was "Printing and Economic Freedom in Latin America." The jury selected the essay of a student in Rhetorique (next to last year) at the lycée of Jeremie and that of a student in his final year at the Lycée Petion in Port-au-Prince as winners of the contest.

In 1943–44 there were 405 candidates registered for the first part of the baccalaureate, with 141 succeeding, about a third of the candidates. For the second part, of 126 candidates registered 65 received, or about a half of those taking it. This was slightly better than the year before. The private schools did better, for out of 117 candidates for the first part 69 succeeded and out of 35 presented for the second part 29 made it. The students who had studied privately did poorly. Out of 168 only 24 succeeded, and out of 39 for the second part only 8 received the degree.

It must have given Maurice and his collaborators some satisfaction to see that the reforms for bringing up-to-date the activities and programs with the introduction of a greater variety of subjects and the greater participation of the teachers and the students in the life of the school had taken hold. Though the criticisms continued, the directors, after the study trips, understood the aims of the reforms better and were willing to go along with them.

Higher Education

As early as the school year 1941–42, Maurice took action concerning higher education, although he had not thought to be able to do this so quickly. He began with the law school (which underwent some repairs), and named a lawyer, Pierre Liautaud, as director. Pierre Liautaud had received his law degree in France and was a practicing lawyer. He was also one of our friends, but friendship had no part in the appointment. He became director because he was capable, serious, and responsible and shared Maurice's ideas. Pierre cooperated in every way in promoting these ideas.

A word about the law school. It was founded in 1850 and had been closed and opened several times, but finally became the National School of Law in 1890. In 1941 it was housed in a recently constructed building, with a large room for gatherings and a law library. It would be here that the summer courses would take place, as would conferences and events of various sorts. With the new director backed by Maurice, regular attendance was demanded of both the professors and the students, with attendance taken. As there was almost no information on the students of former years, a card file was made with information on every student and a new student record booklet given to each. The library was made more comfortable, and some twenty-four volumes of the missing issues of the official journal *Le Moniteur* (in which appeared all decrees and laws passed and appointments) were bought, as were fifty-three books on jurisprudence. Moreover in the spring of 1942 the library instituted an evening service to stay open from 8:00 to 11:00 p.m. to help students to prepare for exams. Some students came from very modest homes. They often studied under streetlights. Permitting them to study in the library in the evenings was of great help. Salaries of the director, teachers, and other personnel were paid by the ministry.

As minister of public instruction, Maurice accorded a subsidy of 1,500 gourdes to the School of Applied Science, a private institution. Therefore, he could in a way have a say in the manner in which the school functioned. He desired that the school have not only qualified professors—they were for the most part educated in France—but he wanted them to be serious in carrying out the work they had accepted to do. He established a contract with the Council of Deans (Conseil des Doyens, to which I shall refer later) stipulating that one of its members must be named by the minister (by him). It was also his ministry that paid the salaries of two of the professors.

Both Maurice and the president accorded great importance to the preparation of cadres. The president even offered a grant to permit a member of the teaching personnel to study abroad. Maurice continued to put aside funds from the budget and make contacts with universities abroad for grants. He was able to send twelve grantees to Teachers' College, five to Hampton, and one to the University of California in 1942–43.

One of the special events of the year was the visit of Alain Locke, an American of African descent, graduate of Harvard University, and professor at Howard University, a university open to all but mostly attended by nonwhites at that time. He gave a series of conferences on the theme of civilization and democracy. One of the conferences was titled "L'Apport des Noirs Dans la Civilisation Americaine." In English: "What the Blacks Have Given or Brought to American Civilization." It must have worried the white Americans in their attitude toward the blacks, for in the National Archives in Washington I found a telegram marked "confidential" sent by the chargé d'affaires in Haiti to the State Department that stated that if these conferences were published in the United States they would cause explosive agitation among the American blacks.

Dr. Locke made us the gift of a beautiful book of which he was the author. It was a study of the contribution of black painters to North American painting, with illustrations of paintings by blacks or in which blacks were portrayed.

Maurice had at heart the creation of a University of Haiti. In Haiti, even in colonial times, there came about an elite and a group of intellectuals, but the members had all been educated in France. It was after independence in 1804 that gradually postsecondary schools were created. In 1823 the first law school opened its doors, then a school for medicine. This school, renovated, is still in service. A dental school saw the light of day in 1898 and the School of Applied Science in 1902. Each one of these schools was independent and had its own rules and regulations. In 1920, Dantes Belle-garde, minister of education at the time, tried to bring these schools together. But it was the efforts of Maurice that permitted the directors of these schools to form the Council of Deans (Conseil des Doyens).

Following the decree of March 1943, this council, without modifying the administrative relationships between the schools, played an important role of coordination in the effort of the government to create the University of Haiti. This was also the year that the grades in these schools were all noted in the same manner, with 6.5 being the lowest acceptable of a possible 10.

For the first time the diplomas of the four schools were given out to the graduates in the presence of the president of the republic at the law school. He gave a talk on this occasion. This ceremony, unknown even today in France, is very impressive, with the graduate who received the highest grades, the laureate, giving a speech and on this occasion Maurice making a short one after the president to compliment the graduates and wish them well. Family and friends were in the audience.

In the year 1943–44, the programs and methods continued to improve. Plans were made to open a normal school for training teachers of the intermediate years (junior high school), with dormitory, dining room, study hall, library, auditorium, and classrooms. It would be used as a university center. Maurice tried to put aside from his budget a sum to eventually buy up properties around the schools of law, medicine, and dentistry for the creation of a campus. The fall of the government in January 1946 would prevent him from achieving the task he set himself. He would leave a sum of ten thousand dollars in the ministry treasury—a unique act in the history of Haiti. It was the first time that such a sum was put at the disposal of the successor. Unfortunately, the sum was used for other purposes and to this day the projected campus remains only a plan. But l'Ecole Normale Superieure, the normal school was created later and functions today.

In 1944 the provisional government of the French republic sent Aimé Cesaire (the poet and playwright of the French Antilles of whom I've already written) to give a three-month course on French literature at the university level. He also took part in the summer school courses. That year, 122 secondary school teachers were invited to take the courses held in the law school. They were grouped according to their specialties: literature, math, physical and natural science, social science, and English. The discussions showed up the problems that preoccupied the teachers.

The program was carried out by both foreign and Haitian lecturers, among them A. Viatte (for a second time); J. K. Sonntag of the University of Michigan; Max Bond, Ph.D, University of California; Mercer Cook, Ph.D., Brown University; and D. Blelloch, Oxford University, from ILO, of Quebec, and Thadeus Poznanski of Laval University, also in ILO (of these two more later). Among the Haitians were L. Hibbert, brilliant mathematician, several times minister of finance; Dantes Bellegarde, former minister; A. Bellerive, a doctor of medicine who would later head the

WHO team in the Congo crisis; and F. Morriseau-Leroy, M.A., Teachers' College, head of urban education, and for special conferences there were W.E.B. Du Bois, Aimé Cesaire, and Maurice Dartigue. It was quite a gathering of highly qualified individuals. It is hoped that the secondary school teachers profited from what these men had to offer them.

It may be of interest to give a few highlights of a report on one of the conferences given by Maurice that summer and published in the review *Cahiers d'Haiti* in September 1944. Its title was "Some Considerations on Teaching Methods." He said he was not going to give a conference of the usual type but make some remarks about what he had observed in schools he had visited and his own experience as a student:

Methodology is the least spectacular trait of pedagogy, but one of the most important. As in all one does, method is needed. In Haiti we form magnificent plans, but we forget to actually put them into action and seem to scorn details. In teaching, the methodic preparation of the lessons and the teachers' control of the results of what he has taught play an important role in the success of teaching.

Certainly the teacher needs first to have a philosophy of what kind of persons he wants his students to become. The process of forming this kind of person begins in the earliest years. It is because not enough attention was paid from the beginning that there are so many failures at the end. Each year is important in constructing a solid base on which to add. Besides the knowledge that the student must gain to go higher up, the teacher needs to develop the taste for culture. One of the avenues is for the teacher to help the student learn how to do research and find the information he needs. It is here that the personal qualities of enthusiasm, sincerity, intellectual honesty of the teacher and his culture can influence and can be communicated to the students. It is under these conditions that teaching ceases to be a routine based on a program of memorization of facts and ingestion of school manuals to become an art and a science. It is here that teaching becomes creative, and the teacher stops being a machine to become an artist.

I have brought to your attention the problem that faces the teacher of Rhetorique [the second to last year at the end of which occurs the examination of the first part of the BAC for which the teacher tries to prepare his students] when he is confronted with students not having the necessary base because not enough attention was given in the grades leading to the "Rhetorique" to the step by step formation of this base on which he can build. This problem can be solved through better controls by the Administration through better testing along the way. Tests are a means of diagnosis but never an end in themselves. If they are used judiciously by the teacher they can be very useful for the teacher to learn if his teaching is effective. "Testing" is an integral part of teaching and can permit the teacher to remedy the deficiencies of the whole class or those of individual students.

The process of education should not be just the control through examinations at the end of the year or at the end of the 6 years leading to the BAC but one of each week, each day. It is here that the patient, humble, but how vital, work of daily teaching becomes decisive.

This talk shows the importance Maurice gave to the job of teaching. There were other talks to graduating classes at Damien, at the reopened normal school for urban teachers, and at various ceremonies. They, for the most part, concerned the problems of education in Haiti and the urgency of improving the lot of the teachers and of 90 percent of the population and the part Maurice's audience had to take in this undertaking.

Minister of Agriculture and Labor, SHADA (Societé Haitiano-Americaine du Dèveloppement de L'Agriculture)

As minister of agriculture, Maurice was involved in the enterprise known as SHADA, which was founded as an expression of President Roosevelt's Good-Neighbor policy. It was conceived as an instrument of Haitian-American technical and economic collaboration. This undertaking came about in the weeks that followed the election on May 15, 1941, of President Lescot. Soon after he formed the cabinet, the president returned to Washington, where he had served as ambassador of Haiti to the United States, to negotiate a loan to give a boost to the economy of the country. It is presumed that talks had been going on earlier. He came back to Haiti with an accord involving $5 million to be used in agriculture to boost the peasant economy.

The main points of the accord were as follows: SHADA was created for the development of agriculture for the benefit of the Haitian peasants as independent producers of agricultural products. For this project money and some American technicians were needed. Among the aims of SHADA were the improvement of existing products, the introduction of new products such as spices, the extension of manual arts, and the development of *Hevea,* the rubber plant mostly referred to in this study as *cryptostegia.* The first idea was that SHADA would administer some large acreages but that financial and technical aid would be given to small landowners to cultivate independently outside the strategic areas decided upon. Although the United States did not declare war on Japan until December 7, 1941, rubber from Southeast Asia was more and more difficult to obtain due to the advance of the Japanese on land and sea. It will be seen that the planting of this crop would take precedence over every other due to the Japanese attack on Pearl Harbor and the takeover by the Japanese of the rubber plantations in Southeast Asia. In the accord there was mention of furthering cottage industries. Eventually an expert in these spent two years in Haiti.

Because of this urgency, the cultivation, preparation, and export of *cryptostegia* would involve several U.S. government and private agencies such as the Export-Import Bank, the Rubber Corporation, and the American

71

Rubber Development Corporation. Also were concerned, because of the war, the Bureau of Domestic and Foreign Commerce, the Haitian ambassador in Washington, the American ambassador in Haiti, the Bureau of Inter-American Affairs, the Haitian minister of agriculture, the Haitian minister of finance and the American president director-general of SHADA; and as a result of the war, the Bureau of Strategic Services and the Bureau of Economic Warfare.

SHADA was not a private American company such as the Standard Fruit or HASCO (the Haitian American Sugar Company), with profits going to American shareholders. It was a joint governmental project. As collateral for the $5 million loan, the Haitian government gave SHADA the right and the profits of the exploitation of the extensive pine forest located on Morne des Commissaires for a fifty-year period, as well as the monopoly and exportation of *cryptostegia,* which was supposed to be a fast-growing rubber plant. The exploitation of these two products was estimated to mean a profit of about a million dollars, which SHADA could give as guarantees to obtain the loan of the $5 million.

President Lescot himself went on tour to urge the peasants to rent or lease their lands as their contribution to the war effort. It is doubtful if they gave up easily their most precious belonging. Even compensation for renting, leasing, or outright sale would not completely reconcile them to their loss and the upset of their lives.

Earlier in this book when the educational reforms were discussed, SHADA was mentioned, as it concerned manual arts. Groups of students and groups of teachers were sent to learn the techniques of weaving and spinning. In this area, SHADA carried out one of its tasks. It also, at the insistence of President Lescot, put aside 24,000 acres for new plantations of sisal to be cultivated in cooperation with independent peasant growers. SHADA also attracted teachers and pupils, making for disruption and perturbation in the rural education service.

It also, at the beginning, made studies for the cultivation of medicinal plants, such as citronella, and even pepper and other spices, which up to that time had come from the Orient. These were for the most part neglected in favor of an all-out effort to grow *cryptostegia.*

The accord was made into a decree in mid-August 1941, permitting SHADA to buy 300,000 dollars' worth of materials and machines from the engineering company J. G. White, which had just finished the dam on the Artibonite River and was leaving Haiti.

The actual direction of SHADA was put in the hands of T. Fennell. His right-hand man was Mr. Hill. A board of directors was created. It consisted of three Americans, the two mentioned above and Mr. Williams, the American head of the Bank of Haiti. The three Haitians were Maurice, vice president; Abel Lacroix, minister of finance, member; and Pierre Chauvet, undersecretary of finance, member. Meetings were to be held once a month. Mr. Darton of the Rubber Development Corporation was present at times.

At first all seemed to go well, as the correspondence is about dates and meetings in the fall and winter of 1941. Until the beginning of the *cryptostegia* project, Fennell, president director-general, stayed within the limits of his prerogatives. The program of action of the first year was properly submitted to the board. Hiring was done within the limits of the budget. The curricula vitae of the upper echelons, both Americans and Haitians, were also submitted. Problems were discussed at the meetings and between meetings with the minister. But immediately after the approbation of the sisal and cryptostegia programs, the attitude and conduct of Fennell changed completely.

It must be stated that the first year, SHADA had more than 17,000 employees, 16,580 day farm laborers, almost all Haitians, 20 Americans, American technicians and engineers, and 398 Haitian and American technicians and supervisors, which made for progress in employment. In September 1942, SHADA began to produce sisal, wood from the pine forest, some essential oils, and rubber for about $89,000. The budget for the year foresaw the exploitation of 12,000 acres in sisal, 8,000 in *Hevea,* 5,000 in various products, and 100,000 acres in *cryptostegia.* This would never be, the most acreage planted being 65,000 acres.

Naturally the Haitian members of the board had complete confidence in Fennell and in no way wished to interfere, so that he could feel unhindered to carry out the complex program. The board thought that at times he had to make decisions in between meetings but would inform the board at the next meeting. This was not the case.

In a small country like Haiti, where there were few large plantations and thousands of peasants had but a few acres, the acquisition by rental, lease, or sale was in itself difficult. Putting together 65 thousand acres from all the bits of land must have been a colossal task. It could and did lead to abuses.

The land was at times expropriated from peasants without proper proceedings in some instances to permit huge cultivating machines to prepare the land. First, trees were cut down, gardens and huts destroyed. Methods used to acquire the lands were not always justified. Agricultural agents and planters sent in complaints. Maurice denounced the methods used. Here is part of a letter he wrote to Fennell on February 16, 1943:

... The representatives of SHADA must take into consideration the mentality of the peasants and the townsmen, proprietors and their legitimate interests. They will have to act with tact, moderation and equity. This is not only in the moral and political interest of the government but also of SHADA, which is not a temporary organization but one that is to stay on in a permanent way and be called to work with and for the peasants in view of ameliorating their standard of living and the economy of the country. Of course there are some unfounded complaints ...

In January he had sent a letter of condemnation of the way the overseers were treating the peasants in some areas.

A complaint as early as October 1942 came in from the pine forest. The overseers complained that the laborers did not work hard enough. What the overseers did not take into consideration was the fact that the laborers were poorly clothed and poorly housed for the cold mountain climate. Sanitary accommodations, if any, were poor; food was a problem. The overseers with their families were simply but adequately housed and could have food sent in. They probably gave little thought to the workers' plight except in that they were not furnishing the labor quota expected. Later the laborers would go on strike and would be punished by wage losses. Maurice would come to their defense, saying that the punishment far exceeded the reasons for it and was illegal.

Then there came a report written in early 1943 by D. Knapp, chief of the planting section of the American Rubber Development Corporation. He stated that there was an increased labor shortage, also that the workers were too slow, which could be due to deliberate slowing down or an act of sabotage, passive resistance for personal or political gain. There were not enough workers for tapping the plants, etc.

Knapp admitted that the Rubber Development Corporation's only interest was to secure rubber during the emergency period, which was 1943–44, since Haiti was never considered a cheap source of rubber. The laborers furnished only one-third to one-fifth of the American laborers' daily quota. Not only that, but neither the land, nor the variable weather, nor the organizational problems gave any satisfaction or encouragement to continue: "Besides some of the plants from the nurseries were improper for planting. Proper spacing had not been observed, nor had planting weather." He concluded that the entire program was complicated. "Contrary to original ideas *cryptostegia* is a demanding plant in its requirements. Experimental planting was done in an irrigated area which has contributed to the confusion as to where and how to grow it." As it is for the emergency of 1943–44 he stated: "What cannot be cleared by the end of the year is a waste of money." The document reveals the cross-purposes of the two governments. For Haiti, the aim was to help the economy and the peasants. For the United States, it was to grow rubber. Where to put the blame? Haste!

More misunderstandings were inevitable. Maurice in April 1943 wrote to Fennell to protest the inconsiderate cutting of fruit trees by the agents of SHADA. He urged that nurseries for fruit trees be started immediately. Again in April, Maurice wrote to Fennell asking him to permit the peasants in a certain area to keep their lands until after the harvest in July. Fennell circumvented Maurice and went to President Lescot directly. Lescot gave in to Fennell and demanded that the 20,000 acres concerned be handed over to SHADA immediately. Although Maurice was upset, it was not so much that Fennell had gone directly to the president, but that the president had given way to Fennell. Reluctantly Maurice carried out the president's request.

The three Haitian board members took their roles seriously and felt that Fennell did not consult them or keep them informed of his actions. It seemed that he began to manage SHADA as if it were his private enterprise. Maurice, as vice president, wrote to Fennell (August 24, 1943) demanding the accounts and budget. In the letter he stated: "As we shall be asking some questions at the next meeting of the Board, and as some questions necessitate research in the account books, we think it is better to give you these questions in advance and in writing." The questions concerned the manual arts, the exact situation of the expenses, the receipts, the indemnities given to those who had been expropriated or where lands had been leased or rented, the indemnity paid for the destroyed harvests, the state of activities in the pine forest, and the income coming from certain payments made by the Rubber Development Corporation. Fennell did not answer this request!

Maurice, Lacroix, and Chauvet wrote to President Lescot on December 6, 1943, to explain the situation to him and the impossibility of their controlling either income or expenditures, because they knew nothing. Fennell had not kept them informed. Lacroix wrote a personal note dated December 6, 1943, to the president:

My dear President,
    During the day you will be receiving the letter written by Dartigue, Chauvet and myself concerning the SHADA situation. I am adding these lines to confirm to your Excellency that which I had the honor to tell you during our conversation the evening before last, on the same subject.
    An enterprise of the scope of SHADA deserves to have at its head a real director with all that that word implies as to prestige, authority and executive capability. It does not seem that Mr. Fennell has these qualities in the measure needed, which gives rise to the difficulties he is undergoing in trying to keep order among the personnel and the impression of instability that his administration gives. The dangers that the enterprise runs are due to the fact that Fennell sees too big, does not occupy himself enough with certain contingencies, gives no importance to his responsibilities towards the Haitian government and is impatient of all serious and thorough control.
    Moreover, it cannot be denied that at the stage at which the enterprise actually is, such a control should exist . . . In presence of the recent incidents and acts, I realize very clearly that the means I have to control the enterprise, the little free time I have to do it, my limited competence in certain matters do not appear to respond to the extensive legal and moral responsibilities that in the actual circumstances the function of a member of the Board of a company of the importance of SHADA should have . . .

This was a very diplomatic way of letting the president know that Lacroix did not wish to stay on the board but also showed what he thought of Fennell's competence.
    On December 6, 1943, the Haitian board members wrote again to the president:

We feel it is our responsibility to let you know that the situation in which SHADA actually finds itself necessitates an investigation followed by a reorganization, with new directives based on the principles and practices of a commercial administration . . . The report of the auditors and according to other information received on the budget and the expenditures confirm their opinion that these are incorrect and must be changed. But Mr. Fennell pretends that all is well . . . What disturbs the three members most is the absence of sincerity in the way the accounting books are kept . . . The Haitian members of the Board submit these facts to your Excellency because they cannot be held responsible.

They esteem that if a change can not be had through the action of the American government and the Export-Import Bank, Your Excellency must authorize these members to resign as members of the Board of SHADA so that the Haitian government will not have to continue to guarantee the repayment of the $5,000,000 loaned by the Export-Import Bank in case of the failure of SHADA.

This was very serious, but the members could not do less, since Fennell refused to cooperate.

Then Mr. Hill, Fennell's assistant, put together a plan of redressment permitting better functioning of SHADA. He had had several confrontations with his boss. He told Fennell that the money was that of the Haitian government and not enough attention was being taken to see that it was spent properly, with economy. He added that Fennell was giving jobs to nonqualified people, often his friends, whom he had fetched from the United States at great expense when there were competent Haitian technicians right there in Port-au-Prince. Moreover, these people were overpaid. Fennell also ordered huge amounts of material without consulting anyone. In fact, he was doing as he pleased. He listened to no one. This plan was submitted December 24, 1943, to the Export-Import Bank, with a copy sent to Maurice. It is wondered if the direction of the Export-Import Bank even looked at it, for to the great surprise of all concerned, the American Rubber Development Corporation on January 13, 1944, proposed that the *cryptostegia* program be interrupted! After having had hundreds of trees cut down, plantations and homes destroyed to make way for the *cryptostegia,* the project was being dropped without warning or preparation. Was it Knapp's report that influenced the decision and the differences with Fennell just the excuse awaited? (I do not know, as I have not had access to the inner workings of the American Rubber Development Corporation.) The rural economy was certainly upset. But the problem did not end there. The

77

Export-Import Bank wished to maintain Fennell and dismiss Hill. This act was countered by the following response, dated January 13, 1944, written by Maurice, Lacroix, and Chauvet to President Lescot.

Mr. President,

In response to the report we had the honor to present to your Excellence, the Export-Import Bank presented a memorandum in which it expresses its will to maintain Fennell as president of the Société Haitiano-Americaine de Developpement Agricole, and demanded the resignation of Hill. This is another proof that the Export-Import Bank exceeds its prerogatives. In the last analysis, whatever the outcome of the activities of the president of SHADA, the bank has nothing to lose, the Haitian government having guaranteed the loan of $5,000,000 agreed upon for SHADA. . .

We want to repeat once more—either the Board functions and acts like all Boards in all countries and in all companies or the Board has no reason for existing and must retire to let the actual president take entire responsibility for his acts.

When the president of SHADA creates new important functions which were not foreseen in the organizational plan, not only without having obtained the consent of the Board but without even informing the Board after having taken the initiative of these measures; when under the cover of a global budget he engages the services of new high salaried people in the US, without afterwards making a report to the Board of these appointments of which the Board learns at the same time as the public through the company newspaper "A Propos de la SHADA"; when the president makes changes in the budget approved by the Board, again not informing it; when he makes agreements introducing modalities of execution in certain contracts without informing the Board . . . We insist that by the nature of its functions the Board has the right to know all about these transactions that have been voluntarily concealed.

To prevent the return of such abuses of power . . . we are of the opinion that steps should be taken by the Haitian government. . . . It is almost certain that the growing of *cryptostegia* will not continue after the war. It is known that the projected 100,000 acres have been reduced to 50,000 acres, and already in the region of the Artibonite River, where properties were rented and permanent cultures destroyed, both the *cryptostegia* nurseries and the plantations have been abandoned without the president of SHADA judging it necessary to officially let the Department of Agriculture know. It is to be noted that Mr. Fennell, who had been a technical advisor to the Department, and who after being appointed president of SHADA asked to keep this post without remuneration, did not once give an opinion or a suggestion concerning the situation or what to do in this instance. In no way did he seek to have an interview with the Minister of Agriculture.

This precedent comes to confirm our apprehensions of the gravity of the agricultural, social and political problems which the government must face after the war, when the cultivation of *cryptostegia* will be abandoned by the Rubber Development Corporation. The representative of this corporation, D. Knapp, declared at a meeting held at the National Palace last November that all that interested the Rubber Development Corporation in Haiti was to grow rubber. It is true that this corporation has no contractual responsibility concerning the problems created by the cessation of its activities outside its obligation to root up the *cryptostegia* plants before giving back to the proprietors the lands which it had leased from them. . . . But it is also true that both the American government and the Rubber Development Corporation, which is after all an American government organism, have a responsibility toward the government and the Haitian people. . . . That is the reason why we think that in view of the approaching end of the war, it is indispensable that a commission of experts be sent without delay to Haiti by the American government.

Maurice also wrote a memorandum of twenty-two pages to L. Duggan of the State Department as a résumé of SHADA since its beginning in 1941 and the evolution of the attitude of Mr. Fennell and the misunderstandings. At the end he states: "SHADA is a company the shares of which belong to the Haitian government. The loan of $5 million by the Export-Import Bank is guaranteed by the Haitian State. In consequence, it is elementary that the president general director of SHADA act in conformity with the Haitian interests and in accord with the aspirations of the Government and the Haitian People." This he sent in April 1944, when he went to Washington for meetings concerning SHADA. He felt that Duggan, although a supporter of Fennell, had more sensitivity as concerned the point of view of the Haitian government.

André Liautaud, the Haitian ambassador to the United States, also contacted the Export-Import Bank. The two, Maurice and André, tried to see how their country could be extricated from such a critical situation. They were able to make the American officials more aware of just what was really going on in Haiti, as Maurice stated in a letter he wrote to Lacroix on April 27, 1944. "These gentlemen seem to finally understand the gravity of the situation."

A few days later, on May 13, 1944, Maurice wrote to President Lescot that the Americans offered grants for Haitian students as well as aid for school construction, etc., but that the Americans could in no way consider these offers as compensation for the enormous damage caused by SHADA. Maurice was determined to multiply his efforts to have the peasants properly indemnified.

Maurice also saw a representative of the U.S. Man Power Commission for the possible recruitment of Haitian labor to cut trees in the forests of the United States. He also went to New York to have an interview at the International Education Institute, where he was asked if the big companies in Haiti offered grants. He said that the president of the republic had sent a circular to the different companies, but up to the time he had left Haiti there had been no response except one favorable one from an English firm.

From Washington Maurice wrote to the president on May 14, 1944, of the three meetings he and Liautaud had had, two with the State Department and one with the Export-Import Bank. Concerning Fennell, Maurice wrote that he explicitly told the Americans that the Haitian government had never chosen Fennell, it had simply acquiesced to the choice, and that "the Haitian government had confidence in him at the beginning but at this point it was not a question of defending anybody but to present the point of view of the Haitian government concerning a project carried out on its territory." Maurice then described the attitude of Mr. Wright, the adviser of the State Department, who stated, "It appears that the government had confidence in Mr. Fennell and now has changed its opinion." A little later he remarked, "It follows that Mr. Fennell ignored the Board." It seemed evident that Fennell had to go. The newly appointed American ambassador of the United States to Haiti, Orme Wilson, was present at all the Washington meetings. Maurice gave his opinion from the few times he had met Wilson that he was better than the former ambassador.

To confirm the conversations and the points of view of the Haitian government, André Liautaud wrote to W. L. Pierson, president of the

Export-Import Bank, to suggest "a better organization of this company [SHADA] which unfortunately has not given the results that we all had the right to expect." He continued to say that there was no reason why after the departure of its president it could not be reorganized with better controls, such as a committee of three, with the minister of Agriculture taking on the position of copresident with the future one, a better and firmer fiscal control, the appointment of more Haitian technicians so as not to have foreigners at far greater expense, giving up the unprofitable projects, and negotiating as to the funds necessary to have the company to begin the activities again.

The American chargé d'affaires in Haiti, Vinton Chapin, presented President Lescot with the memorandum of the American Rubber Development Corporation proposing the arrangements concerning the *cryptostegia* project.

While Maurice was in Washington, he and André were given the proposals of the Rubber Development Corporation as to how it would compensate the Haitian government in the name of the peasants and the cessation of the *cryptostegia* project. At a meeting at the State Department in Washington with the representative of that company, Mr. Allen, they answered in the form of a memorandum that began in a conciliatory manner. It referred to the friendship that united the two countries and would continue to unite them in the spirit of collaboration and mutual aid with which they regarded the problems facing them.

The memorandum continued: "The obligations stemming from the contract; the Haitian government is aware that although no precise obligation was incurred by the Rubber Development Corporation in the contract passed with SHADA as concerns indemnities or compensation to accord the Haitian peasants in case of a brusque cancellation of the contract, the Haitian government is asking for compensation for the following reasons."

The reasons were as follows:

(1) Real damage was caused or will be caused by the cancellation, as was indicated in conversations and memoranda.
(2) The spirit of collaboration brought the Haitian government to come to the aid of the United States, which had an urgent need for rubber. No one can deny that to promote the realization of the program special measures had to be taken, which often displeased public opinion, with the only purpose of coming to the aid of the American government to permit it to carry out satisfactorily its military operations. To tell the

81

Haitian government at this moment that there is nothing in the contract to justify a demand for compensation would be equal to reproaching it for having upheld the war effort of a friendly government without hesitation and without having taken the ordinary and legal precautions, which usually take time.

(3) It is necessary to come to an understanding because the peasants depend on the rainy season for planting and in some areas the rains have begun. The lands must be returned quickly; otherwise grave economic and social injury can come about.

(4) The global sum demanded is $1 million. This results from the calculations as to how much it cost to uproot the trees and plantations to prepare the lands for *cryptostegia* and how much compensation was to be given for the harvests destroyed; the conclusion is that the one dollar an acre offered by the Rubber Development Corporation is too low. A dollar-fifty was estimated by Fennell as the minimum, and two dollars is what the Haitian government feels is the necessary amount. There would be administrative costs, and as of yet the picture is confusing because of the way the lands were acquired, their location, and condition, so that the one dollar offered by Mr. Allen can only be accepted under reserve. The most important point was the adequate compensation to put the lands back into production. Some plants take from four months to four years to produce. Fruit trees take up to eight years. The peasants have to wait for the results and to profit from their work and investment, without taking into account illness, insects, etc. Seedlings, nurseries, and protective trees also must be considered. The cost per acre for a few plants follows: sugarcane, $13; manioc, $10; rice, $10; cocoa, $26; bananas, $26; coffee, $40. Taking the mean average, the amount comes to $1.5 million instead of the $75 thousand offered by Mr. Allen on the basis of one dollar an acre. Therefore, the $1 million demanded by the Haitian government is the strict minimum that would force the government to aid the peasants from its own budget. A better way to come to an understanding is for the American government and the interested parties to send a mission to Haiti to inform itself about the exactitude of the estimates and also the extent of the damage caused to Haiti.

(5) The amount for the construction that the Rubber Development Corporation is willing to give to SHADA is estimated at $483,000. As we have said before, what interests the Haitian government is aiding the

Haitian peasants whose lands were rented or requisitioned for the *cryptostegia* program by SHADA. The money is a fine gesture, but the government will first have to sell the constructions to get ready money for the peasants. As these buildings are far away from cities, they cannot even be rented let alone sold.

(6) Given the difficulty due to the war in obtaining farm tools and machines it would be highly recommended that in the arrangements between the Rubber Development Corporation and the Haitian government, some of the machines and tools already on Haitian soil be given to the Department of Agriculture to be used for the realization of the program envisaged for the Haitian peasants.

To give more force to the government's demands, President Lescot decided or was persuaded to use his influence to back up his minister of agriculture and his ambassador in Washington by writing directly himself. So still in May 1944, the president gave the American chargé d'affaires in Haiti the answer of the Haitian government. In it is stated:

... it has clearly been shown that the proposals made by the Rubber Development Corporation, especially those which deal with the sums proposed as financial aid for the reconstitution of the peasant plantations which were destroyed to permit the culture of *cryptostegia,* are absolutely inadequate and to begin with unacceptable to the Haitian government . . . The immediate and unexpected cessation of the program puts the government into a painful and delicate situation vis-à-vis the peasants whose lands were rented or leased and whose plantations were destroyed. This has created grave economic and political problems which can only bring the government to welcome all generous and kind aid that the government of the United States can accord it, so as to permit it to face the situation.

But the aid proposed in the memorandum delivered by the American embassy is so disproportionate to the necessary sum for a serious job of rehabilitation that it appears to be purely symbolic . . . In the face of the situation that it confronts the Haitian government esteems that the damages caused to the peasants' lands represent the sacrifices consented to by the inhabitants of Haiti for the sacred cause of the freedom of the world. They can be compared to ravages provoked by enemy bombs falling on its territory . . . and, as concerns the effective return of the lands to the peasants and the rooting up of the *cryptostegia* plants on these lands, the Rubber Development Corporation needs only to scrupulously observe its contractual obligations. As concerns all the other points which could be the object of an accord between SHADA and the Rubber Development Corporation, an accord to which the Haitian government can not be a part, as it belongs to the Board of SHADA to talk with the Rubber Development Corporation.

At the end of May, Maurice prepared three memoranda that President Lescot had delivered to the American chargé d'affaires. Number 1 concerned the eventual cessation of *cryptostegia* production. The president explained the exceptional measures taken to oblige the proprietors in the zones declared strategic to rent or lease their properties to SHADA. The president had to visit all the areas where the project was carried out to explain in Creole the importance to the peasants and persuade them to work for and assist SHADA.

He went on:

... The giving up of their lands caused the peasants and certain proprietors considerable injury. In certain regions such as in Grand Anse, the felling of trees that serve in the construction of houses and small boats (wood called tanis) ... the economic repercussion provoked by the destruction brought uneasiness in all the regions where it was practised and affected the whole country. Because of the destruction of food crops, prices have risen considerably. Higher living costs were not compensated by salaries ... From the point of view of health there were notable perturbations, principally in Pilate from where were recruited a large number of day workers to work in a malaria infested area. This illness made many victims among those returned to Pilate: ... it is true to say that not enough attention was paid to the health of the laborers.

... it must also be said that in spite of the optimism of the president of SHADA certain members of the government foresaw the possibility of the failure of the *cryptostegia* program and advised the president of SHADA to come to an understanding with the American Rubber Development Corporation to consider certain measures in view of being prepared for such an eventuality. These recommendations were confirmed in a letter addressed to the president of SHADA dated April 21, 1943, by the Minister of Agriculture. It was not answered . . .

In this memorandum is noted also plans for the peasants' welfare that the directors of SHADA rejected from the point of view of the contract:

. . . it is none the less true that the Rubber Development Corporation and the American government have a moral responsibility vis-à-vis the government and the Haitian people which, by the way, are their allies in the war.

The reparations incumbent on the Rubber Development Corporation must not just be based on the mathematical evaluation of the material damages caused to the peasants and the permanent agricultural program but it should also take into account the psychological and political disturbances resulting from the cessation of the activities of the Rubber Development Corporation and the partial paralysis from which will suffer the affairs of the country. Therefore we think that at least one million dollars in cash should be paid to the Haitian government to undertake reparation and rehabilitation.

This memorandum then gave suggestions as to a plan of action composed of two parts:

I. The First Part
(1) The setting up in the central bureau of SHADA a service to get information from all the employees who were concerned with land acquisition and the technicians who had to do with the land abstracts. The work of this service will consist, first of all, in finishing the payment of the rented properties not yet entirely paid for.
(2) The rapid return of the lands to their proprietors.
(3) The immediate payment by the Rubber Development Corporation to the Haitian Department of Agriculture of part of the sum judged necessary for the uprooting of the *cryptostegia* plants. This will permit the immediate uprooting in certain regions to profit, if possible, from the coming rains to plant fast-growing food crops. This work can begin in the Artibonite valley to extend the culture of soja beans.

II. The Second Part—Program of Rehabilitation

How to go about this:

(1) Payment of $1 million in cash to the Haitian government by the Rubber Development Corporation.

(2) The delivery by SHADA on behalf of the Rubber Development Corporation of some of the pickups and trucks with three sedan cars. Five tires should come with each car.

(3) Augmentation of the quota of gasoline accorded to the Haitian government (rationing of gasoline because of war needs).

(4) The utilization, where judged necessary, of certain Rubber Development Corporation constructions.

(5) The utilization of a certain quantity of farm tools and light machinery.

(6) Transfer to the Department of Agriculture of the service created by SHADA to deal with land acquisition, because it is the Haitian government that will assume the responsibility of continuing to return the lands to their owners.

(Maurice showed himself firm when it concerned the rights of his country. He was willing to cooperate as long as whatever was proposed was for the good of Haiti; otherwise he stood his ground.)

Part II of the memorandum no. 2 established a plan of rehabilitation, always in conjunction with the cessation of the *cryptostegia* program. The government was to take the responsibility of returning the lands and giving tools to the peasants, establishing nurseries, and giving financial aid as well as technical aid and aid for health. It would also begin reforestation, the conservation of soil, and the extension of the production of certain plants.

Memorandum no. 3 was similar to Memorandum no. 2 but took into consideration the disposal of the SHADA constructions, the surplus materials, and the permanent projects, the reorganization of the company, the pursuit of the activities such as the growing of sisal, lemongrass, coffee and *Hevea,* and possible introduction of new plants, and how the unprofitable ventures would be shut down.

In an annex concerning the disposal, it can be proven that Fennell went overboard as concerns constructions both for housing and depots as well as tools and machines—all bought far in excess of what the situation demanded in each of the five areas: Bayeux, Grand Anse, Cape Haitian, Source Chaude, and Jeremie—even personnel. There were also boats and a short railroad line.

In July 1944 Maurice prepared a letter to send to Mr. W. L. Pierson, president of the Export-Import Bank, setting out his point of view, that unless the president of the company was a specialist in rubber growing he should have with him such a specialist, with Haitian superintendents in the division. Maurice went on to point out in what way the company could be structured as to the administration, the two divisions concerned with rubber, the two with sisal, and the one with the pine forest. To this end he states:

I hope there will be better cooperation between the executive direction and the Board and I would wish that outside the formal meetings there would be more frequent exchanges of view between the representatives of the Import-Export Bank and the different members of the Board so that the members could better know and understand the Bank's point of view and the Bank know better the point of view of the Haitian government and the Board.

I have always had the impression, after my conversation with you, that the Export-Import Bank wanted a frank and reciprocating collaboration, and never thought that the representation of the Haitian government on the Board was purely symbolic and illusory.

But President Lescot on hearing about the contents of the letter asked Maurice to wait.

A day or two later Maurice wrote to President Lescot a letter that he would not send because at the board meeting Fennell turned in his resignation as of September 30, 1944, followed by those of three of his closest American associates. In the letter Maurice referred to the board meeting held on June 19, during which he said to Fennell "either the president executes the decisions of the Board or he resigns," to which Fennell answered, "I am ready to do whatever the Export-Import Bank *orders* me to do." Maurice continued: "This statement is significant as it shows clearly that Fennell refuses to recognize the authority of the Board. If that is so then the Board has no reason for existing . . . ."

The unexpected withdrawal of the Rubber Development Corporation, the devastation of the peasants' lands, the inadequate compensation, and the lack of technical aid may have discouraged the peasants and may have been one of the causes of the fall of the Lescot government.

It is evident that in spite of the intervention of the president himself, who compared the catastrophic situation of agriculture caused by the planting of *cryptostegia* and the withdrawal, to the ravages of war, and in spite of André Liautaud's efforts as well as those of Maurice, the compensation given was inadequate to put the lands back properly for production.

However, a small victory was gained. Fennell did leave. In his place was put Robert Pettigrew, who had been in Haiti several years and had been manager of the pineapple plantation near Cape Haitian taken over by SHADA. The grapefruit plantation was permitted to continue. Pettigrew put out a report when he took office. He took his information from the balance sheet of May 1944.

Of the $5 million the sum still not spent was $660,000, which meant that $4,340,000 had already gone to salaries, land acquisition, construction, materials for the exploitation of the acquisitions, transportation, etc., and done without, for the most part, the consent of the board, yet for which the board could be held responsible.

Pettigrew was not optimistic. He foresaw the income from sisal, rubber *(Hevea),* and the pine forest as negative in comparison to the maintenance required. Too much had been spent in all areas, and too little would be the return on the sale of surplus and the sale of products.

The scaled-down SHADA program (the handcrafts section was closed, among others) continued. The exploitation of the pine forest came to a halt when a fire destroyed most of it. Whether this was an accident or a criminal act could not be determined. This loss was another blow for SHADA and the country.

What was the impact of SHADA on the rural economy? First of all, hundreds if not thousands of peasants had their autarkic way of life destroyed. Expropriated, displaced, their lives from one day to the next were, in some sense, ruined or at least completely upset. One could assume that it is from this period that the exodus to the cities began. The lands given back to the peasants, denuded of trees, bushes, and grass, must have been too much to cope with for a certain number. It would take time and an enormous amount of effort before the land became productive. The amplitude of the work to be furnished may have discouraged many. The rural economy, one can say, had been despoiled. It may have been a bagatelle for the Rubber Development Corporation and the United States. It was an economic disaster for Haiti.

What is so sad is that President Lescot had such good intentions for the country concerning the loan of $5 million from the Export-Import Bank. The war, the Rubber Development Corporation, and his sentiments as an ally of the United States against the Axis created a situation beyond the capacities of his country to control.

Although Maurice had many other obligations, which will be mentioned but not enlarged upon, it seems to me important to have taken the time to discuss SHADA not only because of its effect on Haiti, but also because the *cryptostegia* program consumed most of the money, time, and effort of all concerned to the detriment of the original program. It reveals the fight the representatives of the Haitian government carried on so as not to have the rights of their country ignored or bypassed. The greatest problem would be the repayment of the loan. Even the interest would be a heavy burden.

Other Responsibilities

As minister of agriculture and labor, Maurice dealt with other companies, American and European. But with none did he have as much to do, since he was not on any other board, nor were the companies involved in a contract, such as SHADA, with the government. He had contacts with the Standard Fruit Company, which had plantations for export of bananas to the United States. When there were questions concerning control of pests and diseases as well as the purchase of bananas from independent farmers and the treatment of laborers he was involved. He was also in touch with HASCO, for the same reasons, especially the treatment of the cane cutters. There were other companies with which he had contacts as to exploitation, maintenance, quality of the products, and their labor problems, if any.

It is during the voyage with President Lescot to Canada, where they stayed from October 6 to October 14, 1943, that Maurice made arrangements with ILO of Montreal to have two of their specialists come to Haiti, first to give conferences at the summer courses for secondary school teachers and then to make studies concerning social and health legislation for laborers. Maurice wished to have some laws passed to protect workers and start "social security" and "health insurance." With these two men he wanted to study what could be the first steps. Thadeus Poznanski made a study on a possible insurance fund, and David Blellock did a study titled "Recommendations Concerning the Elaboration of Labor Legislation."

Unemployment was high in Haiti at the time, and people were ready to work at anything for any price. It must also be said that some workers were unreliable, often irresponsible, undernourished, and suffering from various diseases such as worms, malaria, and dysentery, so the work they produced was not very satisfactory. The legislation could protect the workers but also the employers.

As minister of agriculture, Maurice had under his control the SNPA and ER, of which the School of Agriculture and the Normal School at Damien were a part. There were times when he did not see eye to eye with the director of SNPA and ER, Georges Heraux, who often forgot the limits of the budget. He was a good agronomist but as an administrator not careful about balancing the books; Maurice had to step in time and again to object to certain expenditures that he felt were unwarranted or beyond the possibilities of the budget.

Of course, Maurice supervised the various aspects of the services both in agriculture and rural education, with his good friend Allan Hulsizer, there for the first two years of Maurice's ministry, during which time he could feel confident that he could give most of his attention to the urban schools. He spent time to see people with propositions for agricultural projects. I remember one such person coming to the house and hearing Maurice say on the man's leaving, "If it's good for the country there is no problem."

There were meetings of all kinds besides those of SHADA. At that time being a board member was an honor but brought no financial compensation. SHADA was an obligation and a duty. Maurice also had a voluminous correspondence. All through his career his secretaries complained of their workload. He had the correspondence with President Lescot, the president of SHADA, the various ministries, and his various services, because he confirmed in writing any decisions taken to be sure they were understood and to have a record of the transaction even when it concerned the salary of a yard boy of a school. All expenditures were noted so he could show how the public funds had been spent down to the last gourde.

A copious correspondence remains, concerning the young people holding grants on leave to study in the United States. Even procuring American visas entailed back-and-forth correspondence, because of the war and travel restrictions. (In 1942 the only reason I was permitted to go to the United States for health purposes was because I was the wife of a government minister.) Besides, the scholarship holders were often dark-skinned and felt isolated in a hostile, cold climate and at times found it difficult to adjust. Solitude, illness, and depression could overtake them as well as money problems. Maurice assumed a role of "father" or "mentor," since he

90

also had been a student in the United States. He answered every letter he received. Perhaps someone someday will look over this correspondence. The study should be interesting.

*   *   *

The bourgeoisie in Port-au-Prince was small enough so the families were known to one another. There were many small circles. Friends and acquaintances saw each other frequently and sometimes more than enough. So it was a pleasure to see new faces from abroad, friends, or friends of friends, officials (from North and Latin America, which is why I learned Spanish; Maurice had already learned it and was fluent), or those interested in Haiti for its people, its culture, and one of its religions, which is voodoo. We greeted all and among them made lasting friends.

One couple, the George Simpsons, came to Haiti, he as a social scientist to study the life and religion of the peasants. He came with his wife and two young children, whom he left in Port-au-Prince, and for six months lived in a hut in a small village near Plaisance not far from Chatard, coming to town about once a month, as roads and transportation were problems. At the time he was on leave from Temple University in Philadelphia. Later as a professor at Oberlin College he studied the Rastafaris in Kingston. Later he became the head of the department of sociology at the same college.

Another friend was Richard Pattee, an American of Spanish origin who came to Haiti in 1936, professor at the University of Puerto Rico and married to a charming Puerto Rican. In 1938 he was appointed by the U.S. State Department to the direction of a service created to augment cultural relations with Latin America. He included Haiti in his activities. It was after the Buenos Aires conference held by the Organization of American States (OAS) that it was decided to create this post. Pattee was one of the first to promote the cultural development between the United States and Latin America for exchanges of visitors, the establishment of libraries, and to make known the Spanish and Portuguese intellectual and cultural values. He also gave conferences in the summer courses. We kept up the friendship for many years. And of course there were Polly and Allan Hulsizer, with whom we kept in contact and, as with the Mercer Cooks, encountered in the United States and Europe later.

Among the visitors was Nelson Rockefeller, for a time undersecretary of state in the State Department for the Latin American republics. (I remember him well, as he sent me a basket of beautiful roses.) Another was Edwin Embree, president of the Julius Rosenwald Fund, who came for two weeks in May 1944 to learn about the education system and offer grants for study in the United States. He was charming, affable, and perspicacious. (I still have the book he offered me, which he wrote. Its title is *Island India Goes to School*. It was on the schools in the Pacific islands of Indonesia, published by the University of Chicago Press.) There was Charles Johnson before he became president of Fisk University, with whom we had contact through the study-abroad program. Fisk, like Howard, was open to all but frequented mostly by Afro-Americans. There was Charles Loram, the Yale University professor who brought twenty-five Yale students to visit the farm and rural schools in Haiti in 1937.

Another friendship was that with Alfred Metraux, who had a position at the Institute of Social Anthropology in Washington. Maurice invited him to serve as lecturer for the summer courses in 1945, an invitation Metraux had to refuse because he had just accepted an assignment from the American government to go to Germany having to do with the war and its effects. Later the men would meet at the Marbial Project in 1951 in Haiti. This project had been conceived by UNESCO and the Haitian government. It was undertaken in 1949. It concerned the creation of a community center with primary school, with evening courses, a dispensary, a workshop, a garden, and raising of pigs, chickens, and other animals. The idea was good but the site not advantageous. There were difficulties in financing and in personnel, so it was not a success.

When we lived in Great Neck, New York, in the early fifties, Alfred lived for a time in one of the UN-leased buildings, but he did not stay long and returned to UNESCO and Paris. Here we renewed the acquaintance until his retirement from UNESCO. His stay in Haiti awakened his interest in voodoo. This interest led him to Brazil. He became an authority and wrote about the subject.

I have written about our friends and contacts from North and Latin America. We also had contacts with the French, due mostly to the war. They were quite special, as they were of high intellectual quality, invited here by President Lescot. Among them were Mme. Geneviève Tabouis, a very well-known French journalist who from New York edited a weekly news-paper, *Pour la Victoire*. It was the winter of 1943–44. Others were Jacques Maritain, French Catholic philosopher; André Breton, the "pope" of surre-alism; Henri Torres, a communist; and André Maurois, the writer of biographies, with whom I had the great pleasure of having several interesting conversations in the course of receptions and dinners. Among this group were several personalities who influenced the young Haitians to begin an opposition to the very government that had invited them to Haiti.

There was also Louis Jouvet and his theater group. They spent several weeks in Haiti and regaled us with theater productions such as *Dr. Knock* and *L'Annonce Faite à Marie*, written by the French poet Paul Claudel. The troupe was making the South American circuit. Musicians also stopped over, on their way either to or from Latin America, as for the time being only the western hemisphere was open to them. So although the war deprived us of certain comforts and at times certain foods, yet it also brought unexpected delights, as these talented people would have passed Haiti by had it not been for the war.

During the time he was minister Maurice made several official voyages. In 1942 he was at the head of a delegation of businessmen concerned with agricultural products to visit Mexico. There is a photo of him being introduced to the Mexican president Camacho.

In 1943 Maurice was included as one of several ministers, the ambassador André Liautaud, Gerard de Catalogne of the newspaper *Le Soir,* and Dantes Bellegarde, former minister of public instruction, and several military personnel for an official visit of President Lescot to Canada, the United States, and Cuba.

The group left Haiti to go directly to Ottawa, where they were received by the prime minister, M. MacKenzie King. The men then proceeded to Quebec City and were met by the lieutenant-governor, Eugene Fisit, and his wife, who invited them to their residence before going to the provincial parliament. The archbishop of Quebec and other personalities had them visit the University of Laval. But it was in Montreal that Maurice and Abel Lacroix met with the representatives of ILO and with the labor organization of Quebec.

After these events the group went to Washington, D.C., where they were invited to dine at the White House and called upon or were called upon by various government officials. President Lescot had a special visit with President Roosevelt. (It must be remembered that Haiti declared war on the Axis powers only a few hours after President Roosevelt's declaration on December 7, 1941, and put its resources at the service of the war effort to the detriment of its own economy.)

On to New York, where the mayor, Fiorello La Guardia, gave them an enthusiastic welcome and a dinner was offered by the president of IBM, Thomas J. Watson, in President Lescot's honor. The IBM president had a 150-page booklet with photos made of the trip to give to the party.

The last stop was Cuba. Here, too, the party was entertained by the president of Cuba, Juan Batista. Finally, they returned to Haiti, bringing back several accords and contracts.

It was during this trip that an incident occurred that illustrates racial attitudes of that time. One of President Lescot's sons was studying at a military academy some miles outside of Washington. The president and his party, accompanied by someone from the State Department, went to visit him. It appears that the journey on the train to the academy was without a problem. On the return, however, once the person from the State Department saw them seated, he left them. A conductor of the train, a few minutes later, asked that they go to that part of the train marked "For Coloreds." They had been put in a compartment marked "For Whites Only." They were the guests of the president of the United States. What to do? They were leaving the train when the State Department person ran up and explained the situation to the conductor. The president and his party were then permitted to return to the train. The separations no longer exist due to the sitdowns and other forms of resistance that took place in the late 1950s and early 1960s.

Another trip with the president took place in 1944, this time to Venezuela at the invitation of the president of that republic, Mr. Medina. This trip was the follow-up to his visit to Haiti. The two countries were linked together by a history that goes back to the time of Bolívar and Petion. In effect, it was through the generous gesture of President Petion that Bolívar, seeking refuge, was given asylum, money, arms, ammunition, and men to return to Venezuela to again take up the struggle against the Spanish and free the country in 1819.

As I have written, Maurice was upheld by the president in all his activities in spite of all the press attacks and probably despite certain maneuvers of certain members of the government and "friends." Not only was the official relationship excellent, but so was the personal one. The children of the family were included in the relationship, especially Eliane, their daughter. We met her again in Rabat. She returned to Haiti years after; there we saw each other on most of our trips.

We kept up our friendship with the Lescots, contrary to many who turned their backs the minute the government fell. I found a letter in my husband's files dated April 24, 1946, in which the president describes his life in exile in the town of Alymer in the province of Quebec. He evidently knew from a letter that Maurice was seeking employment, for he stated: ". . . You, Alex Mathon and Defly are the only ones of my former cabinet members who have written me a word of sympathy. You cannot believe how much this gesture has affected me and my family." Further on he writes: ". . . I think that with a bit of patience all will be well with you. The Lord will help you; you merit it. Your great loyalty, your honesty and your love for work are a capital which should serve you. Of this I am certain . . ."

The future would prove him right, and in a letter he wrote to me (March 27, 1961) when I informed him of my husband's having become chief of the UNESCO mission for the Emergency Program for the Congo (Zaire) and consultant in education in the ONUC consultative group, he wrote:

I cannot hide my great pride in the brilliant promotion of Maurice who at this moment is organizing public instruction in the Congo. It is neither favoritism nor powerful support which has served him. He has been served by his great competence and seriousness. It is not the promotion of a former collaborator, nor that of a dear friend that makes me so joyful. The principal reason for my joy and my pride is to see a Haitian designated for this important work. Our compatriots do not appreciate the magnificent lesson that can be drawn from this marvelous choice. To see one of theirs, descending as all of us, of course, from those unfortunate men, who were torn from their native Africa, sold as beasts of burden in the Antilles, to work for the profit of often cruel owners, now designated by an international organization to organize, direct and administer the educational service in the same Africa, because our ancestors were able to acquire their freedom and liberty in throwing out their aggressors from the land which they had watered with their sweat and blood to become masters of that land. What a subject to meditate upon.

He wrote further: "Permit me to transcribe this passage from the speech I made in Cape Haitian which concerns Maurice particularly." It was his last political speech, to introduce the five-year plan of which Maurice was to be the head as minister of agriculture and labor, but no longer minister of public instruction.

It reads:

I wish to profit from this circumstance to render public homage to Monsieur Maurice Dartigue who, since 1941, with patriotism and courage is bringing about to the satisfaction of our government the reforms in the domain of education that were so necessary. We are persuaded that his circumscribed activities will reveal themselves more and more profitable for our government . . .

We corresponded while the couple lived in Canada. They came to reside in Paris, where we contacted them when Maurice was seconded to UNESCO by the United Nations. They were living in Puteaux and later in Suresnes on a very modest basis, with only a pension of $350 a month. Their home *Manoir des Lauriers* had been sold, but that money was not given to them until much later, after they had returned permanently to Haiti. Here, too, on each of our visits on "home-leave" we paid them a call.

                    *   *   *

The balance of power between the small mulatto group and the much larger black population has always been a delicate problem in Haiti. The mulattoes were often accused of keeping the power for themselves. The truth of the matter was that few blacks had the opportunity to be educated and thus be able to take on the responsibilities and attributes of the higher-echelon positions. (This is one of the chasms Maurice was trying to fill through education and grants.) Just recently I was told that Maurice had been accused of favoring mulattoes. I answered that he favored those who were ready for the job or further study without regard to color or social position. (It was Maurice who helped obtain a grant for François Duvalier in 1943 to study in Michigan.) It is true that the power had been in the hands of the mulattoes since the American occupation; this meant in the hands of the bourgeoisie for the government, commerce, and industry.

I encountered the situation in the winter of 1944–45. Maurice and I were at a dance. I had been dancing all evening. My feet were in such a state I could not take another step. I had just told the table of friends with whom we sat that I would not dance again when a journalist whom I liked came to ask me for a dance. I looked at him. I should have asked him to sit down for a few minutes. All I did was say, "I just can't; my feet hurt too much."

96

He left. A dear friend turned to me. She said, "You should have danced. He thinks that it is because he is black that you refused his invitation."

In my husband's office at home hung a photo that the president had given us. Just before Christmas 1945 I found it on the floor, the glass shattered. I still remember thinking *Oh! Oh! Does this mean he will soon fall?* On January 9, 1946, that is precisely what happened.

In May or June 1945, the Haitian delegates to the UN conference held in San Francisco on their return advised Maurice to leave the government, as the Americans were not going to back President Lescot any longer. Maurice replied that he was not a politician. He had started the reforms and meant to continue with them.

It was in the fall of 1945 that President Lescot announced the five-year plan in agriculture and asked Maurice to give up the Ministry of Public Instruction to concentrate on the plan, indicating that it would be an absorbing and difficult task. By letter Maurice thanked the president for the confidence he placed in him and hoped that he would live up to the responsibilities for this special undertaking. So from November 1945 Maurice held the office of minister of agriculture and labor until the fall of the Lescot government on January 9, 1946.

The five-year plan sounded credible, as the president had perhaps thought to offset the bad effects of the *cryptostegia* project. It was much later that I learned that he had had the constitution changed so as to enable him to keep the presidency until 1952. So it is to be wondered if the five-year plan was made to give him a reason for staying on. This decision angered the opposition and made it determined to become more outspoken.

There are no letters to show that Maurice had a part in the drawing up of the five-year plan. But he must have been involved. The plan concerned the road repairs, the extension of irrigation, reforestation, the intensive cultivation of certain agricultural products, promotion of animal husbandry, the fight for pest control, especially concerning bananas (the Standard Fruit company had left Haiti due to political maneuvering, and those who took over the plantations had neglected to control either pests or diseases, so the banana output had lessened), and the amelioration of the life of the peasants.

In the National Archives in Washington I found a reference to this plan. The American specialists did not think highly of it. Did they think the Haitians could not carry it out? They were against the building of a good road from Port-au-Prince to the Cape, which was part of the plan. In this they were wrong. That road is the most important in Haiti now.

I cannot leave this important part of Maurice's lifelong work without rendering homage to some of the men and women who collaborated with him to put in motion in less than five years some unusual reforms. I've already cited André Liautaud, Pierre Liautaud, and Oscar Boisgris, but there were also Jean Kernizan, André Audant, Pierre Montas, Frank Thomas, Victor Bastien, Abelard Desenclos, Morrisseau Leroy, Max Rigaud, Jeanne and Madeleine Sylvain, and many others among the administration, the specialists, the supervisors, and the directors and teachers in the schools, and all most eager to advance the reforms. After Maurice's death, Oscar Boisgris (the statistician who became director of Rural Education and later was in the first group of Haitian professionals who gave valuable service in the Congo crisis) wrote in August 1983 in the newspaper *Le Septentrion:*

That which distinguishes Dartigue is the work he accomplished, his devotion to public affairs, his capacity to work. . . . Where others hesitated he dared.

Technician of the Technical Services in Agriculture, he was appointed director of Rural Education at its Haitianization in 1931. As soon as he was named he put in the reform of the rural schools which up to that time were directed by the illiterate political protégés who earned but thirty gourdes a month. He doubled the salaries and from then on the teachers were appointed through competitive exams. Never did he interfere personally in these exams. When a teacher was needed in a certain locality, the list of the test results was consulted to choose the most capable . . .

. . . In the rural education services, the most modern methods were put in practice, even though sometimes they were beyond the intellectual preparation of some teachers, even though they were appointed through exams.

Named Minister of Public Instruction, Agriculture and Labor, he reformed urban education in ameliorating work conditions and the obtention of numerous grants for study abroad . . .

In September 1982 there appeared in *Le Septentrion* an article titled "La Pensée Haitienne," which Maurice wrote when he was minister. (This newspaper evidently has always believed in what my husband tried to do.) This article shows quite well Maurice's beliefs and character. It reads:

The efficiency of a public administration implies certain essential factors. First of all it implies honesty in financial and commercial transactions and the scrupulous observance of the rules of the principles of Administration and Control.

Without the most scrupulous honesty, not only the funds destined for definite projects are not sufficient but the morals of the administrative body crumble little by little and the whole system enters into decomposition. The dishonesty of one and the other engenders little compromises which provoke a general slackening of the hierarchical links. Soon comes about lack of discipline, of all ideals, and a general decomposition. [Today he would write: "corruption."]

One should not be content to be strictly honest but even try to prevent all waste of State funds and one should try to obtain the maximum for each gourde spent.

. . . We should prevent the shame that is presented by the dilapidated and unpardonable state of most of the trade schools, with their tools and machines rusted, the schools which were left well-equipped and in good condition by the Americans at their departure.

A chief of Administration who does not work from 8 A.M. to 1 P.M. cannot achieve much. However on a farm working only 8 A.M. to 1 P.M. is not enough. One cannot do research in a laboratory by keeping strictly to the hours 8 A.M. to 1 P.M. One cannot develop a system of education working only from 8 A.M. to 1 P.M. Nor seriously organize and constantly ameliorate an administration working only from 8 A.M. to 1 P.M.

We must banish laziness. The motto should be effort, opinionated effort, intelligent and efficient effort.

(This was asking a great deal, for few had Maurice's capacity for work. However, it was a challenge and some took it up and rendered invaluable service.)

Departure from Haiti and the Ten Years at the United Nations

In a confidential letter written by the American ambassador to Haiti, Orme Wilson, to the secretary of state for foreign affairs, James F. Byrnes (in reality to the assistant secretary of state for the American republics, Nelson Rockefeller) dated January 13, 1946, Wilson stated: "... I have the honor to report that the political disturbances precipitated by the student strike proceeded with unusual rapidity, and finally brought about perhaps the principal object of the strikers, the overthrow of President Lescot ..."[1] There, in a few words, is told how the Lescot government ended, in which Maurice, for almost five years, had played an important part.

As early as July 14, 1945, Orme Wilson had foreseen this possibility. He had been in contact with President Lescot concerning the projected five-year plan. He wrote to the State Department:

> Should the project fail there is little doubt but that it will be alleged that he is losing the support of the U.S. government with whom he has collaborated closely and upon whom he has depended ... Notwithstanding his faults, Lescot has, although undoubtedly for his own interest, cooperated closely with the U.S. and has thereby, however slightly, facilitated the prosecution of the war. Unless therefore it is the Department's belief that it would be advisable to encourage a change in the chief executive of this republic in order to obtain the inauguration of a more democratic regime, it is difficult to see how such a change would greatly improve our relations with Haiti.[2]

So the government fell and Maurice with it. It all happened so quickly. In appearance it seemed calm in Port-au-Prince at the end of the year 1945, although, as usual, there were rumors. But rumors were part of life in Haiti. The Christmas and New Year celebrations passed in the customary manner. However, on the eighth of January 1946 there began a series of student demonstrations with anti-American and anti-Lescot slogans. At first these were passed off as student hyperactivity. They developed into a strike, first in the Excise Office and then in the School of Agriculture at Damien. The army was at the beginning confined to barracks to let the police handle the disturbances. The students were backed by the growing opposition. The various groups, it was rumored, felt that the president favored the mulattoes, that he had become a dictator, that he practised nepotism, and, above all, that the five-year plan was just an excuse to prolong his mandate.

The crisis was precipitated by the resignation of the cabinet and the inability of the president to form a new one due to the refusal of the opposition, whose leader the president had called in for consultation. He desired to choose one or two of the ministers for the new cabinet. A deadlock occurred. In the end the opposition leader insisted that the president resign and leave the country immediately.

The president then made a grave error. Without consulting the heads of the army who had come to be with him in his home, the Manoir des Lauriers, he asked the American ambassador to come to see him, which the ambassador did. When these top army officials learned of the interview they placed the president under house arrest and took over the government. They readied the army in case of invasion, fearing that part of the American fleet that was cruising in the Caribbean might land in Haiti, as had happened in 1915, and bring on another occupation. The president was persuaded to leave the country the next day. He was escorted with his family to a plane. He went into exile in Canada.

The army had to move with great caution so as not to aggravate the excited population or the various political groups trying to foment disorder for a takeover. A triumvirate of high-ranking officers just managed to keep a precarious order and carry out the minimal government tasks. In May elections were held. The triumvirate stepped down, as it had promised to do, for the new president, Dumarsais Estimé. He in turn, several years later would try to prolong his mandate and he too would be forced to take the road to exile.

So the situation of the former ministers of President Lescot was not a pleasant one. Each had to decide for himself what he had to do. In the case of Maurice, in particular, the situation was difficult. One newspaper especially attacked him as well as his foreign-born wife. The family, through telephone calls, was threatened and told that mobs were on their way to pillage. The family was made more uncomfortable by the soldiers sent to "protect" it. Maurice knew he had enemies. His reforms did not please everybody. He freely admitted his preference for the pragmatic American-style education, as he believed that the methods he had seen used and the subjects offered were better suited to the needs of Haiti for improving the lives of the masses.

The failure of the experiment in growing rubber in Haiti, as its contribution to the war effort, was also a great factor in opposition to Americans. As minister of agriculture, Maurice was connected with this failure, as has been noted. Letters brought to light in 1978 prove his constant vigilance for the rights of the peasants. In 1946 this was not known publicly and he could have been partly held responsible for the unfortunate *cryptostegia* project.

The flames were also fanned by newspapers that kept up a barrage of distorted news. So in January 1946 Maurice found himself without a job and surrounded by some hostility. What opportunities would he have had, had he stayed on in Haiti? He was no politician. He had reached the high level of office through hard work and recognition for his achievements. Taking everything into consideration, he preferred to leave the country without knowing what his future would be. Due to the political situation he was unable to receive a passport, so he left Haiti under the protection of the Cuban chargé d'affaires to reside in Havana, Cuba, until he was admitted to the United States a few weeks later as a political refugee.

While in Cuba he immediately began job hunting, writing letters to those eminent Americans with whom he had had contacts while in office. One of the first letters was to Edwin Embree, the director of the Rosenwald Foundation. It was Embree who suggested UNRRA (the UN Relief and Rehabilitation Administration) for work in China. Once in the United States, Maurice applied and for a few days thought he had been accepted. But it fell through; the reason that was given was an excess of personnel. The probable true reason was that Maurice had no passport!

Next it was suggested that he try for a teaching post in the southern United States. To this he gave a categoric "no," realizing how difficult it would be for him, a black, his Hungarian-born wife, and their son to face the social climate and race prejudices prevalent in the American South in 1946.

Maurice wrote to Nelson Rockefeller and to James Farley, then postmaster general and chairman of the Democratic party, whom Maurice had met when he had accompanied President Lescot to the United States and Canada, and to John Winant, in a letter dated May 7, 1946. Winant, the American delegate to the newly created ECOSOC (Economic and Social

Council) at the United Nations in New York, granted him an interview. He wrote to Willard Barber of the State Department, Division of American Republics, and to Lawrence Duggan of the Institute of International Education, who suggested UNESCO, recruiting in New York, which was just opening in Paris and certainly more apt to use his training and experience in the field of education. Maurice did apply and did take the précis writer's examination. He wrote to Ralph Bunche (assistant secretary general in charge of the Trusteeship Department at the United Nations in New York) or was received by him, since the letter of thanks that Maurice wrote is dated October 3, 1946, when Maurice was making daily trips from New York City to Lake Success where the United Nations was housed. There were many more applications, as Maurice thought he had a wide acquaintance and hoped that somewhere someone would be able to help him find a job.

Maurice arrived in the United States in February 1946 and made his way to New York to stay at International House, where there were a few rooms for visiting alumni. It was inexpensive. He could take his meals there. Of course he wanted his family to join him, but where to find lodgings for a mixed couple was a problem even in New York and its surroundings, no matter how distinguished-looking or educated the family. His good fortune was to have a real friend in Allan Hulsizer. Hulsizer scouted around among his relatives and their friends and finally located a small furnished garden apartment on the outskirts of Red Bank, New Jersey. Maurice wired me, still in Havana with our son: "Have found an apartment in Red Bank, New Jersey, shall I take it?" I wired back: "Don't know where it is but take it," which he did, and thus we came to join him in early April. I had rented our home in Port-au-Prince and sold our car. It was this money that carried us through the next months, with the strictest economy. Maurice continued to send out letters seeking employment. At the same time he wrote a monograph titled *An Economic Programme for Haiti,* a special report for the Institute of Inter-American Affairs. It was published in late 1946 and had three editions. I do not know if he offered this report or if it was requested by the institute or if he received payment for this short work. A few friends took the long train ride from New York or came by car to see us; otherwise except for necessary shopping and train catching we preferred to keep to ourselves, not knowing how we would be accepted in the town.

In September, when no job was forthcoming from any application he had made, Maurice decided that the United Nations was his best and last hope; otherwise the family would have to return to Haiti, as funds were getting low and the temporary visa was soon to expire. He therefore took a room in a small hotel in New York City, leaving us in Red Bank. He made the daily journey to the UN headquarters. He hoped that his constant presence at headquarters might be more effective than letter writing. Whether it was the letters, the interviews, or his almost daily presence at the United Nations that brought about the result, the fact is that at last, in the middle of October 1946, he was given a modest short-term position as a documents officer (clerk) for the First UN General Assembly held in the United States. The Secretariat was at Lake Success, the large gatherings at Flushing Meadows. Accepting such a humble task after being one of the most important men in Haiti must have taken courage and humility. Was he foolish to take such a job with his background and experience? Should he have waited for an opening commensurate with his training? Did he compromise his future by being ready to accept such a job? At all events he was grateful to have been offered it, for it would give him a few months to replenish his finances and perhaps find better employment. An interoffice memo dated October 10, 1946, reveals that "this appointment would not prejudice his transfer or appointment to a post for which he is qualified by his education and experience. Mr. Dartigue has taken the appointment as an interim measure until he can be appointed to a more suitable post," and is signed "T. C. Gold, Personnel Officer."

The position carried with it two guarantees. The first was that of being housed in one of the buildings leased by the United Nations for its employees in various cities of Long Island, both in old and new developments. The United Nations understood that it could not attract people inside the United States nor those outside of it of different nationalities and ethnic backgrounds without assuring them security in proper housing. A service for this need was one of the earliest set up in the Secretariat. As soon as Maurice became a member of the organization he applied to this service. Temporary lodgings were found in Long Beach, Long Island, a summer resort quite far from his work and even farther from New York City. Here we spent four months. Fortunately for us, in February 1947 Maurice's short contract was renewed for six months and new housing, in a new apartment complex, opened up in Great Neck, New York, ten minutes by car from the Lake Success headquarters. To this development we moved, and there we remained until we left for Paris in 1956, when Maurice was seconded to UNESCO.

We were fortunate in our choice of Great Neck: Several apartment buildings were leased by the United Nations, housing UN families of many countries. We made lasting friends with some. Our son also made friends. Moreover in Great Neck the residents, many of the Jewish faith, were eager to know interesting and different people. In the ten years we lived there our lives were enriched by their cordiality, understanding, and sympathy. Many remain friends to this day.

The second guarantee was the protection offered by being employed in the United Nations. Maurice's temporary visa had been renewed twice. When it again came up for action in 1948 he was able to give it over to the visa section of the Secretariat, obtaining for himself and us the status of an employee of a designated international organization, which status we kept until our departure for Paris. So there were no more problems concerning the right to live and work in the United States.

It was also in 1948 that Maurice was finally given a Haitian passport. The reason why he had been denied one was that the government that came into office after the elections in May 1946 decided to bring to trial the former president and all of his cabinet, for alleged mishandling of public monies. A law was passed to this effect giving a commission the right to investigate the former administration. In April 1947 Maurice received, through the Haitian ambassador to the United Nations, the summons to appear in court in Port-au-Prince. As he had no passport and none would be forthcoming until after the trial, he wrote a letter in which he exposed his private financial situation before becoming minister and what he had acquired while in office for almost five years. Furthermore, he stated, it was public knowledge that he had administered the state funds with the strictest probity and greatest economy, always trying to obtain the greatest results for each gourde spent. Besides, all the financial reports, bills, and receipts, monthly and annual, were with the archives of the three ministries for which he had been responsible. They were also transmitted regularly to the Department of Finance as well as the Bureau of Control and the National Bank. The various directors and chiefs of all the services could be called upon to bear witness. Proceedings against him as well as some of the other ministers were dropped. The president (in absentia) and three ministers were put on trial. But they, too, were acquitted of the charges brought against them. The investigation and the clearance of his name permitted Maurice to receive a passport, thus enabling him to go to Geneva and Paris for the General Assembly in late August 1948. President Lescot wrote: "They find it hard to forgive us because we were honest."

The United Nations is now well known throughout the world, but a few words about its beginnings might be of interest here. As early as 1942 President Roosevelt had been preoccupied by the period after the war, convinced that the Allies would win it. The League of Nations, of which the United States had not been a member, no longer responded to the aspirations for which it had been created. A new organization would have to be developed. Roosevelt and the British prime minister, Winston Churchill, chose a few men to form a committee to study the problem and formulate plans. It was decided that there would be three main bodies, the Security Council, the Economic and Social Council, and the Trusteeship Council, which later included the section on information from non-self-governing territories. The trusteeships were territories held by certain countries under mandate from the First World War, while the non-self-governing territories were (to give them their usual name) colonies. There would be, to cap these councils, the General Assembly, to which all member states could send delegates and where each state would have one vote. During the time this committee met to put together the basic plan, the countries such as Belgium, France, the Netherlands, and Italy were in no position to give their opinion. Winston Churchill, speaking for Great Britain, was not in favor of the idea, but the United States was bearing the greatest financial burden of the war, so he acquiesced. The fact was that without the United States the European allies would have been in critical straits, so Churchill felt obliged to go along with Roosevelt. Stalin, of course, accepted.

Definite plans were drawn up for a charter for the organization. Much was accomplished at Dumbarton Oaks in Washington, D.C., in November 1944. It was there decided that only those nations that had declared war on the Axis Powers could be members. Several South American countries hastened to do so as late as February 1945.

In April 1945, before the war officially ended but with victory in sight, the first conference of the Allied nations was held in San Francisco, and for two months this group worked out the various articles, rules, and regulations by which the United Nations operates, more or less, to this day. The first General Assembly in the United States was held in New York in the fall of 1946. The very first one had been held in London on January 10, 1946. The service organization called the Secretariat began to take shape, to feel its way on how best to be of use to the delegations, the councils, and the General Assembly.

The Secretariat, headed by a secretary-general, with assistants and staff, was created. Those who were to make up the staff were to be international civil servants, supposedly apolitical, chosen for competence in their field. They were and are functionaries carrying out the resolutions adopted by the different bodies. They were and are technicians, professionals, and general service employees.

The Secretariat is divided into three departments, one for each council, with a director for each, supervised by one of the assistant secretaries-general. Here only the Trusteeship Council and the Trusteeship Department will be discussed. It was in this department that the opening for Maurice came up in February 1947, after his first three months as documents officer for the General Assembly. It is important to remember that the Trusteeship Council was a great departure from the body that had existed in the League of Nations. Therefore, a staff was put together but as yet was untried. It took time to put the right people in the right place for the most effective participation after the resolutions of the General Assembly were adopted and members of the Council selected. The Secretariat was still feeling its way and adding personnel. One can say that Maurice was in the Secretariat almost from the beginning.

A few words to explain the Trusteeship Council: When the United Nations was created, this council was almost as important as the other two organs of the august body. The Security Council attracted more attention and made more newspaper headlines, but it was the Trusteeship Council that became the wedge that forced open the door to freedom for the millions in the colonies and trusteeships. The council obliged the administrative authorities to activate political, economic, social, and educational measures to hasten independence. The mandating powers were to have given independence during the period between the two wars, but some territories under their care were not much further along toward freedom than they had been before. There was little difference in the attitude of some of the Europeans or in their treatment of the indigenous populations. Racial discrimination, lack of upward mobility, and lack of possibilities and opportunities for improvement were the lot of many of the peoples under mandate, just as it was in the colonies.

The Trusteeship Council was given limited powers. The United Nations Charter states that the council may:

(1) Consider reports submitted by the administering authority.
(2) Accept petitions and examine them with the administering authority.

107

(3) Take action in conformity with the terms of the trusteeship agreement.

(4) Formulate a questionnaire on the political, economic, social and educational advancement of the inhabitants of each trust territory. (The administering authority would make an annual report to the General Assembly based on the questionnaire.)

(5) Provide for periodic visits to the trust territories.

One hears little about the Trusteeship Council these days, because it has almost put itself out of business. Only one territory of the eleven that existed in 1946 remains. The trust territories are now the countries of Ghana, Cameroon, Nigeria, Republic of Togo, Somalia, Tanzania, Samoa, Rwanda, Burundi, New Guinea, Papua, and Nauru.

Concurrently through the years most of the colonies or protectorates of Great Britain, France, Holland, Italy, Portugal, Belgium, and the United States have attained nationhood. This means that combined with the trusteeships over 700 million people have thrown off dependence and gained their autonomy. It was in the fall of 1960 at the fifteenth session of the General Assembly that a strong resolution proposed by twenty-five nations was passed urging "the granting of independence to countries under the colonial powers as well as others without waiting for total political, economic, social or educational preparedness." This resolution spurred on those fighting for independence. They felt they now had support of the United Nations.

During the time Maurice worked at the United Nations in the Secretariat, the Trusteeship Department was concerned with all trusteeships and information from non-self-governing territories (colonies). In 1946–1947 there were 60 member nations. Today, with the independence won or given to these territories and colonies, especially in Asia and Africa, there are 184 member states. A great step forward has been accomplished in the recognition of human rights and freedom. Maurice had a role, very small at first, of making known the situation through his and the other staff members' work.

Those years at the United Nations were very exciting. At the time there was strong idealism. The war was over. The search was on for better ways of living together. The United Nations had authority. High hopes were placed in it. Its decisions were respected.

To be part of this vast undertaking at almost the bottom of the scale of hierarchy was a great challenge. Maurice was a black. He was from a very small black nation, the only French-speaking republic in the hemisphere, with little authority outside its boundaries. Moreover, the government that had assumed power in Haiti was not in his favor. In fact, he was told that he must keep a low profile while that government was in office. However, he rose step by step from documents officer, reclassified as political affairs officer in the General Services. Finally he was given professional status in 1949 after he had petitioned the Personnel Board for recognition in this category. He still had to prove himself, for he was given the professional grade two, the grade usually given to recent university graduates or professionals with very limited experience.

While in the General Services he worked as part of a team that produced resource materials, information based on texts prepared and checked by staff responsible for assembling the facts sent in by the administering authorities. In the department there were several sections dealing with different fields of interest and different geographical areas. The staff was also responsible for the annual *Green Book,* compiled from the information received from the aforementioned authorities.

Maurice was given more and more responsibilities as the years went by, but he was happy to be accepted at last in the professional category and felt fortunate to have attained this without the backing of the Haitian government. In January 1951 he advanced to grade three, and in the same year on his return from the visiting mission to Ruanda-Urundi, for which mission he, as secretary, made the report, he was recommended for and given the grade four. In a report signed by Ralph Bunche and Wilfred Benson, Maurice's immediate superior, it was stated that he was recommended, "as he has carried out a number of varied responsibilities with his usual resourcefulness and as a senior specialist he is well qualified." The title of Senior Specialist in Education was given him when he was promoted to grade three.

In 1951, after several short contracts and two-year contracts, Maurice was given a permanent one and the above-mentioned title in the Special Units Section of the division, which post he kept until seconded to UNESCO. He became the anchorman, getting work done no matter what difficulties or short deadlines caused possible obstacles. Not only that, but he knew his field, did detailed research, and produced serious papers in his specialties. Notation was made in a later evaluative report that "he continues to use his considerable diplomatic skills to the advantage of the division."

In looking over the archives at the UN headquarters in New York there is no evidence of correspondence with Maurice's signature. Apart from the short microfiches giving his curriculum vitae, date of entry, and promotion and evaluative reports the only mentions of his name are in the inner office informal directives where from 1950 his name occurs as part of a team, later as head of a team in reference to the *Green Book,* which had to be edited carefully so that no administering authority would be offended by the slightest innuendo, down to the last "it" and "the." Maurice spent hours to get the texts just right. He was also asked to give attention to other reports received from the administering authorities concerning special subjects such as migrant labor, the training of workers, and the definition of literacy, subjects that were to be discussed in the Special Committee of the Trustee-ship Council at the end of the year.

By 1952 he was recognized as one of the few educationalists in the division. By 1953 he was mostly occupied with educational studies. Also through the office memos one learns that the staff was encouraged to initiate research in certain problems concerning education in the trust territories and provide for drafting and gathering of material. Education had been ranked fourth in importance in the development for independence after political, economic, and social advancement. Now it was becoming increasingly recognized as of the greatest importance toward getting dependent peoples ready for self-government. Maurice did a study on compulsory education and another on the education of girls, which showed the existing facilities, the impediments, the provision for improvement, the numbers, levels, and policies of the authorities. These studies were particularly important in 1953, as the program of the Special Committee of the Trusteeship Council was concerned with it.

The next evaluation report was written by Benjamin Cohen, a member of the Chilean delegation for several years, who had recently been appointed under secretary-general in charge of the Trusteeship Division after Victor Hoo, who replaced Ralph Bunche as responsible for the department, had been assigned to other duties. It is dated May 1955. In it Cohen states:

Dartigue's work was devoted mainly these last two years in the planning and drafting of studies on the various aspects of educational conditions in non-self-governing territories for submission to the Committee. Amongst the major studies entrusted to him were those on secondary education, teacher training, and the duties of teachers. In addition, he cooperated on the finalization of pertinent sections of the summaries of official information and assisted in the planning and editing of the volume of the *Green Book* entitled "Special Study on Educational Conditions in the NSGT." He collected and classified statistical data relating to basic information and vocational education and was a member of various teams responsible for the preparation of other studies relating to them. As before he continued to carry out his work with high competence and excellent judgement supported by his background, experience and thorough knowledge of his subject . . .

As stated before, Maurice had missions outside headquarters. His first was to Geneva for the Special Committee of the Trusteeship Council in late August and September 1948 and then to Paris for the General Assembly held there at the Palais de Chaillot later in the fall. (I scraped up enough money for the fare. We lived on his per diem. After three weeks in Geneva, I went to Paris, where I was able to find a room for a dollar a night at the Hotel du Louvre. I ate little but saw much until Maurice joined me at the hotel, in better quarters. After a week together I returned home. What I had been unable to do in 1939 because of the war I achieved in 1948.)

Maurice's most unusual mission, however, took place in July and August of 1951, when he went as a member of the Secretariat with the Trusteeship Council's periodic visiting mission to Ruanda-Urundi in East Africa. Usually the mission was composed of several delegates of the council and several members of the Secretariat of the Trusteeship Division. For this visit to Ruanda-Urundi the members of the mission included four delegates headed by Dr. E. Marchena of the Dominican Republic, and, for the Secretariat, Dr. Victor Hoo, Maurice, P. Rouzier (also a Haitian), and a secretary. Maurice was designated as secretary to write the mission's report for Urundi. Rouzier handled the finances and travel arrangements. They all got along very well. Incidentally, the mission was one of the first to cross the Atlantic ocean by a sleeper air plane. It took twenty-four hours to reach Brussels from New York City. There the mission met with the Belgian authorities concerned with both the Congo (a Belgian colony) and the trust territory of Ruanda-Urundi, for which Belgium was the administering authority. After two days in Brussels, the mission flew to Léopoldville (now Kinshasa), where Maurice was but an observer. He did relate later that he had been well impressed with some of the efforts the Belgians had made to improve living and working conditions of the native laborers.

The group then left for Ruanda-Urundi. There Maurice accompanied the delegation everywhere, to take notes and listen carefully. The mission visited schools, hospitals, fish farming stations (to repopulate Lake Tanganyika), a sanatorium, and other centers of interest. Members of the mission discussed with the Belgian functionaries the political, economic, social, and educational policies in view of the advancement toward independence. They met with leading native dignitaries and were received by the *mwami,* the king (who later was deposed by his son). They also received some petitions by post and others brought by the petitioners themselves. Maurice cites a case of the latter. It was he who made the investigation and wrote up his findings, which in this case showed that the petitioner had greatly exaggerated his ill usage, but the fact remained that he had a real complaint. After the visit was officially over Maurice left the mission and went on to Mombasa in Kenya, Addis Ababa in Ethiopia, and Cairo in Egypt, as a tourist before returning to write his report at headquarters in New York.

This report was published in 1952 as a Green Book (the coverings of the documents printed by the Trusteeship Division were green, hence the name) for the eleventh session of the Trusteeship Council. It was entitled *Report on the Trust Territory of Ruanda-Urundi* (no. 2T/1031). Even for this he received no byline. Except for the higher echelons the work of the Secretariat was produced without acknowledgment, for the most part.

In August 1954 he represented the United Nations at the Caribbean Agricultural Extension Development Centre organized in Kingston, Jamaica, by the Food and Agricultural Organization, the United States Operations Administration, and the Inter-American Institute for Agricultural Services. While in Kingston he visited the Department of Education and the School of Education as well as a few schools for his own information.

Like other foreigners with permanent homes abroad employed by the United Nations, he was entitled to go on home leave every two years. He had not availed himself of the privilege at first because he had no passport. When he was finally granted one he was off to Paris. On his return the pressure of work prevented him from taking the time to do so. This would be the case later, when he would miss several occasions to take home leave while he was with UNESCO. However, with the fall of the Estimé government, after five years of absence from Haiti, in the winters of 1951–52 and again 1953–54 we returned to see relatives and renew acquaintance with friends and country. One of his first visits was to pay his respects to the recently elected president, Paul Magloire, whom he had known when Magloire was chief of the palace guard during Lescot's presidency. Each time Maurice returned to Haiti he rendered this visit. In 1952 when the president and his wife were on an official visit to the United States and were invited to a formal luncheon given in their honor by the secretary-general, Dag Hammarskjöld, at the UN headquarters, we were included.

After Hurricane Hazel hit Haiti, Maurice and others set up a lottery at the United Nations, the earnings of which were used to help offset the dreadful damage, especially in the southwest of Haiti.

During one of his home leaves Maurice stopped in Puerto Rico. He visited schools and low-cost housing as well as new factories specializing in converting imported parts to finished products for export, always with the idea in mind of how these could be installed in Haiti. (The factories did come later.) In Haiti he went out to Marbial Valley near Jacmel to visit the pilot project established jointly by the Haitian government and UNESCO concerning fundamental education. (It no longer exists.) Maurice also returned to his old school in Damien and saw the fish farming experiment at the agricultural station. He talked with his former colleagues about the problems in education. He wrote a report on the Marbial project.

As the early 1950s passed he had more and more contact with the high-ranking officials of the Magloire government, some of whom were his friends, in Haiti and in New York. In fact, as his position in the United Nations became more secure he became reconciled to the very man, the newspaper proprietor, now a delegate to the United Nations, who had constantly tried to undermine, through his newspaper articles, Maurice's efforts to reform the educational system during his term of office as minister. Maurice always kept Haiti in mind and worked out several projects that he presented to the proper minister in Haiti. One such was a more stable method of supplying electricity to Port-au-Prince, where electricity was often unavailable. Maurice was thanked, but nothing came of it.

About that time, too, an offer was made to him by a minister to return to Haiti to direct a proposed bureau of planning. He was willing if he could be given a leave of absence from the United Nations or be detached from the Secretariat to the Technical Assistance Branch of the United Nations and paid by that fund. But at that time Technical Assistance did not send nationals to their home country and there were no real guarantees. Maurice, remembering the difficult situation in which he found himself in January 1946, preferred his more modest but safe position at the United Nations, which depended on competence and not on political circumstances. It was also rumored during his home leave in the summer of 1955 that he might be approached for an important position in the government. He declined, saying he was not a candidate. It was just as well as Magloire decided not to run for a second term in 1957.

So the years might have gone on in the United Nations with a few promotions and perhaps a transfer to another division or a post in the field, as happened to several of Maurice's colleagues with the decreasing amount of work in the Trusteeship division as the trusteeships and non-self-governing territories became independent.

It was in November 1954 that Maurice was a recipient of the medal just created for "Distinguished Services in Education" awarded by Teachers' College, Columbia University. This honor he appreciated deeply.

In 1955 two important events occurred, which incited Maurice to leave the United Nations for UNESCO in Paris. Full knowledge of these was only revealed when a notebook in his handwriting came to light in 1984. One concerned his deception by not receiving the promotion he expected. The other states that he had been offered a post in Paris. I only knew the simple facts at that time.

It appears that as early as July 1954 Maurice learned that the chief of the Caribbean Section of the division was resigning. Encouraged by his colleagues and the excellent reports about his work, as well as his special background and experience, he became a candidate for the post after talking it over with the director of the division and with Mr. Benjamin Cohen, the assistant secretary-general in charge of the division, who had written so highly of Maurice and his work in the periodical report. An American, appointed earlier as assistant to the chief of the Caribbean Section, also made known his candidacy. He had assumed the direction of the section on an interim basis. What interested him was the promotion, not the position. When again Maurice had a conversation with Mr. Benson, the director of the division, he was told by him that Dr. Hoo had a candidate, too, and that he, the director, was in no position to make recommendations, as he was sure they would not be taken into account. The long and short of it was that pitted against the American backed by B. Cohen and a Chinese backed by Dr. V. Hoo, Maurice realized that he didn't have a chance, even with the backing of the Haitian delegate. As expected, the American was selected. What was most unfair from Maurice's point of view was that he had been permitted to go on hoping when the decision had been made weeks before the selection was announced. It was the American who let him know this. The disappointment was great. That this was the outcome of all Maurice's efforts, his devotion and capabilities, it must have been a severe blow to him.

While this was going on, a second avenue of promotion opened up, also in 1955. As Maurice was interested in the position of chief of the Caribbean Section, he took no notice of the job offered at UNESCO in Paris, posted on the bulletin board at the United Nations. It was a Chinese friend who brought it to his attention, saying that he himself did not qualify for the job but he thought that Maurice surely did. It concerned a post in the Education Department at professional grade four. Maurice thanked his friend but said he would consider the offer only when UNESCO would make it and in no case would he accept it at professional grade four. Later in the day another colleague gave Maurice the same news and he gave him the same answer.

A week later Maurice was approached by the UNESCO office at UN headquarters to let him know that his name was being put on the list of possible candidates. Maurice informed his superior, the director of his division, who had not thought it necessary to recommend him for the Caribbean post but who now immediately sent off a letter of protest to the assistant secretary-general Cohen, saying that his division was being raided without his being consulted. No matter, UNESCO went through with the negotiations, and Maurice's demand for professional grade five was accepted. The first we knew of it was when he announced in January 1956 that he had been offered a post in UNESCO in Paris and asked if he should take it (when he had done so already). I was very happy. Our son was less eager, as he would have been entering his senior year in high school in Great Neck, with all the status that year gives.

These ten years in the United States were ones of great enrichment, even though we had done no traveling except to Haiti and back. Our friendships and our contacts were worldwide. The sessions at the General Assembly were unusual, for we were able to be at some of the meetings that resulted in the founding of Israel. We listened to Sylvio Olympio pleading for the Ewe people of Togo. Some "greats" sat in the General Assembly president's chair, such as C. P. Romulo of the Philippines, Paul Spaak of Belgium, Oswaldo Aranha of Brazil, and the first and only woman, V. Lakshmi Pandit of India, until 1969, when Angie E. Brooks of Liberia presided! One cannot forget the American Adlai Stevenson, Britain's Sir Gladwyn Jebb, nor Andrey Gromyko of the Soviet Union.

(In Paris our son stayed for one year in the American school, then went

115

on to Brandeis University in Waltham, Massachusetts. On graduation, after three months as documents officer at the United Nations in New York he entered Columbia University for a master's degree in political science and has had a career in public relations, presently with Warner Bros.

As for me, two months had not gone by in Paris before I was asked to direct the Jardin d'Enfants de l'ONU, a cooperative nursery school (founded by Mme. A. Myrdal and UNESCO parents). I had supervised student teachers in a private school for preparing teachers of young children in New York City and had directed parent cooperatives in Great Neck so was willing and able to accept this position, which turned out to be a very interesting one and which I held for ten years, until we went to Burundi.)

A letter dated January 23, 1956, written by Mr. J. McDonald, deputy director of personnel at the United Nations, addressed to Mr. Gagliotti, executive officer of UNESCO at UN headquarters, states:

> The UN will be happy to agree to the secondment of Maurice Dartigue to UNESCO for two years. As the Committee on Information from non-self-governing territories, at which Mr. Dartigue is presenting a paper, will not adjourn until the end of May, it is suggested that the effective date of secondment be June 9th . . . It is understood that UNESCO will inform the UN not later than June 8, 1957 whether they will be in a position to take over Mr. Dartigue's permanent contract. If the answer is in the affirmative, Mr. Dartigue will be transferred immediately to UNESCO. If the answer is in the negative Mr. Dartigue will complete his two years' secondment and then will return to New York.

Due to his sense of responsibility concerning the work he was doing, Maurice had never used up the annual leaves or sick days. He had accumulated on leaving the United Nations 67 days of annual leave plus 125 days of sick leave, because apart from the ulcer attack he had had in 1954 (due to stress and overwork), which kept him from his office for six weeks, he had been in good health. Moreover, apart from the home leaves, he only took a few days off here and there to settle business matters or relax. He did not do any traveling in the United States, fearing racial discrimination. Therefore, the accumulated days benefited the UN Secretariat.

A letter to welcome Maurice to UNESCO was sent in March 1956 by Dr. Matta Akrawi of Iraq, then deputy director of the Department of

Education at UNESCO, stating that he was happy that Maurice was joining the department as chief of the Section of In-School Education. He stated:

I have followed your trail in Haiti where even some years after you had left people speak of your splendid work. Also I had the opportunity to see you in 1953 at the UN where I was very well impressed with the papers produced under your direction for the Special Committee on Information from non-self-governing territories, and was glad to have some very pleasant chats with you. All of this encourages me and all of us to look forward to very pleasant work together.

This kind, warm, and appreciative letter was welcomed by Maurice. He left for Paris in late May 1956. Our son and I joined him, bag and baggage, in early July after John's school closed. Just as the decision to leave Haiti (though under very different circumstances) was in retrospect a fortunate one, so was Maurice's decision to join UNESCO. Wider horizons and greater responsibilities were to be offered him there. With his culture and language he was much more at home in France.

Notes

1. *Foreign Relations of the U.S., the American Republics,* vol. 2.
2. *Diplomatic Papers,* vol. 9, no. 887, *Foreign Relations of the U.S., the American Republics.*

The First Years at UNESCO, June 1956–August 1960

A few words can be said about UNESCO and about Maurice's position there. UNESCO was created in 1945 in London under the UN Charter, article 57, which made provision for specialized agencies. As early as 1942 ministers of education had been invited to form the "Conference of Allied Ministers of Education" in London. With this group as a nucleus, forty-four ministers met from November 1–6, 1945, at a meeting convoked by France and the United Kingdom to work out and adopt a constitution in which the roles of the General Conference, the Executive Board, the director-general, and the Secretariat were defined.

According to its constitution and following the UN Charter, UNESCO has the responsibility to contribute to peace and security by promoting collaboration among the member states through education, science, and culture, to further these through the universal respect for justice, law, human rights, and fundamental freedoms through a better understanding of each other's cultures. Its action is to further education throughout the world to attain these goals.

It is the General Conference, when the delegates of all the member states meet every two years, that decides upon the organization's program for the succeeding biennium. The program sets out in some detail the activities to be initiated and those to be continued, with corresponding appropriation of funds. A draft program is prepared for the conference by the director-general through the Secretariat, in accordance with the main lines of emphasis. The member states expect UNESCO to serve as a beacon helping them to work out their problems, especially in relation to education, by offering new approaches, methods, and aid that may make it easier for them to solve their problems.

UNESCO has limited resources. It aids governments to make requests and procure funds from such agencies as Technical Assistance (TA), the United Nations International Children's Emergency Fund (UNICEF), the Special Fund (SF), later the United Nations Development Program (UNDP), and BIRD (International Bank of Reconstruction and Development), as well as bilateral, multilateral, and private agencies. It is limited as to how and how much it may undertake, as it is obliged to respect the desires and the limits set by the requesting governments. It is through the director-general that the Secretariat makes its contribution and receives its directives.

The Secretariat is the technical body of UNESCO, with its professionals, experts, consultants, and its general services. As the number of member states has grown, so has the Secretariat, with the director-general having to consider not only competence for the professionals, but also geographic and political quotas. His deputy and his assistant directors-general oversee the various departments. Each department has a professional director and is divided into several divisions. (There may have been changes since Maurice was part of the staff.)

It was as chief of the Division of In-School Education in the Department of Education that Maurice came to UNESCO. While at the United Nations he had had contact with the department because its education services had provided him with information for his studies for the Special Committee of the Trusteeship Council. It was a small division, but with the sudden independence of African countries from 1957 on, its work greatly expanded.

When Maurice joined the organization, its director-general was the American Luther Evans. Before him had been Torres Bodet of Mexico from 1948 to 1952, and before that it was Julian Huxley, who was the organization's first director, from 1946 to 1948. An Iraqi, Matta Akrawi, was the acting director of the Department of Education. It was he who welcomed Maurice into the organization. At the time there were 72 member states, up from the 51 in 1946 and growing to 99 by the time Maurice left in 1963. According to the latest statistics there are now 184 member states.

As the General Conference meets once every two years, a steering body, the Executive Board, made up of a limited selection of delegates, meets at least twice a year with the director-general to take cognizance of the ongoing activities or problems needing attention. In an emergency the director-general may call upon the president of the board to take immediate measures.

The Secretariat was relatively small in 1956. It was housed in temporary quarters on the avenue Kléber, in the former Majestic Hotel, requisitioned by the Germans during the war and hastily repaired to accommodate the new international organization. Quarters became tight as more people were recruited for the expanding work. The atmosphere was cordial and purposeful. In 1958 the first permanent building was completed and the Secretariat moved to Place Fontenoy, to quarters that at the time seemed very spacious. It was able to have under its roof all the services, some of which had been dispersed in various rented quarters. Since then additions have been made to the building at Place Fontenoy and other buildings added within walking distance of the first one to accommodate the ever-growing staff.

The work of the Education Department centered on the countries of South and Central America and certain of the Arab states, and some Asian countries. Apart from reports sent in by the administering powers, little was being done in Africa south of the Sahara. According to hearsay, Maurice was brought into UNESCO because a project concerning universal primary education had been proposed and a professional with experience in this area had been sought. His division occupied itself with primary and secondary technical and vocational education. His division consisted of four units, one for Latin America, headed by Carlos Cueto (Peru) and later by Diez Hochleitner (Spain); one for the Arab states, under a Dutchman, Van Vliet; one for the Asian countries, under A. F. M. K. Rahman of Pakistan, and the Technical and Vocational Unit under G. Rousseau, a Frenchman. Maurice soon showed himself a hardworking administrator. He demanded high standards of his staff and gave as much autonomy as possible.

When Maurice had accepted the position he asked Matta Akrawi about his responsibilities. The list given to him was a long one, very impressive and demanding. Only a few will be noted here. Beside the administrative and budgetary tasks, this latter at times a tour de force, the following were to be his main preoccupations: the extension of primary education and the initiation of proposals for future action for the education of girls as well as boys, the encouragement of public and compulsory primary education in all countries, planning appropriate studies, organizing international and regional conferences, assisting national seminars and experts meetings, and stimulating professional study and interest in primary education. The list went on to include the orientation of primary education toward international understanding and the effective cooperation with other agencies, departments, and sectors, so that the program of any one period is part of a coherent long-term activity.

The most interesting responsibilities and educationally important were the possibilities of initiating, suggesting, and proposing projects that would be sent on to the higher echelons. They would come back to the division later from the Executive Board and the General Conference as directives resolved upon by these bodies.

Maurice took these responsibilities to heart. He wished to prove himself but also to prove that a professional from the third world, of African heritage, could show leadership. At the time there were very few blacks in such a position.

It is through the budget details that some of Maurice's preoccupations can be noted. There were budget demands for technical assistance for a joint UNESCO Liberia project, projects for Haiti, Nicaragua, Panama, and Peru for primary education integrated with teacher-training programs, and for the Fundamental Education Center for Latin America. Funds were also requested for the annual conference of public education held at the International Bureau of Education in Geneva. For the first time large-scale funds were requested for fundamental education and teacher training for Ethiopia, Ghana, and Sierra Leone and special funds for long-term plans for developing a school system for the nomads, with regional training courses.

With each passing year the list became longer as more states joined UNESCO and more requests came in. Some aid was also being given to Sri Lanka, Greece, India, Indonesia, Iraq, Jordan, Laos, Libya, Morocco, Pakistan, Somalia, Thailand, and Vietnam in the form of a few experts for fundamental and/or adult education or fellowships for study abroad in these branches (also Saudi Arabia, Tunisia, Sudan, and Yemen).

The indications given above point out the global interests as concerns primary and secondary in-school education. Four of these interests will be dealt with. They are the Latin America Major Project (LAMP), the International Advisory Committee on Curriculum Revision, the First Conference of Ministers of Education of Tropical Africa for countries south of the Sahara, and the questionnaires in 1959.

The Latin American Major Project

In the fall after Maurice's arrival, the General Conference, held that year in New Delhi (India), passed a resolution covering a major project in Latin America. Several small projects were being carried out in Latin America. Already various experts were in the field. There was already a UNESCO regional center in Havana, Cuba. The OAS, sponsored by the United States, with headquarters in Washington, D.C., also had projects, a few jointly with UNESCO. One such was the Inter-American Rural Education Center (IAREC) created in 1954 in Rubio, Venezuela. Another was the Escuela Superior de Administración Publica de America Central (ESAPAC) in San José, Costa Rica.

The delegates insisted that at least half of the personnel involved in it at headquarters and in the field be from Latin American countries or of a similar background. This explains the recruitment of Carlos Cueto, a Peruvian, and later Diez Hochleitner of Spain. The head of the department demanded that Maurice be included, since he was of the area, spoke Spanish, and had knowledge of the culture through study and travel in Puerto Rico, Cuba, and Venezuela, as well as Mexico and the Dominican Republic. As the project concerned teacher training for primary school teachers, it was normal that he be a part of this program, although he was not at first considered.

The project was planned to last for ten years, 1956–66, which it did. Its principal aim was to contribute to the extension and amelioration of primary education in Latin America. This aim was expressed in a work paper produced by the staff and presented to the Executive Board by the director-general at its forty-seventh meeting, held at headquarters in February 1957. The resolution was accepted by the General Conference. In order that the governments participate more fully in the project, an intergovernmental advisory committee was set up, with twelve delegates chosen from among the twenty member states of Latin America. The delegates were to be rotated every two years.

The aims and the procedures for implementing these aims emerge repeatedly in the correspondence. The most important were as follows:

(1) The need for planning for an efficient and realistic educational system on a national scale. (This is what Maurice had introduced in Haiti.)
(2) The training of teachers to better the quality and augment the number of trainees in the associated normal schools, of which a few were already in existence, with others to be added.
(3) The training of professors and/or teachers for the normal schools at the IAREC in Rubio, where would be added courses for in-service training of teachers, administrators, and inspectors. There would be research on specific problems of education.
(4) The use of associated universities to train professors and other upper-

echelon functionaries, with special courses aimed at rural education. The university at San Diego, Chile, was ready to give such courses.

(5) The granting of inter-American, international, or national fellowships for study in educational problems of Latin America.

(6) Information in the press, on radio and television, and in films to form public support of the project.

(7) General measures to carry out these objectives.

It was an ambitious program. Some of the aims were carried out to a certain extent, but not to the extent desired. Obstructions, delays, and inadequacy of experts and resources would hamper the project, but with perseverance, effort, and constant attack it did permit the extension of education and the training of more teachers.

It was important to try to keep the project running smoothly with the coordination of the working relations with the different governments, the staff in the field, the OAS, TA, which was to fund the project in part, the universities, and the normal schools that participated.

The countries most involved in different ways at the time were: Chile; Colombia; Bolivia; Brazil; Costa Rica; Ecuador; Haiti; Mexico; Paraguay; and Venezuela. For this undertaking the Department of Education set up a special staff that included personnel from the director-general's office, the Department of Social Sciences, Mass Communications, Cultural Activities (for libraries), Exchange of Persons Bureau, the Bureau of Member States, the Bureau of Personnel, and of course Maurice's division, with Cueto the most concerned. One can appreciate the need for patience and diplomacy in this partnership of different sectors of the organization, governments, other agencies, and personnel in the field, especially the coordination with the center in Havana. The necessity of going through the proper channels in proper order for whatever action was to be taken was an important factor that had to be adhered to for good relationships. This made for delays, overlaps, and frustration for those wanting to push ahead with the action.

As chief of the division involved with LAMP, Maurice was involved in the carrying through of the directives, as well as making suggestions for future action. With his two excellent collaborators, this part of his work was of great interest to him. He was asked to make a draft concerning the relationship between headquarters, the field experts, and the coordinator of the project in Havana, after some misunderstandings had occurred as to prerogatives and assumption of authority. This he did.[1]

As early as 1957, a questionnaire, put together by the designated staff, was sent to various Latin American countries to ask about their needs and how UNESCO could be of service. Several experts in the field did spot checks and in a few instances helped government officials to fill in the questionnaires. The answers would lead to evaluating the situation and stressing the action on certain voiced priorities, without letting up on the other aspects. Reports came in regularly from the coordinator in Havana. These were discussed in a group meeting, and decisions were made together as to next steps.

It was decided to have a meeting of the delegates of Latin America to the General Conference to discuss the project, with the hope that the governments would become more interested and offer more funds. The coordinator in Havana was called in to chair the meeting. This would give him status in his travels about Latin America.

Maurice, in concluding a memorandum he wrote on December 15, 1958, on the meeting, stated:

The Latin American Major Project is a complex undertaking. The collective participation of experts and the various departments of UNESCO, the cooperation between headquarters, Havana, the field and the governments needs leadership which a strengthened Department of Education can assume within the established chain of command. [An interesting reflection on the amount of authority the division was permitted or could assume.] A plan for the duration needs to be worked out—priorities, change of emphasis, termination of activities, introduction of new ones—for its success.

Maurice took a part in the recruitment of experts, the selection of "fellows" for grants for the various institutions, and the recruitment of professors for the associated universities, besides the allocation of funds in the budget. He suggested that private institutions having training courses might be associated with the project if they qualified to participate. Another was that the fellows having finished the courses in various universities be given a sort of certificate of accomplishment. The first was later accepted. Malcolm Adiseshiah, deputy director-general, after a visit to the area said that the project in 1958 was catching on and that governments were giving more money. They were also asking for help to set up educational planning services as well as services for statistics. These were good signs.

Maurice undertook one mission to Latin America during the three and one-half years or so he was involved in the program. He represented the director-general at Rubio, Venezuela, on October 28, 1957, to iron out certain problems. He received instructions to go to the IAREC, created in 1954, as one of the projects for the reorientation of rural education and the training of teachers for rural schools. It needed to have its program reevaluated and suggestions given for a more effective contribution. This was to be done through a seminar during which Maurice and the UNESCO coordinator in Havana would guide the participants. After the seminar he was to proceed to Pamplona, Colombia, to look over and evaluate the Institute of Rural Education, near which a new associated rural normal school was to open. His chief concern, however was the seminar at Rubio.[2]

In his report, which was printed and circulated, Maurice stated that he had been able to steer the seminar to the way of thinking of UNESCO. He described the setting, the participants, from fifteen countries, and the various committee meetings, certain of which he attended. He remarked that the coordinator of the regional center in Havana had made a valuable contribution. The committee had worked hard. Some reports were excellent. The director of the Rubio center showed comprehension and skill in conducting the plenary sessions.

The agenda concerned the draft plans for the center for 1958, the program of study, suggestions for 1959–60, suggestions for the improvement of the training of rural education personnel, and inter-American cooperation for improving rural education services.

As to the recommendations, they were as follows: use the services of the professors of the Rubio Center for the summer courses, organized in different Latin American countries for in-service training of rural schoolteachers; consider a four-month intensive course for teachers of agriculture education, home economics, health, and manual arts, who already had technical training but none in teaching methods in their fields; and last, in 1959 evaluate the proposed program of studies by a few experts.

The reorganization might have meant a new agreement with the Venezuelan government, OAS, and UNESCO had not the coordinator suggested a simple amendment to the existing agreement. This was accepted by the minister of education, with whom Maurice and the coordinator met and of whom Maurice asked if legislation permitted changes in the official curriculum. The minister asked that a memorandum be given him on the program and the exemptions requested, as he was to see the president of the country at nine o'clock the next morning. The minister also stated he would consider an additional financial contribution for the center and the school. The men worked late in the night to prepare the memorandum, which they delivered in time.

Maurice's conclusion was that the seminar had been valuable for what it was, well organized and conducted, giving a boost in morale for those involved in it, creating greater interest on the part of the authorities and the public, developing better professional attitudes in all concerned, and giving a feeling of optimism toward the future. It was money well spent to bring the group together, to air problems, to come to a consensus, and for him to get firsthand knowledge of the institute and the people involved. His closing words in the report were:

> Just as the seminar was the first stage in the elaborating of a realistic program in Rubio, the final emerging process will be only one phase of the work of building Rubio as an institution capable of serving the needs of Latin America in the field of rural education and rural schoolteacher training. As conditions vary from one Latin American country to another, major emphasis should be placed on the technique of approach in solving problems in education particularly in the field of community improvement for each one. In the task of adapting the program and the work at the Rubio Normal School, one is faced not only with problems requiring technical and pedagogical solutions but with problems of human and diplomatic relations. The future of Rubio is a challenge for the Organization of American States and to a certain extent for UNESCO.

Maurice accomplished the second part of his mission in his visit to Pamplona, Colombia, to make an evaluation of the Institute of Rural Education there. He was well impressed with the buildings, the activities, the farm and workshops, and the director. Funding was provided jointly by UNESCO, the Colombian government, and the OAS. The year after Maurice's visit, the institute became an associated normal school.

On his way back to Paris, Maurice stopped in New York. He visited the United Nations. But his important task, he felt, was to have contacts with Teachers' College, Columbia University, to investigate possibilities for the recruitment of professors for the two associated universities. He had preliminary conversations with Hollis Caswell, the dean. Maurice contacted other universities through correspondence. Follow-up was done by another sector.

In 1958 the intergovernmental advisory committee for LAMP reviewed the first year's operations, acknowledging successes all along the line. It was evident that with limited means much had been accomplished in organizing and taking steps to carry out the project. A great deal was hoped for of UNESCO, expecting it to wipe out illiteracy in Latin America, when the most in its power to do was, with its limited resources, to awaken governments to the needs and help them initiate improvement.

The General Conference in the fall of 1958 placed confidence in the UNESCO efforts and through the director-general congratulated the Secretariat. UNESCO earmarked $1 million for the project, with $500,000 expected from member states for teacher training, in-service training, determining status of teachers, adaptation of curricula, and training of specialists and administrators, and planning a realistic approach for the continuation of the expansion of primary education, the setting up of competent statistical services, and the study of practical school-building programs. Much of the funds came from TA, administered by UNESCO. Seventeen countries benefited in some manner.

As had been decided in 1957, an evaluation took place in 1959. For this a comprehensive questionnaire was prepared, mostly by Cueto and Diez, supervised by Maurice. It was sent to the different associated normal schools to stimulate them toward more practical and efficient programs. From the answers it was decided as to how to continue the project. One of the suggestions was that other associated normal schools be added to the program. To this Maurice, his immediate colleagues, and all those involved at headquarters with the major project cautioned that UNESCO should proceed with prudence, since those schools already in the program were not yet stabilized.

Surveys were carried out. The evaluation was done. The report was sent to the director-general. He in turn informed the Economic and Social Council of the UN:

As a result of the efforts, the impact of the Major Project on Latin American countries has been remarkable. In most of them comprehensive long-term plans have been or are being prepared and/or implemented by local personnel especially trained in the fields of educational planning, educational statistics and documentation with the technical assistance of UNESCO.

The Latin American Major Project has considerably influenced UNESCO's Technical Assistance and Participation Programs in the region. This is reflected in the sharp increase in projects undertaken at the request of member states in primary education and related fields. It also has evoked active interest of some member states outside the region, in particular France, Spain and Czechoslovakia, in the form of financial and technical contributions . . .[3]

To sum up, by mid-1960 four countries had asked for experts on educational planning. There were 103 UNESCO experts in the field, five associated teacher training normal schools, the two associated universities, one in San Diego, Chile, and one in São Paulo, Brazil, and the rural education centers as well as the already existing regional centers. These activities were joint efforts of UNESCO in conjunction with the OAS, the national governments, and UNICEF. Countries from the Middle East and Asia were watching the progress, as they were interested in similar projects for their areas. LAMP would go on until 1966, with changes in coordinators, programs, and UNESCO personnel. Maurice's mission to the Congo in August 1960 detached him from this program.

The International Advisory Committee on Curriculum Revision

The second educational project with which Maurice was especially concerned was the reform in school programs for which the International Advisory Committee on Curriculum Revision was created. This committee was launched in 1956 by the then director-general of UNESCO, the American Luther Evans. The committee to study the problems of program revision was composed of ten members representing four countries in Europe: France, Germany, Great Britain, and the USSR; three from the Western Hemisphere: the United States, Brazil, and Costa Rica; one from Arab countries: Egypt; and two from Asia: Japan and Burma. The composition was good, but not all the members were specialists in curriculum revision. Moreover, there was a diversity in programs as well as conceptions of education aims and modalities.

Maurice arrived in June 1956. The first meeting took place in October. The role of Maurice was to second the director of the department, who in turn aided the president of the committee during the sessions to give précis on the texts put together by the division. Each text contained ideas concerning educational reforms. The division prepared thirteen for the first session. One of the themes was to sensitize governments to the necessity of curriculum revision. This meant checking off the problems to analyze and evaluate the methods being used. But at first it was necessary to define the role of the committee and its action and define the role of UNESCO in the matter.

A secretary was chosen from UNESCO staff for handling the correspondence, preparing for the meetings, making the documents available, informing members, and deciding on the agenda with the chairperson of the committee. The most delicate task of the committee was introducing reforms without doing violence to the culture and the way of life of the developing countries. It was important also not to overcrowd the curriculum yet structure it to meet the needs of the school population.

The first session took place at headquarters on October 23, 1956. The West German member was elected chairperson. The committee defined its role as contributing in a modest way to facilitating the work of UNESCO in promoting international cooperation for the improvement of education. It stressed that UNESCO had a unique responsibility. It used the prepared texts and asked that those who had prepared them be on hand in case of questions or need of clarification.

The results of the first session were encouraging. Under the guidance of Dr. Akrawi and the president, the sessions were animated. The final report included these points:

(1) the important role UNESCO could assume;
(2) the meaning and conception of curriculum;
(3) factors creating the need for revision;
(4) common problems;
(5) principles and mechanisms of revision.

In the recommendations, suggestions were given as to the content for the second session. It was decided that in 1957 the committee would deal with the primary schools and, in 1958, the lower secondary school curriculum and then the senior cycle.

The second session was held October 14–21, 1957. The president was an Englishwoman by whose side was Maurice, as Akrawi had left UNESCO to become the president of Baghdad University and his successor, H. Loper, an American, had not arrived. Maurice saw that the texts were prepared in English and French and forwarded to the different members. The members sent in suggestions for changes or clarification. He wrote the draft for the agenda. A plan for an abstract and bibliography service on curriculum studies was to be discussed.

The theme of the session was the adaptation of the school curriculum to the age and development of the child. The committee proposed the production of a brochure on the organization of planning services and the mechanisms to put them in place. It also proposed that a plan for a book on primary school curricula be produced under the auspices of UNESCO. The president, Ms. M. B. Denny, wrote to Akrawi to say that they were "plodding" along but missed him. Maurice also wrote when he sent the report to ask Akrawi's opinion and to let him know that the workload was increasing.

The new head of the Department of Education was present for the third session, but as he did not speak a word of French, he relied heavily on Maurice, who now knew the mechanisms of the committee work. The session took place September 28–October 17, 1958. The director-general or his delegate opened the session. Staff meetings were held to finalize plans. Maurice sent a report to the director-general to have him thank the delegates who were to leave and suggest items to be stressed, the approval of the brochure, and the report on the second session. Member states were asked to send in reports for the international conference on public instruction about their activities in curriculum research and the efforts being made to lighten programs and develop studies in social sciences in relation to technical changes.

Dr. Akrawi came as a member to the third session. It was suggested that the committee evaluate its work. The General Conference was held at the same time, with the East-West Project of Mutual Appreciation as one of the points on the agenda. The conference invited member states to elaborate and activate a program favoring the East-West project in a systematic way.

Although the division's workload was made heavier the years the General Conference took place with the Executive Board and the curriculum committee, for which he had special responsibility, Maurice, with a few of his staff, managed to produce the brochure titled *The Mechanics of Curriculum Revision and the Organization of Curriculum Research Facilities.* It was published in July 1958 under the rubric *Education Studies and Docu-*

130

ments (UNESCO/ESD/no.28/A). It gave a brief description of procedures and mechanisms of curriculum revision and research from reports based on work being done in some fifty countries, of which seventeen were particularly significant and were briefly sketched. The one in New York City was set forth in detail. The brochure was very well received. It was made available to all member states and other interested parties. A useful publication, it was described as "an admirable, composite summary. The detailed description of one bureau helped others as to how to organize this service."[4]

The committee went on to state that it made an important contribution in that it reoriented educators in some parts of the world as to the aims of a school program that went beyond just a list of subjects to be taught for the cultivation of the mind. The brochure could only describe in general what had been found to be helpful and stimulate and encourage local moves toward curriculum revision.

Preparations were made for the fourth session, which would be concerned with the lower secondary school cycle. Drafts were made for the contents of the proposed book on curricula for the primary school. Questions came up as to how it was to be financed and who would write it. It was suggested that a member of the staff, with the aid of the Clearing House, do it. This idea was later abandoned, as the workload was too heavy.

Loper proposed that work papers be sent in by members. Papers came from India, Japan, Great Britain, Sweden, and Russia. It had been hoped, when the committee was first created, that half of its members would be educators familiar with principles and problems of curriculum revision. This had not been the case, and it had been the Secretariat staff that had supplied the material and given support to some of the members. Now with the selection of new members more competence in this field was demanded, hence the production of the work papers by members of the committee. These papers were duplicated and distributed to the members by UNESCO both in French and English.

For the agenda of the fourth session, to be held in the fall of 1959, an interdepartmental meeting took place. How much time Maurice gave to the preparations for this session cannot be determined. He was already involved with the evaluation program for LAMP, the questionnaires prepared and sent to the Arab states, the Asian countries, and the African free countries, trusteeships, and colonies. On their return would come the work of analyzing and preparation of syntheses and work papers for the projected conferences in the different areas of the globe that were to take place in late 1959 and early 1960. He traveled a great deal for contacts and progress, going to Liberia in March, Ghana and Senegal in April, Switzerland in July, and to Italy and West Germany, as well as Sudan and Ethiopia, in September. He also went to Madrid in June to represent the director-general, invited by the minister of primary education to the closing of the training school courses and the meeting of the National Commission for UNESCO.

The fourth session, on the lower secondary school cycle, held August 31–September 11, 1959, followed the agenda prepared by the UNESCO staff. It concerned the school subjects, avoidance of overcrowding the curriculum, equal opportunities, orientation and guidance, individual differences, humanizing special education, examination of promotion, adaptation of program to age and children's growth levels, and international understanding. Due to human failures and errors, there were delays in the publication of the report, which finally came out in the spring of 1960.

The fifth and last session was to concern the transition from the lower to the upper secondary school cycle. It was the director-general who opened the session, held from September 26–October 7, 1960. Among the subjects discussed were the problems of adolescence and factors leading to dropouts and delinquency. Teacher education, education of the handicapped, coeducation, compulsory education, and correspondence courses were touched upon.

As no provision was made in the UNESCO budget for its continuance and as the new director-general, an Italian, and his deputy, a Frenchman, did not have the same ideas of Luther Evans on the revision of curriculum, they did not attempt to find funds to continue the committee. The greatest effect that the committee had while it existed was to make member states aware of the need for curriculum revision and the need for special services for this, with specialists to do the work efficiently. It also brought together educators from around the globe with different ideas about education. This in itself furthered the East-West culture appreciation project. Three positive accomplishments were the brochure on curriculum revision, the establishment of the service of abstracts and bibliographies, and the book *The Primary School Curriculum,* written by the Belgian educator Dr. Dottrens, published in 1962 by UNESCO.

The Beginning of the Emergency Program in Africa, 1958, 1959, and Early 1960

To better understand the purpose of the questionnaires for tropical Africa and the first meeting of ministers of education of that area, a few introductory words are necessary concerning what UNESCO could do. It has been brought out again and again that UNESCO can only carry out directives given to it by the Executive Board and the General Conference through the director-general. Up to 1958 the Department of Education had been given directives for the major project in Latin America (LAMP) and for fundamental education, the same for Asia and for the Arab states, with the special concerns of nomads and the education of women.

As early as 1948 the Resolution of Human Rights under the leadership of Eleanor Roosevelt was promulgated at the UN General Assembly, held in Paris that year. This resolution referred to the "rights of children to an education without discrimination due to race, religion, sex, economic or social conditions." It is not in the scope of this work to touch upon the problems of the application of the resolution that needed attention even in some independent industrial nations, nor how much more complex it was to apply it in the countries of dependent peoples.

Suffice it to say that the human rights resolution demanded that an education be assured taking into consideration tradition, language, and religion, and that education not be changed for political reasons. It took ten years for UNESCO to refer to this resolution as concerned tropical Africa. In 1958 the General Conference authorized the director-general to make an investigation in view of elaborating regional programs in Asia, the Arab states, and Africa for the development of school education. The member states were invited to take measures to open education to all by doing the following:

(1) giving education to all according to age and need;
(2) making education universal, free, and obligatory;
(3) training teachers for this undertaking;
(4) taking steps to increase and ameliorate primary, secondary, professional, vocational, and technical education, including the undertaking of a regional program for tropical Africa (the first reference to tropical Africa as such);
(5) considering higher education;

(6) having a yearly international conference on public education (this to be done in cooperation with IBE [the International Bureau of Education] in Geneva);

(7) continuing through the United Nations Relief and Works Agency (UNRWA) the education of Palestinian refugees;

(8) participating, at the demand of the member states, in their action in favor of in-school education.

In the next article of the directives it recommended that UNICEF be asked to participate in the primary education efforts.

As stated, point 4 of the directives was the first official reference to tropical Africa as a region of special endeavor for UNESCO to develop a particular program. This important inclusion opened up a whole new area of work for the Division of In-school Education and led to the questionnaire and the First Conference for Ministers of Education of Tropical Africa, held in Addis Ababa in February 1960.

It was in this connection that Maurice went on a mission in May 1959 to Ghana, Nigeria, Liberia, and Senegal. He was to discuss with the authorities the needs and problems in education and the inquiry to be conducted by UNESCO. He was to look in on the symposium on community development being held in Accra, sound out governments ready to sponsor coming conferences and seminars, and also explain in what ways UNESCO could contribute.

Tropical Africa was already known to some extent through the reports of the administering authorities of trust territories and colonies. UNESCO funds had been allocated in 1957 for a workshop organized for member and associate member states of occidental Africa. Through TA aid had been given in the form of one or more experts in fundamental and adult education to Ethiopia, Sudan, Somalia, Liberia, and Sierra Leone.

Among the items of the enquiry were to be the access of women to education, as well as their availability for higher education, the possibilities for conferences, and preparation of work papers for these. Included also were the teaching of science and the collaboration for the questionnaire, which was being put together at UNESCO, besides finding host countries for conferences and seminars. In his mission report[5] Maurice stated that Liberia wished to be host to a seminar on the education of women, as there were more educated women in Liberia than in any other African country. Names were given of women who could participate in the meetings of experts and contribute to preliminary studies. Liberia was also eager to participate in the various seminars held elsewhere and was ready to collaborate on the enquiry. As exposed by the authorities, the greatest need in Africa was for the expansion of primary education.

Nigeria, which would be independent in 1960, was interested in opportunities for girls. There were both women and men ready for higher education, but there were not enough educational institutions. There were a few women candidates for grants. The needs of Nigeria pointed to secondary education, the teaching of science, higher education, and the adaptation of curricula, a seminar for which could be held in Ibadan. The authorities were willing to answer the questionnaire.

Ghana, independent since 1957, had already agreed to host a seminar of administrators and directors of technical schools to be held in Accra in March 1960. It was concerned with the development of secondary education and the teaching of science, as well as the adaptation of curricula to include traditions but putting emphasis on science. A beginning was being made in producing primary school textbooks. Ghana administrators were ready to collaborate on the questionnaire.

In Senegal, Maurice found the French colonial authorities ready to answer the future questionnaire. They were interested in the seminars on secondary education and the teaching of science and some aspects of the adaptation of curricula. They wished that one seminar be held in Dakar, as the others were scheduled to be held in English-speaking countries. For the seminar on women's education a woman could be found as well as one for a grant. They were interested in having contacts with UNESCO documentation services for publications on LAMP and the General Conference. In each country visited, Maurice asked if there was anyone of recognized competence and with enough training to be invited to Brussels to a meeting on technical and vocational education. As in the other countries, there was not one African ready in this field.

Maurice felt that the trip was worthwhile and useful. It produced valuable contacts and information for the implementation of the projected program, especially the survey and the seminars.

After his return from the mission to West Africa and before going to the IBE conference in Geneva, Maurice formulated the aim of the questionnaire. He stated as follows:

It would permit to disclose and analyze, as far as possible, the most

135

urgent needs in the domain of education which are common to the greatest number of countries of the region so as to make plans as to how to resolve them. It would be a comprehensive questionnaire with various sections—one of the most important being quality (change in program) and the quantity of secondary education, both general and technical. Several countries asked for aid for the primary, others post-primary. These factors must be taken into consideration before deciding which has priority. Outside of Liberia, where girls have equal access, the education of girls has not been developed, therefore through aspects of primary, secondary and adult education, the special problem of girls and women must be determined. Some of the information will be used for the projected workshops in 1960. There is *no* impression that planning in education has been done or that it needs to be done.

An explanation of the inquiry was sent to the different countries. There would be three steps: *first,* a survey of the situation through the inquiry; *second,* spot checks by experts recruited by UNESCO in the field; *third,* a meeting of the directors of education of tropical Africa, using the report made from the analysis of the inquiry as a working paper to identify needs and problems and suggest possible solutions at national and international levels, this meeting expected to be held out of the TA contingency fund in February 1960.

This questionnaire[6] was to be used to formulate proposals for 1961–62 for aid for education in tropical Africa. In early August 1959, Dr. Sen, director of the TA Board at the United Nations, came to Paris to discuss the African program. It was explained that the projected meeting in February 1960 was for the purpose of drawing up a ten-year plan of intensive educational development for which the governments would have to make agreements for annual appropriations for UNESCO and regional as well as multilateral programs. TA would work along closely with ECA (Economic Commission for Africa, a branch of the UN Economic and Social Council), which had held a meeting in July in Addis Ababa attended by the secretary-general of the United Nations and R. Maheu, representing the director-general. At this meeting ECA brought out the necessity of preparing projects for countries and territories of Africa to accelerate their economic and social development. UNESCO was asked to make a survey of the ways and means at its disposal to train Africans in the domains of economics and statistics as part of the overall Economic and Social Development Program.

Most of the work concerning the questionnaire on tropical Africa was done or being done when the fifty-fifth session of the Executive Board took place from November 23–December 5, 1959. There the director-general reported that the questionnaire had been sent to twenty-two states and territories, of which twelve had answered. Four consultants for on-the-spot checks had visited ten countries while members of the Education Department had gone to several for the same purpose. Recommendations of two sorts were made—that for long-term and that for short-term—so as to prepare the program and budget for 1961–62. But it was again through TA that aid in the guise of secondary school teachers and experts was given to Sierra Leone, Ghana, Sudan, Somalia, and Ethiopia.

It was at its fifty-sixth session, April 4–30, 1960, that the director-general reported on the various conferences that came about in late 1959 and early 1960, the Executive Board giving its approval. It authorized the director-general "in collaboration with the competent non-governmental, international agencies to aid the member states to extend and ameliorate school education at all levels in accord with the priority in 1959–60 and to go ahead for '61–'62 with special attention to secondary education," evidently the majority opinion being that secondary education for the time being had priority over primary education.

Behind all this were Maurice and his staff. It was Maurice, with one or two others, who carried most of the responsibility for the new programs. As of yet no special unit had been created as for Latin America, the Arab states, or Asia. So although he supervised these units he also took on formulating proposals, making reports, and carrying out the directives of this new undertaking. The surveys and the conferences took up much time in 1959 and early 1960.

Questionnaires and Conferences for Arab States, Asia, and Tropical Africa

The year 1959 turned out to be the "Year of the Questionnaires" in the division. Maurice, as chief of the division, supervised their production. These questionnaires, the one for the Arab states elaborated by the unit headed by Van Vliet, were sent out in May. This was done to prepare an official document as a working paper for the regional meeting of ministers of education of those countries, already decided upon, to be held in Beirut, Lebanon. There already existed some three hundred documents at UNESCO from which to draw if necessary. There would be delays in the returns, and experts had to be sent to several countries to aid the ministries in replying to the questionnaire.

The other one prepared by the Asian unit, headed by Rahman, was sent out as early as April, with an explanation by the director-general, V. Veronese. It was answered by eleven countries. Returns were compiled and analyzed. Four consultants had been sent to visit some countries, and Rahman went to Karachi in September 1959. This area had had several meetings, the first having been held in Bombay in 1952, so that the mechanisms were already known. Budget provisions had been properly made for both these meetings.

In a report by the director-general to the funding agency at the time, mention is made of these surveys, stating that the plan and execution of the work were well in hand. As to the inquiry for Africa, it was still being prepared, and the location at which to hold the meeting for the African conference was not yet known, as a host country had not yet been found. The questionnaire was put together for much of it by Pauvert (France). Part of it had been prepared for a seminar to be held on secondary education for directors and administrators. Some of the questions and later answers were gleaned from the World Survey on Education made in 1957. In fact, the United Kingdom demanded why the 1957 survey could not be used, as their offices in various areas of Africa were understaffed or staffed by people unable to answer the questions. Others felt there were too many questions. The questionnaire had as title: "The Survey of Needs for Primary and Secondary Education in Tropical Africa." The director-general sent accompanying letters to the ministries of the different countries in September only. Once the questionnaires were sent, consultants were selected to visit the countries for spot checks. There was a great deal of correspondence back and forth, as each consultant had to be approved by the government and/or the colonial authorities and the UNESCO resident representative and the Bureau of Personnel as well as other departments of UNESCO. In the end, the Education Clearing House completed the answering of several questionnaires from documents compiled in former years, because of the insufficient information received from a few countries.

Maurice, as mentioned earlier, went to Accra, Ghana, concerning the questionnaire in August and to Mogadishu, Somalia, and Addis Ababa, Ethiopia, in late September, as well as Khartoum, Sudan. At the same time he looked in on teacher training courses being given there. He also went to Lomé, Togoland (now Togo), and later to Kampala, Uganda, and Bangui, Central Africa, putting out feelers to find a host country for the seminar on secondary education, and the teaching of science, and another seminar on the access of women to education. He was on the move a great deal in 1959 in connection with the various aspects of his work. He also supervised the activities of his division.

As with the other surveys, the answers had to be compiled and analyzed and a report written as to the findings to be used as a working paper for the meeting to be held for the first time ever. With all these inquiries, the division was overworked to meet deadlines and get out accurate and comprehensive reports as well as make arrangements for the meetings.

The meeting December 28, 1959–January 9, 1960, of the Asian ministers of education held in Karachi went off very well. There was little reason why it should not. The meeting was already decided upon by June 1959 and the budget for it approved by TA under the Contingency Funds. Pakistan had early requested to be host for the meeting. Technical papers had been prepared by the Secretariat for distribution to the ministers and interested groups a month ahead. Four consultants had also prepared preliminary studies and were attached to the meeting. Provision had been made for simultaneous interpreters, translators for English and French. The aims of the meeting were defined. The purpose was to take cognizance of the present situation and take concerted action to provide minimum educational facilities for at least 220 million children in the seventeen countries for the future welfare of the region and for peace and prosperity of the world.

As usual, governments sent their ministers and directors of education. But sister agencies, private and nongovernmental groups, were also present. From the Secretariat went the deputy director-general, M. Adiseshiah, Diez Hochleitner to represent Maurice, who was too occupied by the pressing demands of the first conference for African ministers to attend, and Rahman, the unit head, who had borne the heaviest responsibility.

The results of the Asian conference were publicized through press releases and created a positive reaction. Dr. Akrawi, in a letter complimenting Rahman, stated: "You and the Department are to be congratulated on the tremendous effort which was brought to such a successful result" (February 1960).[7]

139

As concerns the Conference of the Arab states, it, too, went off well. It was organized in somewhat the same manner. The provisional report was based on the questionnaire and was used as a working paper. The meeting was held February 9–15, 1960, in Beirut, with Lebanon acting as host country. It was opened by the minister of education of Lebanon and was attended by nine Arab states plus the representatives of the United Kingdom dealing with Arab-speaking colonies. The special problems were the Palestinian refugees as well as the education of nomads and girls. From the Secretariat went R. Maheu, the deputy director-general to represent the director-general, Mr. Guiton, acting director of the department, and Van Vliet, the unit head, who was mostly responsible. Mr. Maheu cabled Mr. Veronese, the director-general.

The cable reads:

Conference adopted Resolutions (proposed certainly by UNESCO) unanimously: 1. Approval of Secretariat Report; 2. Principal problem that of directives for action in Arab states; 3. Six concrete measures decided on with UNESCO aid. Also creation of an Information Center, Planning in Education included in Planning of Economic and Social Development. General atmosphere good. All express gratefulness to UNESCO. Very favorable toward Secretariat.

It was the conference of ministers and directors of education of tropical Africa held in Addis Ababa in February 1960, just after the other two, and the first of its kind for the new emergent African nations, that was Maurice's greatest challenge up to that time, because of the various obstacles including shortness of time and preparation for it. It is true that the second meeting, held in Addis Ababa fifteen months later, was of far more consequence, far more elaborate, and far better prepared for, with ample time, ample funds, and ample publicity. Far more delegates of the highest echelon attended it. But the fact remains that Maurice and his very few collaborators paved the way for it by the success and results of the first one, which was a surprise and satisfaction for everyone. There had been such reservations concerning it that Jean Thomas, assistant director-general representing the director-general in his speech at the opening of the conference, admitted that the preparation was done in too short a time, with delays of several kinds and limited resources put at the disposal of the Secretariat. He paid homage "to the conscientiousness, the devotion and the enthusiasm of those who animated and sustained the collaboration in this difficult enterprise."

The meeting had not been budgeted. As early as July, Adiseshiah wrote to Sudhir Sen (executive chairman of the TA Board at the United Nations) asking for a grant of twenty-five thousand dollars as had been provided for the other two meetings from the Contingency Fund, stating that negotiations had not yet come to fruition and "it would be only towards the end of the year that plans would be finalized and that the African countries would be making requests for the meeting." Adiseshiah went on to state what was being done as to the inquiry and other preparations and concluded: "The meeting has to be in February because *I want* the development plan for education to be drawn up by the Africans themselves . . . and *we* would have to submit this plan for UNESCO's major effort for 1961 for the discussions and approval of the Executive Board meeting in April and the General Conference which will meet later in the year which will act on the approval of the Board" (author's emphasis).

Sen answered that he saw no problem: Ethiopia had offered and had been accepted as the host country. Maurice had been to Addis Ababa in September for a symposium on community development, in which he was deeply interested. While there, he had preliminary talks in relation to the meeting with the Ethiopian authorities, as well as Mr. Mekki Abbas, the director of the ECA, and the deputy director Robert Gardiner (Ghana), whom Maurice had known at the United Nations in the late forties. Maurice thought that these talks were adequate and went ahead at headquarters with the preparation. He prepared a provisional plan, noting the purpose, the possible number of consultants, UNESCO specialists, translation services, interpreters, transportation services, as well as rooms needed for delegates and secretarial help, hospitality, etc.

Perhaps after his talks with these ECA officials Maurice should have sent an official covering letter. It was in November that he sent an informal one asking Gardiner if he could help find local staff for the translating, secretarial, and clerical services. Gardiner wrote that most of the available help would be in Tangier, Morocco, where a meeting sponsored by ECA would be going on at about the same time. Was it that both Gardiner and Abbas were hurt that they had not been invited or consulted through higher channels? At all events, the twenty-five thousand dollars was not granted, for the time being. UNESCO found itself in a very delicate situation.

The director of TA made difficulties. The correspondence is revealing.

What went on behind the scenes is not known, but Maurice did write a conciliatory letter to Gardiner stating that close cooperation between the two agencies, with their common interests in Africa, was an understood fact. René Maheu, deputy director-general, wrote to Dr. Sen saying that a formal invitation had not been sent because the agreement between UNESCO and the imperial Ethiopian government had not yet been signed. Chevalier of the Bureau of Member States also wrote, and finally the director-general, Veronese, cabled Mekki Abbas in the middle of December asking for his personal support. The chief of the UNESCO mission in Addis Ababa was requested to obtain the ECA approval. It was as late as January 15, 1960, that the grant of twenty-five thousand dollars came through at last, with the meeting only three weeks away. For the later meeting, in 1961, UNESCO was very careful to include ECA from the beginning and to insist that the meeting was sponsored jointly.

Maurice, with a very small team, put together the provisional report of twenty-seven pages from material collected and analyzed from the inquiry.[8] It was a major undertaking in itself, because of the pressure and the nature of the answers. It did bring out the need for the rapid training of Africans for professional and supervisory posts and functionaries at various levels for different sectors of public and private activities. Primary education was of the highest priority, as well as general secondary, technical, professional, and vocational education. The ratio of primary school children going on to secondary school was only 5 percent. Also, there was an enormous difference between the number of boys and the number of girls going to school. There was great need for the training of teachers, the revision of texts for African children, the production of manuals, the use of visual aids, school construction, financing, the use of the vernacular, and introduction of European languages. The report suggested that national resources for financing were inadequate and that funds needed to be obtained through TA and the Special Fund, as well as bilateral, international, and private agencies. UNESCO would help as far as its limited resources would go. The budget for 1961–62 to be presented to the General Conference would be based on this report as well as on the conclusions of the conference. This report was very well received and did stimulate discussion at the seminar. It was published together with the report of the seminar (for which Maurice had much of the responsibility) in August 1960 for the General Conference under the identification UNESCO PRG 11/C/PRG/1 in English and French.

This report based on the inquiry was sent by the director-general, along with the formal invitations, the first week of January 1960. In the meantime, His Majesty the Emperor of Ethiopia, Haile Selassie, let it be known that he would open the meeting in person and pronounce the speech of welcome. The director-general did not expect this. More letters were sent to the chiefs of mission in the various countries to try to upgrade the members of the delegations. The emperor would be present again in 1961, with the presence of twenty-four ministers from the newly independent nations.

In the signed agreement the imperial government accepted responsibilities for meeting rooms and other facilities such as transportation and voluntary workers to look after the reception of delegates, the seating, and the distribution of documents. It even provided official photographers. Maurice received several photos, one of which shows him being introduced to His Imperial Majesty and another of the emperor opening the first session. UNESCO expected 50 participants in all. At least 150 persons attended. There were 22 official delegates, among whom were ministers from newly independent countries plus their aides. As observers there were present ambassadors in residence and some educators from various colonies, representatives of specialized agencies, such as Gardiner of ECA. There were nongovernmental groups of Ethiopia and student associations invited for the most part by the Ethiopian government. The Secretariat was represented only by the assistant director-general, Jean Thomas, and Maurice, seconded by R. D. Garraud, the resident representative of UNESCO, and E. S. Osman, a UNESCO expert on mission there. The UNESCO group was a very small one, to say the least.

Maurice arrived in Addis Ababa on February 9 to help Garraud and the Ethiopians to finalize the preparations. The conference opened as scheduled on February 16. His Imperial Majesty Haile Selassie made a warm, welcoming speech.

Then Jean Thomas, in the name of UNESCO and the director-general, thanked His Imperial Majesty and the Ethiopian government for their generous hospitality. After the inaugural ceremony and the departure of the emperor, the officers were elected, with His Excellency L. E. Makonnen (minister of education of Ethiopia) as president and Maurice as general secretary. Jean Thomas presented the Secretariat's provisional report, and the discussions began. Sessions were held every day from Tuesday through Friday, centered on the following topics:

(1) primary education;
(2) general secondary, technical, and vocational education; and
(3) the planning, administration, and financing of education.

Committees were instituted. Several delegates presented papers. The discussions disclosed the same lacks as the provisional report had. Among other conclusions, there were emphasized the need for adequate financing, inclusion of educational planning for economic development, and the recognition and acceptance by the Special Fund and other international funding *that expenditure for education was an investment* (Maurice's insistence.)

At the closing session, Mr. Makonnen, in the name of the conference, expressed gratitude to the Ethiopian government and UNESCO for holding the meeting. He stated that after having studied and discussed the UNESCO Provisional Report, which gave in a concise manner a comprehensive picture of educational needs that, in varying degrees, were common to almost all the countries concerned and after the several meetings devoted to those needs that were the most urgent in their respective countries, the conference recommended the governments take the necessary measures to improve and expand both primary and general secondary, vocational, and technical education. He went on to state in more detail what these measures might be and then requested UNESCO take certain steps, which he enumerated. He expressed satisfaction at the existing cooperation between UNESCO, ECA, and other UN and specialized agencies in the regional activities. He ended, in the name of the conference, offering humble thanks to Emperor Haile Selassie, also expressing profound gratitude for the generous hospitality, the deep interest evinced and the high inspiration the conference had received from the shining example for the cause of education that the emperor had shown.

This conference was truly a historic event. It must not be forgotten that several delegates were from countries that had only recently acquired independence and others from countries about to do so. This was the first time that their voices were heard and their opinions listened to on an international scale, the first time that they were being consulted as a group concerning the educational problems of their countries. From that time on they would exert more and more influence and become active participants in the international organizations.

The contributions to the success of the conference made by the president, Maurice, and his few coworkers were the guidance for a smooth-running, productive meeting, the subtle control, and, with the help of the Ethiopian government, the efficient management. The participants also helped make the conference a turning point. They were serious, enthusiastic, appreciative, and cooperative and showed that they were cognizant of the problems and were eager to find solutions.

All this is best stated in a long letter in French written by Jean Thomas to the director-general the day before the conference closed. In it he stated:

> . . . I must say the President is excellent. He possesses the courtesy, the patience and the necessary authority. One could not expect better . . . So far there have only been compliments . . . [He goes on about the receptions and other social activities and how well he was received as representing the director-general and UNESCO]. . . . As to the debates, you know I was not without uneasiness on the manner in which the conference was going to be held and the conclusions that might result. You are not unaware that the Secretarial report was prepared under such conditions that criticism was possible. But I must say my fears were in no way justified. On the one hand, the Secretariat report was very well received and gave the discussions an excellent basis. On the other hand, from the first moment the atmosphere has been extremely cordial and even friendly, not only among the delegates themselves but between the delegates and the Secretariat. There has not been a false note. The participants were very competent and very serious people, anxious to bring a precise and efficacious contribution . . . I do not want to exaggerate the importance of this meeting, nor the results which may be attained, but the general opinion is that this is an extremely successful conference which will mark a date in the history of tropical Africa.
>
> The needs of tropical Africa are immense, and I do not know if the report will take this into consideration, but it will reflect the spirit of realism and seriousness which pervaded the debates. Mr. Dartigue, who has been designated as Secretary of the conference and who is participating in the committee which will make the report, has been striving as I have been to present the problems in a very realistic manner and the conference has echoed us. . . . I have insisted on the importance of education in relation to social and economic development and on the fortunate coincidence that makes Addis Ababa at the same time capital of a great country and the seat of ECA. I underlined

the strong desire of UNESCO to collaborate with ECA. In this way I obtained from Mr. Gardiner a more positive declaration in the desire to reciprocate . . .

I would not wish to give in these first impressions a too optimistic note. One must not expect to attain miracles of precision nor revolutionary ideas in the final report. But given the haste in which this inquiry and this conference were prepared, I cannot but underline the serenity, the seriousness, the spirit of cordiality and the confidence which have presided, to the present time in our debates, which will continue to be held until tomorrow evening . . . The press has shown an exceptional interest . . . useless to say that for the local press, the presence of the Emperor suffices to explain this enthusiasm . . . *without a doubt UNESCO has a very good press in this country* [author's emphasis].

Maurice wrote thank-you notes to all those who collaborated in Addis Ababa to make the meeting a success. He also had a great deal to do with the provisional report of the conference, as he had had with the working paper for it, for when it was published on March 18, 1960, he sent copies to the delegates, his collaborators, and other interested parties. The director-general, Mr. Veronese, also sent many copies with his thanks for the enthusiastic participation in letters to the delegates. There were many positive replies.[9]

In late June 1960, Maurice made another trip to Nigeria, this time to help the government formulate a request for the Special Fund for aid to set up a training school for the training of secondary school teachers, especially for the teaching of science and modern languages. He first stopped off in London to talk with officials of the Colonial Office, who all emphasized that it was wise to proceed slowly. Maurice must have been encouraged by the reactions to the questionnaires and conferences of some officials in London. It was thought there that they constituted one of the happiest initiatives of UNESCO. The result had the effect of arousing a sort of general movement, but it also created the danger of proliferation of activities leading to duplication if there was not coordination of effort among the various agencies. To this Maurice must have agreed. The American assistant secretary of state expressed the opinion that at the General Conference in the fall of 1960 it would be good to organize a meeting among representatives of all countries and agencies giving help (France, the United Kingdom, the

146

United States, UNESCO, ILO, the Food and Agriculture Organization [FAO], etc.) and the countries that were to receive aid to come to an understanding as to the most appropriate ways to effectuate this coordination of assistance. Another observation was that few graduates of universities went into teaching, as private industry attracted them.

There was a need in Nigeria for at least four training schools to provide an adequate number of teachers for the expanding numbers of children enrolled as well as to replace unqualified teachers. (This would be a problem in most countries of tropical Africa.) A project of the Carnegie Foundation was being studied for Africans to go to Teachers' College, Columbia University, in New York City, and the University of London, while professors from these universities would have terms of teaching in Africa. A special African section in the Education Department of Teachers' College was being set up.

In Lagos there already was talk of *manpower* targets for economic development for agriculture, commerce, industry, education, and government. Maurice had several contacts with the chief of IDA (International Aid for Development) there as well as the president of the Nigerian WCOTP (World Confederation of Organizations of the Teaching Profession), members of the ministries, and representatives of the TA Board, UNICEF, and ILO for the UNESCO proposal. A project was proposed that was more elaborate than the UNESCO one—this concerned a federal advanced training college to train normal school teachers for the training of teachers for all levels and kinds of schools.

During the discussions Maurice made some suggestions: one was that some form of research be included in the project; second, that since building costs were so high, all space should be used to the maximum, with night school and summer courses going on as well as the regular sessions, refresher courses and in-service training; third, that since science equipment was so expensive not all regional schools could be equipped; fourth, as to teachers of art and music, the training should be reserved for one central institute. Better training would be the outcome. Maurice went about to the various government officials to be sure that their approbation would be forthcoming: the minister of education, the minister of finance, and the prime minister, who would get a favorable response from the council of ministers. He also received the approval of the ICA (International Cooperation Administration) representative who was sure aid would be accorded if the U.S. Senate approved the special allocation for Africa that President

Eisenhower demanded. This it did in the fall. This was Maurice's last mission before finishing off administrative tasks at headquarters to go on holiday.

As has been stated, Maurice was involved from June 1956 to August 1960 wherever UNESCO had projects dealing with primary and later general, technical and vocational secondary education and institutions and personnel concerning them and then also with the beginning of the Emergency Program for Africa decided upon in 1959. These just described— LAMP, the International Advisory Committee on Curriculum Revision, the questionnaires and the Addis Ababa Conference in 1960, were the tasks taking up most of his time outside of administrative obligations before he was sent on mission to the Congo.

Notes

1. Home Files, "Division of Responsibilities between Department of Education and the Coordination in the Implementation of LAMP," MD/FER, November 24, 1954.
2. UNESCO Regular Files 372 (8) MPOI, parts 1–4, LAMP 5243/ES WS/117/119 6982, December 9, 1957.
3. Ibid.
4. UNESCO Regular Files 371.214 A-022, parts 4 and 5.
5. Edso 1/59—426, May 11, 1959.
6. "Questionnaire for a Survey on Needs for a Primary and Secondary Education in Tropical Africa," ED/834 051, annex 59, UNESCO Archives 37(6) A-64/20.
7. Ibid., UNESCO ED/173, December 28,1959–September 1, 1960, Report on Regional Meeting, February 29, 1960.
8. First draft of Provisional Report, UNESCO ED/Africa 2, January 1, 1960.
9. UNESCO/ED 174, Meeting of Ministers of Tropical Africa (of Education) 37(b) A-06(63) 60 TA, March 18, 1960.

The Congo Crisis and the UNESCO Emergency Program, August 1960

The years 1960 and 1961 would be the years during which quite a number of African colonies threw off the yoke of colonialism to become independent states. Most of them made the transition without too much turmoil. One that did not was the Belgian Congo, which became independent on June 30, 1960. Its independence would be the greatest challenge that faced the United Nations and its sister organizations—especially UNESCO—since their inception. Through his activity in the name of UNESCO, first as chief of the UNESCO mission, then also as member of the Consultative Group to advise the chief of the UN civilian operations in the Congo, it would also be the greatest challenge for Maurice since he left Haiti. He would be the first UNESCO professional to be sent to the Congo. In his capacity, he carried out immediate measures and worked out long-term plans for the educational system of the country. His feelings about this mission can be judged by the two letters he wrote, one to Dag Hammarskjöld, the secretary-general of the United Nations, the other to René Maheu, acting director-general of UNESCO, at the end of his term in August 1961, on the eve of his return to headquarters.

In the letter of August 7, 1961,[1] he thanked the Secretary General of the United Nations, Dag Hammarskjöld, for the opportunity given him and the confidence placed in him as a member of the Consultative Group of the United Nations to the chief of its civil operations in the Congo. He appreciated the chance it gave him to participate in this historic experience and to bring his modest contribution to such a vital work under the secretary-general's direction. He went on to state: "Permit me to say that your untiring devotion to the UN cause, the lucidity, the patience and courage you have shown during the most difficult and distressing moments were for us a source of inspiration in the execution of our task."

To this D. Hammarskjöld, on August 14, 1961, sent a letter of acknowledgement and thanks. In it he states that he wished to personally express his thanks "for the contribution you brought to the United Nations and to say that the Organization was privileged to be able to profit from your services in such difficult circumstances as those we have encountered in the Congo. I hope that another occasion will present itself when you can again be associated with our work."

On August 9, 1961, Maurice wrote to René Maheu:

At the end of my mission to Léopoldville I want to thank you for the confidence you showed in naming me head of the UNESCO mission to the Congo and the support you accorded me in the accomplishment of the task assigned to me. I very much appreciate the opportunity that you offered me to participate in this historic experience which was rich in learning for me, in spite of the frustrations and numerous difficulties which we have undergone. I believe that in spite of the difficulties and the budgetary restrictions which were imposed, UNESCO has been able to establish and successfully initiate a realistic program which one hopes will give positive results in the future.[2]

Maheu's reply[3] of August 18, 1961, states: ". . . in spite of the numerous difficulties of all kinds which you encountered and which often could not be surmounted except at the price of patient efforts, you arrived at laying down the bases on which our future action in the country will be established. I congratulate and thank you . . ."

As early as February of 1960 the secretary-general of the United Nations visited the Congo, then still a Belgian colony. He sensed that the granting of independence on June 30 would not be without problems, believing that the Belgians had not prepared the Congolese to assume the responsibilities of running the country and that the Congolese would need support and aid. Therefore, he asked Ralph Bunche, one of the under secretaries of the United Nations, who had acquitted himself so well in the Palestine crisis of 1952, to represent him at the independence ceremonies and stay on in case the new national government needed assistance.

It turned out the way the secretary-general thought it would. The ceremonies for the inauguration of the first president, Joseph Kasavubu, and the first prime minister, Patrice Lumumba, took place in the presence of King Baudouin of Belgium, who had come for the independence celebration. No sooner had the two men taken office than the problems began.

Most of the administrative services had been run by Belgian functionaries. These had departed, leaving the services in the hands of personnel untrained and thus incompetent to carry out the tasks before them, causing nearly chaotic conditions in the public administration. The national treasury was almost empty, so neither salaries nor debts could be paid. Rival political and tribal factions began to cause disturbances. Finally the army, resenting the continued presence of some of the Belgian armed forces, and especially the Belgian officers, began to rebel, as it felt the presence of these officers was an encroachment on the sovereignty of the country.

Ten days after the assumption of office, Lumumba went abroad to seek help. On the twelfth of July he appealed to the United Nations, first for military aid and then assistance in all the public services, education, health, agriculture, as well as economic help, in fact, in every field of public service. This he did through the secretary-general, Dag Hammarskjöld. Lumumba had been encouraged to do so by the U.S. government, to which he had turned first. The United States promised help through the United Nations.

On July 22 the secretary-general convoked the Security Council to deliberate on this unusual appeal. The Security Council adopted the resolutions necessary to give him directives. The secretary-general took immediate steps. He quickly recruited an international military task force, which soon numbered twenty thousand men and their officers. Furnished with proper equipment, this armed force arrived in the Congo to keep the peace and protect civilians. It installed itself in record time throughout the country. It was the first time that a UN force was called upon to keep peace within a country. He then set up a team for the civil operations. He called upon the sister agencies of the United Nations to give their aid. First, the Famine Relief Service went into action in the regions hit by food scarcity. Also, the FAO, the World Health Organization (WHO), the International Children's Emergency Fund, responded, among others. They withdrew experts from other areas to send into the Congo.

As for UNESCO, Andrew Cordier, right-hand man of the secretary-general, cabled the deputy director-general Maheu in Paris. "We need a very high-level educationalist to join the Consultative Group to advise the chief of the Civil Operations, Sture Linner. He will be adviser to the UN team and also be available to the Congo Government on request, not only to advise on all aspects but assist it in organizing the education system." Further on the cable read: "Please propose as a matter of urgency the name or names of candidates with sketch of backgrounds and appropriate emoluments for the approval of the secretary-general."[4]

As early as July 24, André Paté, head of famine relief, had notified UNESCO that several specialized agencies already had experts in the

Congo.[5] A critical situation was foreseen in education with the reopening of schools, due to the massive departure of the Belgians. He thought that UNESCO could send representatives to survey the situation. Both Linner and the Technical Assistance Bureau (TAB), the funding agency, concurred.

This information was circulated in the Department of Education. Maheu, in the absence of the director-general, assumed responsibility for this urgent request. He, with the chief of the Division of Relations with International Organizations, Carlo Pio Terenzio (Italy), had been to Geneva to attend the meeting of a section of the Economic and Social Council of the United Nations where the problem of the Congo had been discussed. From there they proceeded to Léopoldville to learn about the problems in the educational sector. Mr. Maheu left Terenzio there to continue the preliminary contacts with the various officials. He issued a communication concerning the UNESCO participation in the Congo effort. In it he declared:

> The most urgent problems in the Congo are the reopening of the schools, the taking of decisions concerning the opening of the universities, Louvanium in Léopoldville and the state university in Elizabethville in the province of Katanga, the filling of vacancies in the administration, the preservation of the scientific research installations in the interior of the country for which the Director-General asked for a UN military force for their protection, and the setting up within the country as well as abroad of intensive training of administrative functionaries and technicians necessary for the social and economic life of the country.

It continued:

> ... the director-general preferred to designate as chief of mission, a person outside the Secretariat.[6]

(Maheu would later admit that he had made a mistake.) Soon after, Edmond Sylvain, a Haitian, former dean of the law school in Port-au-Prince for two years, was appointed to be the chief consultant in education to the chief of ONUC. Maurice, as chief of the UNESCO mission, was to give technical support to him. It was to be a joint effort. They were to share the responsibilities. Until November both would sign some of the communications.

The news of his appointment reached Maurice in Amsterdam, where we were stopping before going on to Copenhagen for a brief holiday. He must have been aware that he might be designated, as the first cable, dated August 1, 1960, from Maheu in Léopoldville reads:

For Dartigue—following our conversations have decided to name you chief of the UNESCO education mission for the Congo. Initial period three months STOP This mission ought to support and back up the efforts of the Education Consultant—not yet designated—on behalf of Linner, United Nations, without being under his authority STOP Regret to ask you to join us in Léopoldville Sunday 7 August. Please contact Van Vliet. Signed: Maheu (3261).[6A]

It took some time to locate Maurice and me, as we had asked our son, who knew where we were, not to tell anyone for two or three days so that we could at least return by way of Bruges, Belgium. Therefore, Maurice called headquarters from Bruges to say he would be back in the office the next day. He would be ready to go to the Congo but had to settle certain private matters first.

The second cable sent by Maheu, on August 8, 1960, read: "You are *instructed* [author's emphasis] to proceed to Léopoldville for an initial period of three months as head of a UNESCO educational mission."[6B] Maurice again wired that he was ready to go, but that since he was to be gone for three months, he had to take certain measures to ensure the financial security of his family during his long absence, under the uncertain conditions prevailing in the Congo.

Maheu returned to headquarters on the ninth of August. He issued the note concerning the participation of UNESCO in the emergency program as part of ONUC. By August 12 he was on his way to Léopoldville with Maurice, Osman, the expert recalled from Addis Ababa, and others. Maheu had decided to introduce them personally, probably realizing that the men would have more prestige and authority with the Congolese government and the UN officials if he did so.

On August 11 a UN note appeared stating that "it is necessary to give to the experts utilized for these activities which demand responsibilities at a higher level, a new status without precedent."[7] In another communication the UN secretary-general was cited as saying: " . . . the Specialized Agency concerned, appoints a local representative of such seniority as to correspond to the duties which he will have in the field, taking fully into consideration, on the one side, the scope of the operation, on the other side, his senior responsibilities as advisor to the government at its request."[8] Such representatives had already been appointed in several cases.

A General Assembly resolution had appeared on July 14 requesting that all states refrain from supplying arms or other material for warlike purposes. Further on, it set forth that the purpose of the UN Civil Operations was to train the largest possible number of Congolese in the various fields, as many had been inadequately prepared for their new responsibilities. They had had no opportunities to exercise authority, make decisions, take initiatives, make plans, etc.

To better appreciate the situation in the Congo that the United Nations and its specialized agencies, such as UNESCO, faced it is necessary to make some remarks about the past of the Congo before and after it became a Belgian colony. Today, the country is known as Zaire, the name that President Sese Soku Mobutu gave it in 1968. In 1960 it was known as the Congo or Congo-Léopoldville to differentiate it from Congo-Brazzaville, the French Congo across the river.

As early as the late fifteenth century Portuguese traders had opened up some coastal towns of West Africa. However, it was not until the latter half of the nineteenth century that interest was shown in Africa, when it was penetrated by several European explorers. As concerns the Congo, it was the journey of David Livingstone, a Scottish explorer and medical missionary, that made news. He had started from Capetown in South Africa and worked his way up into the area of the great lakes of East Africa. The British journalist Henry Stanley was sent to find him. This he did in July 1871 in Ruzizi, a small outpost on the west side of Lake Tanganyika. Stanley returned to Great Britain, where several brilliant articles on Stanley's unusual exploit were published. These events, it is presumed, led to his being hired by Leopold II of Belgium to explore as much of the Congo territory as he could in the king's name. This Stanley did, financed by the king, with the result that what he explored became the king's personal property.

At the time of the king's laying claim to the vast territory there were many petty kingdoms inhabited by many ethnic groups, the best known of which were the Bantu (by far the most numerous), the Sudanese, the Nilotic, the Hamitic, and the Pygmies. With the advent of the Belgians this pattern was broken up. Large investment consortiums for mining, mostly from Europe, were set up, often with forced labor and brutal management. Huge

154

plantations were acquired through various means for single-crop production, doing away with the self-sustaining village agriculture. In many instances, customs and mores were modified to the detriment of village life. The hold of the traditional web was torn and shaken, though not completely done away with, as tribal identity still remained, to cause violence after independence.

At the same time, Protestant and Catholic missionaries, mostly of Belgian origin, arrived to spread the gospel. They set up missions throughout the territory and put up so-called primary schools in 1906 to teach reading and writing, often using the pupils as free labor in the mission gardens. For these schools they trained "monitors" in special normal schools. The training was elementary and some monitors were not much more literate than the children they taught. But they answered the missions' purpose.

In 1908 the king ceded this land (his private preserve) to the state. The Belgian government set up an administrative structure to control the colony through a special government authority in Brussels whose agents worked out of Léopoldville, carrying out instructions decided upon in the Belgian capital. Slavery was abolished and health was improved somewhat. To administer the huge area it was divided into a confederation of six provinces with the central administration in the capital, Léopoldville. The provinces were Léopoldville (the same name as the capital), Equator, Katanga, Kivu, Oriental, and Kasai (which at independence became North and South Kasai). After independence, Katanga seceded until brought back into the fold in 1963, causing three years of disturbances. At the time of independence there were more than ten thousand Belgian functionaries in the Congo. It is for this reason that their massive departure caused near-catastrophe. For the most part, the Congolese were clerks, secretaries, stenographers, and typists—what in UN parlance are referred to as "general services"—while the Belgians were classed as professionals and held the higher administrative posts.

As far as the educational system was concerned, the central government in Léopoldville fixed the general policies and coordinated the programs. The provincial governments had a certain autonomy but were expected to go through the central ministry for most demands and operations. Two universities had been created in 1954, that of Louvanium on the outskirts of Léopoldville, and the other in Elizabethville in Katanga. On the eve of independence, most of the students were European and most of them (as did many European secondary school students) returned to Belgium.

Although 1,800,000 children were in primary school in the Congo in 1960, the greatest number of all African countries, only 55,000 went on into postprimary and/or secondary schools—a very small percentage. Many stayed in primary school for only two years, far below the minimum schooling needed for literacy. Of the few who finally finished high school, most were able to get higher training only through seminaries for the priesthood. At the time of independence there were 120 college graduates for all of the Congo. It is with this situation that ONUC and UNESCO were confronted when appealed to by Kasavubu and Lumumba to come to the aid of their country.

The first contacts made by the UNESCO mission with Maheu were with the then education minister Pierre Mulele; Sture Linner, chief of ONUC; and Robert Gardiner, UN representative for administrative affairs, most closely concerned with UNESCO and its program, especially concerning financing. The minister immediately verbally agreed to the proposed UNESCO program for the urgent needs as well as the modalities for implementation. He estimated that 1,567 secondary school teachers would be needed if the Belgians did not come back, otherwise less, depending on how many returned. A special statute for the to-be-recruited foreign teachers would have to be worked out. Headquarters hoped Maurice would work out a plan in eight days. By the twenty-seventh of August, the estimate was lowered to five hundred, as some Belgian teachers did come back. The government was against recruiting new teachers from Belgium but accepted those already in service who had been on holiday. Teachers could be recruited from French-speaking countries such as France, Canada, Switzerland, and Haiti. Non-French-speaking countries could be asked about teachers who understood and spoke French.

It was urgent to constitute the basic school files that were lacking. Osman was already there for this. A specialist for organizing the administration and the school budget was needed. Murray Chase, chief of the Section of Administrative Procedures Program and Budget at UNESCO, was speedily sent for a short term from headquarters. A judicial adviser was needed to prepare the agreements between UNESCO, the United Nations, and the government. Maurice would make the first drafts. Technical experts were also needed for the six provincial ministries, to keep those offices afloat.

Maheu returned to Paris on August 18. On the nineteenth, the first of several incidents between the Congolese army and UN functionaries took place. Ralph Bunche, the representative of the UN secretary-general, made a statement that was circulated among all the international civil personnel in the Congo: "This A.M. some of our colleagues were made to disembark from their plane by Congolese soldiers and roughly treated; one man is in hospital, not seriously injured. . . ." He thanked the UN military for the restraint, forbearance, and patience they showed. He continued: "May I also say that the civilian members of ONUC, who have had their share of harassment, have conducted themselves in an exemplary manner. They are due the highest praise."[9] Ralph Bunche himself later was roughly treated by members of the Congolese army. The possibility of this kind of occurrence was part of the daily life there at the time.

As to Maurice's and Sylvain's activities, they again met with Gardiner. They worked out a plan and program with the then minister of education, and sent them to Maheu in Paris on August 22, 1960.[10] They outlined the following points: (a) recruiting teachers for general and technical secondary schools with a 50 percent contribution toward salaries; (b) demanding the services of Osman for statistics for three months; (c) demanding the services of Chase for one month; (d) demanding the visit of W. Carter (exchange of persons, grants, etc.) for eight days; (e) demanding the visit of Bertrand (civil administration) for eight days. Gardiner thought that the United Nations was too generous. He said that there had been too many well-paid Belgian functionaries; with judicious promotions and accelerated training, the Congolese could take over and the country would be run with less personnel. If the United Nations did too much for the Congolese government, it would spend too much and not recognize its responsibilities. Maurice informed him that a budget man and a statistician were needed for at least a year to be of real use to the government and to initiate those who would replace them to these tasks. Gardiner was not convinced but acquiesced. He did accept Carter and would put him in contact with representatives of countries that might have fellowships to offer. Maurice also brought up the subject of the special status of the teachers to be recruited. To this Gardiner answered that he was working on statutes and would collaborate with Maurice on this. So, after only a few days, a plan had been put together and most of it accepted by Gardiner. At the same time Maurice, Osman, and Chase developed a long-term technical assistance plan in a larger perspective for the reinforcement of the cadres in the Ministry.[11]

It was the United Nations, through the special contributions of member states, that underwrote most of the Congo operations, with the specialized agencies paying within their limited resources for some of the personnel sent from headquarters for short missions. All the functionaries directly paid by ONUC had to have the approval of the chief of ONUC as well as that of the Congolese government. At times there were delays in allocating funds, due to delays in contributions or differences of opinion between the agencies and the UN officials in New York as to the necessity of certain projects. There would be differences of opinion within UNESCO or with the mission and headquarters because of misinterpretations, misunderstandings, or plain negligence. However, it was remarkable how much was accomplished with such a diversified group at such a difficult time, with the disorganization in Congolese public life.[12]

There was to be a great amount of cabling from Léopoldville to headquarters, from Léopoldville or Paris to New York, or vice-versa. The diplomatic pouches with reports, questions, decisions, information, and consent seemed to take too long. In spite of all the goodwill, problems in communications came up several times. A very good example of this is shown in the message sent to Terenzio at headquarters from Maurice and Sylvain in Léopoldville dated October 3, 1960, in which Maurice, after informing Terenzio of the complex political situation due to the fact that the prime minister and his cabinet had been relieved of their duties by President Kasavubu (and the latter had set up a group of commissioners to carry on the government and that these college students were incompetent to do so), went on to state that the mission was making headway in having the government ask for aid of UNESCO despite an adverse press and some hostile Belgian counselors. He continued that he had been called in with Sylvain to attend the UN Consultative Group and was asked about a cable sent by Sir A. MacFarquhar, the UN official heading the Congo effort in New York, concerning a project, the recruitment of 500 teachers submitted to him by Maheu. It was impossible for either Maurice or Sylvain to answer precisely, as they had not been informed by headquarters. Maurice quickly decided that this project must be in reference to the 500 teachers who were to be supplied through TA without waiting for a formal agreement to be signed with the government. This seemed plausible and he advanced an answer according to this assumption.

Later they were asked about measures being taken for the development of the training of teachers at the postsecondary level in agricultural and vocational fields. Again, they were unable to give an affirmative answer. Maurice asked Terenzio if this referred to the idea that he (Maurice) had advanced, but about which he had had no answer, of organizing a technical training school at a former air base training school at Kamina, which he hoped to visit with Rousseau, head of the Technical Education Unit at headquarters. He also mentioned the exchange of views about which he had written on September 29, concerning the possibility of creating a training school for secondary school teachers. He went on to state: "I do not know up to what point the cable from MacFarquhar refers to the above-mentioned projects or goes counter to them. But it should not be that one set of projects are discussed here and another set in Paris. The mission in the Congo should be kept informed of the intentions, projects, preparations and decisions . . . It is the best way to permit us to serve UNESCO."[13]

The early part of September was taken up by the problem of the financing of projects determined upon and the way in which the recruited secondary school teachers would be paid. But political crises absorbed the attention of the United Nations. The UNESCO mission found it difficult to know whom in the government to contact, as Kasavubu had ousted Lumumba and his cabinet. Sylvain and Maurice together reported on September 8, 1960: "The crisis which burst the day before yesterday has hindered our negotiations. The statute has been approved but now all is being held up." However, by the middle of the month the UNESCO liaison officer at the United Nations in New York could write: "School budget and administration posts approved. Secretary-General asks for $100,000,000. If this accepted UNESCO has green light for recruitment. Status of teachers more than normal OPEX [Operation Executive Personnel] arrangements." Another exchange of letters showed that Akrawi of Iraq, the new head of the UNESCO office in New York, needed to be informed concerning recruitment. He wanted to know what UNESCO responsibilities were, who was to recruit, make contracts, arrange travel, per diem, security coverage, health, accidents, and tax problems in the home country, manner of salary payment, and in what currency?[14]

It was evident to the UNESCO mission that for the time being, the Congolese government could not take on new financial burdens because the treasury was almost empty. Some civil functionaries, such as teachers, had not been paid. The university had not been given its subsidy. Moreover, the Bank of Belgium had blocked the Congolese funds, leaving the government in critical straits as concerned foreign exchange. The government was also unwilling to levy taxes, fearing uprisings.

The education minister threatened to bypass UNESCO, since he felt recruitment of teachers was going too slowly. UNESCO did have at headquarters files of over a thousand applicants; still, very few met the special needs of the Congo. Moreover, as in most countries, school terms were about to begin or had already begun and the supply of possible teachers was reduced. It had taken time, too, to get exact information from the ministry as to the specific numbers and types of secondary school teachers needed. The opening of primary schools did not present difficulties, since most of the teachers, such as they were, were Congolese, but for the secondary schools it would be a grave problem unless Belgian teachers returned. Many did eventually come back. This came about after a critical situation caused by differences of opinion between the central government and those of the provinces was smoothed out. The central government at first refused the return of the Belgians. The provincial governments maintained that they knew better the realities of the secondary school problems and were directly responsible vis-à-vis the population. If the schools could not open because of the lack of teachers, there would be social problems. To avert catastrophe, the Belgian teachers had to come back. The minister from Léopoldville Province saw the president and the minister of education of the central government. In consequence, the consent was given. Maurice agreed with the provincial minister's opinion.

Maurice found himself doing a great deal of the work. Sylvain did not know, nor could he know, about the ins and outs of an international organization, its demands, its limits, and its procedures, nor how it negotiated with officials of member states or how it aided them in making requests, and helped them decide on responsibilities, nor how to implement projects once they had been agreed upon. The Congo crisis was a more complex set of circumstances than even Maurice had had to deal with, but at least he had the background and experience of working in the United Nations and UNESCO and with member states.

Transportation was a problem. At first there was only one car, which had to do service for everyone and everything. A small bus was added. But when either broke down, the problem became critical. Cars had to be begged and borrowed from ONUC and/or other agencies. By late spring another car was added, and by the fall of 1961 the problem disappeared, as enough cars were provided, some through UNICEF.

Because of the government crises, although Maurice had worked out a project for an accord with the government, due to several changes in the education ministry it was difficult for the mission to know if the next official would approve of what his predecessors had agreed to, thus placing UNESCO in a delicate position. It was decided that a definite agreement could not be negotiated until a stable government was formed, so the accords for each project would be initialed only. However, the accords would define explicitly the responsibilities of each of the participants. But before this took place, Maurice and the two UNESCO experts in the ministry worked out a project and sent it to headquarters for approval. On its return with complete acceptance or suggested changes or amendments, Maurice presented it to whoever was occupying the minister's chair. The same procedure was followed for each project. Finally, after the UN officials had approved it for financing, it was ready and the special representatives came from headquarters for the purpose of initialing. Maurice as well as those who succeeded him had to be very careful not to overstep the prerogatives of advising and suggesting and make decisions that rightly belonged to the Congolese officials. On the other hand, the Congolese were wary of shouldering responsibility and making decisions, thus causing procrastination and, for the mission, the need for great patience.

Dwight David Eisenhower, president of the United States, let it be known in July that the United States was willing to help the Congo, but only through the United Nations. He expected the other nations to do likewise. The Secretary-General of the UN reaffirmed that no member state could unilaterally aid the Congo. This was especially aimed at the USSR, which, stated the *New York Times,* had sent planes and personnel to the Congo at the demand of Lumumba. The USSR asserted the right to do so. President Eisenhower urged the Soviets to end such aid.[14A]

On September 15 it was finally Colonel Mobutu who, having become head of the Congolese army and the strongest man in the government, gave the Russian embassy and technicians forty-eight hours to leave the Congo. He invited other embassies of socialist countries to do the same. He then, on the sixteenth, put Lumumba under house arrest. On the eighteenth, the secretary-general of the United Nations convoked a special session. After hearing an explanation of his actions, the General Assembly gave him a vote of confidence. On the twentieth, Messrs. Kasavubu and Mobutu created a "caretaker" government that included the college students as commissioners of the government. This made the work of the UNESCO mission more complicated, as the commissioners knew even less how to run a government.

On the twenty-fourth, in New York, the Soviets demanded the secretary-general's ouster because they felt he had overstepped his prerogatives. He refused to resign. It was at this assembly that he said:

It is not the Soviet Union, or indeed, any other big power who needs the United Nations for their protection; it is all the others. In this sense the Organization is first of all *their* organization. . . . I shall remain in my post during the term of my office as a servant of the Organization in the interests of all those other nations as long as *they* wish me to do so . . .

There would be more confrontations between the Soviets and the secretary-general as the assembly continued and events occurred in the Congo.

In spite of the political uncertainty, the mission worked on. It produced a short-term plan, most of which was accepted by headquarters; this was a plan for the restructuring and strengthening of the central education and provincial ministries. Maurice was to obtain a formal request from the education minister; only then could the experts be recruited now that funds had been made available. The problem would be to find qualified experts. Maurice had suggested that all the activities relating to teacher training and cadres be under one head, those concerning statistics, research, planning, and documentation under another, and also the creation of a unit charged with the questions of cultural relations, technical assistance, and fellowships, all guaranteed financially by the United Nations, with security guaranteed by the government.

On the twenty-seventh of September an important official document was circulated in UNESCO titled "UNESCO Educational Assistance to the Congo." It gave the main points of the plan and program that were to be applied, some points of which have already been mentioned. The immediate task was twofold: (1) to recruit 500 teachers for the various secondary schools, requested as early as August 17 by the minister Mulele; and (2) to strengthen the administrative structure of the central and provincial education ministries by providing TA experts, for whom there was still no formal request but who would provide accelerated training for postsecondary personnel and higher echelons jointly with the ILO and FAO to strengthen technical and vocational training. The estimate was for eventually employing fifty-four experts. References were made as to provision for payment, family plus educational allowances, health, travel costs, etc., estimated at $3,349,200.

Maurice wrote to Terenzio concerning a conversation he had had with Cardozo, a new interim general commissioner of education on October 6. The Congolese government had not yet completely decided to accept the UNESCO program. Although the full text of the accord was transmitted to the minister Mulele on September 8, Cardozo was waiting for the report of his Belgian adviser, Mr. Ceulemans, on the project of the statutes for the incoming foreign teachers; only then would he bring up the question of the entire project before the Council of Commissioners. The mission was waiting for this. Maurice let Cardozo know that if UNESCO wished to restructure the Ministry of Education it was so that he, the general commissioner for education, could accomplish in an efficient manner the formidable task that had been entrusted to him. It was up to him to make known the needs in a request to TA. Training could be instituted for Congolese teaching personnel for secondary schools, with accelerated formation for certain primary school teachers. Maurice continued in the note to let Cardozo know that there was an urgent need for trained teachers for technical and vocational schools. He could ask for financial aid for these from the United Nations, UNESCO, and TA. The Kamina base, where a school already existed, could receive trainees for technical education.[15]

As of yet the new republic had not formally accepted admission to UNESCO. Terenzio wrote to Maurice to urge Cardozo to encourage the government to do this. Maurice gave Cardozo a copy of the letter in which Terenzio (August 17, 1960) advised the then secretary-general of the Ministry of Foreign Affairs that the Congo Republic had been admitted as a member to UNESCO, with an annex of a facsimile of the instrument of acceptance contained in the Constitutive Act of UNESCO, which should be deposited at the Foreign Office in London by a plenipotentiary named by the Congolese government. Evidently, the Congolese government had not yet deposited the requisite papers by the proper person there.

Already Maurice was considering the tasks he still had to do before finishing the three-month mission. He wrote to headquarters on October 10, 1960,[16] that he was studying the possibility of two teacher training institutes for the regular high schools and one for teachers of vocational and technical schools. If feasible and desired by the Congolese authorities, who would need assistance from the United Nations, the Congo Fund, and the Special Fund, he needed the assistance of the man who had worked on the questionnaires to draw up a good plan and have it approved before his departure, which was to take place on November 12. Before that he wanted to go to Kamina, to Bukavu, and to Elizabethville, then meet in Léopoldville with the mission to draw up conclusions. At the moment, he wrote, developments were slow because of the political upheaval. The central government was not in control of the provinces, nor were the provincial governments masters of the situation, as the army put fear into all by their lack of discipline and their aggressions.

By October 11, it was Charles Bizala, who had been a delegate to the 1960 ministers' meeting in Addis Ababa and had some education, who was in charge of the education ministry as general commissioner. He wrote an official letter stating that a preliminary study had been made of the suggestions on the restructuring of the ministry and that it had been approved in principle. He begged that thirteen experts be put immediately at the disposal of the ministry out of the total of twenty-four offered, and as one (R. H. Ardill, who had replaced Chase) was already in the Congo, it would mean twelve to be recruited. He gave thanks to the United Nations and UNESCO for the help being offered.[17]

Terenzio came to expedite matters since the formal request by Mr. Bizala had finally been made. He wrote on October 13 to the director-general that there was progress. He added:

With a great amount of patience and flexibility, it may be possible to arrive at a result in a week or so. A welcome committee (in theory at least) for the incoming experts and teachers has been constituted. A search for lodgings for them has begun. The disorganization and irregularity of communications is such in three or four provinces that arrangements for a man of ours should be made to keep the needs up to date, welcome the teachers, take care of them and inform Léopoldville.[18]

This request was ignored at headquarters. He admitted that the political situation was bad and that it was hard to obtain decisions. The commissioners were suspicious and incapable of appreciating the impartiality on which the United Nations was founded. They were also being influenced by the Belgians to boycott the United Nations as well as TA.

It was in this letter, too, that the possibility of Maurice's being given Sylvain's job, as well as keeping his own, was brought up. It was suggested that since Sylvain was to go to the ministry as adviser to the general commissioner, it would be better to strengthen Maurice's authority by making him not only chief of the mission, but also a member of the Consultative Group to aid the chief of ONUC rather than to try to replace Sylvain. Terenzio also suggested that if necessary to speed matters, UNESCO could withdraw experts from other areas, as some specialized agencies had done, to send them to the Congo. He added: "Unfortunately Bizala's demand must yet be approved by the Minister of Planning and Coordination. Contacts are difficult and the final decision is put off from day to day." He wrote by hand at the end: "The decision has just reached us." Maurice and he must certainly have been relieved that at last action could be taken. In the meantime, the schools had opened.

Because of the uncertainty of the political outcome it was decided and Maheu sent a cable on October 14, 1960, to that effect to the secretary-general of the United Nations stating: "There will be specific work arrangements, initialized memoranda, described as interim which later will be subject to approval or modification when a constitutional government authority is established. The temporary arrangements are to be concluded for which approbation will be given by the Executive Board when it meets."[19]

There was a flurry of cables between headquarters and Léopoldville on the seventeenth, nineteenth, and twentieth of October concerning the signing of this first accord, its content, and its financing by the United Nations. The general commissioner of education released a communiqué to the press concerning it. UNESCO headquarters and the mission had to encourage and persuade not only the representatives of the Congolese government, but also the chief of ONUC in the Congo and, through him, Sir A. MacFarquhar, who held the purse strings at the United Nations in New York, especially since, for the time being, the United Nations would have to bear the total financial responsibility for the program, as the Congolese treasury could not contribute. The UN General Assembly was meeting in New York. It would have to be made cognizant of the steps taken by UNESCO in the field of education. For this purpose, Dr. Akrawi, at the United Nations, had to be kept informed in detail to be able to define the interests of UNESCO with all the UN officials connected with the Congo program.[20]

There had recently been established an Agency for International Development (AID), mostly funded by the United States, to which the newly independent nations could turn. President Eisenhower, present at the General Assembly on October 20, 1960, urged the expansion of the TA program, especially for newly independent states in Africa, special action in education for training of personnel in all areas of public service. He demanded that UNESCO develop further action and that private agencies and nongovernmental organizations (NGOs) do so, too. President Eisenhower promised increased aid to Africa.[21] Dr. Akrawi urged UNESCO to augment its assistance to Africa in cooperation with the other specialized agencies in matters of health, child care, and agriculture. Maheu, the director-general, and Terenzio went to the General Assembly in New York to assist at the sessions concerning the UNESCO program.

The fifteenth session of the General Assembly had some stormy sessions. The Soviets, angered by the fact that they could not take unilateral action and bitter for having been ousted by Mobutu, who, they were convinced, was backed by the United States and the United Nations, attacked the Secretary-General, Dag Hammarskjöld, on several occasions. On October 17, he finally demanded to be allowed to speak in defense of the UN policies as implemented through him, and the action that was being carried out in the Congo. He referred to the needs of the Congolese people and the work of the United Nations in assisting the Congolese authorities whose responsibility it was to meet these needs. He went on to praise the services rendered by the hundreds of unnamed Congolese who tried painstakingly each day to maintain a minimum of order to keep an administration—on a minimal level—running: "They are never mentioned, they have chosen to serve instead of to rule. They have chosen to subordinate themselves instead of searching for power. May I pay tribute to these men and to what they have done to give life and sense to the independence of the Congo. It is those with whom the United Nations has had to work, it is those we have been able to consult, and those we have tried to assist."

He referred to the various accusations made of him and the United Nations, especially the accusation that the United Nations was trying to reinstitute some kind of colonialism. This he denied, stating that the men from many nations of Africa, Asia, and Europe serving the United Nations "are there, working against the heaviest odds under a continuous nerve strain, having endless working days, not knowing whether all they do would not be swept aside by new waves of political unrest, giving their best." He

166

paid them tribute as pioneers for the growing group of men all over the world who regarded service to their fellow members of the community of mankind to be a reward in itself, guided by a faith in a better future and maintaining the strict norms of behavior that the charter requested of an international civil servant. He went on to say that "decisions taken could be criticized, might have been different but that doubt must not be thrown on their motives—the well-being of the Congolese people in a life of peace and true independence . . ."[22]

He talked about the breakdown of the army and its incapacity to keep public order. He felt that the unrest was a passing phase. The civilian operation was of decisive importance; what had been achieved had required the services of all the UN agencies to their full capacity. Further on he said:

We have tried to consult to all the extent there was anybody who could be consulted and who paid any attention to the needs. . . . We have avoided taking decisions for which we could not get authoritative approval, but when a specific situation reached the stage of acute crisis, requiring immediate counteraction, and when we could not find those whose support we wished to have, we have had to act as responsible human beings facing a desperate emergency.

Finally, he said that the birth of an independent Congo had come to coincide with the birth of true cooperation of the UN family of agencies in the service of a member state:

. . . we will be even prouder, when through all the joint efforts, the stage has been reached when our services are no longer necessary in the Congo and we can leave the country solely and fully in the good hands of its own people, with its independence, peace and prosperity safeguarded by its own means . . .[23]

Although there were human frailties and human errors, such men as Maurice did have the will to serve, as well as the idealism that Dag Hammarskjöld upheld. Unfortunately, Hammarskjöld's early death prevented him from seeing this rescue operation through.

It was in the middle of October when Maurice learned of his promotion. He received a short letter of welcome from the secretary-general and a cable from Terenzio stating that his contract as chief of the UNESCO mission *and* consultant in education to the chief of ONUC would be dated from August 1 rather than November 1. Already on September 22, Chase, on his return to headquarters from Léopoldville, had written that at a meeting with Veronese, Maheu, Terenzio, and Henri Saba, Maheu had said that "he made a grave error in not nominating you as UNESCO's representative."[24] He (Chase) added that everyone at headquarters was much impressed by the work Maurice was doing and hoped he would stay on. It was only on November 16 that he learned by cable from headquarters that he had been formally named for the post after consultation with the Executive Board. It was signed by the director-general. Maurice could now take action and accept the full responsibility for the UNESCO program.

Both the Executive Board and the General Conference met on November 4, the first for its fifty-eighth session and the latter for its eleventh meeting. As was usual, the director-general gave a report to the members of the Executive Board.[25] He brought it up-to-date on what UNESCO had tried to do in the Congo and why. He said that he had contacted the president of the Executive Board immediately on learning of the UN appeal to UNESCO and kept him informed. Together they had decided that it was not necessary to convoke an extraordinary session. Although they recognized the urgency, they could take no steps before being assured by the Congolese government and the United Nations as to judicial and financial matters. This took some time. He then went into detail about the short-term program of the pressing needs of opening schools, recruiting secondary school teachers, recruiting experts for the minister, the granting of fellowships for study locally and abroad, and working out a budget. He spoke of the long-term plan worked out by Maurice, aided by Chase and Osman, and of TA for the reinforcement of cadres in the ministries and administration. It was only after his trip to New York and discussions with MacFarquhar that the proposed budget of $3,400,000 for UNESCO action was assured. He alluded to the frequent changes in ministers and the uncertain political situation that created the necessity of only initialing each accord, until a stable constitutional government would be instituted (this would take place in September 1961), when these accords could be duly ratified. He referred to the critical situation of the Institute for Scientific Research in Central Africa (IRSAC) and how that was eased, as well as the demand of ONUC to have UNESCO study jointly with ILO the possibility of a technical secondary school to be set up in a vacated section of Kamina Air Base.

The director-general's report to the General Conference on November

4 was very similar to the foregoing one. The Executive Board approved the director-general's action taken in the Congo. It invited the director-general to take all useful measures to satisfy the changing needs of the Congo and other tropical states in the framework of the international action.

It was in a private letter from Terenzio that Maurice received the most interesting news of the conference. It was written in December after the debate on the Congo had been terminated. Terenzio stated:

> In fact there were two debates. The political one on the powers of the Congolese delegation which appeared for the first time and provoked a tumult and disorder without precedent, with interruptions, cries, shouts, fists on the desks, etc. The other on the program was excellent. The Commission on Program approved the plans contained in Document 11C/34, even the Russians who had voted against it, somewhat embarrassed and only for political reasons. There were two abstentions: Guinea and Ceylon. All the rest voted favorably . . . In presenting the document Mr. Maheu rendered homage for your work and that of your collaborators.

He went on to say that everything was slow and difficult and that there were, as yet, very few volunteers for the Congo (partly because of the newspaper accounts on the aggressions in Léopoldville and the provinces). This information about the meeting must have been heartening to Maurice, as he had worked hard to draw up the plans that were exposed.[26]

The ministries of the provinces began to ask for help. The mission received official requests, approved by the commissioner, Bizala, from the provinces of Léopoldville and Kivu (with Kasai, Equator, and Oriental provinces pending) for 167 teachers in the fields of general, technical, agricultural, and business education on the secondary level. Maurice cabled this news to Terenzio, with copies to go to the Bureau of Member States, the office of the director-general, and to the acting head of the Education Department (the American, Loper, had left and a new head had not yet arrived) as well as other members of that department, personnel, personnel for technical assistance, etc. It was a real breakthrough after months of effort due to the suspicions of the provincial ministers that UNESCO wanted to take over the education system. It was the Belgian counselors who inspired these unfounded suspicions. Maurice insisted that only experienced teachers be recruited.

This result came about after Maurice had made a trip to the interior to try to convince the different ministers of the sincerity as to objective offers of UNESCO to come to their aid. He had been to Coquilhatville in Equator Province. On November 24 he had written to Terenzio that he had been to Bukavu, where it took him some time to convince the various school officials and the chief of the minister's cabinet (the minister being absent) that he was not there to advise them or decide for them, but that he was there to let them know of the possibilities of assistance that UNESCO could offer them. However, it was up to the minister to judge and decide. Maurice told them that he had heard that an unqualified Belgian was being brought back to teach in the technical school at a high price. UNESCO could provide qualified teachers for little or no payment. He also tried to dissipate the fears that the United Nations would insist on the departure of the Belgians. (While in the area he visited IRSAC. The personnel were in good spirits.) Maurice doubted that 500 teachers would be needed, as there was a determined effort by a group of Congolese for the return of the Belgians. He had been told that eighty Belgian judges had already returned, as well as some doctors. That Maurice was able to go to the interior was due to the kindness of UN pilots. The roads were not safe. It was difficult to know when and where fighting might occur. Chase on his return to headquarters at the end of September had written that UNESCO would have to be more energetic and go forward quickly.

Then came the other occurrence, rather important, of noncommunication between headquarters and the mission. On December 2, Maurice protested to Terenzio, as he had done in the communication ONUC/UNESCO note dated October 3, that he had not been informed of the dealings going on between UNESCO and FAO or about an agreement in Rome signed September 15 and October 31 that put him in a very difficult position, as he had been negotiating with the FAO representative in Léopoldville. Maurice had just seen the document. He wrote: "It is too bad I did not see the document before. It is impossible for me to represent UNESCO if I am unaware of the agreements . . . UNESCO has let itself be taken in by FAO."[27] Maurice felt that the courses in agriculture in the secondary schools should continue to be under the Ministry of Education, while FAO was trying to have them put under the Ministry of Agriculture. The acting head of the Education Department at headquarters was in accord with Maurice, noting "this was not the moment to upset the educational system in the Congo." He suggested that the two ministers (education and agriculture), the FAO man, and Maurice work out the plan already proposed by Maurice and the FAO man in Léopoldville. Evidently Maurice's protest and the department head's backing carried weight with Maheu, for on December 6 he wrote to M. Boerma (deputy director-general of FAO in Rome) that it was best not to compete and, in the Congo, not upset existing structures.[28] Therefore, according to the agreement procedure, UNESCO asked FAO to recruit a French-speaking expert in agriculture instruction, since it was UNESCO that had received the demand from the minister of education of Equator Province. Not often did the specialized agencies bump into each other in this way.

On December 5 the USSR at the General Assembly spoke out again against Dag Hammarskjöld and the United States, NATO, France, Belgium, and the United Kingdom, stating that these powers were "liquidating" the Congo's independence under the cover of the UN flag. The declaration went on:

> . . . we are assisting at the division of influence between these coun-
> tries [named above] to pillage the Congo riches. . . . The events of the
> Congo dissipate the patriarchal confidence that yet existed in certain
> places. The secular oppressors and their valets in the persons of
> Hammarskjöld, Bunche and Kasavubu exploit the divisions and dis-
> cords between the tribes. They are trying to reestablish the colonial
> system . . . The army sent in by the United Nations has become the
> instrument of these aggressors and these colonists . . .

It demanded the liberation of Lumumba, the disarming of the "terror-ist" bands of Mobutu by the UN troops, and the creation of a special committee representing countries of Asia and Africa to investigate who was giving arms and money to Mobutu. It demanded the expulsion of all Belgian troops and functionaries and the examination by the Security Council of the whole situation. The USSR was ready to accord "all friendly aid as well as its support to the Congolese people in their fight against colonialism . . . " Again, Hammarskjöld had to defend himself and the UN action.

Maurice had asked to return to Paris for a briefing as well as home leave, the latter because he had arranged his affairs for a three-month stay only and now was to be in Léopoldville a year, the former because he felt contacts with the headquarters staff were necessary and as beneficial to the staff as they would be to him. This was accorded. Most of the correspondence before his departure on December 17 concerned the delicate matter of funding by the United Nations. Once the projects proposed had been approved by all parties concerned—the Congolese government, UNESCO, ONUC (Mr. Linner), and the United Nations (Sir A. MacFarquhar)—it was important that funds be allocated. Contributions were not as forthcoming as had been promised by member states. UNESCO could not implement accepted projects without being assured that the outlay of monies would be guaranteed by the United Nations.

In the meantime, Maurice had been working on a long-term plan for education. This he presented to the chief of ONUC, Mr. Linner.[29] It is called in French "Programme Provisoire d'Assistance de l'ONUC dans le Domaine de l'Education." Maurice drew it up at the demand of Balinski, who had replaced Linner for a time. It presents projects already begun and those possible of execution in 1961, needing the technical and financial aid of ONUC. The problem is presented. It points out the penury in secondary education, the lack of indigenous secondary school teachers and the need for training schools, the inadequacies of the administrative personnel at all levels, with the need for their further training in the country and abroad, the very poor quality of primary school teachers and the need for their amelioration, the underdevelopment of technical and vocational education, the lack of equipment, school housing, and school manuals adapted to the milieu, and the present educational needs of the new republic. He outlined seven projects, four of which were already being implemented—secondary school teachers, IRSAC, aid to the university, service of experts, and three projects being studied for implementation: the training and further training of personnel of the various ministries of education, in the country and abroad, the training of general secondary school teachers, and teachers for technical and vocational schools.

Maurice stated that the list could be longer, but these were the most pressing in view of the present situation. For one of the future projects he drew up a plan. It was the first draft for a National Institute of Pedagogy (IPN), which would be public and nonsectarian, with no religious affiliation. He defined its aims, discussed location, dimensions, possible date for implementation, modalities of admission, and, most essential, financing.

The plan's conclusion was as follows: "The implementation of this project would constitute a contribution of major importance to the development of education in the Congo. The expenditures, very necessary, constitute, without a doubt, an investment which is amply justified from the point of view of social and educational progress, economic development and political evolution of the country." Maheu congratulated him on this project.

These were two important papers for which Maurice was responsible in the fall of 1960, besides the director-general's report to both the Executive Board and the General Conference, which reflected to a large degree the information gathered and plans made by Maurice and Chase, the drafts on the agreements, and the early draft on a statute for the incoming foreign secondary school teachers. But he was also called upon to do extra tasks. He spent twelve hours over the folders of 100 candidates for various fellowships sent to him through Sylvain from the ministry. Overworked as he was, Maurice still took the time to reduce the number to 40. He wrote to Terenzio that it was impossible to occupy himself with everything at once, which obliged him to neglect what he thought was his mission: to concern himself with the major problems of education in the Congo. He had to have an assistant.

Throughout the fall the political situation was chaotic, with ousters and changes and finally the takeover by Mobutu. At one period there were four contending governments. Maurice did not know with which it was proper to do business until the situation cleared. In November, according to the *New York Times,* there were constant incidents, some with the uncontrolled and undisciplined national army. On November 1, a thousand refugees poured into the UN compound in Kolwesi. There was rioting in Léopoldville, with the arrest of a former government official who was released a few days later. On the twenty-first, fighting broke out in Léopoldville between the UN troops and the national army for the first time. On November 29, at least twelve UN personnel were savagely beaten by Congolese soldiers. (During those weeks, Maurice telephoned me in Paris to reassure me of his well-being and to learn how I was faring in Paris, due to reports of bomb throwing by members of the Algerian liberation movement.)

Little has been noted here concerning the mission and primary schools, as they were open and running. Some help in the way of personnel was requested for the various provinces, both in the public and private sectors. For the time being, the secondary school situation was far more urgent. The religious sectors from the primary schools up to the university were, for the most part, hostile to the United Nations and UNESCO, fearing that their status and government subsidies, as well as their influence, would be greatly diminished. Maurice had discussions with diverse officials and took their views into consideration. It would be the creation of the teacher training institute that would cause him differences of opinion with Monsignor Gillon, the rector of the Catholic university. Maurice had trouble with the rector, who wished to appoint his candidates, who were inexperienced, to be paid by UNESCO/ONUC, especially for the methods in teaching, etc. Monsignor Gillon had made a trip to Paris in late November to consult directly with headquarters, passing over Maurice who protested to headquarters that he was sure that Monsignor Gillon had consulted representatives of WHO and FAO in Léopoldville, so why did he bypass the UNESCO representative? On December 12, Linner, chief of ONUC, called together the heads of the various agencies to choose a coordinator for the ONUC aid to be given to the university. As Maurice was soon to leave for Paris, the representative of the judicial body was decided upon, as he had less to do than had been expected, since so many Belgian judges had returned. Compared to the other Congolese institutions, the university was deemed quite well off.

On November 26, Terenzio had sent around to the various staff concerned at headquarters a note of clarification as to who was to be paid by UNESCO, who by the United Nations, staff on loan, needs in recruitment of experts, numbers changing as the Congolese officials changed their minds as to numbers needed, also procedures for recruitment, and the difficulties of recruitment due to reasons cited earlier and reiterating his suggestion that experts be withdrawn from their posts in other member states on an emergency basis.

Maurice returned to Paris on December 17. What had he accomplished for UNESCO and the Congo, first as technical adviser and then as chief of mission with the temporary help of two collaborators and a secretary during the first few months of the mission? The most important accomplishment was to convince the different holders of the ministerial chair, as they succeeded one another, of the sincerity and impartiality of UNESCO, in spite of the hostility of the press and some of the Belgians who had stayed on as counselors to the government, so that the Congolese began to have confidence in what UNESCO was attempting to do and began requesting aid. By the end of the year requests were coming in faster than they could be filled, with the fear on Maurice's part that if UNESCO did not hurry the Congolese would resort to the Belgians more than they had been doing, to the detriment of the UNESCO effort.

The second accomplishment was the opening of the secondary schools, and third was the short- and long-term plans for the program as well as the plan for the pedagogical institute.

Before the first of the New Year, Maurice went to headquarters several times for discussions and meetings. There is a communication by the assistant director-general, Adiseshiah, referring to the latter, in which he recommends the transfer of Terenzio and the unit responsible for the Congo from the director-general's office to the Department of Education for more efficient coordination with the UNESCO mission. This communication is dated December 27, 1960. Adiseshiah also defined the roles of Maurice and Terenzio and admonished the unit to speed up its search for experts and teachers. Thus ended 1960. (Terenzio stayed in the office of the director-general and continued to work out of it.)

Notes

1. ONUC/UNESCO L228.
2. Home Files, ONUC/UNESCO L230 MD/JC.
3. Home Files, ODG/UNESCO PHG/77.
4. UN Ar., DAG. 12.21, Box 63, IS (UNI), NY 12727, July 28, 1960.
5. 2 LEO 7824 1252 (UNESCO Gen. Reg. 37 [675] A-64-66), part 1.
6. UNESCO DG/214, August 11, 1960.
    6A. Home Files. Cable August 1, 1960, no. 3261.
    6B. Ibid.
7. Security Council UN Gen. Dist. S/4417/ Add. 5.
8. IIC/34, annex 2 (Eleventh General Conference UNESCO).
9. ONUC Ad. Circular no. 21 to all International Civil Servants.
10. UNESCO Ar., Dartigue Files, 37(675) A-64-66, part 1, LEO/ONUC/UNESCO, note 1.
11. UNESCO Ar. 37(675) A-64-66, part 1.
12. UN Ar., DAG I 260, Box 25.
13. UNESCO Ar., and Dartigue Files, ONUC/UNESCO, note 20.
14. UNESCO Ar. 37(675) A-64-66, part 1, ONUC/UNESCO/12.
    14A. United Nations General Assembly Records, Fall 1960.
15. UNESCO Ar. 37(675) A-64-66, part 2, ONUC/UNESCO/22.
16. Ibid., 121, no. 32.
17. Ibid., 121 NOCED M/588 to Sylvain and Dartigue.
18. Ibid., 121 Terenzio to director-general.
19. Ibid., UNESCO/Paris 287/90101/USA TEX MR 105 793.
20. Ibid., 06/USA TEX Akrawi 182.
21. Ibid., 06/USA TEX Akrawi 182.
22. Before the General Assembly, October 17, 1960.
23. Statement of Operations before the General Assembly, New York.
24. Private letter, Dartigue Home Files.
25. General Conference 113/34 and EX 57/22, 1960.
26. Home Files, UNESCO/ODG/CONGO A22.

27. UNESCO Ar. 37(675) A-64-66, part 2, ONUC/UNESCO/119.
28. Ibid., Home Files, UNESCO/ODG/Congo/213.
29. Ibid., ONUC/UNESCO, note 43, November 14, 1960.

Return to the Congo in January 1961

Maurice's sojourn in Paris was beneficial for himself as well as the staff at headquarters involved in the Congo Emergency Program. Not only had he had a much-needed change from the stress of the political, social, and physical climate of the Congo, but his presence could bring home to the headquarters staff the realities of the situation and his need for their support and energetic action. He had consultations with the deputy director-general, Maheu, and the assistant director-general, Adiseshiah. An administrative assistant did join Maurice in the Congo to deliver him from some chores he had been obliged to perform.

Maurice left Paris in late January 1961 via London, where he stopped off for consultations with the British Council, which offered to provide an inspector of English and would search for a head for the English Department of the proposed IPN. During Maurice's absence, several experts had arrived. The Congolese could then see tangible evidence that their demands were being considered and met. An approximate schedule was made for the arrival of other experts and teachers, as facilities were not adequate for a large number to come at once. Maurice with his new assistant became busy with details on housing and transport for the first contingent, which was to arrive at the very end of January. The matter of transport was critical and remained acute for the rest of the spring.

By the end of the month, twelve experts had been placed or were about to be placed in the offices of the ministry, in Léopoldville the capital, and two provinces for general services and information on personnel and cadres in general education, educational studies, planning, and technical education. More would arrive at the end of February. Maurice wished to set up a document center at the UNESCO mission until such time as the ministry could take it over. He begged headquarters to send documents with the experts coming to the Congo. He had a difficult time convincing both Khiary and Balinski, who replaced Linner temporarily, of the necessity of such a center.

A more critical problem for UNESCO was that of the negative influence of the Belgian counselors advising the high officials of the government. The Congolese members of the government had asked Khiary,[1] the chief

UN adviser in public administration matters, to join them in a roundtable discussion to air their so-called grievances. This took place on January 21, 1961.

Khiary made a report to the chief officer of ONUC and the Consultative Group. He stated that the discussions at times were very animated, sometimes marked by a lack of maturity and by misinterpretation of reality or by tendentious information. Khiary several times had to correct information or redress errors of judgment. He clarified the purposes and principles of the United Nations as well as the position of the chief officer of ONUC.

Out of the conference came certain proposals:

(1) All foreign aid should come to the government through the UN channels.
(2) The Congolese government alone had the right to decide on the foreign technicians from a list presented by the United Nations, and to place, transfer, or dismiss them.
(3) The delegates to this conference hoped that an interministerial commission would be constituted to study, in collaboration with the United Nations, the methods of hiring these technicians.

In his report Khiary stated "that nothing should be changed until the Conciliation Commission had finished its work." He was referring to the commission charged by a resolution of the General Assembly of the United Nations passed September 20, 1960, to go to the Congo to attempt to reconcile the factions to accepting a unified government. The advance group arrived on December 19, 1962. The commission stayed for several weeks. The secretary-general came for three days in early January 1961 for discussions with Dayal[2] and his colleagues in relation to the political and constitutional situation and the widespread outbreak of violence, the unresolved question of Katanga, the difficulties of the UN troops, and the refugees from Kasai. The secretary-general went on to South Africa.

The arrest, the flight, and the assassination of Lumumba complicated the efforts of the UN commission. It was because of these difficulties that Khiary suggested that nothing be changed for the time being. However, he did suggest that a study group be formed within the Consultative Group to look into all aspects of the work of ONUC and its related agencies with the Congolese to transform, if necessary, the way of carrying out the work, then make definite proposals to the secretary-general and await his approval before taking steps with the Congolese government.

The roundtable, the complaints, and the recommendations pointed out the delicate nature of the human relationships and the susceptibilities of those whom the United Nations and UNESCO were trying to help and the need for insight and comprehension on the part of those giving the aid.

The political confusion is referred to in the report given by Khiary. Maurice referred to it, having been asked by Terenzio to enlighten him. In his reply on January 29, 1961, Maurice stated that it was a very difficult task and that it was just as muddling as the month before but was shifting. Some felt that there would be long palavers and conciliations. Others, like himself, felt that it could become a test of force.[3] There were rumors of plays and counterplays, various alliances of factions. There was a Congolese Commission of Conciliation, but it was not known how successful it was. There was also to be a second political roundtable to be held in Elizabethville, but it was not sure that the president would go and, if he did, how strong his military escort would be, not because he feared the Lumumbist faction, but because he was not sure of the president of Katanga Province, Moise Tschombé, and his Belgian mercenaries. Maurice could have added that few days went by without incidents between the factions or the ANC[4] and the population in some part of the country, or the ANC and the UN troops. There was no real security anywhere. However, the situation in the area of Kivu was more acute and for the time being experts were not being sent there.

At times there were differences of opinion between the Central Ministry and the provinces. At present, the minister of the province of Equator, who at first wanted only Belgian teachers and no UNESCO aid, was now ready to accept twenty Canadian teachers. But the Central Ministry had decided that there should be no concentration of one nationality in any one region. Until that was settled only a few teachers could be sent and those only to the subsidized Catholic schools and only to those localities where their safety was assured by UN troops.

At about this time, Sture Linner, chief officer of ONUC, sent out a recommended program for the civil operations for 1961 after consulting with the Consultative Group. Only the introduction is in the files. In this he stated:

The 1961 program submitted is a most tentative one, subject to the exigencies of a constantly changing situation. For obvious reasons,

179

since last July, the activities of the United Nations in the Congo were directed towards filling the gaps in various essential public services left vacant by the departure of the Belgian employees and technicians and by lack of properly trained Congolese personnel. This situation will remain to a great extent in 1961. Consequently, in accepting this force majeure, the program attempts to provide for the preparation of Congolese civil servants and technicians to take over in due course the responsibilities temporarily taken by the UN. It calls for a system of advisers in many branches of the administration, for an extensive training program for Congolese officials and technicians, for the granting of fellowships abroad and the organization of courses locally—above all—for the provision of technicians in numbers sufficient to run the basic services of the country.

It should be fully realized that in preparing the program it has been impossible to follow normal UN procedures, namely to have a program discussed with and approved by the national authorities. Approval has been received on certain phases of UN plans, and even that is tentative; otherwise, the suggestions are made almost unilaterally by the UN and agency representative. At this time there is no guarantee that the program as a whole will obtain government approval or even its cooperation . . .

In early February there was a flurry of cables, Telex, and correspondence with Terenzio and Maheu at headquarters and the United Nations. A meeting at headquarters had been called by Terenzio January 26, 1961, as had been demanded by Adiseshiah in December to bring the headquarters staff involved in the Congo Emergency Program up-to-date concerning the recruitment of teachers and experts for 1961–62, the courses to be held in Geneva for administrators, the aid to be given to the university, the use of the UNESCO coupon system,[5] the Documentation Center, the IPN plan, proposed by Maurice, IRSAC, and the courses, to be held in Dakar, Senegal, in communication, radio, and newspaper reporting. This was a new field for many Africans, but for which ONUC had no grants and the Congo no candidates. Also, at last, the United Nations had approved financially an assistant chief of mission of P5 rank, an assistant administrator P2 (already there), and two secretaries (being recruited). This tied in with the decisions made while Maurice was in Paris.[6]

It was in response to parts of the report of this meeting that Maurice sent two cables to Terenzio on February 3. The first concerned IRSAC. He had received a telegram from the team at IRSAC stating that it would not be fear that would make it leave the center, but acute lack of funds. It had sent its records and archives to Brazzaville, as the ANC had visited it and dismantled the government-owned radio transmitter. If funds could be supplied by airlift, all would be fine. This was done after Maurice alerted UNESCO, which alerted the center in Brussels, which then sent the funds, which Maurice transferred by airlift to IRSAC.

The second cable concerned IPN, for which Maurice was determined to fight. He had consulted the chief officer of ONUC for a Special Fund appropriation. Maurice was told that the request would have to come from the government, which should assume part of the financing. He had sent a cable to Hammarskjöld on February 3, 1961, conjointly with Linner concerning the Special Fund. He had also consulted Balinski. The result: another cable from the United Nations: the government must assume a counterpart in the expenses. Maurice wired UNESCO. He remarked that a week was insufficient to revise the first draft and obtain even a conditional accord from the government. He called UNESCO: "New York has approved general program and assistance concerning provisions for UN contribution for expenses for personnel, grants and equipment. MacFarquhar (UN) arrives Léopoldville shortly to discuss details of program and budget. It is understood we ask ONUC guarantee expenses for additional constructions for IPN if impossible to obtain funds from other sources. If ONUC impossible recourse to Special Funds will be attempted."[7]

When Maheu learned that MacFarquhar was to come to Léopoldville he telexed Maurice to sound MacFarquhar out on the financing of the secondary school teachers for the year 1961–62, since the recruitment in the framework of the urgent program came to an end in the beginning of March. Second, the present salaries of the teachers would be insufficient, in view of the inflationary tendency in the Congo, so Maurice was to look into raising salaries with him and the government. "Third, authorize look into financing IPN under the base indicated in telex of February 3. Fourth, the formation of education administrators must take place locally with the aid of our experts in the framework of the cooperation between UNESCO and the National School of Administration. The projected courses in Geneva are excluded."[8]

Maurice replied to the telex on March 6:

Steps will be undertaken with MacFarquhar concerning points one, two and three of your cable. Congo authorities will be consulted on point two as relates to training of specialists in education. *I permit myself the following observations* on two points—Specialists in Education—It would be more suitable to have them trained at IPN. As to the experts assigned to the Ministry, they could give a few lectures for seminars of short duration but cannot undertake the responsibility for full courses of several months, and as to the training locally to the exclusion of training in Geneva it would be best not to apply this measure retroactively for those candidates already designated. The Congolese authorities who have requested grants and decided on candidates will insist on getting fellowships from other institutions and foreign governments. The training will be dissimilar and will be done outside UNESCO and in their minds *despite* UNESCO[9] [author's emphasis throughout].

Maheu replied on February 2, 1961:

Reference to your cable on 6/2—In accord for regular training of specialists of Education in framework IPN. Our experts will be charged with only short-term courses. Maintain principle of formation locally as preferable *but accept* [author's emphasis] not to apply this rule to the candidates already designated. The concentration of this work appears reasonable but will be happy to receive details of your plans and measures for this particular project before final approval.[10]

On these points Maurice's ideas were accepted, and he now had to correspond with Geneva and negotiate with the government to determine arrangements and program. On February 7, a memo was put forth by the deputy director-general's office concerning assistance to the Congo from which the foregoing points were included, plus the facts that a report containing the appropriate propositions would be sent to the Executive Board by April 30 at the latest, that Terenzio would go to the Congo to aid Maurice in the discussions with ONUC and the Congo authorities, and that Maurice would be invited to inform Gardiner (head of the Public Administration Bureau) concerning the University of Louvanium, and informing headquarters of the fate of the demand formulated by the Congolese government in view of obtaining a specialist in radio and the experts to carry out the inquiry on the needs in providing information through radio and the press. Headquarters would intensify its information through broadcasting and the UNESCO *Courrier*.[11] When Maheu later suggested that the UNESCO *Courrier* be sent to Léopoldville for distribution and information about UNESCO to be broadcast on the local radio, Maurice gave a categoric "no." He could not take on this responsibility, too, until he received assistance from added personnel. The last point in the memo concerning personnel upset Maurice. It stated that it would be expedient to replace the post of deputy chief of mission at grade five to the post of assistant at grade three or four. In case of absence of the chief of mission, he could be replaced in the Consultative Group of ONUC by the assistant or one of the experts.

To this last point Maurice responded with some irritation. He wrote to Terenzio on February 12, 1961:

It is to be regretted that I was not consulted as to the grade of my deputy who, ipso facto, will succeed me. One cannot ask an expert to take my place just like that. Moreover, it astonishes me that you proposed a purely administrative functionary. It is to ignore the nature of responsibilities and the activities of the consultant, chief of mission. At any rate, I hope to be consulted as to the choice and that this question will receive the consideration its importance merits.[12]

Maurice was heeded, for his deputy, D. Najman,[13] who arrived in late April, turned out to be a hard worker and competent, and it was Terenzio himself who would succeed Maurice for three years, after which this same deputy would then take on the job as head of the mission. In a recent interview Najman stated that the position of consultant to the chief of ONUC was more important or significant than being chief of the UNESCO mission.

Maurice prepared the report for the deputy director-general as pertained to the courses in Geneva. He wrote that all the grant recipients would follow the same course, in the same place, in the same institution. There would be at least three professors and he to give the courses. The participants could have experience in the ministries of Geneva and/or be attached to inspectors or administrators. Visits would be arranged for them. Before leaving the Congo, these grant recipients, inspectors and assistant directors in the ministries would attend a seminar in Léopoldville planned for May.

He was now seeking a person who would supervise them (it would be P. Rossello of IBE) in their studies and be on hand to help them with their personal problems. As to money, MacFarquhar had allocated $20,000 (later raised to $25,000). He would ask the Swiss, TA, and the Emergency Fund for more. The contact in Geneva, Rossello, had not yet sent the program. Stipends, travel costs, salary payments, etc., would be worked out. By March 19 this program was approved.

At the same time, Maurice reported the arrival and placement of experts and their tasks. He also stated that the minister of education (Mobutu had dissolved the group of commissioners and replaced them by ministers, so Bizala now had that title) had constituted a commission for program revision of representatives not only of the public schools, but also the Catholic and Protestant schools, along with two UNESCO experts. In spite of the Belgian interference, Maurice, who was present at the first meeting and meant to drop in often, proposed R. Hennion, one of the UNESCO experts, as technical secretary, with some of his staff for studies and research. A Catholic prelate supported Maurice. He then urged headquarters to seek an expert competent in program revision. He suggested that headquarters address itself to known educators for recommendations. He added: "If you do not go fast the Belgian refugees from the provinces of Kivu and Oriental will infiltrate the ministries."[14] He went on concerning his visit with a few experts to Binza, not far from Léopoldville, the locale proposed for IPN, along with members of the ministry and the ONUC architect, to suggest renovations and possibilities.

His last paragraph deals with transport—still only one car in spite of his repeated demands. Finally, after talks with its representative, UNICEF agreed to give a number of cars for the experts in the provinces who dealt with primary education. (One of the experts from Haiti stationed in Luluabourg had been making his rounds on foot, which the others felt they could not do, because of the hot sun and dust. This was an act of heroism under the circumstances.)

The contingents of teachers had begun to arrive. The welcoming committee of Congolese did not show up. Fortunately, Maurice now had an administrative assistant, G. Gallai (from Italy), who pitched in, and together they hunted about for bedding, utensils, etc.; this was not easy in Léopoldville. It was they who prepared for the teachers. (The Congolese were too preoccupied with their personal or political affairs.)

Some of the darker Haitian teachers sent to the provinces met with opposition. Supposedly they were not needed and supposedly some were not qualified. Eventually they were accepted, though reluctantly. They gave an impressive performance, showed themselves to be serious, competent, and they did more than their jobs called for, so much so that more were requested for the fall entry.

In February, Dag Hammarskjöld had again been attacked by the Soviets, who blamed him for Lumumba's death, which had been revealed the tenth of the month. (Mystery still surrounds the capture and assassination of Lumumba.) It is outside the sphere of this work to discuss this. (Maurice hardly mentioned it.) The atmosphere in Léopoldville for several weeks was agitated because of these events. The USSR again asked for the secretary-general's ouster. This was rejected. The USSR then refused again to contribute to the UN fund for the Congo. Later the USSR through its delegate at UNESCO asked this organization to break with the United Nations, since it insisted on keeping the secretary-general, who in the USSR's estimation was no longer worthy to hold that office. This communication embarrassed the UNESCO director-general. He was able to bypass the request by answering that it was not in his competence to take such a step, as only the intergovernmental organs of UNESCO could examine the request, if the USSR decided to address them. This the USSR did not do, so the matter was dropped.

A few weeks later France also refused to appropriate funds to the United Nations for the Congo. It was France's president, Charles de Gaulle, who decided this, referring to the United Nations in a derogatory way as *"ce machin"* ("that thing" or "that thingamajig"), refusing to honor it by using its proper name.

In contrast, the United States, through its recently elected president, John F. Kennedy, supported and backed the secretary-general and the United Nations in opposing unilateral aid or action by any member state and insisting that all aid be channeled through the United Nations. The United States gave more than 40 percent of the funds for ONUC. The problem of funds would be critical time and again as expenses mounted and member states were not forthcoming with contributions. The Congo almost broke the United Nations financially. This caused the seesaw of approval of projects.

For Maurice, in some measure, what he had learned at Teachers' College, seen in the United States on his trips, then put into practice in Haiti gave him the precious background and experience that he could apply here.

Not only that, but some of the first contingent arriving from Haiti were those who had worked with him there and were imbued with his principles and methods. They were to give valuable service in often difficult physical, social, and political conditions. Whether this was realized or appreciated to its full extent is debatable.

That the deputy director-general had confidence in Maurice and trusted his reasoning there is no doubt, as is evidenced in the reports. However, when Maurice wrote to the head of personnel at headquarters to ask if his grade and salary did not merit upgrading in view of the unusual position and tasks he had in the Congo (the secretary-general of the United Nations had recognized Maurice's unusual position and stated: "It is necessary to give to the experts utilized for these activities which demand responsibilities at a higher level a new status without precedent"), he was answered: "I have shown your letter to both A. Roseman [the new assistant director-general in charge of the Department of Education] and Maheu and talked to them about the whole problem of your position in the Congo. The result of this is that my letter of 9/1 stands but that Maheu has authorized me to say that he will personally take action when you return to headquarters to give tangible recognition to the work you have done in the Congo . . ." It appears that Maurice had not even been given his proper title in the personnel office. This the head of personnel promised to correct. Maurice was finally accorded a step to the D1[15] category only in May, when his deputy arrived. It will later be shown whether Maheu honored the promise.

The experts and teachers had settled in and begun their tasks. Most were sent to the various provinces when possible, and those who could not join their posts because of fighting or insecurity were given jobs in and around Léopoldville to perform tasks there until hostilities ended. Most of the Haitians integrated well, since they were Catholic, thus appreciated by the church and church schools. The salary differences between the Belgian teachers and those recruited by UNESCO would be a bone of contention in spite of the explanation given by Maurice, that to attract recruits to come to the Congo UNESCO was obliged to pay the prevailing salaries in the home country for people having qualifications and experience in addition to indemnities. Even with these incentives it had not been easy to procure personnel.

Terenzio's visit, as had been announced concerning the recruitment of teachers for 1961–62, coincided with the departure of a contingent of teachers for Luluabourg. No arrangements had been made by the government of the provinces for their reception, so it was Terenzio who accompanied them and commandeered lodgings, linens, and other household equipment. These were later paid for by ONUC after Maurice and Terenzio asked for additional funds the Congolese government had promised to furnish but had not done.

While he was in Luluabourg, Terenzio noticed that the opposition to the UNESCO personnel, especially the Haitians, was lessening. The minister of education with whom Terenzio met had only praise for the latter. He said that L. Bourand, a Haitian expert in administration and budget, had become indispensable. He did much more than the work for which he had been hired, as did some others.

In his report to the director-general of April 12, 1961, Terenzio stated that the level of experts was very high and they constituted a team capable of contributing efficiently to the task of reorganizing education in the Congo if circumstances permitted. Why not turn to Haiti, as Maurice guaranteed their technical competence and they were available? They were willing to come, while UNESCO had had to forego eighteen candidates from ten countries, and this often after long negotiations. Terenzio added that there were sixty-four teachers in the Congo, of whom twenty-nine were Haitians.

As to the main purpose of his visit, Terenzio and Maurice had discussed with Linner the modalities of recruitment. Maurice was encouraged by the importance that Linner and his colleagues now attached to the program, for which Maurice had drawn up a budget until the end of 1961, and by the rapidity with which Linner had recommended it to New York for ONUC approval and made requests for provisions for it in the budget. Terenzio was later to go to New York to reinforce the UNESCO budget demands worked out in consultation with Maurice.[16]

The budget for 1962 had been agreed to when MacFarquhar came to Léopoldville. However, the figures would come up again and again, bandied among UNESCO, ONUC, and the United Nations, then added to as more requests were to be made. The budget for 1962, the discussion of it, and the sources that were to feed it were constants in the correspondence. To this was added the delay in the final approval pending confirmation of available funds (this availability already referred to) and the assumption of local costs by the Congolese government.

Because of this very important factor, Maurice on March 14, 1961, advised Terenzio by cable that although UNESCO negotiations with FAO had been going on since the fall as concerned courses in agriculture in the schools

> . . . the representative of FAO thinks the present moment is not good for any new activity in the Congo considering the present general situation and lack of interest of the Congolese authorities. Linner and Balinski share this opinion. Personally I believe the political situation would not permit an effective job in all the provinces. It is necessary to take into consideration the desire of the government or not to assume its part of the responsibility in any new activity and its capacity to carry out the responsibilities it accepts.[17]

The experience of eight months of dealing with the changing governments forced Maurice to offer this opinion.

More than once the lack of understanding of the government of the country's financial predicament was made evident to the UNESCO mission in its dealings with the Congolese officials. The emptiness of the treasury was so obvious that on March 23, the *New York Times* headlined an article on the front page "Congo approaching financial collapse." The United Nations itself was in difficulties due to the drain on its budget because of the needs of the Congo. The United States was already bearing a great part of the financial outlay; Great Britain and Canada offered extra funds. Finally, $8 million a month was appropriated by the United Nations, which would not be enough.

During this time Maurice, Hennion,[18] and Ardill were busy. The latter, among other work, was attending the commission of secondary school program reform and acting as technical secretary as well as aiding Maurice in the preparation and execution of the projects concerning the improvement by refresher courses of the quality and level of the education in primary schools through improved school supervision and by raising the level of the qualifications of school directors and teachers. Maurice submitted a project for four itinerant teams for organizing in-service training in the provinces. The members of each team would include a teacher in agriculture and one in home economics. The team would be made up of six people.

Preparations were also being made to hold the first seminar for functionaries of the education ministries in May in Léopoldville.

Some of the correspondence is taken up in this connection in April, as well as the courses to be held in Geneva later. Maurice had prepared a detailed budget, which had been approved. He was in correspondence with the Belgian educator Dr. R. Dottrens, who was to give lectures at the seminar in Léopoldville and at the course in Geneva later. Maurice kept begging for a deputy to second him. He wrote to Terenzio that he had worked till 3:00 A.M. to prepare for the seminar, at which he would give several lectures. When finally there was hope the post would be filled, Maurice insisted that there should be a probation period of six months. As stated earlier, it would be D. Najman who would come at the end of May and it would be Terenzio who would really profit from his services.

Maurice in Léopoldville was getting ready for the first seminar, while in Paris intensive preparations were being made for the second Conference of Ministers of Education of Tropical Africa, to be held in Addis Ababa in May 1961. This time UNESCO went all out, with plenty of money and several of the higher echelon, including the director-general, the deputy director-general, two assistant directors-general, and the director of the Department of Education, several consultants, and staff members to arrange and carry out this conference. It was a very important meeting. Plans were to be drawn up that would chart the way education was to go for the newly independent countries for twenty years.

The meeting would also bring the visit, on his way to Addis Ababa, of the newly appointed director of the Department at Education at UNESCO, a post that had been vacant for a time. He was an American, formerly provost in a small New England college, who was trying to become acquainted with the various aspects of his new and far more important position. So Maurice would not only have to concern himself with the seminar and give the opening talk, but have Mr. S. McCune on his hands. Mr. McCune did come and did spend a day at the seminar and did meet various officials and members of the UNESCO mission who were in Léopoldville. (A year and a half later, he left UNESCO.)

While Maurice was getting ready for the seminar, he prepared the mission report to send to headquarters for Maheu, who would use it as a base from which the director-general would derive his report to the Executive Board meeting in Paris on the fourth of May at its fifty-ninth session. Some of what went into the report has been discussed, but some important elements are referred to here.

The director-general reported that according to the resolutions taken at its fifty-seventh session and the resolutions decided upon at the General Conference held in November 1960 in Paris, he wished to inform the

Executive Board that progress had been made in carrying out the program approved by the directing organs of the organization and drawing attention to the problems relative to the pursuit and development of the activities in aid of the Congo.

The director-general brought out the urgent character of UNESCO's action: (a) for secondary education; (b) for putting into place experts to reinforce the services of the Central Ministry of Education and Culture as well as those of the provinces; and (c) for the safeguarding of the existing scientific institutions. He then stated that he had sent an appeal to member states on November 30, 1960, for recruits for secondary schools. He cited from which countries response had come, how many had finally gone to the Congo, and the subjects they taught. He noted that the needs had diminished, since many Belgians had returned. However, due to the bad news coming out of the Congo through the mass media, thirty percent of the candidates had withdrawn. The political situation had restricted the number of posts foreseen. In a few instances neither teachers nor experts could carry out their tasks efficiently, because the Congolese officials were not able to furnish transportation, proper lodging, or equipment, though promised. Fortunately, in some cases the situation was improved through help from ONUC. However, he estimated that the work accomplished answered the possibilities offered by the situation in the Congo in February and March 1961. "One must point out," he said, "that in getting to work under, at times, precarious conditions, these teachers furnished a fine example of international solidarity with which one must associate their country of origin."

It was Maurice who in his report stated: "The following programs of assistance constitute an organic whole and require a concerted action of experts of different specialties. Some of these are still in the discussion stage with the UN which furnishes the financing of envisaged activities." They were: (a) technical assistance for ministers through experts who might be called on to collaborate in the programs of improvement; (b) creation of mobile itinerant teams for in-service training, starting with a pilot project for successively aiding inspectors, directors, and monitors of primary schools; (c) the founding of the National Institute of Pedagogy; (d) the organization in Geneva of a course for further training of administrators and inspectors; and (e) recruitment of secondary school teachers for 1961–62: "For the present, 80 teachers are envisaged." (These would prove far too few, and a special Congolese team would go to several European countries, Canada, and Haiti to recruit more.)

The director-general pointed out that the program outlined and initiated would contribute usefully to the economic and social development of the Congo. This was also the opinion of the United Nations, as well as the Congolese who asked that the collaboration continue:

> This action of UNESCO was in the framework of the Civil Operations of the United Nations in the Congo as defined by the Secretary General in his statement to the Security Council 11/8/60. In this framework, the Executive Board, if it held to the line of conduct it adopted at its 57th session, needed to authorize the director-general to answer the request for aid formulated by the central and provincial authorities transmitted through the United Nations, it being understood that conforming to the practice already being followed, the granting of aid did not imply the taking of a position by the organization concerning the constitutional problems that exist in the country.[19]

The Executive Board approved the report and asked the director-general to send a message of goodwill and encouragement to the UNESCO personnel in the Congo. It also passed the following resolution:

> *Conscious* of the importance of secondary education in the Congo— *preoccupied* by the need for teaching personnel in the secondary schools of this country and by the difficult situation which appears to be that of the teachers who are actually teaching there invites the Director-General: (1) to consult the Secretary General of the United Nations on the subject as to measures to be taken in the framework of ONUC on the subject of the teachers of secondary schools in the Congo; (2) make a report to the Executive Board at its 60th session on the measures taken or to be taken to remedy this situation [author's emphasis].

As stated, Maurice and his staff prepared for the first seminar of its kind in the Congo for directors and inspectors. It took place from the eighth to the twentieth of May, held under the auspices of the minister of national education and arts. The committee of organization was headed by Hennion, seconded by another expert and two Congolese. It was attended by sixteen administrators from the Central Ministry, two from Kasai, two from South Kasai, and two from Equator, making twenty-two in all. As observers there were six experts, ten representatives of Catholic institutions. Among the speakers were high-placed Congolese officials, several experts, Dr. Dottrens, and Maurice, who tried to bring out the seriousness of the task and the inherent problems that demanded constant vigilance and application.

The other lecturers gave talks in their special fields. The participants made various visits and were invited by Monsignor Gillon to see the University of Louvanium. Evidently, Maurice felt it turned out well, for he wrote to Terenzio: "It was a big success." The participants asked for more seminars of this kind and showed real interest. Other work prevented Maurice from attending all the events, but he was encouraged by the results. He was able to save on some of the estimated expenditures, and this was heartening for him, as he was so careful about spending monies entrusted to him.

On May 9, there was another political disturbance, this time in South Kasai, where the Baluba political leader Kalongi was trying to extend his domain farther, to include parts of North Kasai. There were clashes between the army and the UN troops. The chief of the UN troops decided that as he did not have enough men to defend the area properly, he would leave with his troops, thus exposing the civil UN and UNESCO personnel to the mercy of the army. This Maurice learned when he was called away from the seminar to join the representative of WHO and other ONUC officials in the bureau of the Service for Refugees. A decision had to be made whether or not to withdraw the UNESCO personnel from the area. Maurice was in a delicate position, as Bizala, the minister of education and the arts, was a Baluba and had assured Maurice that Kalongi had given his personal word as to the security of the UNESCO personnel. Their withdrawal could compromise the ongoing negotiations. However, due to the uncertainty of the feelings of the army in case of further clashes with the UN troops, Maurice felt he could not risk the lives of the UNESCO teachers and their families by leaving them in such a precarious situation.

After discussing the crisis with the chief of ONUC, Sture Linner, and the other officials assembled, Maurice decided it was better to withdraw the UNESCO personnel, even though doing so might cloud the relationship established between the UNESCO mission and the minister of education. Maurice first sent a cable to Maheu, then a long letter on May 15, 1961, explaining his decision and the reasons for it. In reply he received a letter from Maheu thanking him for the explanation and expressing his satisfaction for the action Maurice had taken. This incident is an illustration of the kind of quick decision making that had to be done without consulting headquarters or waiting for its approval. Fortunately, the situation was not often so critical or so delicate. On June 13, according to the *New York Times* headlines, Dag Hammarskjöld said: "Crisis in Congo Appears Ended." Yet on June 16, the *New York Times* announced: "Mobutu Seizes Sixty in Abduction Plot." It seemed that he had learned that there was a plot to poison or kill him and other leaders. For example, Tschombé, president of Katanga province, had been seized while in Léopoldville, and then was freed, having agreed to become president of the Congo. He returned to Katanga and decided, in the safety of his province, to refuse. He announced he preferred to secede. This put the Congo into off-and-on disturbances for more than a year. Two years later the tribal and regional fighting became so acute that Terenzio, as chief of the mission, had to order the evacuation of those not directly employed, such as wives and children, from the Congo. In the spring of 1961, few families had yet arrived, so the problem was not as complicated. As can be judged tension continued in the Congo.

The teachers recalled did not remain idle. Several were sent to Kamina, the air base (which Maurice had visited in the fall and recommended for a postprimary technical school but where now a primary school was functioning), to aid the teachers to prepare those pupils who were to present themselves for the terminal examinations, by giving intensive courses in French and math, as well as giving tests to determine their capacity for further postprimary study. They also did in-service training of teachers through seminars. A few were sent to a school in Léopoldville, subsidized by the Salvation Army, and there aided experts to formulate tests.

The newspaper *Courrier d'Afrique* accused UNESCO of keeping the foreign teachers in Léopoldville to lead an easy life and be highly paid for it. It also accused UNESCO of wanting to close half the schools. This was deliberate falsification to create hostility by a hard core of Belgians and extremist Congolese. Maurice through Rossborough denied this and said, on the contrary, more schools would be opened (this came about in 1962) and the quality of teaching would be improved.

A grievance of the Belgian teachers was that ONUC had instituted a commissary for all ONUC personnel with prices not to be had at the local markets to offset the shortage of foodstuffs and household needs. To this the Belgian teachers did not have access. Less than two years later, Terenzio would win for them access to the commissary as well as salary and health protection and other indemnities and benefits received by ONUC, UNESCO, UNICEF, FAO, and WHO personnel.

By the end of May, Maurice proposed the renewal of contracts for most of the teachers and experts, but he did ask Terenzio not to renew the contracts of two of them, as these experts had not measured up to expectations. Because of the greater number of Haitians in proportion to the other nationalities, there would be more problems concerning housing—adaptation, health, faculty discipline, etc. (In fact, outside the Belgians, they made up the greatest number, since so many were later recruited in Haiti itself by the Congolese recruitment committee.) Early in June the minister of education, Bizala, asked Maurice if UNESCO would hire more secondary teachers. To this Maurice replied that UNESCO had a very limited budget, which included only eighty teachers, but he thought that if the minister made the request in the name of the government, UNESCO could look for and process candidates for the government, which would be responsible for contracts, salaries, and other indemnities, but that he would have to receive directives from headquarters if such a request was made. The minister said he wanted teachers of other nationalities besides Belgian.

At last in May Maurice's deputy, Najman, arrived and Maurice now had more time to give his attention to preparing the long-range program, job descriptions, project descriptions such as the one concerning the itinerant teams, and the courses in Geneva, as well as keeping contact with the experts in the field. He left many of the mundane obligations to Najman, as he was too absorbed by what he deemed were the important tasks, such as budget calculations and approvals by the government's officials, by ONUC and United Nations in New York, and of course by headquarters in Paris.

The urgent requests for more adequate transportation for personnel in Léopoldville and in the field finally brought results. Two buses were bought, one for Coquilhatville and one for Luluabourg, but due to the discontinuance of the ferries between Brazzaville and Léopoldville, the buses could not be delivered until that situation cleared up. The mission was authorized to buy six station wagons, but there were none to be had in either Léopoldville or Brazzaville. This caused more delays, continued frustration, and much time spent begging and/or borrowing cars for the experts and teachers to get around in. Some had been able to purchase cars and in this way relieve a little the aggravating problem that had plagued the mission since the beginning. One problem had diminished. More housing had been made available both in the capital and in the provinces, for lodgings and offices.

Much of June was taken up in defending the projected IPN (Institut Pédagogique National) as an independent, national public institution. Maurice had worked on this project since late November 1960. It had met with approval but now faced opposition by Monsignor Gillon, who hoped to incorporate pedagogical courses in the private, subsidized Catholic University of Louvanium. Maurice said he had no objection to these courses. However, the IPN was to be a national "nondenominational" institute that would go far beyond the mere training of teachers. It was to be created for the special needs of the Congo. He insisted that it was only such an institution that could help the Congolese take over their education system from foreigners.

Money was being held back by MacFarquhar in New York, although plans had been worked out, estimates for renovations of and additions to the buildings consented to. The main reason appeared to be that the funds expected by the United Nations from member states and other sources had not materialized to the extent necessary. New York demanded supplementary explanations of salaries and other expenditures, which Maurice felt was just a stall. Then Rossborough, representing MacFarquhar, asked for a confidential memorandum. This was just another case in point that showed that those holding the purse strings did not always see eye to eye or understand the education needs as Maurice and UNESCO understood them. Maurice continued patiently to supply the demanded information. Then he received a boost from the head of ICA (which later became IDA), which promised that part of the funds from the sale of flour by the United States to the Congo could be used to help finance the project if the United States and the United Nations were in agreement.

Maurice went immediately to Rossborough, who referred him to Linner's Economic Council, which in turn referred him to Mr. Van der Aord, who was in charge of the UN public works project and dealt with this question with the Congolese government. At first, Van der Aord refused to listen to Maurice and Najman, who accompanied him, but on their insistence Van der Aord said he would find 4 million Congo francs to put the buildings in condition to receive the students if Maurice could obtain consent from the minister of planning and finance to add the project to the proposed budget. Off to the minister went Maurice. The minister consented to do this if the minister of education put in a formal demand. Armed with two projects for letters of request he had drawn up, Maurice went to see the minister of education. After more than ten days of negotiations, letters were finally signed and sent. He, Maurice, invited certain persons to dinner to expose to them the importance of the project so that they could use their influence to obtain the approval of the monies to be thus allocated. At last Van der Aord telephoned that the accord by the government had been granted.

Maurice was urged to announce in the newspapers that recruitment for students for the proposed IPN would soon begin when the news came from New York that MacFarquhar was still hesitant to approve the financing of the project as the cost was too high. Maurice began to go over his figures to see what could be reduced and if some of the experts approved by the United Nations could be used in the IPN project. But he wrote to Terenzio: "It is really discouraging." However, Maurice plodded on.

Later he learned that the Congolese parliament was to meet, and to ensure its running smoothly the United Nations was sending a special contingent of a hundred security guards. It was possible that expenses for the parliament and the guards would be high and could absorb a large portion of the available funds for salaries, the trip, and indemnities for a month or two. This represented a fourth of the budget for the recruitment of the teachers. All this he wrote to Terenzio on June 26, 1961. He begged Terenzio to bring pressure on the UNESCO office in New York to support the project with MacFarquhar. As Maurice was convinced of the necessity of this special form of the IPN, he was willing to fight for it. He was proven right, for in the years to come more and more IPNs would be set up in Africa and would become permanent parts of the education systems in the different countries, whereas some other projects did not.

A communication by Maurice entitled "Report of the Activities from August 1960–June 30, 1961" gives a recapitulation of the work for the year of the UNESCO mission, whose chief, Maurice, was the only one who was there throughout the year and who headed such a small staff, first consisting of Chase and Osman, followed by Ardill and then Hennion, all of whom proved invaluable. That so few men shouldered the enormous task undertaken by UNESCO and carried out such important work is in itself remarkable. More help came after the first of 1961 and later in the way of larger staff, many experts, and hundreds of teachers. But it was Maurice and his staff who took the first difficult steps and they who had to face great obstacles. This they did in spite of political disturbances, incomprehension in the Congo, and often at headquarters, the drawn-out negotiations for accords, the uncertainty of funds, and the constant efforts of undermining done by hostile groups. The results achieved were exceptional indeed.

As most of the report repeats what has already been mentioned, only a few items will be included here. It refers to the Institute for Research in Central Africa (IRSAC), as well as Kamina, assistance to the ministries, further training of persons, the seminars, the revision of programs, and the courses in Geneva.

Important studies were made to analyze the functions and needs of the ministries and suggestions given for their reorganization and the number of experts needed to carry out the reform until the Congolese could take over. A series of statistical studies were undertaken, easily usable, which furnished data permitting interpretation of the teaching situation in the Congo and the elaboration of a long-term program.

The system of UNESCO coupons had been begun to facilitate the buying of school manuals, equipment, and school materials, for which UNESCO would allow at first $200,000. The report also concerned the IPN, which during the next ten years would graduate a minimum of 250 secondary school teachers each year to give this country of 14 million people native secondary school teachers with proper training.

The report also refers to projects being studied, one for a higher school for the training of teachers for technical and professional secondary schools and another for the training of rural leaders. Finally, it refers to the sale and distribution of the UNESCO *Courrier,* which, since the arrival of his deputy Maurice could give some time to, to decide on how and where it was to be done. The report does not refer to the radio and communication project, as it was primarily in the hands of another sector for the time being. Later on Terenzio would organize a program for training technicians in this field.[20]

From this report was taken the material for the deputy-general's communication to the sixtieth session of the Executive Board held in Paris October 10, 1961–November 27, 1961.

Between June 29 and July 7, 1961, Maurice carried out an urgent mission to New York and Paris. I presumed that he had gone to New York to plead the cause for IPN with MacFarquhar. This was not the case. It concerned the secondary school teachers recruited by UNESCO, paid for the most part by the United Nations, and about whom there was a problem of salaries and indemnities. All is not clear as to what precipitated the trip, as the correspondence is incomplete.

Maurice argued that unless guarantees that were provided by the United Nations for the daily subsistence allowance of twenty dollars a day and which had become a status symbol were not met, ONUC would lose the teachers already there and make it harder to recruit others. However, if the terms the United Nations offered were satisfactory, he was sure that at least fifty-two of the present teachers would stay. He also wanted to get many posts into Congolese cadres, as UNESCO was trying to do. (Evidently MacFarquhar was unaware of the very few Congolese prepared to undertake responsibilities and the efforts UNESCO was making to try to prepare those few available.)

In a final cable, sent on July 5, 1961, by the secretary-general in answer to two sent by Maheu, and to one that MacFarquhar had sent, the decisions concerning the problem became known. They were the following:

I hope Dartigue, your representative and my consultant in ONUC has meanwhile seen you and explained our thinking—I am confident you will not wish to abandon a project so recently started whose full effect has still to be felt. Personal regards.

Did Maheu suggest or threaten (is this too strong a word?) to abandon the project of supplying experts or/and secondary school teachers because the terms offered by the United Nations did not appear satisfactory, bringing about this cable?

Dag Hammarskjöld took part in the discussions. It is most interesting that the secretary-general of the United Nations took time to be personally concerned with this one area of endeavor in the Congo. Was it because funds were so low at the United Nations that summer that MacFarquhar felt he had to bring this item of the budget to the attention of the secretary-general to see if the expenditure could be decreased? Was it because MacFarquhar could not understand the necessity for the expatriate secondary school teachers and hoped to persuade the secretary-general to cut the budget? Also, how much was Maurice able to persuade the secretary-general and/or get the backing of Maheu to insist on certain conditions to arrive at the results indicated? Until the Maheu archives at UNESCO are available this will not be known. In a few months' time UNESCO would be processing hundreds of expatriate teachers for the Congo, with certain guarantees coming from the United Nations.

Maurice returned to Léopoldville. He learned that during his absence Monsignor Gillon, rector of the University of Louvanium, after a talk with the minister of education, Bizala, had thought up and proposed a project incorporating in the university program certain educational studies for training of secondary school teachers. This Maurice wrote to Terenzio on July 12. He continued to say that Monsignor Gillon had sent a delegation of professors with the project to deliver it to the minister. This was communicated to Maurice by the minister himself, who let Maurice have a copy of this project, but not another counterproject proposed by the BEC (Bureau of Catholic Education), which offered to give upgraded courses in their primary school teachers' training institutions. The minister said that he was going to call together Louvanium, BEC, and BEP (Bureau for Protestant Education) as well as Maurice. Maurice requested that he put off the meeting for two days so that Maurice and his experts Ardill, Hennion, and A. Chiappano could look over the project and revise the one UNESCO had proposed and had thought accepted!

Maurice, the same afternoon, called his experts together to study the Louvanium project and set down a new, simpler project. This was done during the night and in the morning was ready to be delivered. The meeting was not altogether positive for UNESCO, remarked Maurice in a letter dated July 22. It became apparent that Monsignor Gillon was trying to confuse the minister by using indifferently and perhaps deliberately the indication of the institution being "public" (that is non-denominational) and/or an institution being "recognized as a public utility." More discussions with the representatives of BEC and BEP took place, with more maneuvers by Monsignor Gillon. It is presumed that certain texts were again revised. At last, just before Maurice's departure from the Congo, the UNESCO project was accepted. The decree was formulated and published in late August after Terenzio's arrival.

It had taken since December 1960, when Maurice had produced the first draft, patterned after the one created in Nigeria, for the IPN project to finally be approved by the minister, after much vacillation on his part due to the various influences that tried to cause him to change his mind, as well as the reticence of MacFarquhar. Maurice did have the satisfaction of having brought about the creation of this most-needed institute for the training of nationals for the secondary schools, although it would be Chiappano who would become known as the "father of IPN." IPN opened its doors on December 5, 1961, with Maheu being present for the inaugural ceremonies earlier.

Of course, as chief of mission, Maurice concerned himself with the experts sent to the ministries of the provinces. Referring to the letter he wrote to give encouragement to one of them, he stated:

Even if you but put a little order in the administration system, even undertaking tasks that seem humble to you such as establishing lists and making files, putting together a simple system of school accounts as well as preparing the annual budget and helping to organize the courses for the seminar, which are all of great usefulness and considerable importance, you will have justified your presence. Your very presence is of significance. With tact, great patience and tenacity you will succeed in your work.[21]

For the most part, the experts managed. They worked hard to organize the courses in Luluabourg that were held from July 3–15 for inspector candidates, July 24–August 5 for directors of primary schools, and August 14–24 for primary school teachers. For the first of the three there were nine attending, for the second forty-five, and for the third eighty attending. Considering the situation, the shortage of help, equipment, lodgings, and other necessities to make them a success, these must have been a tour de force. The experts not only organized them, but gave lectures and carried out demonstrations, besides showing the participants how to make simple school materials from what could be found locally. These seminars, though a small contribution toward the amelioration of teaching in the face of the enormous problems, were a beginning. They were a success not only from the professional point of view, but also from the cultural and above all from the human aspect, with the getting together and the exchange of views. It must have been satisfying to both the organizers and the participants.

Maurice felt it necessary to suggest a program to be undertaken in the matter of administration by the experts in all the ministries. He outlined a plan for the organization of the various sections and asked that the experts make a detailed plan, which would be sent to him before its presentation to the minister of the province. Maurice recognized the difficulties they faced due to diverse circumstances, especially the lack of competent Congolese collaborators, but urged them "to try to obtain the best results possible with the inadequate means at your disposal." He hoped that the other experts, although occupied by their respective tasks, would give their assistance so that, thanks to teamwork, the reorganization could be accomplished. Maurice hoped to unify the system for all the ministries, indicating the establishment of lists of schools and of primary and secondary teachers, statistics, etc. He then requested monthly reports on their activities.[22]

One of the most assiduous and most appreciated of the experts was Bourand in Luluabourg. He sent in full reports detailing the various activities. A glance at one of his reports dated August 7, 1961,[23] gives an idea of the different aspects of the experts' work. He stated that he spent his time between the cabinet of the minster, who was not very cooperative, and the Office of Public Education, where he concerned himself especially with accounts. At the latter there were frequent meetings and exchanges between the director and his collaborators. Bourand then outlined his part in the seminar held for directors, inspectors, and later teachers. He mentioned receiving Maurice's directives. Bourand was working very hard to overcome the difficulties due to the incomprehension of some and the apathy of others. He was assembling the information necessary to set up the files and working on the bulletin, the organization and functioning of the ministry, and the Bureau of Education. He aided in the preparation of the in-service training program for the administrative personnel, done by the director of education. Bourand ended by stating that he was happy to relate that the group of experts and teachers was in good health and excellent spirits, which gave hope for success.

At this time came also the renewal of contracts. Maurice gave a list of those experts and teachers to be kept to Rossborough, who asked him to make a list of the undesirable or malevolent Belgians in various positions in the educational field and those who should not be in certain high positions, especially those who were counselors to the ministers. It is interesting that in some cases it was the Congolese themselves who revealed in confidence the machinations of the Belgians.

Before leaving the Congo, Maurice had the satisfaction of seeing one decree concerning the reform of the school program published. He made a report on the educational operations of ONUC dated August 11, 1961. In it he gave a recapitulation of the events that led to the UNESCO effort and the first urgent measures taken by the mission, the first accord on October 19, 1960, for the recruitment of secondary school teachers and the difficulties encountered, and the final number of sixty-five teachers in Léopoldville and the provinces. Then he noted the mission's longer-term program to attack certain problems at their base. IPN is mentioned as well as in-service training both locally and in Geneva. The new minister had just approved the creation of a technical normal school. A project for adult education was being studied. The UNESCO coupon system had already absorbed $160,000.

Sture Linner in the tenth report he made to the secretary-general, in July 1961, summed it up in much the same way—that we must open schools, find teachers, restructure the central ministry; difficulties, delays, unrest, the work of UNESCO to aid in the hiring of secondary school teachers, IPN; and the reform of the teaching program and methods. He referred to the creation of the Congolese commission with UNESCO experts for this, the bolstering of the administration by sending experts and offering in-service training, and transfer of funds to IRSAC. He did add that the reconvening of parliament would make for the formation of a new government. He stated that the way was clear for IPN at Binza, with the government giving funds for the renovation. He also mentioned the coupon scheme, for which an accord had been signed.[24]

Just a few days before leaving the Congo, Maurice made a quick trip to Luluabourg to see how the experts and teachers were doing and how the first and second seminars had gone and about the third, which was being prepared. The UNESCO personnel were happy to see him, and he was happy to see the situation at first hand, visiting the schools and lodgings. He received high praise for the personnel from the director of the Catholic secondary school. Maurice was informed that the candidates for the various seminars were of low professional level but full of interest and zeal. He hoped that the level could be improved through radio lectures, correspondence courses, and more pedagogical directives. All this was good publicity for UNESCO and made for a new way of looking at schoolwork. He sent this information to Maheu in a report dated August 7, 1961, for which the deputy director-general wired: "Thank you for the interesting report on your mission to Luluabourg."[25] He wrote notes of departure to those interested stating that he would be concerned at headquarters with the African program.

Maurice worked hard during the last few days to finalize the preparations for the fellows who were to go to Geneva. Just before leaving, he wrote the two letters cited in the beginning of this chapter on the Congo crisis to Dag Hammarskjöld and René Maheu to thank them both for the confidence they expressed in him in letting him partake in the extraordinary operation. Maurice reported to headquarters on his return to Paris. We then took a much-needed holiday in the Swiss mountains.

Changes of persons and changes of policy did vary the relationships as the years went by. The cohesion of the first year was of necessity closer, but the United Nations continued to rely on UNESCO and the mission for this vast educational program.

Notes

1. M. Khiary (Tunis), Chief of Administration, September 1960–September 1962, and chief of ONUC, September 1961–September 1962.
2. A. Dayal (India). special representative to D. Hammarskjöld, October 1960–May 1961.
3. UNESCO Ar. 37(675) A-64-187.
4. The national Congolese army.
5. UNESCO Coupon System—Schools and ministries exchanged local currency for coupons which enabled these institutions to have foreign exchange to purchase materials abroad.
6. UNESCO Ar. 37(675) A-64-66, part 2, January 30, 1961, green sheet.
7. Ibid., 107628 LEO 12503 10322, February 3, 1961.
8. Ibid., 05/3 UP 147 31830, February 3, 1961.
9. Ibid., 107677 3F LEO 157 6 14294.
10. Ibid., 03/8 UP 677 1700.
11. The *Courrier* is the UNESCO monthly review, then published in five languages, now in many more.
12. Ibid., ONUC/UNESCO 21.
13. DragoLub Najman of Yugoslavia later became one of the assistant director-generals.
14. Ibid., ONUC/UNESCO 22.
15. DI Director step 1.
16. UNESCO Ar. 37(675) A-64-66, part 2, DDG/Congo memo 37.
17. Ibid., Fm 108552 AF LEO 140 13 16032.
18. R. Hennion, French program specialist.
19. 159 EX/7, Paris, May 4, 1961, Point of Order 7.1.5, Aid of UNESCO to the Congo Republic in the Framework of the Civil Operations of the United Nations.
20. Report of Activities August 1960–June 1961, UNESCO Ar. 37(675) A-64-66, part 3, June 30, 1961, 25 pp.
21. Home Files, UNESCO 226/JC, file 111 B.1, June 27, 1961.
22. UNESCO Ar. 37(675) A-64-66, part 3, ONUC, July 26, 1961.
23. Dartigue Files, ONUC, Luluabourg.
24. UN Ar., DAG 221, Box 56.
25. Home Files, UNESCO 226/JC, File 111 B.1, July 27, 1961.

At Headquarters in the Fall of 1961

The autumn of 1961 would be a very trying one for Maurice. He returned to headquarters after a well-deserved vacation, expecting to resume his former position. The verbal as well as the written expressions of appreciation by the assistant director-general, Adiseshiah, the deputy director-general, Maheu, and the Executive Board permitted him to anticipate a certain recognition of the successful accomplishment of his mission to the Congo. This was not to be. Was this the reason that Adiseshiah in 1986 from Madras, India, where he had retired, in answer to my request for a testimonial wrote the following words: "There were many times when there seemed to be some injustice done to him in not rewarding his outstanding work, some inhumanity in passing him over because of impersonal political considerations, and some unfairness in judging his many and varied accomplishments. On all these occasions, Maurice showed qualities of patience, quietness, forgiveness and refused to be deflected from his path of service . . ." It appears that Maurice's return from the unusual mission in the Congo in the fall of 1961 was one of these occasions.

A circular put out in December 1960 designated him as chief of the division, on mission, replaced for the period of his absence by Rahman, head of the Asian Unit. In July 1961, Rahman was named director of the Asian Regional Center and left for Karachi, Pakistan. He was replaced by Van Vliet, head of the unit for Arab states. Both men had been on Maurice's staff. He expected that on his return he would resume his post, as he had had a conversation with the new director of the Department of Education, the deputy director, and a member of personnel in Paris in August 1961. It was then agreed upon. But when Maurice reported for duty on the fifth of October, he was informed at a meeting that a special structure would be maintained in the department until January 1962 and that this structure would keep a unit on the Congo within the division as a separate activity and would be headed by him. The paradox was that the former head of a unit had become the chief of the division and that the former chief had become the head of a unit.

Maurice was also informed that during this period "he will acquaint himself with the rapidly expanding work in Africa which the Department

has undertaken, and after 1/62 will be in charge of Area II into which the supervision of the African program will be incorporated." This must have made him smile. Of all the staff of the Department of Education it was he who had been the most involved in matters pertaining to Africa, dating from the time he had been senior specialist in education in the Trusteeship Division of the United Nations. It was he who during 1959 was on the go continually on short missions to East and West Africa for projects involving UNESCO. If anyone in the department or even in UNESCO knew about Africa, it was he. In a way, insult was added to injury. He accepted the transitional position, but he did protest that his former unit head, temporarily given a P-5 grade, was kept and paid at this level while he, who was also in the same program, was reduced to his former level even though he was being paid out of the Congo fund, under which he had had a higher grade. The last sentence of the letter reads: "It is not so much a matter of having or not having a temporary D1 grade during a period of four months, but rather a question of what seems to me to be the application of a double standard." This he wrote to Roseman, assistant director-general, on November 23, 1961.[1]

Maurice sent a second letter of protest on December 21, 1961, to his immediate superior, McCune, who had visited Léopoldville in May and given Maurice high praise in the periodic report made in the fall of 1961. This letter was in connection with McCune's memo to Roseman in reference to the organization and staff of the new proposed division of the department for the expanding work. It was to become the African Division, dealing with all of the African countries receiving some form of aid in education, with the Congo a special program. Maurice, who had headed four units before going to the Congo and there had been chief of the whole UNESCO operation, was now to be part of a trio or, as he put it, a "troika," with Van Vliet who had replaced him and R. Ochs transferred from another service, both with far less experience, to be his partners. Evidently Maurice had not been consulted nor had his counsel been taken into consideration, for he wrote: ". . . after a year of successful mission in the Congo at the request of the Acting Director-General, during which mission I was replaced by Van Vliet for 8 months, I found the resumption of my post in the Department is made conditional to unprecedented negotiations and restrictions." (He revealed nothing at home. The only sign was that he was somewhat short-tempered. He kept calm in the office, as everyone attested.)

If I understand correctly, your proposed memorandum gives me the impression to partition the Area II Division between three individuals with me as a theoretical senior partner, whose competence, except for the Congo program, is restricted to collaboration with various units of the Secretariat on certain specific matters, while the last paragraph of your memo institutes a virtual "troika" as far as the administration of the Division is concerned, which, if applied, would contain the seeds of discord and anarchy in the Division . . .

In the spring, an Indian colleague had warned me that Maurice should come back or he would be without a job. Did he know that there was something going on in the department?

"I had presented to you, on your request after discussion with Van Vliet and Ochs, a tentative plan for the organization which took into account the organic as well as the logical aspects of the various projects and of the need for coherence, efficiency and staff distribution." Maurice went on to outline the plan he had thought out for the different activities. In ending the letter, he gave a pointed message to the new director of the department. He stated: "As for the details of the organization of the Division it should be left to the head of the Division to work them out with the staff." He added: "I have had considerable experience in the field of education . . . Therefore I do not see why the resumption of my post in the Department of Education, which was expected, should give rise to all these discussions and compromise arrangements."[2]

The African Desk was finally created in January 1962. Van Vliet was not included, while Ochs became part of Maurice's staff. Also on the staff were some of the first professionals coming from the newly independent African countries: F. Bartels of Ghana, Tchicaya of Congo (Brazzaville), and Madame Finkelstein, daughter of Félix Eboué. Soon afterward came Rex Akpofure of Nigeria and Songué of the Songué tribe. It was the latter who said to Maurice, "How is it you are the boss yet you are the first one here in the morning and the last to leave in the afternoon?" Little did he know that Maurice often worked far into the night and on weekends to keep on top of the workload and the extra challenges that faced him. In the fall of 1961, all this was yet to be. There was no African Desk as such. Maurice applied himself to the Congo Emergency program.

Maurice left the Congo on August 19, 1961, a week after Terenzio's arrival. While together they negotiated with the education minister to

establish a final text for the decrees of the president for the establishment of IPN. They also visited the premises where the future IPN would be located and decided on the renovation plans. They hired two professors out of the seven needed and definitely designated Chiappano, a UNESCO expert, to assist the future Congolese director. In a 1985 interview Chiappano, then at headquarters, stated that when he was appointed he told Maurice he had never done such work. Maurice said, "I'm sure you can do it. Give it a try." Maurice and Terenzio also brought arguments to bear on the UN financial representative to use pressure on the government to make the funds for salaries of personnel the first priority. They studied with the minister the distribution of the fifty-one secondary school teachers. After Maurice's departure, Terenzio asked the chief of ONUC to guarantee the security of the Belgian teachers by the UN troops as they did for ONUC personnel.

In his first report, August 19, 1961, Terenzio stated that the former minister Bizala was on a recruiting mission in France, the United States, Haiti, Lebanon, etc. Terenzio felt that the most important and durable result would be the effort of UNESCO to sustain and expand the secondary schools, starting with the program of the first cycle and the studies being carried on to reconcile opinions and opposing interests. He complained, as did Maurice, that one of the most difficult tasks was to obtain statistics upon which to build estimates.[3]

Terenzio sent in a report on September 16, 1961, to the acting director-general to let him know what had occurred in the Congo during Terenzio's first month as chief of the UNESCO mission. The decree for the creation of IPN, though published in August, had not yet been signed; however, a preliminary selection of students for IPN was going on. Negotiations with ICA were in progress obtaining a grant for IPN to augment its resources. Belgian teachers, now reassured as to salaries and protection, were returning in larger numbers. The most urgent problem, however, that faced the mission was that of the sixteen thousand primary school graduates who could not be accepted in the first cycle of secondary school for lack of space and teachers. It was imperative that this problem be solved as quickly as possible. If more Belgian teachers returned and the best primary school teachers could be used for the first year, the situation could be improved. The Congolese government had made an appeal to the UN secretary-general for two thousand teachers.

Terenzio learned that on his recruiting mission Bizala had had unkind words for UNESCO in Brussels (whether to ingratiate himself with the Belgians or because he felt that UNESCO was too attached to the United Nations cannot be known); therefore, if he came to Paris, he should be received without enthusiasm. On the other hand, the minister of South Kasai had received several UNESCO-recruited secondary school teachers and had only praise for them. He expressed sincere thanks and rendered vibrant homage to UNESCO for its efforts to put qualified personnel at the disposition of the Congolese Republic in general and South Kasai in particular. The new minister of education, N'Galula, recognized the great lack of cadres and asked UNESCO for more such experts as Hennion and Ardill to assure the rational functioning of the administrative services, as he did not want to depend only on bilateral aid from Belgium.

On September 17, Dag Hammarskjöld was killed in an airplane accident along with those who accompanied him just nine kilometers from N'Dola, on his way to attempt a reconciliation between Tschombé, president of Katanga (who threatened secession), and the central government. It was a shattering blow to the United Nations and the member states. Katanga seceded and was brought back into the fold and Tschombé made prime minister of the central government only in 1963, after two years of negotiations and fighting.

Dag Hammarskjöld had planned to visit various countries of Africa, especially the Congo, to get a firsthand view of the work being done by the affiliated agencies. Terenzio, as chief of mission, had been called into conference with him, and another meeting was scheduled on his return.

U Thant (Burma), already on the list of possible candidates for the post of secretary-general drawn up by Hammarskjöld, who had not wished for another term, was elected on November 3, 1961, to finish out Hammarskjöld's mandate. He then became secretary-general in his own right in 1962.

MacFarquhar, still beset by the lack of adequate funds, wrote on September 29, 1961, that the aid to the Congo was unusual, the financial burden was too great, the experts must retire as soon as possible, and the government make an effort to reorganize its offices to cut down and control expenses. He insisted that the national army was too big and cost too much and that the financial and economic situation of the country was catastrophic. The government had contracted debts illegally, and measures of redress had to be taken. It is not known how MacFarquhar expected the agencies to get all this across to the government, but as he had the final say in the dispensing of the UN monies, Terenzio in Léopoldville as well as Maurice at headquarters in the name of UNESCO would now have the headaches and frustrations concerning the budget estimates and the allocation of funds, the projects proposed or begun and then held up for insufficient means.[4]

At the same time, Khiary, who had become chief of administration, wrote: "The state should have a manner of living corresponding to its financial responsibilities. It should, of necessity, suppress all the sumptuous and useless expenditures . . ." Evidently he, too, thought that the Congolese government was spending far beyond its means and that it did not understand its financial responsibilities.

One of Maurice's first communications on returning to Paris was a note to Terenzio in early October concerning funds to be allocated for Hennion and Ardill to travel to headquarters, the first for consultations and briefing on a long-term plan of development and the latter for drafts on legislation for a "Fundamental Law for Cadres." The note disclosed Maurice's concern as to the competence of UNESCO to make laws for the Congo.

Then on October 9, 1961, a letter from Tchicaya to Jean Guiton, assistant director of the department, with carbons sent to Van Vliet and Maurice, stated among other items referring to the Fundamental Law to be formulated that "the danger would consist in 'legalizing' the transplantation in Tropical Africa of the foreign methods and programs which would not eliminate the failure of fifty years of education in the Congo."[5]

Maurice agreed with Tchicaya. The Congo program had to be revised to meet the new national needs. Laws and statutes behind the programs had to be constituted to reflect the reorientation and aims of the nationals. Maurice was concerned that certain of the staff at headquarters did not realize the implications of the limits imposed by the principles of the UN charter and the deceased secretary-general. He later stated that he already had sent material on the subject of the Organic Law on Education to the mission. He had spoken to the UNESCO legal adviser, who said that the law had to conform to the new constitution. Ardill could make a first draft after looking at models of legislation, then have it examined by specialists for constructive comments. The legal adviser agreed that UNESCO was not competent to elaborate laws for a member state, juridically speaking. Maurice was afraid that the visits to headquarters might be misinterpreted by outsiders already critical of the United Nations and UNESCO and their supposed hold on the Congo, as well as by the Congolese, who could object to their laws being made in Paris. He had always been most scrupulous to delimit his and his colleagues' attributes as advisers and counselors, insisting that it was the Congolese who must make requests and make decisions.[6] He made his opinion known in letters to several of his superiors during that fall.

N'Galula (minister of education) on October 17, 1961, wrote to the acting director-general after the acting director-general's visit to Léopoldville, to insist on an emergency program for the recruitment of more secondary school teachers and the establishment of more secondary school classes for all the extra students who had finished primary school. In the letter N'Galula did ask for an expert on the Fundamental Law as well as one on schoolbooks and one on a history of the Congo. He solicited experts for adult education and popular education, experts to help set up an international body of inspectors, an expert for development plans, one for school construction, and one for a professional orientation center.[7]

This letter Terenzio answered on October 19, 1961, sending a copy to Maheu, Maurice, Gagliotti in New York, Hennion, and Ardill stating that his requests were being attended to but there were two problems.

Hennion would make a first exposition of a plan of development. If your views coincide, Hennion would go to Paris to document himself to do the best he can as to the Organic Education Law. The Director-General underlines the fact that the preparation implies a certain number of decisions of a political order outside the competence of UNESCO. UNESCO must limit itself to technical matters. Ardill can transmit to you a number of points on which it is necessary we know your directives. For this Ardill will go at the same time to Paris as Hennion to study the problem as there is a correlation between the two . . .[8]

Thus Terenzio hoped to allay Maurice's fears and possible UNESCO critics.

After more interoffice exchanges of notes and opinions, it was agreed that it must be Terenzio who should decide how and where the first drafts were to be made and when the two experts were to come to Paris. Terenzio was being careful, as a letter dated November 23, 1961, to the minister N'Galula shows. He stated that the ONUC authorities delegated to aid the Congolese government concerning constitutional matters had been consulted. The draft put together by a team had been delivered by the chief of ONUC to the prime minister to show him what had been done. The next step was up to the prime minister, who, at his convenience, was to call on the ONUC specialists in constitutional texts to present suggestions after appropriate consultations, "then taking all the suggestions, opinions and factors into consideration, another draft would be made, hopefully giving the Prime Minister satisfaction."[9]

In the middle of December, Terenzio sent a draft, sending carbons to Maurice and Khiary, that concerned only the statutes for public school, the private and subsidized schools to have a special statute. In writing to Maurice, Terenzio made it clear that he was being careful not to implicate UNESCO in any political responsibility and that such documents were objects of discussion for all concerned. It was finally at this time that Hennion made the trip to Paris. The reason the correspondence for the Teaching Profession statutes and the Plan of Development involving the two UNESCO experts, Ardill and Hennion, have been cited is to emphasize and bring out the complexities involved and limits imposed on the UNESCO efforts to aid the leaders of nascent nations to make laws for their new status.

Back to the events and the work going on during this time at headquarters and the mission. Maheu visited Léopoldville in October. He was much impressed by the work being done by Terenzio and his team. Maheu met the highest officials of the Congolese government and ONUC and the other agencies. For the time being, the government was stabilized after the meeting of the parliament. The prime minister, Adoula, the minister of education, N'Galula, and the minister of information, Ileo, by their requests showed their appreciation for UNESCO's aid. For the minister of education the most urgent problem was the schooling of the thousands of primary school graduates. He asked for two thousand teachers. He begged Maheu to find $2 million to cover the financing of this unexpected emergency program. He was willing to examine all candidates proposed by UNESCO. (It was later agreed that UNESCO would aid in recruitment, but the government would take the responsibility for contracts, etc.)

It was within the means of UNESCO to provide the experts. Teachers and classrooms were a different matter. It was a tremendous challenge for Terenzio and his staff to scout about for possible schoolrooms and possible teachers to be found locally as well as for the Bureau of Personnel and the division engaged in the Emergency Program of the Congo, meaning Maurice and his staff. (The head of the department, Mr. McCune, encountered twenty-four years later, said that what he remembered most was Maurice's constant preoccupation with recruiting teachers and experts.) Terenzio asked if the standards could not be lowered to make it easier to find teachers, which it is presumed was done, and later might have been one of the causes of adverse criticism leveled at some of those teachers.

It was the financing, apart from the off-and-on political instability, that would be a major headache. On October 27, 1961, Terenzio tried to convince the temporary chief of ONUC, D. Dumontet, of the validity of the UNESCO demands. Terenzio brought up the requests of the minister and reminded Dumontet of the conversations between himself, Linner, Khiary, and Maheu, which implied supplementary financial aid. He reiterated the problem of the lack of schools for the fifteen thousand primary school graduates. He reminded Dumontet that $10 million had been accorded to the Congo in June to facilitate importations. It could be liberated proportionally. Some of this money could be advanced as a guarantee. When a counterpart would be obtained from outside sources such as UNICEF, the money could be put back into the Congo treasury. He outlined the possible double uses of classrooms, one group for mornings, one group for afternoons; the consolidation of underused classrooms; and redistribution of teachers, as well as fixed payment for extra hours for teachers. He even suggested the use of excess staff in the administration services as teachers, the use of the best primary school teachers for the first year of the secondary school cycle, and the recruitment of foreign women in the Congo as teachers for this emergency. As Terenzio felt that the schooling of the fifteen thousand children was absolutely necessary, he was ready to grasp at all possibilities, whether very wise or not, to accomplish the task. In fact, he went ahead without waiting for a definite approval to make a survey of possible housing.

At the same time, negotiations were going on at headquarters with UNICEF representatives for its participation in financing the training of teachers. It was in connection with the in-service training of primary school teachers, directors, and possible inspectors through itinerant mobile teams that the discussions took place, in which Maurice certainly took an important part, as Terenzio advises the UNICEF representatives to address themselves to Maurice, since he was the "chief of the Congo operations at HQ," as confirmed in an administrative circular, no. 68-12/10. The draft for the agreement came in for discussions. It concerned the teachers for home economics, handcrafts, and basic principles of agriculture as well as academic subjects. It was hoped that it would soon be signed by the director-general and UNICEF. In a letter to Terenzio dated October 23, 1961, Maurice confided to him that he had kept silent concerning the failures of the Congolese to carry out the obligations they accepted. He added that the emergency program for the schooling of the fifteen thousand children was discussed. The representatives wanted to see the first draft of the proposal. Perhaps the Executive Board of UNICEF would accept that UNICEF pay one-fourth of the expenses.

There was also the matter of the group of Congolese educational administrators who had been selected for the courses in Geneva. Fellowships had been obtained, a few from the Swiss government. Housing in Geneva had been found. They were finally off and in Geneva, they were received by P. Rossello, the coordinator for the program. Piaget, the Swiss educator, director of the IBE, wrote to Maheu to ask who of the UNESCO staff would give conferences. By the middle of November classes were in full swing. Maurice, as he had promised, gave his lectures in December. He made an interesting report. Four other UNESCO staff members went to give a few talks. Terenzio was so busy that it was only when Maurice wrote to him to ask that he look into the cases of three of the grant holders, who had learned from their families, left behind in the Congo, that their salaries had not been paid, that he remembered these courses in Geneva. At the same time, Maurice urged Terenzio to have a list made of all the fellows abroad, branch of study, academic level, experience in the Congo before departure, length of stay, etc., to make sure that on their return suitable positions would be found for them; otherwise they could be lost to education, being drawn into private enterprise. Although Maurice had thought that sending people abroad for further training, as he had done in Haiti, was a necessity, he arrived at a different opinion, asserting that after the 1962–63 session in Geneva only one or two fellows needed to be sent abroad.

The report Terenzio sent on November 2 was particularly interesting in that he started it off with this statement:

I have just traversed one of those exasperating periods such as you must have undergone a certain number of times while you were here. The minister, absorbed by politics, seldom showed up in his office. It has been impossible to obtain any decisions from him either on the request for the emergency program campaign, or for the candidatures I transmitted to him. You must have noticed this delay. At last, today

I have been able to send off the cables which I have held back for some time.

The general TA accords were not yet signed, and the OPEX forms were still being discussed.

Terenzio continued to say that he was preparing the program for 1962 to discuss the projects with MacFarquhar, who was to arrive on the eighth of November. Terenzio added:

There have been several preparational reunions of the Consultative Committee of ONUC to dissipate the extreme confusion that reigns concerning the manner in which the activities are to be carried out in 1962, and the way to present them to MacFarquhar. Each member will present an inventory of his organization's needs—Congolese and foreign personnel, bilateral and international aid, OPEX and A.T. with the priorities (Hennion doing this). It is necessary to aid the Congolese to prepare their budget on an absolutely unrealistic basis because it concerns maintaining 1960–1961 teaching salary levels although these have been tripled.[10]

The interesting communication was that there would be held in Léopoldville the first conference of the ministers of education of the provinces and the central government on November 15. For this meeting, N'Galula was pressing the mission to present a first draft of the Organic Law on Education. Ardill was working on this, putting some ideas on paper so that the draft could be discussed and reactions expressed. He ended by affirming that he would send Maurice the reports, but to Maheu only those for which he had to have directives.

In a later letter, Terenzio noted that he had had to tell Khiary that he should occupy himself with the budget and permit him, Terenzio, to decide which projects in education should be pursued and how this was to be done. Adiseshiah in a communication from the United Nations in New York observed that the greatest confusion prevailed there concerning the program in the Congo.

On the same day, November 2, Maurice sent a recapitulative report to Maheu on what was being or had been accomplished, pertaining to the requests formulated by the ministers N'Galula and Ileo. This report would be used as part of the report for the Executive Board on November 27, 1961.

The Executive Board had been meeting since October 10, 1961, and at that time Maheu had given a report of the preceding activities culled from earlier reports received from Maurice and Terenzio. In the recapitulation Maurice brought Maheu up-to-date and at the same time permitted himself to make certain observations.[11]

The relationship that had existed between Maurice and Maheu because of the special circumstances of the Congo mission no longer held, and the relationship reverted to what it had been before Maurice left for the Congo. However, the fact that he did make the following observations shows that he could go directly to Maheu.

In the summary, Maurice touched on the campaign for the enrollment of some fifteen thousand primary school graduates. He expressed the opinion that if five thousand could be enrolled that would already be an achievement. (He proved almost correct, as six thousand finally were taken care of.) He reminded Maheu that the minister had promised that the government would manage to pay half the cost of the necessary four hundred teachers to be recruited for this project. Maheu had offered to try to find the other half of the required $4 million.

Maurice continued his report, referring to his reservations in connection with the Organic Law of Education and his actions concerning the minister N'Galula's request for an expert for the writing of the history of the Congo, one for the production of school manuals, one for adult education, as well as funds for these. As to the minister's request for ten international inspectors for secondary school as well as the setting up of this service, it could be done through OPEX, as Terenzio had suggested, unless ONUC withdrew its approval. The British Council had offered one inspector for English. N'Galula had also requested an expert for the evaluation of a plan for the development of education and a psycho-technician for a projected "Professional Orientation Centre," plus a statistician, and although Hennion was already there, Maurice observed, it would be too much for him, as he was deeply involved in program revision and other activities. The minister of information, Ileo, asked for aid for developing dissemination of information and radio broadcasting. This, too, was being looked into.[12]

On November 27, 1961, Maheu gave his report to the Executive Board at its sixtieth session.[13] He recounted his visit to Léopoldville in October, when he met with heads of the government, ONUC officials, and UNESCO staff. He had attended the inauguration ceremonies of IPN, the first of its kind in the Congo. He brought back an excellent impression "of the work, begun under Dartigue and now continuing under Terenzio, with its three staff members, and the 19 experts provided by UNESCO. I received very satisfactory reports on the competence and devotion to duty displayed, often in difficult circumstances, by the fifty-one teachers and experts also supplied by UNESCO."

Maheu had brought to the attention of the minister that not only UNESCO teachers, but also foreign teachers, whose assistance was at this time indispensable to the functioning of certain branches of education, particularly secondary schools, should enjoy satisfactory conditions as regarded security, accommodation, and food supplies, as well as regular payment of salaries and allowances without which normal service could not be maintained. He mentioned the requests of the ministers (as Maurice had reported) and what was being done about them. Maheu went on to enumerate the program of action for 1962, of which the in-service training of teachers in the primary schools through mobile teams was the latest development. He cited their composition. An agreement had been worked out and approved by UNESCO, UNICEF, and the Congolese government. He was waiting for the approval of ONUC. It was hoped that as these teams traveled around the country they would discover candidates for primary school inspectors.

As to secondary education, hundreds of teachers were needed. Those fifty-one supplied by UNESCO were far too few. The need was for seven hundred. A mission sent abroad by the government to recruit personnel had found only 350. The total cost would be $4 million. The greatest difficulty was financing. UNICEF and IDA had been applied to. A decision from the United Nations was awaited. The mission was in consultation with ONUC to convince it to bear the cost of the foreign inspectors of secondary schools demanded, as no such service existed and it was indispensable until Congolese nationals could be gradually trained. He also went into the financing of IPN and the Organic Law on Education and the kind of aid UNESCO could permit itself to give the requests for experts for planning in education; the producing of school textbooks, especially in the revision of Congo history; adult education, almost nonexistent; and mass communication. The mission had obtained 1 million Congo francs a month for six months from the government for IRSAC and 2,223,000 Congo francs toward the upkeep of the national parks for this period. The government had asked for an expert to advise it in matters relating to these.

Terenzio came to Paris in late November. He sent a happy cable after the general approbation of the program given in a resolution offered by the Malagasy Republic and accepted by the Executive Board. A press release announcing the recruitment of the four hundred teachers (the largest scale of aid ever given) came out on December 4, 1961. Both the mission and Maurice were happy, but not for long. As happened with IPN, budgets were made and accepted, then monies held back for more information, more explanation, more revision. Maurice at headquarters and the mission in Léopoldville went through this procedure again and again. This happened once more with the three new projects: the setting up of the itinerant teams for in-service training of primary school teachers, the recruitment of four hundred secondary school teachers for the overflow of primary school graduates, and the recruitment of the corps of inspectors for secondary school supervision. The UNESCO liaison officer at the United Nations in New York was begged to plead the cause. That he did not succeed is revealed by the later actions of Maheu.

To make for more efficient and cohesive teamwork with the various sectors at headquarters and the mission in the Congo, meetings were held and prerogatives and responsibilities defined. A circular dated October 12, 1961, as to "Organizational Arrangements and Attributions of Responsibility for the Congo Operation" enumerates these, giving the head of the Education Department the overall coordination of planning and supervision with Maurice, chief of the Congo operation at headquarters, and Terenzio, chief of the operation in the Congo. It was a shared responsibility. It will be noticed that as Maurice became more involved in the whole program for Africa, of which the Congo was an important unit, more and more would be done directly by the mission in the field.

By December 14, 1961, Terenzio was back in the Congo, at which time he wrote to N'Galula that he had submitted the first draft of the proposed statute for teachers, elaborated by Ardill, to the UN adviser on public administration matters for observations and comment, as had been suggested by Khiary.

On the fifteenth Terenzio sent an SOS letter to Maheu. Terenzio had seen Khiary concerning the urgent program and the need for four hundred more teachers. The Congolese ministers were ready for the reorganization of education with priority for secondary education, thus placing the UNESCO-proposed projects within the framework of the government's policy. Khiary was in accord that the various projects be transmitted to

MacFarquhar. Terenzio feared that MacFarquhar might refuse funds for the four hundred teachers, dreading that the United Nations would have to bear all the expenses, since he had noticed while he was in Léopoldville the government's inability to apply budgetary discipline. Terenzio had insisted that only UN guarantees could make recruitment possible. He then asked Maheu if MacFarquhar held back, would it be possible to use Funds in Trust, never before used on so vast a scale? This was the reason for his SOS.

As to the emergency program for secondary school enrollment, here, too, Terenzio found hard going with Khiary, who opposed using matching funds until he learned that the Congolese had given 45 million Congo francs out of the 85 million needed and that the campaign had already begun. Only then was he ready to grant 22 million Congo francs out of the fund. Terenzio asked Maheu to beg Gagliotti at the United Nations to try to obtain 20 percent of the total from UNICEF. This would help.

Maheu was so concerned about the turn of events, he felt the situation so critical that he made a quick trip to the UN headquarters in New York to consult with MacFarquhar to defend the UNESCO projects. He thought his trip mostly successful, for he sent a wire to Adiseshiah to be transmitted to Maurice at headquarters and to Terenzio in the Congo on December 22, 1961: "MacFarquhar promises letter—UN guarantees salaries if really necessary. UNESCO can recruit if government pays UNESCO expenses. He accepts three or four mobile teams. Request must come from government. Accepts five inspectors. Will see later for more. He is ready to employ matching funds if government takes entire responsibility. UNICEF in accord but wants to know role of UNESCO." To this he added: "Joyeux Noel. . . . Merry Xmas."[14] A real victory, or so all thought.

Had Maheu not gone to expose directly the delicate situation of UNESCO vis-à-vis the aspirations and determination of the Congolese government and the attitude of the Congolese toward UNESCO, there would have been a serious crisis. Fortunately, the problems were averted for the time being. At headquarters the staff concerned must have been relieved, as action had been begun in several sectors to recruit and process candidates. Maurice made the suggestions: to appeal to all nationalities speaking French for the teachers and use Funds in Trust if necessary.

Just before the end of the year an important document with the title *The Analysis of the Education Situation in the Congo* was published on December 27, 1961.[15] It was an assessment and results of UNESCO action in the Congo since August 1960 (less than a year and a half). It was done by Hennion and Ardill. Maurice had first seen it a few days earlier and immediately wrote to the two men to compliment them on the excellent work they had accomplished. They merited the praise, as they were the two men who, without fanfare or publicity, worked the hardest to aid the Congolese in formulating new laws, statutes, and programs for educational revision.

The report noted the difference between the program in the Congo and the one used in Belgium; another, the decline in special postprimary education in favor of secondary education. Because of the departure of Belgian secondary school teachers and administrators, unqualified personnel had taken their places in many instances, making for temporary lowering of standards in teaching and disorganization and confusion in the administration. UNESCO, with its limited means, and ONUC had filled the breach to a certain extent.

They suggested certain reforms. The secondary school system needed to be unified as to the number of years for the various cycles, with the maximum use of teachers and classrooms. Until there were enough Congolese teachers, foreign teachers would be needed. IPN was the first step. Also there was a need for a national technical normal school for the training of teachers and workshop technicians for secondary technical schools. They even suggested teacher training for higher training schools and engineering. (These Maurice questioned, as they were a little too optimistic.)

As for administration, they reiterated the lack of training and the need for competent personnel and noted how this was to be obtained. They mentioned, however, the often paralyzed services, due not so much to incompetence as to the *"prebendal conception of the Congolese of the administrative function—the immovableness and immunity enjoyed by subaltern functionaries.* There was a need to have hiring tied to competition and probation before titularization."* (Just what Maurice had done in Haiti.) For the administrative services foreign experts would be needed to reform the services and encourage Congolese to take over the work and to take responsibility. The problem of inspection was more acute, as all the secondary school inspectors before independence had been Belgians. In this area, foreign personnel had to be used. A very limited number of primary school inspectors existed. Through seminars, courses, and selection of candidates, a group could be reactivated, with the hope that the inspectors would actually visit schools.

As to adult education, the two experts learned that there were about one thousand adults in different groups dispersed throughout the country for youth and/or community development. An organized program was needed for the present social and cultural disequilibrium. Too many young people were in the streets, leaving small towns and villages to go to the big cities. (Maurice expressed the opinion that only industrialization and economic development could absorb this group.)

They estimated a budget of 6,880,736,000 Congo francs. Quite a sum for a country whose treasury was almost empty. To bring this amount down, subsidies would have to be reexamined; certain standards had to be requested. The political repercussions needed to be considered if this were done. Evidently the Congolese accepted this report as neither Hennion nor Ardill were decried or denounced.

One of the last communications from Terenzio in 1961 referred to the actual opening of IPN on December 5, 1961, with seventy-six students. He stated that it was going strong with both students and professors happy. He would send the program as soon as approved. AID was willing to give some funds. The urgent program for the scholarization of the thousands of primary schools' graduates was in full progress, "against high winds and high water." Several classes had already opened. He referred to the political trouble in South Kasai, which had repercussions on the work of UNESCO both in the province and in Léopoldville. He wrote that N'Galula had not appeared in his office for days: "He stays at home surrounded by a guard of his partisans." Terenzio saw him a few times there on business. N'Galula was to have left for Italy, but he renounced the trip. He, Terenzio, was off to Bakwanga to solve the problems of eight teachers. He had just been there to meet UNESCO teachers and experts. As an aside, he reported that the 140 teachers from Haiti recruited by Bizala were held up in Miami on their way to the Congo.

It is fitting before closing this chapter to cite a few notes from Sture Linner's reports sent to the secretary-general of the United Nations in New York, Dag Hammarskjöld at first, then U Thant after Hammarskjöld's death. The salient points were the reconvening of parliament, with the formation of a new government (when N'Galula and Adoula were appointed) and the final acceptance of IPN at Binza, with the government furnishing funds for the renovations necessary. He made references to the seminar held in Léopoldville in May and those in Luluabourg in July and August.

The report for September and October showed the first draft of the codification of legislative laws governing the school system and the revision of school programs, the preselection of the students for IPN, the revision of the business school curricula, and the beginning of the reform in primary school teaching, as well as the rise in numbers of graduates demanding secondary school entrance, with the need for far more teachers and school-rooms.

The last report, no. 13, for 1961 concerned the opening of IPN; the production by certain experts of an overall plan for future educational development prepared for the first conference of the central and provincial ministers including others concerned with education (Catholic and Protestant missions); the outcome of this first conference, showing a decided priority for secondary schools limited only by resources; the secondary school emergency program for more teachers and classrooms; and the decision taken for the opening of a technical training school in October 1962 financed by the UN Special Fund.[16]

Notes

1. Home Files, UNESCO/ED/Congo/A.231.
2. Home Files, UNESCO/ED/Congo/memo 208.
3. Home Files, ONUC/UNESCO no. 46, Report to Maheu.
4. UNESCO Ar. 37(675) A-64-66, part 3, ONUC/UNESCO/456.
5. Ibid., ED/4110/1.
6. Ibid., ED/Congo/memo 65, October 31, 1961, to McCune.
7. Ibid., ED/NAT/CHB/621/61.
8. UNESCO Ar. 37(675) A-64-66, part 3, ONUC/UNESCO/456.
9. Ibid., ONUC/UNESCO/L300B.
10. UNESCO Ar. 37(675) A-64/186, ONUC/UNESCO/467.
11. UNESCO Ar. 37(675) A-64-66, part 4, November 1, 1961–July 1962.
12. Ibid., Ed/Congo/memo 67.
13. Report to 6C EX/10, add. item 8.1.5.
14. UNESCO Ar. 37(675) A-64-66, part 4, cable 7/6/22.
15. UNESCO Ar., *Special Reports,* 39pp.
16. UN A., DAG, 2.60.25 583.

The Creation of the African Division, 1962: The Emergency Program for the Newly Independent States of Africa

In January 1962 Maurice became the first chief of the African Desk, again heading a division with several units. While he was on mission in the Congo, work had begun at headquarters on an Emergency Program for Africa as dependent people obtained their freedom to become self-governing. Certainly Maurice must have worked on the report that the director-general gave at the Executive Board's fifty-sixth session, which met at headquarters to April 30, 1960. At this meeting, he was authorized to have studies made for the planning and development of education, short- and long-term plans in detail, and plans to adapt programs and train primary school teachers. Governments of tropical Africa would need to reserve a large portion of their budgets for the formation of middle and higher cadres. It is on this basis that UNESCO conceived its action in favor of the development of education to train African personnel capable of assuring the functioning of the public administration services, as well as commercial and industrial enterprises.

Before proposing new activities, the director-general referred to those already undertaken by UNESCO, such as the sending of consultants to several countries and territories, especially for the teaching of social and natural sciences. It had, in cooperation with ECA, made studies, arranged the Addis Ababa conference, and hosted a study group on technical education in Accra and another in Abidjan on the education of women. All studies and conferences pointed to education as the greatest need. There was the urgent need for planning and for training of nationals in both teaching and administration to replace foreigners. There was need for financing such necessities as textbook production, libraries, school construction, and educative radio. National resources were not enough. Funds had to come from outside.

Maheu suggested that a work committee be constituted, to study the available documents and formulate action that UNESCO could undertake. A committee of twenty-three delegates with Adiseshiah as a member was

222

set up. It held six sessions and came up with several conclusions, among them that the recommendations of the Addis Ababa conference of February 1960 had to be revised, with priority going to secondary education, for the time being, the importance of creating a regional center for pedagogical documentation and research, and a practical training session for specialists in textbook production.

It is these proposals and the advocacy of others by the General Conference that inspired the Addis Ababa conference of May 1961, to bring about the creation of the regional centers, the planning missions, the increase in the number of experts, secondary school teachers, and professors for higher training schools, and the creation of such schools; in short, most of the work of the future African Division.

The main objectives of the General Conference and the Executive Board were the following: (1) school construction; (2) production of auxiliaries for teaching (textbooks, laboratory equipment), both new and old types; (3) the recruitment of teachers and experts for secondary, normal, general, and technical schools and professors for higher training establishments; (4) evaluation of the needs (surveys, planning missions) in the matter of education. These would be considered at the Addis Ababa conference.

Thus the follow-up of the General Conference and the fifty-eighth Executive Board session was the intensive preparation of the Addis Ababa conference, held from May 15 to May 25, 1961. The title was the Conference of African States on the Development of Education in Africa. To it were invited delegates not only from tropical Africa, but also from North Africa, meaning the Arab countries. Its special interest was the inventory of the exigencies for economic and social development in relation to education. It was held jointly with ECA.

The meeting opened on schedule, with some 250 participants from thirty-nine countries, of whom there were twenty-three ministers of education, and observers from twenty-four governments. Adiseshiah was the guiding light. This was *his* meeting.

In his enthusiasm, Adiseshiah was so far carried away that in his opening speech he stated, "Six months ago Africa did not exist for UNESCO." There were many speeches, four plenary sessions, and four commissions. The emperor welcomed the participants, and the minister of education was elected to preside over the conference. It was an impressive gathering.

The recommendations that came out of this conference, which determined UNESCO action in Africa for years, were a short-term plan of five years to increase total school enrollment from 11 to 15 million children with emphasis on secondary school expansion and an output of forty-five thousand additional teachers a year (!!!) with increased expenditure for these, and special attention to adult education and literacy campaigns, as well as those concerning the creation of institutes for research, book production, the need for foreign teachers, the reform of programs, and education of girls.

"The costs are staggering but the will of the African people is strong. However, they will need aid. States and institutions will be called upon to contribute. Already some help has been given; much more is needed. The Africans have established these goals as essential to achieve their rightful place in the world community. These goals are a gigantic challenge. Africa calls on its more fortunate brothers to share the burden of the program." Thus spoke Adiseshiah. (It would be interesting to verify to what extent these goals have been attained. In 1985, emphasis had returned to fundamental education.)

What the conference did do was turn the main focus from fundamental education or primary education to secondary education. Opinions differ as to the wisdom of this move. Africa was desperate for trained personnel in all areas of endeavor, especially education, and perhaps the bottleneck between primary and secondary schools and higher education justified this priority. Some feel that a more balanced program could have been worked out, with fundamental education keeping an important place to raise the level of the general population. This would be more Maurice's opinion.

The 127-page report of the conference, including statistics, speeches, etc., came out in record time. By May 31, 1961, the first conclusions were distributed to the members of the fifty-ninth session of the Executive Board, which met May 25–June 15, 1961. The board expressed satisfaction. It agreed that the director-general present the report of the conference and the outline of the plans to ECOSOC (Economic and Social Council of the United Nations) at its thirty-second session. It invited the member states and associate member states in other regions to implement the recommendations aided by the various agencies to help in the realization of these plans.

The Executive Board invited the director-general to submit proposals at its next session, including the establishment of the machinery within the framework of UNESCO to implement the objectives and report the progress accomplished. Judicious allocations had to be considered for a balance between the various projects. Publicity was done to encourage countries as well as private and international agencies to offer more funds.

During the year, advisers in educational matters were sent to fourteen countries to awaken the new states to the need for planning in education and aid them in the creation of offices for this activity. But before this could be brought about, surveys had to be made to determine how much was necessary and in what manner it was to be done, as each country was at a different level of development and each had its specific strengths and problems. So it was with the first surveying missions that the division was occupied, Van Vliet through correspondence to recruit teams and Ochs through his preliminary survey mission to several West African countries in July 1961. Ochs traveled to Upper Volta and reported that it recognized its problems but was financially handicapped and would need aid. The political situation in Sierra Leone, at the time, was uncertain. Tribal rivalries were evident. The minister of education said that a planning mission was too expensive and unrealistic. Ochs went ahead with a well-developed plan, bypassing the financial problem. In the end UNESCO had to fund the missions to both countries.

Earlier in June the new director of the department held a meeting for the first planning teams on the problems and techniques of educational surveys to set up guidelines. As good as the guidelines were, they did not always prove of value, depending on the local situation and the persons taking part, both in the teams and the governments that received them. However, the one to Upper Volta and the other to Sierra Leone became lessons for future missions. Not all members of the staff or division or other sectors or countries were in agreement as to the importance or usefulness of the planning missions. They claimed other priorities for the limited budgets of UNESCO, TA, and the Special Fund. Even the status of the members of the mission caused differences of opinion. Maurice on his return to headquarters in October 1961 was perhaps so involved in the Congo and his own status, the ambiguity of his responsibilities, and other duties that his signature concerning the planning missions does not appear until 1962, when he finally became the first Chief of the African Division in the Department of Education.

The director-general made his report to the Executive Board at its sixtieth session, held from September 29, 1961, on, concerning this program. He referred to the planning missions, procedures, objectives, and problems, but especially to funding, as each planning mission could cost from $65,000 to $100,000. He went on to the other areas having to do with the Emergency Program for Africa, such as the request of twenty-six countries for 600 teachers, school construction, textbook production, and school equipment (the pittance of ten thousand dollars being allotted to this). The Executive Board thanked the director-general for all that had been done but expressed the hope that only that for which money was available would be undertaken. It consented to the holding of a conference of ministers of education of tropical Africa to be held in 1962 to examine the national education plans of each country, country by country, then reflect on the possible action, methods for procedure, and how the action was to be financed. The conference would be carried out jointly with ECA.[1]

Survey missions were not new to UNESCO, but the planning missions begun in 1961 were. Due to the sudden independence of unprepared nations, aid was urgent to plan for a program that reflected the new aspirations. As in the Congo, many nations were ill equipped in cadres and personnel to instigate or carry out planning; therefore, the Department of Education of UNESCO was called upon to aid in this task. The need for special guidelines for the survey and planning missions was acknowledged and the circular sent out with an introduction by the director-general. In light of the two missions already carried out, the need for great flexibility, adjustment to difficulties of several kinds, and correct timing was made evident.

The program really went forward in 1962, when the African Division became a specific division, with Maurice as its designated and accepted chief.

Maheu, just elected director-general, summed it up at the General Conference in the fall of 1962. He stated that the Executive Board had already noted in August what a great evolution had taken place between 1960 and 1962 in the work of UNESCO as a consequence of the rapid decolonization of the African countries, the considerable increase in the number of member states, the considerable augmentation of extrabudgetary funds, and the acceptance and recognition of the central place education occupied in economic and social development. For UNESCO the mobilization of resources for the promotion of man was of historic importance. UNESCO now managed vast sums. Its position in the United Nations was reinforced. It concerned itself with the development of education in all its aspects at all levels . . . concrete action limited in time, with definite results.

The General Conference now included the new independent countries of Africa, and the delegates of these countries made their voices heard. They, as well as others from other nations, approved the UNESCO program to provide services for primary and secondary education, especially for solutions to the following problems:

(1) adaptation of school curricula for African needs;
(2) the training of teachers;
(3) provision of adequate school facilities (construction and equipment);
(4) preparation and training of supervisory and administrative staff;
(5) collaboration with FAO and ILO (for planning missions and program);
(6) the planning of technical and vocational programs (with experts sent for this purpose); and
(7) the approbation of international and regional studies and surveys and the giving of advisory services in reference to planning organizations, with continued priority for secondary education.

These resolutions and directives gave wide scope and opportunities to the new African Division. When one looks them over one can appreciate Maurice's responsibilities in collaboration either with other sectors of the department or with other departments or other agencies. When the director-general referred to the vast extrabudgetary sums, he included, outside the regular program, TA, Emergency TA program (EPTA, or Enlarged Technical Assistance Program), the Special Fund, the Emergency Fund for Africa, the Emergency Fund for the Congo, possible funds from UNICEF, and U.S. aid, from contributions of member states and other funds for which requests had to be made, proper projects presented, and estimates calculated. According to Francis Bartels [Ghana], the man who succeeded him, Maurice had entire responsibility for the budget and allocation of funds as well as the supervision of the division and its program.

Also through Maurice's small office went the furnishing of documents for the sector, the formulating and elaborating of possible projects, and documents for delegates and for ministers of education. Besides there was the supervision of the organization of the planning missions, meetings, seminars, or participation in them. Moreover, there were the propositions for the formulation of resolutions as well as suggestions to the office of the director-general as to plans for action, proposals especially requiring careful phrasing and diplomatic awareness. Bartels remembers Maurice sitting at his desk writing, writing.

When Maurice became chief of the African Division, he outlined the different areas of endeavor mentioned earlier, concerning policy, planning, and administration of the different projects. Bartels, with Tchicaya, Ochs, Finkelstein, Bergeaud, and Lightfoot, among others, worked out a distribution of responsibilities. The staff was very small for such a vast program. To be sure that each of his staff as well as the other divisions knew for what each was responsible, he put out a circular in August 1962[2] giving details of the work of each unit setting out the general responsibilities as formulated in an administrative circular sent around February 27, 1962, and the specific responsibilities. He gave autonomy but supervised when necessary. He was fortunate to have several of his staff who could carry on without much supervision.

Maurice was careful to see that assignments were carried out properly. Even minor details, often quite important for the success of the program, took time and explanation, as the following note shows, which Maurice wrote to Terenzio on January 30, 1962, "concerning the complaint of Chiappano [associate director of IPN] in Léopoldville. . . . He has no idea of the administrative formalities [Chiappano was a field man, and only after service in the Congo did he join headquarters] to which we are obliged to submit. The list he sent was transmitted to the Clearing House, which cannot order directly but does so through the library. On the other hand, the library only handles books and not other teaching materials, so the Clearing House had to send the list of the latter to another service. As certain references were vague, Tchicaya (of the Congo unit) had to make several trips to the editors to get prices on the books and determine just what to order. The same goes for the equipment. For the history of the Congo to be written, there, too, Tchicaya had to do research to obtain documents and books. When you came to headquarters you gave a partial list and later Hennion, when he came, a further one. But the real slowness and a virtual stop came about when the Bureau of Accounting and Control blocked all orders under the pretext that the bureau had not been authorized by ONUC through UNESCO to spend money for the acquisition of books and material for IPN."[3]

The following was a three-page hand-written interoffice note from Maurice to Miss Smith of the Bureau of Accounting and Control for the Department of Education. It was written in such a hurry that it is less than perfect. It reads:

Miss Smith

The acct. number for the approved budget (approved by UN) for the Léopoldville Pedagogical Institute is 20-60. This budget contains provision for staff, fellowships and equipment including library books. We received a request from Terenzio to buy certain books for the library and for teaching and a few pieces of zoological laboratory material. BOC would not approve the order prepared by the library because they have not been notified by ONUC that they are authorized to make such purchases and charge them to ONUC although I show these evidence that the budget for project 20-60 has been approved by the competent authorities in UN. They say this does not constitute an authorization for UNESCO to buy any material for the Institute.

I also informed them that the ICA (U.S.) has contributed $130,000 to the Institute for fellowships and library books, etc. to be administered jointly by the UNESCO mission and the Director of the Institute. BOC wants to see the agreement between the mission and the Director of the Institute on the administration of the fund.

But in the meantime, the school has been in session since the 10th of November; the students are there and the professors are there, but no books for the students (for teaching). This will make a very bad impression on the government authorities and the community, which is not good for UNESCO.

Chase, budget expert, has suggested and Rao of Budget and Control has agreed that the Department of Education accept to charge temporarily these purchases to one of its projects, until the formalities required by BOC can be met. I do not have the exact amount, but I do not think that all the requisitions exceed $2,000 or even less.

Please make the necessary arrangements so that the requisition can go to the "fournisseurs." This is urgent.

M. Dartigue

This long note was in response to one sent by Miss Smith demanding clarification as to what budget to charge it to. A Congo project was found until the agreement was reached and the amount put in its proper place. This shows, however, the rigor for the accounting and control services. The checks and counterchecks were necessary, but in many cases making for regrettable delays. Some, accustomed to the greater freedom offered by the field, were, on entering headquarters, irked or frustrated by the bureaucracy and either sought other field assignments or resigned as soon as their contracts permitted. Maurice took the interventions in his stride for the most part, on occasion not awaiting communication through the regular channels but going himself or sending one of his staff from office to office to get the necessary approvals and visas.

The vast increase of work was recognized by the directorate, to judge by the administrative circular sent out late in January 1962. It stated:

The volume and complexity of UNESCO activities are continuing to accelerate rapidly. The new programs with which the organization is charged have been integrated with the regular program. Although staff has been added to compensate partially for the increased workload there has been relatively little increase in supervisory personnel at the division chief [Maurice] or director [head of the department] level or in the ODG [Office of the Director-General]. Therefore important senior staff should be relieved of routine work so their time and energies can be used for planning and supervising the program. The achievement of this objective can be facilitated by the delegation of authority.[4]

It is certain that Maurice assumed the responsibilities to the full often, so one of the periodic reports states: "He is apt to shoulder too much responsibility himself."

The Emergency Program for Congo-Zaire, 1962

As the Emergency Program for the Congo was Maurice's most direct concern as coordinator of the program at headquarters, it will be the first program touched upon. Continuing from 1961, at Christmas Maheu had sent a cable from the United Nations expressing success in his demands, and Maurice took for granted that the program for the Congo could go ahead. He therefore on January 10, 1962, cabled Terenzio that some funds were to be made available for most of the projects either through TA, Special Funds, or the regular program, such as the mission to be sent for adult education, a two-week mission sent for the development of mass communications, more experts for the reinforcement of the administrative structure of the Ministry of Education in the various sections in Léopoldville and the provinces, as well as inspectors for secondary education, professors for IPN and personnel for three mobile teams, specialists, one each for textbooks, primary teacher training, mass media, and home economics in conjunction with UNICEF. As for the recruitment of the four hundred teachers, this would be done by the Bureau of Personnel [PER] in consultation with BOC and Education. Recruitment was also going on for teachers for technical and normal schools. Other projects (on which Maurice must certainly have been working) were a program for adult education and a training school for training teachers for technical schools.

The assumption that Maheu's quick trip to the United Nations had cleared up the financial obstacles was short-lived. Sir A. MacFarquhar made more obstacles by sending to Terenzio a note for further information if funds were to be granted. It included the following: (a) requests for all the projects had to be accepted by the interministerial coordination committee (this did not exist); (b) the expenditures were to be written into the Congolese budget (this budget would not be decreed for some months); (c) the contracts for the experts should be only for three months; and (d) the program was to go from an emergency one to a normal one as soon as possible.

These conditions were a severe setback for the program. Terenzio had at first been optimistic and had written that the emergency program for opening the extra secondary school classes for five thousand pupils was going on "come hell come high water." He added that the minister had not shown up for days because of the political situation. In the provinces there had been imprisonments, which hampered the work of the experts. Moreover, because of the unsettled condition in Bakwanga, eight secondary school teachers could not be sent there.

In his letter of January 9, 1962, Terenzio added that the conditions demanded by MacFarquhar made the task of recruitment even more difficult. The UN officials in Léopoldville were as powerless as he was to change MacFarquhar's attitude. The experts were unhappy about the short-term contracts MacFarquhar had demanded, and to go on with the reforms a minimum of experts was necessary. Contracts had to be for at least six months. If the demands of MacFarquhar persisted, the situation would be so desperate that in order to keep the experts already there it would be necessary to take them off ONUC funds and put them on the TA program, withdrawing TA funds from other countries.[5]

He suggested to Maheu that he give instructions to Gagliotti at the United Nations in New York City to learn from the assistant secretary-general what the UN intentions were concerning recruitment and authorization of contracts for six months or a year: "If United Nations could not renew contracts for 6 months then it was up to UNESCO to do it if it did not want to see the Congo operation fail."[6]

On January 26, 1962, Maheu felt obliged to write directly to the secretary-general, U Thant (the letter drawn up by Maurice), stating that the United Nations and ONUC had to have confidence in the technical judgment of their specialized agencies. The concentrated and integrated efforts to come to the aid of a country could not be held up by the incomprehension of the program by the UN officials in New York.

Maheu stated that in spite of the conversations he had had in New York, funds were still blocked. He knew the difficulties that threatened the United Nations, but he had hoped for positive action after the conversations he had had with those immediately concerned yet after a month there was no confirmation. MacFarquhar had demanded acceptance by an interministerial committee that did not exist. UNESCO presumed that the minister of education had the authority of the government to act on its behalf. To question the authority would be tantamount to interfering in the internal affairs of the government. UNESCO had undertaken the work in the Congo at the request of U Thant's predecessor. Now an urgent decision was needed. If the United Nations could not guarantee finances, then UNESCO would find it difficult to carry out major responsibilities in the development of education in the Congo and the scope of its work would have to be reviewed by the Executive Board.[7]

On February 1, 1962, U Thant replied to this strong missive. He stated that the resources of the Congo Fund were not enough to cover all the projects. The Congolese government had to absorb operational personnel and other expenses. Since there were not enough funds, they (the United Nations and UNESCO) must resign themselves to ending direct provisions concerning teachers guaranteed by ONUC by June 1962. There was no objection to UNESCO serving as agent for the Congolese government, and as many teachers as the Congo budget could absorb could be hired. There was no objection to the projects, but the United Nations had to minimize the burden on the Congo Fund. He was anxious to have revised plans worked out so that they could be approved formally. MacFarquhar was not at variance with Maheu. There just were not enough funds.[8]

Finally, on April 1, 1962, a cable from the chief of UN operations in the Congo informed headquarters and the mission that the United Nations was ready to guarantee the salaries, etc., of the four hundred teachers to be recruited. It approved the six-month contracts for the experts and accepted a reduced number of in-service training mobile teams and urged that work had to be done with a minimum spent for the maximum benefit. This guarantee had taken four months while the program had had to go on.

The approval might have come about because MacFarquhar had been replaced by Amachree (an Indian), who on assuming his post had gone to the Congo to see for himself what the situation was. Terenzio, in a report to Maurice of March 7, 1962, stated that he had informed Amachree of the different projects and the difficulties with the United Nations that were partly responsible for some of the problems especially as to the secondary schools. Terenzio wrote: "It's a vicious circle. We need their guarantee yet must push ahead without it with what we have undertaken."

In the meantime, on February 23, 1962, the annual report was put together from Terenzio's reports with Maurice's additions in preparation for the director-general's report for the Executive Board's sixty-first meeting, to be held in April. The report noted that in spite of the insecurity in the provinces and the restricted budget, progress had been made and projects begun to be carried out because of the enthusiasm and devotion of the experts and collaboration of the government. The material and moral difficulties of the teachers, especially in the provinces, did not prevent them from doing as much as they could. However, better guarantees should be given to foreign teachers, sixty-six altogether from eleven countries, 50 of whom were in the provinces (despite the adverse press insisting that they were concentrated in the capital). These teachers were those hired directly by UNESCO. The other items have already been mentioned in the various reports.

Terenzio on March 5, 1962, suggested the creation of a special bureau to treat problems of the foreign teachers directly, as there were often delays in payment of salaries, indemnities, etc., due to strikes and the handling of different matters by bureaus scattered in the various ministries. He added that due to the disorganization of the administration at all levels, which seemed to have increased instead of lessened, with the experts paralleling administrative personnel to get things done, as of yet they had not succeeded in training counterparts to take on responsibilities. This bureau was shortly created and did ameliorate the services necessary to aid the foreign personnel.

From New York in late March came another request for clarification and justification for the various projects, by Gagliotti for the UN group for Congo affairs in New York. It was Maurice who answered this new demand in a strong report. Once more he stressed to Gagliotti for transmission to the UN officials that there was almost a complete lack of trained personnel at all levels in every educational field. In the central and provincial ministries there were only one Congolese university graduate, two with postsecondary diplomas, and not a single qualified secondary school teacher. There was a complete lack of inspectors and administrators. Out of thirty thousand primary school teachers, fewer than a third had training equivalent to four years postprimary. The most urgent need was to expand the secondary school system and at the same time assure continuation of existing schools. The number of high school graduates in this country of 14 million was 300. Also, curricula had to be adapted to the new conditions of the country. There was a great need for proper textbooks. School housing was inadequate. More experts were needed to support the work of the ministries and to help reorganize the school system. UNESCO experts were working on much-needed legislation governing employment and the status of teachers. He emphasized the opening of the added classes for 6,500 secondary school pupils, the presence of sixty-six UNESCO teachers, with the need for 400 more, the opening of IPN and its indispensable expansion, and the need for the in-service training mobile teams. He mentioned the coupon scheme and the aid for the scientific centers and alluded to the elaboration of long-term plans. (It is interesting how often the plans and projects had to be repeated to get hearing and action.)[8A] At times, United Nations inner politics obstructed the carrying out of the UNESCO program.

The projects that were secured were those mostly accepted in late 1960 or early 1961: the sixty-six teachers to be paid until June; the experts in the ministries, the IPN with eighteen UNESCO experts needed as professors and administrators, and specialists with the IPN expansion to 205 students; the training of administrators, which involved one expert and eighteen fellows; the training of inspectors for primary school supervision; the recruitment of five foreign inspectors; and the in-service training program with three mobile teams, this project in collaboration with UNICEF. These were all pioneering projects of unusual proportions for UNESCO-ONUC, given the shortness of time to organize them.

Maurice reassured Terenzio as concerned IPN. He wrote on April 24, 1962, that even if the Congo Fund dried up, IPN would be financed by the Special Fund. Terenzio had sent a cable to Amachree to urge him to approve the recruitment for 1962–63 of those secondary school teachers who were already there in order to keep them, as their contracts would be up in June.

At the sixty-first Executive Board meeting in April the director-general included the report made earlier, stating in addition that the secondary school classes had increased through the exceptional efforts of the UNESCO mission and the Congolese government, although in some schools standards were lower than in others due to lack of adequately trained teachers. The Congolese provincial and central ministries had organized a national conference in December 1961 of the higher echelons of those responsible for education, a first such meeting. The major lines of a policy of development and amelioration had emerged. At the same time, UNESCO experts gave the first results of their studies as to how best to aid the government to define its objectives and best adapt its action. However, the execution of certain projects demanded of UNESCO by the government had been delayed because of the uncertainties that reigned as to the availability of UN funds. He referred to the special urgent program for the secondary school pupils to diminish the enormous loss of potential human resources. The program depended on French-speaking secondary school teachers, of whom there was a worldwide scarcity, so that recruitment had to begin early and the posts made desirable enough to attract candidates. He spoke of the difficulties with the UN financial officials and the creation of the special service for foreign personnel.

He mentioned new projects: an institute for construction and public works and the request for a normal technical school, which was submitted in November 1961 to the Special Fund. A school of mines to train inspectors and engineering technicians was being considered. He remarked that the success of the courses held in Geneva for eighteen upper-echelon ministerial functionaries encouraged UNESCO to repeat a similar course in the winter of 1962–63. Funds had already been allocated by the United Nations.

A committee had been formed of government officials, Catholic and Protestant school representatives, and two UNESCO experts to evaluate the reforms inaugurated immediately after independence. The first drafts of the Fundamental Law of Education and the Statutes for Teachers were being examined in preparation for their reshaping once the texts of the constitution and the general statutes for all state employees had been adopted. Planning in education for development was being pursued in accordance with the 1961 Addis Ababa conference.

Maurice on April 27 worked out another statement as to how to handle finances if the United Nations was no longer able to furnish funds. He did this in view of the meeting on May 18 of the CAC (joint FAO and WHO Codex Alimentary Commission), to which Maheu would go and which would be attended by Amachree. In these observations, Maurice stated what financial conversion was necessary to keep the programs going in the Congo. He suggested creation of an economic and social development fund, which would save the Congo from having to compete with other countries for TA assistance, by transferring the institutions to the Special Fund and thus relieving the Congo Fund. This would give them more stability. International agencies could offer experts for short-term missions, it being understood that the present ONUC system would give way to another. The value of the creation of this fund would be facilitating the planning by international organizations of their activities and permitting gradual and orderly disengagement. It would also permit the common use of transport, commissary, and medical services and salary payments.[9]

The new communication was a cable of May 17, 1962, from Gagliotti in New York to Maurice. It read: "Present at meeting where cable was drafted for Khiary, which set forth . . . wish you to be assured UN will approve $1,500,000 for the 400 teachers, funds paid to UNESCO by United Nations rather than to the Congo Fund. Consequent contract change may increase to $3,500,000."[10]

Maurice had in late April passed on to Terenzio the needed total disbursement to that amount for the entire program. ONUC later gave the details to the control office. So, after all the months of uncertainty, of searching for other ways to go on with the program, the United Nations finally accepted the projects about which there had been such confusing stands taken on the part of the UN officials in New York.

In early June, Maurice was in Léopoldville for consultation and to make suggestions relating to the eight-week training course to be given at the university from August 6 to September 29 for intermediate cadres of the education administration. Courses on planning, administration, revision of program, problems of teaching languages, and general subjects on Africa and economic and social development were to be offered. Conferences were planned on public hygiene and development of agriculture. The trainees, forty in all, would come from thirteen different countries. The usual problems of selection, transport, and agreements with the governments arose.

The trip to the Congo was only one of a series Maurice undertook from May to October 1962. He was in and out of the office. He first went to Accra on May 22, 1962, to investigate problems at the regional center that had been created under the Emergency Program for Africa. Then he went on to Léopoldville. From there he visited the Regional Training Center in Kampala, Uganda, and the Polytechnical Institute in Nairobi, Kenya, which was part of the regional center. He returned to Paris on June 17, to leave on June 30 for the conference in Tananarive, Madagascar, on the adaptation of secondary school curricula July 2–13, for which he and several of his staff were responsible and at which he represented the director-general. After a few days of leave of absence, Maurice was off again on August 31 for Tananarive to attend the meeting on the future of higher education in Africa, which was prepared by the Higher Education Division but in which he was involved because of the IPNs that were being created throughout Africa by the African Division. On his return, he stopped off in Khartoum, Sudan, to visit the Regional Center for School Construction already in operation.

Maurice submitted a report on June 16, 1962, to Maheu in which he discussed the problem of IPN in Léopoldville. The Congolese director appeared on the defensive. He suggested that a grant be obtained for him to study abroad. He also noticed the lack of real teamwork among the group of expert professors. They had little contact with the students or each other, giving their courses and hurrying away. (It is doubtful whether Maheu appreciated these observations, as the professors' behavior was the same as that current in France.) Maurice added that the mission worked with devotion and zeal. It was preoccupied with the recruitment of the four hundred secondary school teachers.

While he was still at headquarters in late June, Maurice wrote to Terenzio concerning the financing of the projected 1963 program, what UNESCO could do, and the conditions of the Special Fund. On July 9, Terenzio sent in the revised 1963 program. He also informed headquarters that experts had joined the Congolese to recruit teachers abroad with a mission to Rome, Damascus, and Beirut and another to Madrid and Warsaw. Governments were appealed to. He announced that ONUC had accepted the employment of an expert to process the candidates in Léopoldville thus relieving headquarters of the task. He went on to state that most of the teachers already there had signed up for a second year. The committee on secondary school reform was progressing.

A committee for primary school reform had met June 26–July 3. Its aim was the unification of the various programs and diverse structures, with the obligation of six years' schooling, free for all, limits as to age and entry and exit, and the adoption of the French language as the vehicle of teaching. The documents produced were sent to headquarters.

The mission in the Congo was very active. The Fundamental Law of Education was being revised. The first year of IPN was coming to a successful close in spite of several crises. It seemed that there were 1,000 candidates for the fall entry. As the problem of school construction was acute, Terenzio consulted with the education minister concerning prefabricated schoolrooms with the result that financial credit was accorded for them. Thus more classes could be opened.

The African Division was informed of a new complication in the Congo. On August 21, 1962, the five provinces were split up to form twenty. The reason that this was done was not clear. It may have been either to please various tribal leaders or to weaken the power of certain possible rivals of Mobutu. What the measure did do was make it much harder for UNESCO. There were not enough experts. This measure increased the workload and travel time of those attached to the provincial ministries.

The full impact of this development was communicated by Terenzio in a report at the end of September: "The move has engendered a second Congolese chaos less spectacular than the first but more profound, the national patrimony scattered, administrations destroyed, files have disappeared."[11] Gardiner, who had replaced Sture Linner as chief executive officer of ONUC, suggested that UNESCO take fifteen of the best foreign secondary school teachers and place them in the new provincial ministries (perhaps with the five earlier experts acting as guides and advisers). This was done, with funds obtained from ONUC by the central ministry of education.

Amachree had gone to the Congo in August and finally had approved the UNESCO program for 1962–63. Terenzio elaborated on this in his report. Approval for 110 experts and 500 teachers, at the cost of $4,598,000, had been given. Of the 1,400 secondary school teacher candidates, 400 had been selected and 300 were already at their posts, but because of the extent of the territory and the difficulty of communications and transport (with not enough planes, because due to the "political events many had been requisitioned"), it had been a problem to get the teachers to their posts, but the schools had opened without major incidents. IPN was operating almost normally, but due to bureaucratic obstructions, the dishonesty of some, the wilful damage by others, and the lack of materials, the School of Mines would only open in November. The School of Construction and Public

238

Works created by the United Nations with the help of UNESCO experts was placed in the UNESCO program. Two mobile teams were composed, and one was working in Kivu, the other in Oriental Province. The mission began a course of four months for the Information Services. He added, finally, that the food situation for foreign teachers was disastrous outside of those of the United Nations and UNESCO. He urged that all foreign personnel have access to the UN commissary in Léopoldville.

Adiseshiah made a trip to the Congo in early September. In a confidential note to the director-general September 20, 1962, Adiseshiah praised Terenzio for his leadership and Najman and all the experts for their fine work. Adiseshiah felt the UNESCO mission was doing an excellent job. In his opinion, in spite of the moment-to-moment crises (at this time Tschombé in Katanga had started a plan to undermine the UN secretary-general's efforts to bring Katanga back into the fold), this vast and delicate operation, the biggest ever undertaken by UNESCO, was going as well as it possibly could under the circumstances. He added: "This is not technical assistance, it is so massive, it is like running a country. The Congo has made United Nations a reality . . ." It was almost a

trusteeship and it was a challenge not to go beyond the limits of the aims and purposes of the UN and UNESCO. The very scale of the operation exposed UNESCO to a systematic campaign of vilification by a small but powerful reactionary group. But it was important that the UNESCO program go on. The Congo had to have continued financial help from the regular budget, Technical Assistance, Special Fund and USAID. All the new schools of higher training needed long-term planning and advice. Bergeaud of the African Division was needed for IPN and the Special Fund program. He thought that the Prime Minister Adoula was first class, and N'Galula, the Education Minister, a strong man who knew his mind. But there would be a problem in turning over the responsibilities the UNESCO experts had taken on to the Congolese as the latter appeared reluctant to assume them.

Later Adiseshiah wrote to Terenzio from New York, where Adiseshiah was having discussions with the officials dealing with the Congo: "Really I have not seen anything like the mess there is on the Congo. I am surprised we have operations going on smoothly in the field."[12]

At the same time, he also wrote to Gardiner: "I have been trying to get some order out of the confusion here in New York concerning EPTA." Adiseshiah also wrote to Ahmed, who was to take Gardiner's former position: "You and Khiary have one view, Amachree here another. The Bureau of Finance still another."

Someone had suggested that a program as had been carried out in the Andes be applied to the Congo. It was far from encouraging there, and as Terenzio pointed out, the conditions in the Congo were quite different, with a vast country, very poor transportation and communications, insecurity, difficult living conditions, and no rural local leaders, so it could not be applied. The possible project was suggested by the deputy director-general of ILO, Abbas Ammer, in a letter to Maheu on September 21, which Maheu sent on to Maurice. (In parentheses was a note urging Maurice to take action concerning the implementation in the field of integration of a program for rural communication in the Congo.) The letter stated: "Please send an exploratory mission to assess the nature of the problem and establish appropriate contacts." The ILO deputy director-general was going to the Congo, and the UNESCO chief of mission should receive instructions to be available for on-the-spot consultation. On the deputy director-general's return there would be interagency consultations. The instructions were sent by Maurice to Terenzio. Already in June the Congolese minister of labor had sent a request to ILO for aid to the rural regions, as there was serious economic degradation. (Evidently the ILO people thought it a good idea to collaborate on this project with UNESCO and as Maurice was the coordinator for the Congo program, the request was sent to him.)

Late in December, Maheu, now elected to the post of director-general by the General Conference, sent a note around stating that the project was chimerical and visionary considering the actual state of the Congo. After six years, even the Andean project was not successful. In the Congo, conditions were much worse. For the time being, at least, this project of rural integration got no further at UNESCO. Adiseshiah also thought that it was not the time to launch another major project. Although there is no evidence as to what Maurice thought, it is almost certain that he would have been very cautious about such an undertaking in such circumstances.

Maurice informed Terenzio on October 6, 1962, that it had been decided not to present a special report on the Congo for the General Conference, but he would prepare a short paper for the director-general for his oral reports. He needed explanations of certain items in Terenzio's report as to the number of grant holders. Were there 300, of whom fifteen were abroad? He had no report on the 110 grants given to train or further train inspectors for primary schools. Had UNICEF given $90,000 for vehicles and materials plus $104,000 for the mobile teams? How much did ONUC give? Did USAID give $130,000 or not? He needed a list of the experts listing nationality, position and the area to which each was sent.

The director-general made the oral report on the Emergency Program in the Congo as part of his report on the UNESCO activities in Africa, as he did for Asia and the Arab states rather than as he had done in 1960, when the problems were acute and needed urgent action, which he had described in detail. However, he mentioned what UNESCO continued to do for primary and secondary education especially in the solution of certain problems such as: the adaptation of curricula, the training of teachers, the struggle for adequate school facilities, the preparation for and the training of supervisory and administrative staff, and the joint FAO/ILO project for the creation of a polytechnical and vocational school for trade, industry, and agriculture. It was felt that education in agriculture should be an integral part of the national school system. UNESCO would do the necessary research and surveys.

As Adiseshiah had stated, there was crisis after crisis. Terenzio informed headquarters that the minister of education had resigned and there had been no minister since the middle of September. The minister of the interior had taken on the job but could not give his time to it, so it was practically impossible to make decisions. Even the prime minister was inaccessible. The success of the UNESCO program depended on the stability of the government, and at the moment the program was jeopardized. The finalizing of the Fundamental Law of Education was suspended, as there was no minister and the expert who had worked on it was gone. Terenzio went on to state that he had gone to Luluabourg, Kasai, and Bakwanga to take in the situation of the hundreds of teachers. (It had been a problem to find lodgings, etc., and administer to such a large number.) Most of the teachers were satisfied, as were the experts, who were doing good work on secondary school programs, introducing such subjects as African sociology, philosophy, an introduction to art, and political economy, among other subjects. What did strike him was the violent tribalism in Kasai. He felt it was no time to set up a technical normal school there in view of the instability.

The system of UNESCO coupons was also doing well. The volume of sales had reached $4 million. It was decided that a special bureau and depot be set up to handle the volume of orders and distribution of purchases. An expert for this was assigned as well as secretarial help.

Before I leave this chapter on the Congo, a few reports from experts in the field should be mentioned. It was too early at the end of 1961 to give a report on the efforts of the experts in the provinces, except for those of L. Bourand in Luluabourg. By 1962, reports came in from several. Moreover, as Maurice had done, Terenzio made trips to the interior of the country, usually because problems needed to be solved as to housing, transportation, and altercations. Only a few of the reports are found in the UNESCO Archives. In reading them several observations crop up frequently, concerning insecurity, the Congolese counterparts, and working conditions.

One of the experts reported "to enter the province of Kivu was a heroic act, to get out, an act of prowess." There was pillage, imprisonment, fires, raids, curfews.[13] Another wrote that it was fratricide, thousands killed by insurgents among them numerous intellectuals. Everywhere the rebels passed, either in towns, villages, or the countryside, they left only ruin and devastation. Loss to the Congo was some 25 billion Congo francs. Whereas before independence, the Congo was an exporter of cotton, rice, and maize, in the 1960s these were imported.

As for the counterparts, which the experts were trying to train:

Many have no sense of discipline, nor professional conscience, and the technical level is often inadequate to profit from the training. They let themselves be discouraged by the least difficulty. The simplest remark on an error can degenerate into tension, distrust, or violent conflict not propitious for work. There are traps at each step so that a person risks to become the victim of his good intentions. In one course in which there were 12 participants, there were 25 changes of personnel before it was over. Only two finished the course.

The expert thought this was a waste of TA funds, and he wondered if he had wasted his time. However, he persevered. Another also stated that the frequent changes in personnel and the general low level of training had by the Congolese functionaries delayed the training or even prevented it.[14]

As to the working conditions, one expert on school programs who traveled about in the interior had this to write: "The bad roads, the scarcity of transport, the lack of any hotel accommodations make it difficult to do the work."[15] However, the expert could act as a liaison officer between the central and provincial governments, as communication was uncertain and often the latter were not aware of the new laws and reforms. Moreover, they mistrusted the central government. There were not enough school materials, such as blackboards, etc., furniture was elementary and for the most part dilapidated, and there were no tools and no apparatuses in the technical schools. The teachers were underprepared and had caused disorder through strikes and protestations. There were not enough buildings.

In spite of such drawbacks, the experts did try very hard in most cases to carry out their assignments. Bourand in Luluabourg was especially assiduous. Bourand helped the minister in every way. He set up the first statistical bureau and introduced planning. Out of desperation, after interminable proceedings, he set up a housing service and through Terenzio obtained transportation. He worked out the budget. He carried out inspection trips to encourage, advise, and suggest. With his staff, he organized the seminars. Over and over, he tried to prepare nationals to take over the responsibilities.

The expert in school programs admitted he fought resistance to change through persuasion and information, but that the elaboration and revision of programs were difficult. He hoped to simplify the history being taught, but so much was needed in terms of production of texts and manuals, diverse publications, pedagogical documents for the use of both teachers and administrators, and libraries. He felt that the modernization of the program suggested by UNESCO was valid, but given the difficulties, he wondered if it could be done.

Recognition should be given to those in the field such as the experts and the secondary school teachers for their devotion and courage in working against such odds. Terenzio estimated that apart from a few, not more than 10 percent were found incompetent or unworthy of the trust put in them: "Many did more than their jobs called for, and carried out their assignments in spite of all sorts of obstacles." It is certain that some of what they tried to do disappeared after their departure, but no one can criticize their attempts to improve and better what they found. There were not enough of them in the first place, but despite the disorganization of the public services, the fact remains that they kept these afloat and were a stabilizing influence in those troubled times.

243

The Emergency Program for Africa, 1962

Although less spectacular than the Emergency Program for the Congo, some other activities of the African Division were as important in the long term. They took a great deal of deskwork, especially in calculations, allocation of funds, and recruitment of personnel.

The planning missions, the setting up of regional centers and training schools, all recently innovated undertakings in Africa, and the continuing selection and dispatching of experts and secondary school teachers through OPEX and EPTA to the different countries of tropical Africa were vital to the expansion and reorientation of education for economic and social development. Not to be forgotten are the three meetings for African education organized by UNESCO, which influenced or reflected the work being done in the division.

The biggest and most important conference was the one held at UNESCO March 26–30 for ministers of education of Africa. It was organized for the most part by the Division of Comparative Education and presided over by the deputy director-general, Adiseshiah. The second was the meeting in Tananarive of experts on the adaptation of curricula for secondary schools in Africa. The third was held in the same capital under the auspices of the Division of Higher Education and dealt with the future of higher education in Africa, with Adiseshiah the guiding light representing the deputy-general.

At the meeting of the ministers of education at headquarters March 26–30, three problems were to be examined: first, the problem of national plans for the development of education in the framework of social and economic development to aid in modernization; second, what to do in 1963 concerning financing and the arrangement of the mechanisms and procedures for greatest efficiency; third, establishment of the mechanisms and procedures to follow the execution of the program.

Letters by Maheu to the various ministries and administering authorities of dependent peoples were sent starting October 20, 1961, requesting the educational plans. When answers were slow in coming in, the chiefs of mission and experts were called upon to contact the ministers to accelerate the replies. By November 16, 1961, Maheu sent invitations to the ministers.

The first meeting opened with the inaugural speech given by A. Dourmond-Hammond, minister of education of Ghana. Maurice called him to prepare a speech. In making the speech he thanked UNESCO for all it had done. He said that the Addis Ababa conference of 1961 was already obsolete, as the countries were looking forward to next steps and there was an urgency, a pressing need to telescope in a few years what had taken ages to achieve elsewhere. He hoped there would be open exchange of information on failures and successes: "This conference would advance our work."[16]

Dourmond-Hammond, a day or two later, made another speech. He wanted it known that he was for Pan-Africa and would vote to include Morocco, Tunisia, the United Arab Republic, and Libya as full-fledged members of the conference but would refuse to give his vote for the four colonial powers present: the United Kingdom, France, Belgium, and Spain: "It should be the Africans, still dependent, who should be admitted to see how far their free brothers have advanced," he declared.

Thirty-one of the thirty-four ministers invited came. This was a work meeting, with no long speeches except to open and close the gathering. Adiseshiah made the final speech, one of his simplest and most direct. He stated:

This meeting was for you. You paid your travel [expenses] and stayed at your own expense . . . This will go down in the annals of UNESCO history.

You examined each other's plans and internal financial arrangements in a spirit of cooperation . . . the sole purpose being to advance your social and economic development. You have set a pioneering example. The program for the next two years is to speed up educational development quantitatively as well as qualitatively . . . using self help if you can.

He summed up:

(a) take steps to increase national investment; (b) establish firm education planning machinery with the help of UNESCO; (c) begin teacher-training, in-service training and the establishment of teacher-training institutions; these are priorities; (d) accelerate secondary education in all its aspects; (e) renew efforts for rural and adult education; (f) make this meeting a permanent and continuing organism.

The second conference concerning the adaptation of curricula was the responsibility of the African Division. It was a small meeting, as it dealt with only one aspect of the many problems confronting African educators. Maurice was still in the Congo when it was first broached. It took most of the fall of 1961 to decide that only secondary school curricula would be considered. The title, Adaptation of Secondary School Curriculum to Meet African Needs, was approved by the juridical office in January 1962. It was to be a workshop, with mostly experts in curricula attending. Bartels made the first draft of the aspects to be discussed. Among them were the origins of African curriculum, attempts to modify and revise them, principles and mechanisms of curricula revision using documents produced in 1958 for the International Advisory Committee, present possibilities, and coordination of experience and evaluation through collaboration among the African states.

Although the government of Madagascar agreed to be the host country, the accord was not signed immediately due to various delays by the government, one of which was a national budget deficit. Headquarters was so concerned that it begged Pauvert, the UNESCO chief expert in Tananarive, to make every effort to have the proper officials sign the required documents. It was not until June, with the seminar but a few weeks away, that UNESCO received the signed agreement.

Documentation had been solicited of the member states concerning the nature of the secondary school curricula, what if any efforts had been made to adapt or revise the program, etc. The first documents arrived in February 1962 from Accra, Ghana (English), and Fort-Lamy, Chad (French). It is interesting to note that in looking over the program from a French-oriented country, out of forty-two lessons on history in a year, thirty-nine were devoted to French history, much the same for geography. Nothing in the program indicated lessons in health, hygiene, home economics, or physical education as in the English program.

The agenda, finally accepted, was sent May 5, 1962. The purpose of the meeting was defined. Its title was "The Aims of Revision," designed to satisfy the aspirations of the African peoples to meet the requirements for (a) the physical, intellectual, emotional, and moral development of the African child and adolescent; (b) the economic and social development of African countries; and (c) education for international understanding and peaceful cooperation.

The date selected for the opening, July 2, 1962, was that demanded by the president of Madagascar. It was vacation time, a good time for experts to travel, but precluded demonstration classes or visits to schools. Maurice left Paris on June 30, accompanied by Bartels and Mrs. Richardson. Pauvert, the expert on mission in Madagascar, was designated as general secretary. Forty-five experts from twenty-nine countries attended. Experts from two countries had to refuse only because African transcontinental travel was too difficult. An interesting side note was the demand by the Madagascar Secret Service (which had been told that the meeting had been organized by the Communist party of Prague) of the French security services to send a list of all those attending the seminar. This service passed on the request to the African Division of UNESCO with the notation "secret, confidential, urgent 28/6/62." It is presumed that the Madagascar Secret Service was satisfied, as the meeting was permitted to proceed.[17]

Mr. Botekeky, the Madagascar minister of education, welcomed the group. Maurice then took the podium and, in the name of the director-general of UNESCO, thanked the president, the government, and Mr. Botekeky for hosting the seminar. Maurice went on to enlarge upon the reasons for the gathering, the first of its kind in Africa, and the readiness of UNESCO to put its resources and experience to aiding the countries in studying their problems and helping them to work out solutions. He stressed the principle of UNESCO that the question of curriculum and program was the prerogative and decision of each government. He insisted that it was appropriate that the seminar be devoted to the secondary school, since it was at this level that the most urgent needs were evident. Moreover, it was a follow-up of one of the resolutions of the 1961 Addis Ababa conference. In ending the speech, he said that the meeting would attain its aim if it produced a wide exchange of views, if it opened up avenues for future action and decided on the means and instruments for this, which, in order to succeed, should eventually involve regional, national, and international collaboration.[18]

After the work of small committees, the groups, and the plenary sessions, three resolutions were adopted. First, after considering previous statements on curriculum revision, including that of the International Advisory Committee, it set down its own views of the objectives of secondary education for Africa. It recommended the application of general principles of reform of curricula to specific areas of study: mathematics, science, geography, and history. It also expressed the need to give greater status and financial remuneration to the teaching profession. It desired to constitute a committee of seven experts with UNESCO backing with a number of responsibilities: collaboration with regional documentation centers, collection and distribution of reports on revision, organization of meetings at various levels, and advising on curriculum reform, etc.

What came out of the gathering of experts was the desire to reform the curriculum to reflect the African point of view, the African approach, as most of the curricula were European-oriented, transferred or imposed with adaptations, if any, considered insufficient. The group did concede that once an African child had learned about his own heritage, culture, and environment, he could go on to learn about those of others. But it was most essential to reinforce African identity and African unity. Outdated and obsolete material needed to be discarded to lighten the program to include subjects of vital importance to Africans, with insistence on languages and studies to meet present needs. In other words, reforms were necessary to bring about the Africanization of the programs so as to build in the African child a new and worthy self-image. Maurice must have been greatly in accord with these aspirations, as this was what he had been working toward when he was minister of education in Haiti—an autonomous, independent culture, built on the recognition of new needs.

Maurice in a confidential note to the director-general on August 31, 1962, had the following to say about the seminar:

Despite problems and lack of efficient general services, the work of the seminar unfolded satisfactorily although the atmosphere of some of the debates was at times not of the highest quality. The intellectual and pedagogical levels of the participants were not the same. Besides most of the English speaking had little idea of the French-oriented system of education. The same could be said for the French speaking for the English system. This made for some problems in semantics. The French oriented had a central system. The English oriented did not. However, most of the participants were in accord that the programs needed adaptations. They also stressed the need for the training of teachers. Sometimes the debates tended to go beyond their purpose and had to be brought back to order. One of the positive results, and not the least, was the opportunity for the exchange of views. Most of the participants came out of the gathering with clearer ideas about the problems posed by curriculum revision. Together they elaborated and adopted a definition of the objectives of secondary education in Africa,

248

and proposed to set up a committee of experts to promote regional cooperation to stimulate and support action on the aims suggested.[19]

It was not until January 1963 that the report was published and sent by the African Division to educators of interested countries, with requests for comments and appreciation. Some felt that a meeting of this sort was valuable and suggested follow-up workshops and the integration of new subjects so as to aid local staff in revision. Ghana, however, felt it already was taking all the proposed measures and expressed the sentiment that Africanization could go too far. One official stated that it had to be kept in mind that whatever was undertaken by UNESCO could be lost once UNESCO withdrew. This intimated that projects had to be modest enough to permit them to be carried on after UNESCO's withdrawal.

Maurice was already at the second meeting in Tananarive when he wrote to Bartels to prepare a letter concerning the seminar and the proposal for the establishment of an African committee of experts (later there were several exchanges of point of view as to whether the experts should all be African) to inform the African member states that the acting director-general intended to submit the proposal to the General Conference in presenting the budget for 1963–64. He had already received the approval of the Executive Board in August, for which body a shortened report had been drawn up, as for the General Conference.[20]

The committee of seven, later changed to eight members, would be entirely African. The Executive Board and the General Conference accepted the constitution of this committee. Now the problems appeared. Who should be chosen as members? How often and when should they meet? What attributes and statutes should the committee have? For how many years should it meet? Maurice explored the problems of geographical distribution and the number of English speaking and French speaking, as well as specialties. Should they all come from tropical Africa, or should North Africa be represented?

Maurice sent two circulars around the department to collect names of possible candidates. He also sent personal notes on the whole topic. It was only in April 1963 that an alphabetical list was made up with country, language, discipline, and specialty noted for each candidate. In May the list was sent to the head of the department, to the Bureau of Member States, and to the legal section, the last two for help in formulating the invitation to the possible member to be sent through proper government channels. It was finally in January 1964 that the committee was constituted, by which time Maurice had taken up his duties in Dakar. It was Bartels, as chief of the division, who carried on. The committee did meet in December 1964 and again in June 1965 in the Accra Regional Center. In 1966, as the Accra center could not receive it, the meeting was postponed until 1967. It was an ad hoc committee and, as no budget was provided for it, ended without having accomplished much more than formulating its statutes. Had Maurice remained at headquarters to direct and encourage the project, perhaps more would have come of it.

The third meeting held September 3–12, 1962, which concerned Maurice and some of his staff, was titled "The Future of Higher Education in Africa."[21] It was organized by the Division of Higher Education. Maurice's presence was due to the setting up of IPNs and teacher training schools in several countries of tropical Africa.

Many of the thirty-one universities in Africa had only recently been established, most with a European outlook and basis, and courses in European thought. It was time to orient them toward Africa, African needs, and African thought. The meeting held in Tananarive was opened by the vice president of Madagascar. Adiseshiah represented the director-general. Botekeky chaired again. The three problems examined were: the urgent need for the Africanization of the universities and need for personnel; the problem of finances; and, finally, the adaptation of the program for present needs. The conference recommended that the task of the universities was to dispense education and advance knowledge of Africa through research in respect to norms of universities elsewhere, create conditions for the unification of Africa, encourage the study of African culture and patrimony, and redress the deformed image of Africa and Africans.

The ninety-seven articles in the recommendations reflected those that came out of the other meetings, conferences, and seminars. Among them were the need for planning, maximum use of space, better salaries and status for the teaching profession, foreign personnel until enough nationals were formed, reduction of expenditure by giving courses at night and/or by correspondence, and the making of universities more accessible without lowering standards. Adaptation of program content and methods at all levels were of the first necessity. The important thing was to start in the right direction with aid and self-help. Hope was given, as was inspiration, at all these conferences, the largest of which, at the highest echelon and with the greatest impact, was the one held at headquarters in March of that year. Financial needs and sources for funds were included.

The Planning Missions, 1962

Another recent activity for which the African Division was responsible was the sending of planning missions. Maurice as head of the division was involved with the planning missions giving advice, suggestions, and encouragement, but it was Ochs who carried on, turning to Maurice when questions or problems arose that needed higher authority. It was difficult to find experts and specialists for short missions. They could be found during summer holidays, but at that time the schools were closed and administrative services not fully staffed, so information was hard to obtain as well as contacts. Moreover, there was political pressure from delegations to UNESCO and upper-echelon functionaries who had candidates for missions. Ochs felt that the missions should be international rather than from one country or one university. Maurice, although in accord in theory, was still of the opinion that "the choice of experts went beyond background and experience. The characteristics of educational statesmanship, the ability to apply judiciously past experience in a new situation were needed. These were far more important qualities than nationality, cultural background or personal opinion."[22]

A Dutch team was selected for Somalia, an Australian group for the Cameroons, and an Indian team (Adiseshiah's recommendation) for Liberia. The result of the mission to Somalia was the creation of a planning service, with one of the team returning for a year to prepare a document to be used as the basis for an educational plan. A second mission would be sent in 1963. A special mission for adult and technical education was sent to Upper Volta. For Tanganyika, a team from Great Britain had been recruited. Preparations were under way to send the Indian team to Liberia, including experts in comparative education, statistics, finance, and teacher education. For Madagascar, a set of experts was being recruited for textbook production, statistics, and economy. For the Ivory Coast, experts were needed for comparative education, youth problems, agriculture, and economics. For Rwanda and Burundi, a technical planning group for development under the Emergency Program was being sought. The preparation and dispatching of the various teams and their reports and assessments as to further developments took time and effort for their success. In 1961 and early 1962, the missions to Sierra Leone and Upper Volta had been sent. Now during 1962, six more could be reported as being prepared for or already in the field, each with some similar areas of investigation as requests for specific needs were made by member states.

Ochs as well as Maurice was concerned with the UNESCO image. Over and over again its political neutrality had to be expressed. It was international and objective, a civil service without political views or political pressure. The experts had to conduct themselves in a way to give this image. They needed to be diplomatic in their behavior and in exposing their recommendations to the governments. Reports had to be concise and objective, in good English or French, without political overtones or judgments. It was difficult to find the right kind of expert. At times the experts did not live up to their curriculae vitae or references. Sometimes the difficulties came from the situation in the countries to which they were sent. At all events, this development of sending planning missions to aid in the reorganization of school systems was needed. It was estimated that only half the missions were successful. This did not discourage Maurice or Ochs from going on, revising methods, recommending conduct, and trying to find better men and ways to be of greater service.

The Regional Centers and the Creation of GRPE (Groupe Regional pour la Planification en Education, Regional Group for Educational Planning)

Another way of coming to the aid of the countries needing help was the regional centers. It was from ECOSOC that came the first impetus for the creation of regional centers in tropical Africa. There were such already established, one in Havana for the Latin American Major Project, one in Beirut for the Arab states, and one in Karachi for Asia. For Africa, the centers, each with a different purpose, were created to extend the aid ECA and UNESCO could give to developing countries in specific matters. Suggestions that propositions be formulated for a mechanism to disseminate and receive information on these matters within the framework of UNESCO were made. In the resolutions, school construction, textbook production, teacher training, and planning were mentioned to designate the purpose of each.

In the spring session of 1962, the director-general reported to the Executive Board that the Regional Center in Accra, Ghana, for educational documentation, research on textbook production, teaching aids, studies on the language of instruction, and workshops on textbook layout and printing, as well as workshops for authors of textbooks, had been opened in January 1962. Forty grants had been given for training courses in educational planning, administration, and supervision. In Kampala, Uganda, a training center created at the same time had as its first project a training course for twenty-nine instructors for primary teacher training schools. These two centers were for English-speaking persons.[23]

For French-speaking countries, thirty-seven grants had been given for the training center begun in Bangui, Central Africa, for the training of secondary school teachers. In November 1961, a center had been set up in Yaoundé, Cameroon, for textbook production in French and later perhaps in English. The one in Khartoum, Sudan, was being put together for school construction, study of plans, giving out of information, and later having courses for school constructors. A center for Abidjan was being studied. Other similar institutions were foreseen for Brazzaville, Bamako, Lagos, Zazin (Nigeria), and Dakar. There was a polytechnical institute in Nairobi.

Some of the centers rendered real service and expanded with increased expressed needs: one or two of the centers, due to certain circumstances, ineffectual leadership, or too hurried or too ambitious a program, did not.

One that did not succeed was the center in Accra. Problems of various kinds cropped up as early as May 1962. Maurice was sent there on a special mission and made a lengthy report. He went at the request of Adiseshiah. There is an inter-office note from him dated May 30, 1962, to Maheu, stating: "It is necessary to establish clear-cut lines of authority in the Education department under which this center must function under Dartigue as the Asian Center under Eagleton. We should give Dartigue the means of exercising his authority."[24]

On July 10, 1962, Adiseshiah wrote another note to Maheu, probably having read Maurice's report: "The Accra Center needs your review. Dartigue was back 18/6. I sent you the papers. Can you conduct it with him, PER and BMS on 19 or 20/7. It is in a bad situation."[25]

In the report, Maurice revealed that part of the problem was that at its creation the authority for the center had been divided at headquarters between the African Division and the Clearing House due to the reorganization by Maheu of the Education Department to institute the operational division of which Maurice was chief. The director of the center had been informed to get in touch with him. This did not clarify the demarcation of the attributes of the new division concerning the center and the Clearing House, which controlled the technical and administrative aspects of the center. Maurice was simply informed in a collective note of certain decisions taken without his being consulted. The confusion of authority at headquarters reflected on the Accra Regional Center.

Maurice learned in his on-the-spot investigation that there was confusion as to the responsibilities of the director and the executive officer. The direction appeared to be two-headed. This caused friction and misunderstanding. Moreover, there was not enough exchange between the specialists working at the center. Each wished to be his own boss and submit to no higher authority. In his report, Maurice's conclusion was that it was important for the director to know whom to deal with at headquarters. The question of authority and general responsibility was too vague to make for productive activity.

As to the program, the installation of the center had had delays that retarded the execution of the program. The director had written to governments for their acceptance of staff for visits to be made for various studies. No answers had as yet been received. Twenty-two studies had been proposed in PADS; only ten had been done. The documentarian had visited three countries out of fourteen for documents decided upon, but as of yet had submitted no reports even on the three visited. The projected ten-day course for textbook writers had not taken place. From what he observed, Maurice remarked that no method as to how to approach the problems had been thought through. There had been trial and error and improvisation. One expert said that preparations had been too hurried and courses premature. Not enough time had been taken to appraise the situation or study the problems in the passage from dependence to independence that put education into a transitional state. Courses at this time could not reflect the new curriculum or consider new syllabi. It would be preferable to have a workshop of government functionaries to decide on these. There was a need to know what the IPNs were doing so as not to duplicate their work.

Among the conclusions Maurice made was that although the accords generally defined responsibilities, these could only be taken on progressively by sufficient and qualified personnel who could decide just how to work out a program. Given the situation, the center must limit its activities to what it could do with a limited staff and materials. He suggested responsibilities for the director, with a certain autonomy permitted to the chief of each section. There should be effective control of the execution of the program and the application of administrative rules and adherence to budget. Authority needed to be flexible, with the director acting as coordinator and keeper of harmony among the staff. Maurice recommended that the center have two sections, one in program and texts with language studies as part of it, the other a documentation center (inferring that the section on operations could be connected with the African Division and the documentation center with the Clearing House). He then discussed the type of personnel needed for these. At the same time, he indicated that it was important that at headquarters the African Division know its own attributes if it was to give effective aid to the center.

Whether the meeting with Maheu took place and/or clear demarcations were made both for the center and for the African Division is not known. What is known is that Bartels visited the center in 1963 and wrote a negative report, that the chief executive officer resigned in 1966, and that the center floundered until 1967, when it was finally closed.

A real success was to be the center in Dakar started by Maurice in the autumn of 1963 as the GRPE, which later became BREDA.[26] It was projected in 1962 for planning in education under the auspices of ECA and UNESCO. A center was first decided upon by ECA as an Institute for Economic Development and Planning (IDEP). To this institute UNESCO thought a unit for planning in education should be attached, education being an integral part of social and economic development. It was argued that the institute would not be complete without this unit. Its purpose would be to promote instruction and research in educational planning. Maurice and staff at headquarters worked out the resolution for presentation by Senegal to the General Conference. Reference was made to its creation in a long report dated June 5, 1962. The division worked out how this group, to be called GRPE, would be of service. It would have three major functions: (1) training of planners; (2) research; and (3) an advisory service. A plan was produced by the division as to how the group could collaborate, what courses it could give, the number of students, the costs, and relations between it and the Accra center. The General Conference approved the initiatives taken. The project was elaborated by the division and submitted to the Special Fund in December 1962 for financing. The institute was to begin operations in January 1963 with the director and a staff of four professionals. It was hoped that by its fifth year it would have a staff of twenty-five.[27] It began in October 1963 with a staff of one: Maurice.

At the same time, a project sponsored by Maheu and Adiseshiah was proposed. This was to set up an international institute for educational planning in Paris. One hundred thousand dollars was taken from the UNESCO regular budget for this purpose. A consultative committee was formed. A resolution put together by the African Division was presented. The importance of planning was discussed at the United Nations in New York, with the acceptance of such an institute in Paris. The Executive Board proposed it officially in August 1962. A committee sponsored by UNESCO, composed of education planners and delegates of several countries, and the International Bank of Reconstruction and Development (BIRD) met in Paris in June 1962 to define the purpose of the institute and decide upon its organization and its bylaws. Its purpose: to promote instruction and research on educational planning in relation to economic and social development. Its broad objectives were to advance knowledge, provide courses, and assist regional centers such as GRPE and IDEP. It would be multidisciplinary, for educational planners, planners in other areas of endeavor, top-level government officials, and experts who wished to concentrate on educational planning. It would have an interdisciplinary faculty. It would explore new ways of thinking and new practical tools for educational planning to promote economic and social development. It would conduct investigations in the economics of education, educational planning techniques, technology of education, and comparative education. It would do research in human resources and send out missions. It is through Adiseshiah's interoffice notes that references to this new UNESCO/ECA venture are exposed with instructions concerning the resolutions.

The creation of these two institutions shows the kind of pioneering being done at that time by UNESCO. It also brings out the work done by the African Division without fanfare in preparation of resolutions and projects, as other divisions did in their spheres.

The General Conference of 1960 had already opened up the possibilities for such institutions aiding the new African member states in the same manner as planning missions. But it was the General Conference at its twelfth session in the fall of 1962 that adopted four resolutions concerning planning in education. It authorized UNESCO to aid the member states and associated member states that requested the establishing or the reinforcing of their services and the training of cadres necessary for planning in education. It authorized the director-general to favor planning by means of conferences, seminars, and courses of study and aid member states to establish and develop planning services by facilitating the training of personnel for these. It authorized the creation of IIEP (Institut International de Planification en Education) in Paris, which through courses and seminars would contribute to the syntheses of existing knowledge and acquired experience in matters of planning and do research for new ways. It authorized the director-general to favor the establishment of sections of planning in education in the heart of institutions of planning for economic development associated with the regional economic commissions of the United Nations in Latin America, Asia, and Africa (12 C/PRG/17).

The director-general was charged to continue negotiations with the regional economic commissions in view of setting up educational planning sections. This the Executive Board at its sixty-fifth session felt was the logical follow-up to the cooperation already existing between UNESCO and the commissions. The Executive Board showed satisfaction with what had already been done and authorized the director-general to go ahead with IIEP and GRPE. So the work was cut out for the African Division.

National Institutes of Pedagogy and OPEX

Besides the Emergency Program for the Congo, the three meetings, the planning missions, and the regional centers, with the beginnings of IDEP and IIEP, there were two other undertakings of the African Division under Maurice's supervision. They are the creation of national institutes of pedagogy, some independent, some attached to higher-training institutes, and some in the regional centers, and OPEX.

As to the training schools, there was the one projected by Maurice in the Congo. Others were requested by governments; some were readily accepted when they were proposed. Others took time, effort, and the surmounting of obstacles. Bartels in a recent interview revealed that Bergeaud for the French-speaking countries and Lightfoot for the English-speaking ones spent a great deal of time traveling in the field to sell the idea of the necessity of such schools and trying to set them up. It is presumed that they reported to Maurice and received advice from him but were quite on their own. The Special Fund was instrumental in funding for grants and personnel. The fund could not be used for housing but could be used for material equipment. Housing or construction had to come from other sources.

Between 1961 and 1962, besides the one in Léopoldville, there were six national institutes of pedagogy in operation, one each in Yaoundé, Abidjan, Lagos, Zaria (Nigeria), and Omdurman (Sudan), with a total enrollment of 424 students, with UNESCO providing 26 experts. By the year 1965, sixteen were open, with 5,116 enrolled and 1,291 graduates, and 193 experts recruited by UNESCO as advisers or professors. Some training colleges were opened with other funds, such as Makerere in Kampala. Twenty-seven countries asked for help to formulate demands of the Special Fund. By 1967, there were twenty assisted training colleges. To these can be added those in a few Arab countries, one in Kabul, Afghanistan, and another in New Guinea, making a grand total of twenty-five set up from 1961 to 1967 with UNESCO aid through the Special Fund.

As to OPEX, in the files there are a few letters either signed by Maurice from 1962 on or given the visa approved by him. The recruiting of the experts was done for the division by Mrs. Richardson in collaboration with PER, BMS, or the field staff of PER. Teachers, from one or two to several in a country, were sent to Somalia, Burundi, Guinea, Mali, Nigeria, Upper Volta, and Sierra Leone, among others. Demands were also made for professors for universities that had education courses as well as requests for professors to advise on courses in higher education. In June 1963, for example, it was reported that 112 teachers were recruited for 17 countries. Demand far exceeded the supply of experts and financial resources. Hundreds of experts and teachers were requested. Even with all combined resources of UNESCO and other funds, it was too much, and judicious selection had to be made as to numbers and countries. Moreover, in certain fields recruits were very hard to find. UNESCO, or rather the divisions concerned, did what they could with the funds made available. It appears that although those involved in OPEX and other funds for teachers were hard pressed, the work went on smoothly for the most part. Recruitment for the Congo was done there more and more, except for experts. One of the few complaints that were registered was from the office of the prime minister of Rhodesia pointing out that, in his opinion, certain aspects of the OPEX agreement were outside the competence of UNESCO. Another came from the delegate of Rwanda, who stated that he alone could make decisions concerning candidates for employment in his country.

Just finding enough teachers and experts with proper qualifications and the required language was such a problem that in some instances standards were not always kept as high as UNESCO usually insisted upon. Maurice had many requests from his countrymen in those years. He was always scrupulous in his recommendations. In the Home Files and in the UNESCO Archives there are many letters from Haitians offering their services.

The task of finding personnel for these various undertakings—planning mission experts and professors for the different countries—must have been time-consuming, when it was not a headache, so rapid was the expansion of the work. But the division managed.

In conclusion, the year 1962 finished much better for Maurice than it had begun. The difficulties he had faced after his return from the Congo to regain his rightful place in the Department of Education turned into a challenge with the decision by the Directorate to have a special division in the department for tropical Africa.

As in the field, Maurice was at headquarters under great pressure to carry out assignments often thrust suddenly upon the division, which he made a point of honor to carry out before deadlines, often working far into the night. He recruited the first African professionals group (as political and geographical exigencies demanded) from the newly independent member states, as he did the first professional woman from an Arab country.

Maurice had much deskwork what with budgets, funding, drafts for resolutions, projects, and reports. He also had correspondence with demands for jobs from his countrymen who, trained, were eager to work abroad, where higher salaries and opportunities for constructive contribution beckoned. The brain drain from Haiti profited the newly independent French speaking nations. Several times Maurice had to take the defense of his countrymen when he felt their cause justified. He also had correspondence with friends and collaborators in the field as well as contacts in different countries on a professional basis.

Fortunately, Maurice had the backing and the support of the Indian Adiseshiah. This comes out in the interoffice notes time and again, as in the following cases. In a note to the acting head of the department October 4, 1962, Adiseshiah insisted that Maurice be on the selection committee for candidates for the recruitment service requested by Ethiopia. In another note to Maurice dated August 29, 1962, Adiseshiah asked Maurice to get together material concerning TA 1963–64 and finalize the Rwanda-Burundi project as well as the report on the Congo for TA, as he wanted to take it to New York City to the United Nations in early October. At the end he added: "If you have an urgent problem in the Congo send it to Mr. Correa. I shall be glad to look into it."

Maurice did not often appeal for support outside of the department, but in the following instance he turned to Adiseshiah, as he felt that there was negligence or deliberate bypassing of his authority as chief of the African Division. He had been away on mission, after which he had taken a few days of needed vacation. When he returned he learned through a chance conversation with a member of another sector that three of his very small staff were being sent to a meeting in Tunis without his having been consulted. This would paralyze the activities of his division for weeks. He was stunned and felt he had to make it known to both the acting head of the department, J. Guiton, and Adiseshiah. Maurice wrote that he was shocked, since it was not a last-minute urgency. It appeared that the acting head had sounded out two of the staff a month or two before, but up to the time of his return, Maurice, their chief, had had no note either to him or other interested staff. He went on: "These facts are serious enough to give attention to the necessity of re-examining certain conceptions and certain administrative practices in the department or in a certain branch of the department." He further mentioned that as chief of a division responsible for a vast program in different fields of action needing coordination and supervision, with a staff already too small for the work to be accomplished, he could not be considered a simple employee of the department.[28]

Adiseshiah sent back a note to Guiton: "This is shocking. I saw and approved a list of the staff over a month ago submitted by Van Vliet through you. (I assumed your signature meant Dartigue was O.K.) I distinctly ruled out Lightfoot. He is going in sheer defiance of the General Directorate. Whoever is responsible for this must be reprimanded. Please take steps accordingly. There must be some discipline in the House."[29]

In spite of such a vexation, the year 1962, having started as a major challenge for Maurice, ended with his having managed to become master of the situation and having gained stature as he approached and solved problems with his collaborators and had contacts with delegates and others concerned with education in tropical Africa. (Just a year ago I had a conversation with a retired staff member of another sector. He said, "Your husband had great influence during the time he was at UNESCO.")

Notes

1. 60 EX/Decisions/PRO 813 and 814.
2. Memo Org. of Division of ED/Congo/61, August 16, 1962.
3. UNESCO Ar., Special Reports, ED/Congo/memo 24.
4. UNESCO Ar. 137(675) A-64-66, part 4.
5. UNESCO Ar. 137(675) A-64-66, part 4, ONUC/UNESCO/no. 688.
6. Ibid., 666.
7. Ibid., ED/Congo/07/A.
8. Ibid.
   8A. Ibid., April 9, 1962, cable.
9. Ibid., ED/Congo/memo 106 to director-general.
10. Cable 273 BER, Paris, 1362256.
11. Ibid., ONUC/UNESCO/memo 579.
12. Ibid., October 15, 1962.
13. BMS Reports to Director.
14. BMS Reports to Director Mirville, Ed. Sta. 62–65.
15. Ibid., ED/Congo/3, Perrot P. School Prog., 1963.
16. Report, The Conference of Ministers and Directors of Education in Tropical Africa, February 16–20, 1960, in Addis Ababa; UNESCO Ar., 37(675) A-06(44) "62," Ed. 4109/3.
17. UNESCO Ar., 371.214 (6) A-06(691) "62," TA.
18. UNESCO Ar. Report, UNESCO/ED/196, Paris, October 31, 1962, originally French, p. 23.
19. UNESCO Ar., Dartigue Files, Report on Seminar, ED/41/11.
20. Ibid.
21. UNESCO Ar., UNESCO/ED/62/0.20/A, 1962.
22. UNESCO Ar. 37(6) A-64/20/57.
23. 61 EX/4 Add., May 9, 1962.
24. UNESCO Ar., ODG Files 4–7, Memos and Mission Reports, Adiseshiah.
25. Ibid.
26. BREDA, or the Regional Bureau for Educational Development in Africa.
27. UNESCO Ar. 37(6) A-64/20/57, part 2, ED/4111, June 5, 1962.
28. UNESCO Ar., Dartigue Files, ED/41/7, August 27, 1962.
29. August 30, 1962 to Guiton, ED, cc. Dartigue.

The African Division, 1963: The Creation of the Regional Group for Educational Planning in Dakar, Senegal

The year 1963 would be Maurice's last year at headquarters as chief of the African Division and the Emergency Program for Africa. He would reach the mandatory retirement age of sixty on March 14, 1963. As early as August 1962, he had asked Maheu, then the acting director-general, for the prolongation of his contract until October 1963, so that with the years at the United Nations and those at UNESCO he would have 17 full years of service in the international organizations, giving him better pension rights. For the first time, he addressed himself to Maheu in a personal matter concerning his position. The prolongation was accorded.

As in 1961 and 1962, the Emergency Program for the Congo continued to be the urgent concern of the division though the planning missions, the setting up of National Institutes of Pedagogy and/or "Ecoles Normales Supérieures," the sending of secondary school teachers, experts and professors through OPEX or UNESCOPAS (UNESCO Operational Assistance), the expanded TA, EPTA (Enlarged Program for Technical Assistance), the Special Fund, the regular UNESCO program, and the attention to the regional centers would take up time in supervision for the chief of the division.

Maurice again had a direct part in the courses being given in Geneva for Congolese functionaries a second time. There were problems concerning the second special group of functionaries from the Congo to be sent to Geneva. The granting of fellowships, the travel costs, the lodgings in Geneva, the organizing of the courses, and the visits later took time and much back-and-forth correspondence as to health records, visas, verification of documents, etc. The grantees who had finished with the Geneva courses in 1961–62 went in May 1962 on visits of information in Paris, where there were conferences, sightseeing, and trips to places of interest. At the same time, planning was done for the second group. IBE felt that the first courses had been successful. It was willing to continue the agreement with UNESCO.

A flurry of cables took place between the African Division, the Department of International Exchange, Geneva and Léopoldville, in late October and early November because the rooms had been retained and the courses organized to begin, but the grantees had not shown up. It turned out that although the names of the grantees had been sent to headquarters, the medical records, which were needed to obtain visas, had not arrived. The reason given: there was no one to examine the candidates in the provinces. Maurice cabled: "Have this done in Leo." He cabled again: "Date of courses fixed IBE anxious at situation." Finally, in desperation, on November 15, 1962, he wired: "Send the five of the eighteen who are ready."[1] By December all the grantees had arrived. The same problem concerning salaries that were to be paid to their families at home during their absence in Europe plagued certain members of the group. Again both Rossello and Maurice had to ask Terenzio to intervene.

Maurice gave his lectures in Geneva February 28–March 8, 1963. He wrote a mission report to Maheu, now director-general. In his report, Maurice stated that instead of giving the lectures in the usual way he had the fellows describe their work and their responsibilities. Maurice then explained the aims of the course and the method he wished to use. He asked them to present their problems and to set forth the difficulties that were special. These they discussed, taking the most typical and together examining them to find possible approaches to solutions. From this they went to general notions and principles. They tackled a number of problems in this manner and looked at them from the theoretical, then the practical, viewpoint in the light of the national experience. The reactions to this method were very good. Pertinent problems were evoked and questions posed. The fellows showed a high level of professional maturity and an interest in the amelioration of the educational system.

Rossello had asked that UNESCO send a few UNESCO staff members to give lectures, as Maurice had. Fernig of the Education Clearing House and Diez Hochleitner, now in the new Planning in Education Division, were able to do so. Maurice, of course, besides his participation, his reports and the evaluation, worked on the expenses. It is presumed that after the program this group of fellows also visited centers of interest in Geneva and Paris. Maurice suggested to Terenzio in early June that steps be taken to select and process the candidates for the 1963–64 courses, as "there were so many difficulties inherent in all undertakings in the Congo." Whether these special courses continued is not clear; the correspondence ends with a plan for a seminar for math teachers to be held in Léopoldville early in 1964. Grants for study abroad were given under other auspices such as bilateral agreements and universities.

The Emergency Program for the Congo

All was, as usual, not serene in the Congo on the first day of January 1963. Among other things, the students of IPN had gone on strike against the Congolese director of the institute. It is not clear what exactly the reasons were, except that he was ill equipped for the job he was holding. Only the intervention of the UNESCO mission convinced the students that they give up the strike before the minister of education closed the school. Moreover, the prime minister, A. Adoula, was almost overthrown, which would have had serious repercussions for the UNESCO program, and N'Galula was replaced by Colin. (Problems due to tribal factions continued to disturb the stability and security.)

As Maurice had done on a Sunday in 1961, Terenzio, stating he could find no other time to do so, wrote on January 1, 1963, concerning the work of the mission. He felt that the year 1963 opened with better prospects for the program. He stated that Amachree, UN undersecretary for the Congo, had given him assurances that the project for the foreign teachers would be extended, which presented certain practical advantages. It would stabilize the teaching body and recruitment could proceed under better circumstances. UNESCO could request certain conditions of the government, especially as to lodgings and placement of teachers and experts (often arbitrary due to tribal preferences). It would permit the preparation of the 1964 budget of USAID and ONUC. He wished to work out the problem of the University of Elizabethville (as Katanga had returned to the fold). He demanded directives and a few days later suggested that he come to headquarters to discuss these with Maheu and the African Division. He again referred to the visit of the representative of the Special Fund, who expressed the opinion that the three institutions—IPN, the School for Public Works and Construction, and the Technical Training School of Mines—were "technically sound but that the Special Fund could provide only for IPN as the Special Fund had at its disposal for funding in all countries only $30,000,000, so could ill afford to give $7,000,000, almost one-fourth of the entire amount, to the Congo alone. The other two could be aided by the

UN which had been instrumental in their creation." This must have been a blow to both Maurice and Terenzio, who had counted on the Special Fund in case the United Nations failed to provide the necessary money. There were two other possibilities. The United States and Belgium were ready to help but had not yet intimated to what extent.

There was much ado at UNESCO about the rural community development project put forward by the ILO. There was to be a meeting in Rome for further discussions between ILO, the United Nations, FAO, and UNESCO. It was decided that Terenzio come to Paris for consultation on program and budget, then go on to Rome to represent UNESCO after briefing at headquarters. It was to Maurice that the office of the director-general turned for documents for the consultations and the briefing.[2]

Maurice prepared a document for Terenzio, after looking at the material at headquarters, the correspondence of the prime minister and Terenzio, and the cable from the UN headquarters in New York City inviting UNESCO to take part in the project. He first made the observation that UNESCO should be extremely prudent and the concerted action should be thought over thoroughly. He stated that the idea of rural community development was of vital interest in the restoration of native agriculture to its level before independence. Coercion did not work. Other methods had to be tried. It would be worthwhile to do a trial project first. A demonstration farm could be set up, as well as an experimental station to raise animals, with an agronomist and a veterinarian in attendance, both Congolese, an ambulatory clinic manned by Congolese nurses, a specialist in cooperatives, an engineer for roads and road repairs, and a rural school organized after community education principles, with an attached adult education program. All this would have to be preceded by a thorough study of the locality and its conditions, the way to go about the project, and its chances of success. But even before launching such a study it needed to be verified if the project could be financed for at least five years.[3]

Terenzio, armed with the document, went to Rome on January 22, 1963. His report to Maheu on January 24, 1963, was not optimistic. He, too, was cautious. His conclusions were that although it was a high-level meeting, not one person was able to define the nature, the reach, the duration, or the cost of such a project. It was decided, however, to send a joint mission to the Congo to study the situation. The program seemed parallel to what UNESCO was attempting to do. It would be good if this program could be attached to that of UNESCO. Terenzio remarked that the project supposed a passage from tribalism to administrative structures and organizational forms such as cooperatives and unions. There already had been studies, but the application would be difficult and could be dangerous for the international institution that became involved. UNESCO needed to wait until the conclusion of the mission to see if action by sociologists would be necessary. It was a bold undertaking—were there enough people and finances for such a project?

The Congolese minister of education, Colin, expressed gratitude for the 560 teachers UNESCO had helped to recruit, but now at least another 500 were needed. This was in January 1963. Amachree wished to be informed concerning the project of the 250 more demanded (not 500 as Colin requested). This did not mean that the Bureau of Control at the United Nations would authorize the acceptance of the responsibility. For Terenzio it appeared hopeful. He stated in a letter that although the 500 teachers already there had been recruited hastily, they were, on the average, good. Their general qualifications were higher than those of the Belgians. In a few areas, if it were not for the UNESCO teachers there would be no secondary school. In one school, four UNESCO teachers had full charge of 200 pupils. They worked with enthusiasm under great difficulties. They were appreciated by the population. In the town of Goma, the twenty-five teachers of fifteen nationalities worked in harmony.

He went on to state that the four mobile travel teams made up of sixteen experts had given the accelerated one-month course to more than sixteen hundred primary teachers. They were working hard. He felt that the 1963 program was in full swing, to continue in 1964. The one negative comment was the strike of students at IPN.

Maheu answered Colin, who had requested 500 more secondary school teachers for 1963–64, first stating that the 550 teachers already there could have their contracts renewed, as the Control of the Congo Fund of the United Nations had accepted this, but as to the extra 500 or even 250 he could not at this time (February 22, 1963) give a definite answer. He was having discussions with the UN authorities to see what could be done. He submitted to Colin the text of an agreement that defined the obligations of the Congolese government and UNESCO. It was the same as that accepted for 1962–63. He wished that Colin would let him know if he was in accord with it.

Knowing about the financial difficulties at the United Nations concerning the Congo Fund, Maurice wrote to Terenzio in mid-February that it might be necessary and would be possible to transfer certain ONUC/UNESCO experts to TA and the Emergency Program for Africa. At the same time, he advised Terenzio *not* to encourage the government to set up new projects such as the proposed normal school for the training of primary school teachers, as there was no budget provision. There was money for in-service training for those already employed, but not for the training of new ones. However, if ONUC and UNICEF agreed to finance salaries, equipment, and the expenses of certain experts to teach in such a school, the project title could be reshaped and accepted. If UNICEF wished to finance secondary school teacher training, then a special project for this had to be submitted to headquarters for examination. It is assumed that Terenzio had forwarded to headquarters a project for a primary teachers' training school requested by the Congolese government.

In April, Terenzio was no longer as optimistic as he had been in January. He wrote that the financial prospects were as vague as ever, even for 1963. He thought it might be good to orient the Congo government to self-financing "Funds in Trust" in strong currency, at least for the 250 extra teachers, if the minister of education and the prime minister could be persuaded to accept the proposition. Terenzio went on to state that there had been a conference of the education ministers similar to the one held in December 1962. They had made recommendations for a reform of the primary school program. This program, which had been worked out by a Congolese commission, helped by UNESCO experts, was designed to unify the various programs in the different categories of primary schools into a single national system better adapted to the present needs of the Congo and better controlled. Some private sectors feared they would lose their autonomy, their privileges, and perhaps their subsidies. The secondary school revised program had been accepted without adverse propaganda, but the primary program involved so much more that various groups felt forced to undermine the work of reform. In spite of some negative reactions, the conference of ministers approved the proposed program. This result had been achieved because they had participated in the preparation of the texts.

In the area of planning of education, the work carried out by Hennion for a long-term plan was hampered by the absence of an overall economic and social development plan. However, he presented the objectives of primary and secondary education, taking into consideration the budget, and the needs of the market, and employment sectors. He wrote that work on the revised plan for IPN and the School for Construction and Public Works was going on. Another major achievement was the plan for the Information Services, which was terminated. Several fundamental documents were ready for headquarters for comment, such as the statutes for radio broadcasting, the organization of information services, statutes for the Congo magazine, and statutes for the press agency. (This was pioneering work for UNESCO and the Congo.)

On March 29, 1963, the Executive Board began its sixty-fifth session in Paris. The director's report was drawn from a printed document. It is a concise recapitulation of what the correspondence reveals, but it refers only slightly to the negative aspects or the day-to-day frustrations, contentions, and disappointments. In such documents for presentation to the delegates, UNESCO is mostly supportive of the governments as the determining agents in all decisions. Maheu remarked that this report was the first balance sheet to be presented on the ensemble of the work accomplished by UNESCO in aid of the Congolese government:

- to develop secondary education and ameliorate primary education to better meet the needs of the present in the Congo;
- to create new institutions of higher learning and further train education functionaries, teachers, and administrators;
- to establish organic structures that favor the development of a national educational system;
- to safeguard the activities of the important scientific institutions; and
- to develop the means of diffusing information.

It was at the end of the sixty-fifth session that Maurice, on June 4, 1963, informed Terenzio that the Executive Board had passed the following request: "The director-general to report at the 66th session on proposed measures for the continuation of the UNESCO activities in Congo/Léopoldville in 1964 and for the regularization of the cooperation between UNESCO and the Congo in 1965–66." Maurice then asked Terenzio to send him the program for 1963–64 by the end of June, so that it could be submitted to the session that would meet in September. It would be extremely useful, he added, to send separately suggestions concerning projects in which the experts who would be taken over by TA were involved, keeping in mind that the Emergency Fund would cease to exist on December 31, 1964.

At the Executive Board session of April 29–May 17, 1963, the director-general reminded it that in 1960, although there were 1,500,000 children in primary school in the Congo, that is, 71 percent of the eligible primary school population, a very high percentage in developing countries, only 152—that is, about 1 out of 10,000—graduated from secondary school, these having been taught by foreign teachers, as there were no Congolese teachers at that level. It was feared that with independence and the massive departure of foreign teachers even this low number would decrease. Therefore, the first, most urgent action of the independent government with the aid of UNESCO was to call on teachers from other countries, adapt structure and programs to present needs, augment the number of secondary school graduates, train Congolese teachers, and ameliorate and simplify administration methods for more efficient service.

At the same session, the director-general reported that UNESCO had received the accord of the United Nations to put in action a program employing 110 experts, 560 teachers, and giving 600 grants (15 for study abroad), plus indemnities for inspectors and primary school teachers for the in-service training courses. The total expenditure would reach $4,528,000. At the twelfth session of the General Conference, it was decided that UNESCO would provide $200,000 of its own funds for 1963 and 1964 with the Congo under the same title as other African states.

By spring 1963, the four mobile teams had held sixteen courses for over sixteen hundred teachers. An expert was sent to evaluate the work of the mobile teams. In his report made on April 4, 1963, his conclusions were quite discouraging. He reported that there was an adequate number of primary school teachers throughout the country. The various normal schools, mostly run by missions, turned them out by the hundreds. Those with whom the teams had come into contact, although friendly, cooperative, attentive, assiduous, and at times appreciative of the course, were of very low professional level as well as low cultural and linguistic achievement. There were very few women, who had even fewer abilities. So the teams had very poor human material to try to improve. There was anarchy as to programs, with so many different ones. There were few books. They were of very poor quality, and unadapted, as were the few teaching materials. The primitive furniture was degraded, as were the school buildings. The schools were subsidized by the government, but they did not follow the official program and were not supervised (there being almost no primary school inspectors) on the professional or financial level. They were given subsidies en bloc and did as they pleased. The teams and the expert thought the schools and the teachers could slide backward culturally, over which no training could hold. It is for these reasons that Terenzio was not optimistic about the impact of the teams.[4] They probably left little trace on those they were able to touch. The teams encountered a similar situation as to the hopes of finding among the better teachers possible trainees for inspection. Not only lack of qualifications was responsible, but inertia, often due to poor pay or absence of pay for months. This made it difficult for the teams to help constitute a corps of primary school inspectors.

On May 6, 1963, Terenzio wrote that if the extra 500 secondary school teachers were not recruited the program would fail. The Belgians could offer 250 teachers. UNESCO alone had the means to recruit such a large number rapidly, as had been proven. He complained of the difficulty in the continuity of certain programs because of the quick succession of functionaries in the provinces who appeared and disappeared. Therefore, to keep the ministries going, at a minimum it was essential to maintain in 1964–65 two experts, one as technical adviser, in each original ministry and ten for the others, making twenty in all. Though there were no special problems in the central ministry in Léopoldville, still it was nevertheless important to extend the contracts of the experts there. As Amachree was to go to Paris, Terenzio wanted to make sure that these needs would be gotten across to him.

Amachree made the visit to headquarters on May 10, 1963. He had discussions with Maheu, who gave his accord for IPN until the Special Fund could take over in 1964. The Special Fund also accepted the School of Construction and Public Works and later the School of Mines. The in-service training by the mobile teams, the preservice training for education admin-istrators, and the secondary school inspection project with a later takeover by EPTA were all agreed to. He approved the extension of the experts' contracts for a year but wanted their effectiveness evaluated as well as whether the government was using them to the best advantage. However, Amachree would not yet take a stand on the 250 extra secondary school teachers. It depended on future funds. In fact, he was supposed to have said, "Impossible," and to have added that it was high time the government took over the entire responsibility for the secondary school teachers.

One last request of Amachree was to ask Maheu (who was French) to consult with the French government to give aid to the Congo. It is to be remembered that at the United Nations in 1960 France, along with the USSR, had refused to contribute funds. The director-general was to give the French a clear idea of the needs of the Congo. The director-general agreed to do this if the Congo government made a formal request to UNESCO. Amachree said he would speak to the prime minister, Adoula.

On May 29, 1963, before giving a written confirmation to the director-general as to what he had agreed to verbally, Amachree wrote to Prime Minister Adoula to inform him that expected funds were not forthcoming and the United Nations was forced to curtail activities unless the Congo government found means to finance certain projects. He realized it would be difficult for the government. The School for Construction and Public Works and the agriculture rehabilitation projects would not be affected. The United Nations would assist the government in recruiting staff for the Bureau of Economic Coordination and the Congo Finance Administration. The United Nations would release the matching funds for 1963, but they were to be used as specified in the accord. He pointed out the possible deficit, due to expenditure over income after all assets and liabilities were set down. The Monetary Council would provide hard currency where needed for salaries, etc., against Congo francs, so that certain activities could continue. On June 3, 1963, Amachree wrote to Maheu giving him the gist of his letter to Adoula. On the same day, Adoula informed the director-general that he accepted the conditions, stating that his government appreciated all that UNESCO had done and that it was indispensable for the progress of the country that the activities continue. The government was ready to create the "Funds in Trust." He would contact friendly member states for contributions to the fund. This letter would serve as the accord between the United Nations, UNESCO, and the Congolese government.

With this acceptance of the conditions by Adoula, the director-general decided to go ahead to give such aid as was in UNESCO's power. On June 6, 1963, the director-general wrote to Adoula that he, the director-general, would make every effort to find sources of possible financing for the extra 250 secondary school teachers; at the same time he submitted the text defining the responsibilities of UNESCO and the responsibilities of the government regarding the teachers recruited by UNESCO. It was the same as that of 1962–63; Adoula's acceptance of this text would act as an accord.

Terenzio wrote that the result of Amachree's visit to Léopoldville had been to obtain from the prime minister the establishment of the "Funds in Trust" in foreign exchange. He added that there was good news from the recruitment missions sent to the various countries. The selection of the candidates would take place July 1 in Léopoldville. The quality appeared higher and there were more applicants. He went on that thousands of primary school teachers had not been paid, some for two years. This had caused intermittent strikes. Terenzio had brought this information to the attention of the UN authorities time and again. The 1963 Congo budget had not yet been voted on, for which the United Nations was partly responsible. The budget did not reflect the realities of the debt of the government. He had signaled the enormous wastage and ways to clean it up. Either the government would not or could not apply measures if it did not pay the arrears owed. Terenzio felt that the situation had become very serious.

Terenzio also discussed the conference of provincial ministers, which he felt was a victory for UNESCO, since it was the UNESCO experts who had prepared the plans for the reforms in programs and long-term planning. The reforms were now accepted in spite of the violent campaign against them and UNESCO.

Following Adoula's acceptance of the conditions of the agreement between the Congolese government and UNESCO for the recruitment of secondary school teachers, PER, certainly after consultation with Maurice, and with his signature, sent a cable to Terenzio to be sure that the government was aware of the detailed conditions:

(1) the minimum funds required before recruitment could begin;
(2) the amount of 12 percent in hard currency to be deposited for administrative purposes;
(3) the secondary school teachers hired under this fund had to have the same conditions as those hired by UNESCO;
(4) the government must deposit one-third of the salaries and indemnities in hard currency and another third transferable abroad;
(5) the government must give sources of funds that make up the Trust Funds; and
(6) PER underlines the need to apply the same method of recruitment administration as for other secondary school teachers.[5]

It was in early July that Terenzio replied to Maurice's inquiry as to the program for 1964–65 and possible projects. He suggested that the background might be useful for the text to be presented at the sixty-sixth session of the Executive Board. He stated that following an exchange of letters between Prime Minister Adoula and Amachree, Ahmed[6] re-examined all the programs to determine which after 1964 should be entirely financed by external contributions (training and consultative services) and which, such

272

as operational personnel, would need to be funded by the Congo government in case the Congo Fund (UN) found itself in difficulties.

Maurice probably had some part in the preparation of the document that was used for the basis of Maheu's report to the Executive Board for its sixty-sixth session. It is dated July 19, 1963—66 EX/20, with a mention written in red: "Approved by DG." The main points are as follows: First, the Special Fund Board had approved the project for the School of Construction and Public Works and had designated UNESCO as executor of the project. Maheu hoped the Special Fund would do the same for the IPN when the Congolese government made a request to the Special Fund for this as well as for the School of Mines, which the Congolese would continue to finance until the Special Fund could take it over. Second, after three-way discussions among the Congolese government, Amachree, and Maheu the path was cleared for UNESCO to recruit for 1963–64 the extra 250 secondary school teachers in the same manner as those already there. Thus the year 1963–64 was secure.

As to the future UNESCO action about which the Executive Board wished to be informed, the director-general explained that the needs of the Congo in education would for several years be as great as at that time. Progress had been remarkable, but the difficulties would not be surmounted by 1964. The Congo would still face serious problems in the administration services, especially in education. It was most important to form cadres for this service. As secondary and higher education needed to be expanded, foreign teachers and professors would still be needed. It was evident that the aid UNESCO could offer was not enough, but it could help the gradual transition from the extraordinary aid now being given to the normal program. It could help in planning, in accord with the Congo authorities, UNESCO's future assistance for as coherent and efficient a program as possible. This meant that UNESCO had to maintain a representative in the Congo as chief of mission. Maheu then gave in detail the numbers and kinds of experts and their placement and through what funds financing for these could be obtained if the Congo made requests. He hoped that bilateral agreements would offer to take over more and more projects.

Before the sixty-sixth session, a departmental meeting was held at headquarters on July 17, 1963, on the subject of aid to the Congo from 1965 on. Maurice, the director of the Department of Education, and the staff concerned, as well as the deputy chief of mission to the Congo, Najman, who was in Paris for consultations, discussed various projects that have

273

already been noted, especially that of the 250 extra teachers. As the program was to be normalized, the chief of mission post would become a P5, down from the D1 grade it had been for Maurice and Terenzio. No new ideas emerged as to how the extra teachers would be recruited or how the government of the Congo would finance the project, except that the teachers would be recruited with some sort of guarantee. The great expansion in numbers in the secondary schools necessitated at least 3,000 teachers, 1,200 Belgians, 1,000 religious, the 550 UNESCO teachers already there, plus 500 more.

Then the blow fell. The United Nations was cutting back on financial aid for the Congo. Ralph Bunche had just become undersecretary for special political affairs, which included ONUC, replacing Amachree. It was his decision. Maheu wrote to Bunche (the text produced by Maurice). Maheu referred to Amachree's letter concerning the Funds in Trust. He wrote that he needed details for the purpose of financing the operational services of UNESCO in the Congo, hitherto paid from the Congo Fund. The exchange of letters related to the hiring of the 250 secondary school teachers, which the prime minister had approved. Ahmed had advised UNESCO to go ahead with ONUC's guarantee that necessary funds were available for the 500 teachers whose contracts would be extended and for the extra 250 to be recruited.

To this Ralph Bunche replied, on September 6, 1963, that the United Nations could not guarantee or assume liabilities for posts that were now or were to become the responsibility of the Congo government in 1964. The 250 teachers were under the sole guarantee of the Congo government. He doubted that the member states would contribute to the Congo Fund in 1964. The program of recruitment of secondary school teachers was out for the United Nations as of September 1, 1963. This answer must have been a shock to Maheu. He took immediate steps to apply measures in view of this. He wrote to Bunche that he had informed Terenzio of the inability of the United Nations to guarantee the extra 250 teachers.

Adiseshiah offered various solutions, as had Maurice. Maheu on September 12, 1963, sent instructions for the changes in the UNESCO effort in the Congo to all departments—education, natural science, social science, Bureau of Member States, personnel, control, relations with international organizations, program, and budget, among others. Normalization was to begin immediately. Negotiations were to begin to put under UNESCOPAS certain members of the mission, and there was to be intensification of preparation of counterparts and UNICEF was to take total charge of the mobile travel teams for 1964–65. The secondary school inspectors could be financed. The Congo government would have to demand help from IDA and the missions on how to finance education. The center for purchase and distribution could carry on until December 21, 1964, if it had a UNESCO or UNESCOPAS director, and the 2 percent commission coming from the sale of the coupons could be given back to the government. It was a swift mobilization to save the UNESCO program by curtailment and drastic adjustments. The director-general would do his best to help the government to recruit secondary school teachers without UNESCO financial aid. This concerned the sixty-six teachers directly hired by UNESCO. *A la rigueur,* transfer them to UNESCOPAS. As for the UNESCO experts, sixteen vital posts had to be maintained, so proposals were to be prepared for TA to take over. Depending on possible financing, other posts could be kept through UNESCOPAS, Funds in Trust, or suppressed. Fifteen days later Terenzio informed the director-general that the government accepted the proposals.

On top of this came another crisis. The primary schools had not opened. Forty thousand monitors and primary school teachers had gone on strike for higher pay. Their salaries had been tripled in 1960. Now they wanted more. The UNESCO experts had not taken this possibility into consideration in the preparation of the 1962–63 budget, so they carried a heavy responsibility. It was election time and this show of force was troublesome. (The strike must have ended in one way or another, as there are no more references to it.)

To the relief of the mission and headquarters, the United Nations revised the drastic cuts first decided upon. The posts now foreseen by the different regular sources would be financed by a fund that would take the place of the Congo Fund, handled by the United Nations and fed by foreign contributions given directly or indirectly and by the Congo government in foreign exchange or Congo francs. Certain projects would be financed by the United States. In this way the UNESCO program could go on to normalization without too much sacrifice. A special effort would be made to accelerate the training of Congolese counterparts.

What took place in the Congo after Maurice's departure is gleaned from the director-general's report to the Executive Board at its sixty-seventh session, April 23, 1964. The program is concisely presented for 1964, 1965, and 1966. The government and UNESCO signed an accord on October 25, 1963, to apply a special system concerning the recruitment for the newly created center for purchase and distribution of school supplies. Eight hundred secondary school teachers were authorized by ONUC in November 1963, plus six professors for the official University of Elizabethville in Katanga. UNESCO became the executory agent for IPN and the School of Mines when the Special Fund took them over in January 1964. The School for Construction and Public Works had been taken over earlier. Some of the eighty-seven experts were transferred to the enlarged TA while some dealing in primary school matters were taken in charge by UNICEF. The normalization began to take place with the normal budget, extended TA, UNICEF, and the Special Fund.

Terenzio returned to headquarters in mid-1964. He handled the Congo program through the Bureau of Member States, as far as is known. His place was taken by Najman. He returned to headquarters sometime in 1965 to take up duties in the African Division. He was replaced by Mr. Bille, under whom the program was finally normalized.

In summary, the program remained one of the most challenging, if not the most challenging, and vast undertakings of UNESCO. The collapse of the civil services of the whole country after the sudden departure of the Belgians could have led to anarchy and chaos had not the United Nations and its sister agencies quickly mobilized their forces to support the country and keep it afloat. It was a privilege and an extraordinary opportunity for Maurice to make the first plans for the necessary reforms under very difficult circumstances and with a skeleton staff.

The Emergency Program for Africa, 1963

Besides the emergency program for the Congo, which remained most urgent, the African Division continued with the projects undertaken in 1961 and 1962. The most concise report of the various activities was given by the director-general to the Executive Board at its sixty-fifth session, held April 29–May 17, 1963. He stated that there were 137 teachers in 16 countries recruited by OPEX in February and the first stone for the construction of an IPN in the Sudan was laid in late 1962. The Regional Center for School Construction in Khartoum had been set up. In Yaoundé (Cameroon) the center for the production of school materials was functioning; another was being negotiated with the Ethiopian government.

France offered funds to create a regional center to train administrative cadres outside the emergency program. Maheu proposed to accept the 300,000 French francs on deposit. It was up to the Executive Board to decide on the use of this generous contribution.

Maheu then summed up the work of the planning missions. There were two in 1961, to Sierra Leone and Upper Volta. In 1962 there were those to Cameroon, Somalia, Tanganyika, the Ivory Coast, and Ruandi-Urundi (since become Rwanda and Burundi). A mission had gone to Madagascar in early 1963. A mission to Liberia was under study. New demands were coming in from Uganda, Bechuanaland, and Rhodesia. The missions would try to initiate counterparts in techniques of assembling statistics. It was urgent to find specialists for the six-to-eight week missions.

Maurice put together work plans, based on an inquiry and compilation of the needs of each country, which included the possibility of organizing courses and training, types of courses both local and regional, indications as to which functionaries might best profit. He also specified who could give courses or lectures, including experts, bilingual agents, and specialists from other organizations. He stated: "The educational system is a vast enterprise with its specialists, teachers, auxiliaries and administrators with obligations of funding, housing, maintenance, etc." He tried to show the interrelationship of the different activities that must be considered in the training.[7] He added that the governments must keep the public informed concerning the various projects for better cooperation and understanding.

In a memorandum, Maurice wrote that since 1961 twenty-two missions had been sent out to help governments to plan. Some missions had aided governments already having a plan but needing scientific amelioration, while some missions had gone to countries that had none. The time had come to unify the operation to better coordinate the effort. The missions were similar as either coming under the African Emergency Program, USAID, or IDA, or from plans decided upon at Addis Ababa in 1961, which were later elaborated in Tokyo.

Maurice thought that some missions tried to do too much. The real task was to aid the governments to establish or reinforce those services participating in planning, to train personnel for this service, also to assemble and analyze necessary information, facts and figures, to evaluate the available resources for appraisal of costs so as to examine with the competent authorities the possibilities of making an appeal for foreign and international aid. It was important for the missions to realize how much they could counsel for long-term policies and the limits beyond which they could seem to interfere with the prerogatives of the national government.

Missions were in preparation for five countries, the first of short duration, and second teams sent later, perhaps in two years. Experts were placed for longer terms. More would be considered if money became available. For 1963 other projects were planned, such as a joint UNICEF project to Niger for the development of primary education, the granting of fellowships for studies in planning, and courses for further training of planners, these to be within the countries as less costly than study abroad. Maurice reiterated the aims of the African Emergency Program. They were school construction, school equipment, production of school materials (texts, manuals), and recruitment of expatriate secondary school teachers and college professors for the countries asking for this aid.

The director-general's report to the Executive Board at its sixty-sixth session, held September 19–October 29, noted that mobile travel teams were constituted for primary education in Niger, Upper Volta, Mali, and Central and West Africa. More would be created in 1964. Two IPNs teachers' training colleges were in action. These were Makerere and Bangui, while four new projects funded by the Special Fund for five years were being set up in Niger, Ghana, Madagascar, and Rhodesia. On May 1, 1963, another IPN opened in Oweri, Niger. Altogether thirteen IPNs had opened, with the prospect of four more in 1964.

At the Executive Board meeting, Maheu explained how the various projects could be financed. He described the new regional center IDEP (Institute of Planning for Economic Development) that was to open in Dakar and the IIEP (International Institute of Educational Planning) to be inaugurated in Paris. The last preparations were being made. Negotiations had been going on with agencies for funds. BIRD had given $150,000, as had UNESCO for eighteen months. The Ford Foundation gave $200,000 as its definite contribution. The French government had offered the premises, furnishings, and necessary installations. A five-member board had been constituted of which the UNESCO director-general or his delegate was one. The board had met at UNESCO for the first time in April 1963. The first director, an American, Ph. H. Coombs, began his functions in May.

The project for a course to be held in Cairo on manpower and education for economic development had already been discussed as early as February 25, 1962, when a starting team met in Addis Ababa, headquarters for ECA, to draft a program. A team met again on April 5, 1963, and produced a draft that one assumes was sent for comment to UNESCO. It must be this draft and the changes he made in it to which Maurice refers in a note he sent to Bartels on April 25, 1963, asking him to look over the "work" and give his comments.

On April 16, Adiseshiah, referring to the courses to be given in Cairo, expressed doubts to A. Rahman, the director of the Economic Planning Institute in Cairo, stating:

> I have doubts about these courses and the difficulties. I am reluctant as both manpower techniques and educational planning techniques are at the early stages of development. Separate courses are difficult enough, to combine them in a single course in the present state of our knowledge and for a new area like Africa argues a degree of sophistication that I feel neither the disciplines concerned nor Africa possesses. However, we are working on it on our side.[8]

Although Maurice was familiar with educational planning, having done it throughout his career in Haiti and UNESCO, manpower as a subject in itself was new to him, as it probably was to most of the UNESCO staff and the wider public. Now here he was working on a program for courses that included these subjects. Maurice had sent a copy of the draft he had produced to the director of the department in response to a directive sent from the office of the director-general to Adiseshiah that UNESCO prepare a syllabus of two different main courses and review how planning in education was to be presented in the main course outline with an analysis by the Division of Social Sciences, for a meeting of UNESCO, ILO, and ECA on April 30, 1963. Maurice titled it "Draft Outline for a Special Course on Manpower and Education in Economic Development to Be Held in Cairo." Maurice asked Adiseshiah, Bartels, and staff members of different sectors and departments for comments. Maurice put down several formulas and propositions. (As the field was new, he believed that it would take collective thinking to work out a coherent program. To him it was a collective thought process.)

Gardiner, now director of ECA, in early April in Dakar had met with the group involved from ECA and the future IDEP to decide on the length of the courses and the type of trainees. At UNESCO, a meeting took place on April 19, 1963, that Maurice and Ochs attended. At this time a report was given of the Addis Ababa meeting of April 5, 1963. A general discussion followed as to the part UNESCO had in the program and points as to how the courses would be taught, the teaching staff, the languages to be used, the material organization, the calendar, the budget, etc. This course would be another "first."

The next meeting took place at headquarters May 1–4, 1963, to decide on details. There would be thirty-six participants, the language English. IDEP would issue the invitations to the governments in the names of ECA, ILO, and UNESCO. The latter would select the candidates, with the final choice being made by the director of the course, Rahman (Cairo Institute), Doos (IDEP), and Hussain (UNESCO). When the course began, these men were no longer involved. It was at this time, too, that the African Division was asked to work out a program for a course to be given in Dakar.

It was on May 18, 1963, that the announcement was made that Maurice would assume the leadership of the group of experts for the new GRPE in Dakar. The qualifications for this post are listed in the description recorded at the sixty-fifth Executive Board session. They are as follows:

Preference for a university degree in education, with several years of experience in the highest domain of an educational system either in direction or administration, plus teaching practice implying knowledge of theories and practices of problems posed in rural and urban systems in matters of organization, administration reform and planning of education. The person should have knowledge of national, regional and international educational problems. He should be acquainted with theory and practice in economic and social questions of development of education in under-developed countries. He should be perfect in either French or English with capacity in the other language and enough Spanish to read documents on education.

Who else in UNESCO besides Maurice fit the job description so well?

Maurice accepted the appointment. He would be the first director of the new venture in Dakar. A few days later he was designated by Gardiner to also head the courses to be organized in Cairo. To this there was some opposition. A letter to Adiseshiah from Gardiner states that he had received several protests from UNESCO staff and ILO. He then received a direct protest from ILO stating that if Maurice was maintained as director of the course, ILO might withdraw. Gardiner refused to be swayed. ILO then called Adiseshiah, who answered that the decision belonged to Gardiner. As will be seen, Maurice directed the course and ILO did not withdraw. It is difficult to know the reasons for the protests, especially as it turned out that Maurice and a few of his collaborators carried the burden of the course through several crises. Perhaps the objection was that he was not African.

Maurice now produced another outline of the course and set about to procure eighteen grants, later reduced to fifteen, as UNESCO's contribution. Another meeting held in early July brought about the decision to use both English and French, with an intensive one-month course being given for those who knew but one of the languages. It was in late July that Maurice learned that his appointment for two years as creator and director of GRPE was definite.

In the meantime, Maurice accomplished his last important mission as chief of the African Desk. He was asked to do so by Adiseshiah, who in a testimonial written in 1986 stated that this mission was delicate and decisive. His words are: "I was faced with a very difficult and delicate educational problem in Nigeria . . . I turned to Maurice Dartigue, who, at my request, went to Nigeria, talked to political leaders, educators and people there and came back with an agreed program of teacher education, which was put into effect, and as a result, since, never looked back educationally . . ."

Adiseshiah was referring, it is presumed, to the mission to Lagos, which Maurice undertook May 19–23. There is an interoffice note from Adiseshiah to Maurice dated May 6, 1963, stating: "Please arrange some one from your Division to go down to Nigeria, perhaps yourself, as soon as possible for discussions. These discussions should *not* be held in Paris. Ask T. Wilson [chief of UNESCO mission in Lagos] to postpone his departure for home-leave till June 1st. Ask him to prepare your visit and you can visit Nigeria 20–25/5/63. All this should be cabled to Wilson after discussion with the Director of the Department." It concerned the problem of the relationships between the UNESCO-recruited principal (or director) of the Federal Advanced Teachers Training College and the six professors from the University of California, one of whom was the leader.

Maurice had been sent to Lagos in June 1960 to take preliminary steps toward an agreement between UNESCO and the Nigerian officials for the setting up of this higher-training school, jointly with funds from the Special Fund, USAID, and the Ford Foundation, with the collaboration of UCLA, which was to send the group of professors referred to. UNESCO was to recruit the director. The agreements, of which there were at least four, were signed by the spring of 1961. The college opened its doors soon after.

It appeared to be running smoothly until the spring of 1963, when the UNESCO Secretariat was given to understand that all was not well with the project in Lagos. The UNESCO chief of mission in Lagos was asked to investigate. This he did, and stated in his report that the Nigerian permanent secretary of the Federal Ministry of Education had received a letter with serious accusations against the director. Moreover, the permanent secretary, M. Awokoya, insisted that the director had to leave. The chief of mission, T. Wilson, felt the accusations too grave to judge without a serious investigation.[9]

When he returned Maurice reported that the essential aim of his visit was "to make contact with the Nigerian authorities, the chief of mission, those of USAID concerned, the UCLA professors and the UNESCO experts, to gather more information and proceed in an exchange of views relating to the problems of direction and the functioning of the establishment in view of the problem raised in the 'Wilson report.' "

From the talks with the various parties, Maurice received the feeling of disappointment at the turn of events. USAID and UCLA had placed high hopes in this special project. The professors had been selected with great care, especially the leader, who had had wide and long educational experience and had accepted the post because he had been told that the project was unique in the field, multinational in its structure and yet national in character. An important contribution to furthering education in the newly independent country could be made.

Maurice learned that the director had disregarded the accords. The leader of the group from UCLA did not allude to his personal grievances but expressed the opinion that at the moment the college had a competent, devoted corps of professors whose enthusiasm had been dampened by the frustration encountered. The professors needed to feel they were taking part in the common endeavor and not just giving courses. Although a board of study, of which the department heads were members, had been created, there had been no faculty meetings where common problems could be discussed.

Maurice, always accompanied by T. Wilson, had a long conversation with M. Awokoya, permanent secretary of the Ministry of Education, whose attitude he had hoped to soften. To no avail. Awokoya had no confidence that the director could conduct the project as it had been conceived. The institution required harmony and collaboration. Neither now existed. He had come to the conclusion that the director should be a Nigerian and the objectives of the college determined in consultation with Nigerians. He was ready to accept another UNESCO expert to fill in until a Nigerian was found.

Maurice realized that UNESCO could not impose the director on the government. Therefore, he and M. Awokoya came to an agreement, with the reservation of the approval of the director-general of UNESCO, that:

(1) a counselor would be named by UNESCO to fill in until a Nigerian was posted, then, during his absence abroad for study, replace him temporarily;
(2) while awaiting the nomination of the Nigerian and/or the UNESCO adviser, the college would function under the supervision of T. Wilson, according to administrative arrangements to be established at headquarters.

T. Wilson had made a visit to North Nigeria during Maurice's stay to contact the Ministry of Education of that region to ask if the director could be sent there to head the new normal school being set up in Zaria. He received a negative answer for professional and political reasons. Therefore, concluded Maurice, the problem for UNESCO was to find another position for the director outside Nigeria until the end of his contract.

In finishing his report Maurice credited the success of the mission with a minimum of delay to the aid given him by T. Wilson. This had greatly facilitated his task.

While Maurice was carrying out his responsibilities as chief of the African Division, he prepared for his future activities away from headquarters as an expert under TA for the creation of the GRPE in Dakar. In view of this he combined home leave to be taken in New York (from where he had been recruited) with a mission, as he preferred not to go to Haiti at the time, since conditions there were too unsettled. The timing was good, as the field budget did not provide for a mission. It is possible that it was Maurice who decided what he needed to do, where he needed to go, and whom he needed to see and had the mission directives given to him to put an official stamp on his visits in New York and Washington.

Maurice returned to Paris encouraged by what he had been able to accomplish. In his mission report,[10] he stated that in Washington he had encountered A. Da Silva, the head of the UNESCO office there, who arranged appointments for him. Among the first was one with Diez Hochleitner, formerly on his staff for the Latin American Major Project. He was now with USAID but would soon return to UNESCO. At USAID, Maurice was asked if he would go on mission to the Congo. His answer was that as a staff member of UNESCO he was at the disposal of the director-general, who alone could decide whether it was feasible to second him to USAID at this time. He doubted this because of UNESCO's previous commitment to the Dakar project. While at USAID, he talked with those responsible for education and documentation especially for planning in Africa, so as to be supplied by them in Dakar, as he would set up a documentation center there. He received sympathetic attention everywhere.[11]

In New York, Maurice went to Teachers' College to contact its president, Dr. Fisher, to discuss the training of African educational administrators and planners in Africa and abroad. He dropped in at Columbia University to see Andrew Cordier, former executive assistant of the UN secretary-general, now retired, who was dean of the School for International Relations and with whom he had kept on friendly terms. Maurice had a talk with Dr. Luther Evans, the former director-general of UNESCO and now director of the library. He also met the director of African studies, who was to have undertaken a research project on the influence of politics in the implementation of educational planning.

Maurice visited schools to observe programmed instruction in English and social studies. He visited, at the suggestion of Dr. Evans, the "Educational Facilities Laboratories," Inc., which gave small grants to universities and other institutions for research in architectural problems in school buildings. It then published the research reports. Maurice obtained documents for Dakar and for the Regional Center of Khartoum. Before leaving for Paris, he called at the United Nations to chat with Ralph Bunche and Victor Hoo, always a pleasure. Maurice also had a talk with Sir Alexander MacFarquhar, formerly engaged in the disbursement of funds for the Congo and now chief of personnel. Besides these men, Maurice saw the director of the Special Fund in the Department of Economic and Social Affairs, others concerned with IDEP and, finally, Dr. Rahman, who was to have directed the courses in Cairo but was now at the United Nations.

The organization of the courses in Cairo fell on Maurice's shoulders. He had let it be known that since it was he who was to establish and direct the new GRPE, he had enough to do to take part in the Cairo courses, without having to direct them as well. But he took on the responsibility. Two other specialists, not yet recruited, were to join him. After some time, Dr. Bahr of

OECD was selected and Hussain from headquarters, who would go as a member of the team and perform such duties as were assigned to him. The Department of Program and Budget was seeking funds for running the course. Gardiner had asked six African states to make requests of TA. Grants for the participants would come from the Contingency Funds.

After one or two office parties, Maurice was off to Dakar. On arrival at the airport, he was greeted by sporadic shooting. In fact, that night at the hotel, close to the airport, all present had to lie on the floor of the lobby to be safe from cross fire. Maurice did not know what it was all about, but this did not prevent him from going into town the next morning to find lodgings and make contacts. He was there only a few days before he left for Cairo for discussions and contacts with the Egyptian officials and others concerned with the Cairo course. The course had been outlined in June at headquarters and had been unanimously adopted in Dakar in October. Now on the mission to Cairo, the details were to be worked out. (He sent his report to the acting director of IDEP.)

When he took up the talks in Cairo, Maurice learned that the accord had not yet been signed by the Egyptian government. One of the reasons was that the minister delegated to sign it was in the hospital. This put Maurice in a vexing position, since it was difficult to work out details without the official signature. Finally the undersecretary of planning was designated to sign, but not until the accord had been translated into Arabic as well as French.

Maurice was well received by the new director of the Institute for Planning, Dr. Hamza. It was he who smoothed the way about the accord. He stipulated that the future participants be approved by his government and that the professors of the institute, who would give some lectures, be remunerated. Maurice pointed out that the professors' time was part of the Egyptian contribution, as understood by UNESCO. As to the students, Egypt, through its immigration service, could check on the students at their entry into the country. Dr. Hamza acquiesced to this and added that there were enough professors at the institute to fill in if those from Dakar could not come. He himself would offer his wholehearted collaboration and accepted the deputy directorship of the course. He would help to find reasonably priced lodgings for both the visiting professors and the students. Maurice met some of the staff of the institute and the undersecretary for education, who had been recruited for six months by IDEP to give lectures but who proved later to fail in his accepted responsibilities and thus make more work for the others. The problem of honorariums for the Egyptian professors and Dr. Hamza stayed unsolved for the time being.

Before going to Cairo, Maurice had stopped off in Beirut, where there was a regional center for the Arab states. He met the director, Dr. A. P. El-Koussy, visited the center, and even went on an excursion to Balbeck with the trainees who were taking a seven-month course. They were young Arab educators being given further training to later be promoted to more important functions in planning and administration.

Courses were going to be given in Tunis on the teaching of theories of agriculture, so on his return to Dakar Maurice stopped off in that city (he had left Cairo at 4:00 A.M.), where no one met him. He had not been informed that on Fridays, the government services were closed and on Saturdays and Sundays United Nations Technical Assistance was closed, so he had only the half-day (it was a Thursday, November 24, 1963) to see the government officials. This was arranged and Maurice was able to get the information on certain points concerning the courses that needed clarifying. As the Tunis course was being done jointly with FAO, he had talks with its representative and made a telephone call to its headquarters in Rome. Not only would the course be held in Tunis City, but also on weekends in the provinces in Arabic. To help set up the course, IDEP was to send two professors to work with the preparation committee two weeks ahead of the opening.

Maurice on his return to Dakar worked on the lectures he was to give there before going to Cairo and on those for Cairo. He was in contact with headquarters and with Bahr, the economist from OECD who was to give a series of lectures at the Cairo course.

The last month of 1963 and the first month of 1964 were also used to set up and organize his working place. This was one room that he shared with his secretary. Adiseshiah had come to Dakar for talks with Gardiner and with the IDEP staff. Maurice accompanied him on most of the visits. The first draft of the agreement between UNESCO and IDEP was drawn up, prepared by the UNESCO Secretariat. Adiseshiah felt it was a good work session. When he returned to headquarters, he admonished the director of personnel at the slowness of the repatriation of the one expert sent to second Maurice. He stated, "Before another accident occurs." This indicates that there had been a problem. It also indicates that Maurice must have been working alone, in the new venture, and for him a challenge in a new field as a lecturer. He had given lectures or talks in the seminars in Léopoldville and Geneva for the Congolese. Now the field would be wider and the level of the participants even more varied, as they would be coming from several countries. He had had invitations to speak before groups interested in African affairs during the years, but the pressure of work had kept him at his desk or on missions and he had had to decline. He was better in group discussions than as a lecturer. He combined the two in this new activity.

With the independence of the Congo and the need for secondary school teachers and experts, many applications came to Maurice's desk from Haitians for work in either the Congo or other French-speaking African countries. In the early sixties, Haiti passed through a very difficult period. The political climate was uncomfortable, and salaries in the teaching profession were low. Educated Haitians were very ready to seek their fortunes outside their native land when they learned about the salaries and indemnities being offered by UNESCO and other agencies. Neither the heat nor the less-than-easy living conditions in some areas stopped them.

Maurice was very careful to be as objective as he could, recommending only those who, he thought, would make a real contribution and explaining to others the reasons he could not promote their candidacy. A few times the persons he recommended did not live up to expectations. But for the most part his recommendations or assessments were justified, and he could be relied upon to give an impartial judgment in the evaluation of a candidate up for promotion, as letters attest. A subtle kind of neocolonialism might have been unconsciously present in the thinking of some Europeans in the field and at headquarters, which Maurice tried to combat diplomatically.

Maurice was leaving headquarters as head of the African Division, but the work initiated by him and his colleagues continued. Bartels became the chief. He held a central coordinating role with two junior officers. It was decided that the work which had been done by Maurice was too much for one person, so the responsibilities of the chief of the division were divided, with the Congo program being taken over by Terenzio on his return and Richardson assuming responsibility for appeals for contributions and OPEX. Bartels felt that the team worked well, except for one person, who was soon transferred to another sector. The work for the Emergency Program in Africa kept on with the setting up of more pedagogical institutes, of which there were finally thirty throughout Africa for the training of secondary school and primary training school teachers. OPEX continued, as did the giving of grants for study abroad and locally. Professors were sent to some universities, especially to those with teacher training sections attached. By 1966, 10,000 Africans had been trained or were being trained, some abroad.

As to the planning missions, which were more complex in their makeup, purpose, and relations with the governments, some were effective and a few were not. At least twelve were sent for one survey. To a few countries went second missions. What resulted from this special UNESCO undertaking was the installation of offices of planning attached to the education ministries in several African states where even the concept of this need had not existed. The difficulty of recruitment of qualified personnel and the cost of the initial missions held back some governments from the services offered by UNESCO. Maurice had laid down the foundations. Now others could build on them.

Notes

1. UNESCO Ar. 37(675) AG-4-06, cables October 8, October 19, November 8, November 11, 1962.
2. UNESCO Ar., ODG (CAB) 37(675) A-64-66, memos 17 and 18, January 19, 1963, part 5.
3. Ibid., for Rome Report on Integration of Rural Development, January 22, 1963.
4. UNESCO Ar. Special File Reports, Garraud, "Meeting of Mobile Teams," April 9–11, 1963.
5. UNESCO Ar. 37(675) A-64-66, cable PER, June 5, 1963.
6. S.H. Ahmed replaced Gardiner as representative of Secretary-General.
7. UNESCO Ar., ED/291/C402.
8. Adiseshiah, Special Notes and Correspondence.
9. Dartigue Files, ED/2060/3005, Confidential Report to Director-General, November 30, 1963.
10. Home Files, ED/41/11, ED/3400/3010, October 30, 1963.
11. UNESCO Ar., ED/3400/3010, ED/41/11, to Assistant Director-General, October 30, 1963.

The Regional Group for Educational Planning, Dakar, Senegal, 1964 and 1965

With the Congo crisis, Maurice had been thrust into a sudden vast emergency program. By comparison, in Dakar he initiated a small, planned action; still, both IDEP and GRPE, having just been created, were not yet in working order. It would take time to define responsibilities, prerogatives, and relationships among the two groups; the Senegalese government, and UNESCO. It would take diplomacy and sensitivity to keep on an even keel. Maurice was older and had had far more experience, yet he was to be the director of a UNESCO section affiliated to a larger institution of another organization, whose chief just recruited had been a consultant a few weeks before but was from an African country. As far as is known Maurice and Vieyra (Dahomey), the head of IDEP, got along well.

Whatever position Maurice held, he gave it dignity and raised it to its highest possibilities. He had prepared lectures, as he was to give four in January 1964 to the students of the nine-month course being held in Dakar in connection with the central theme "Africa Today." The titles were "The Importance of the Role of Education in Economic Development," "The Structure of Education in Africa," "The Fundamental Problems of Education in Africa," and "The Planning and Administration of Education." He worked hard to prepare the lectures for Dakar and Cairo.

By January 1, 1964, Maurice wrote to the head of the Department of Education at headquarters stating that he had been alone almost from the time of his arrival two months before, to organize the Cairo courses in two languages and prepare not only the Dakar lectures, but those for Cairo, each with a different theme. He also had to make various reports and attend the IDEP meetings, plus deal with correspondence. This was not too much work, but too much given the shortness of time for preparation. He was to have had local help. He had been promised by Adiseshiah (who had come to Dakar in December) that money would be put at his disposal for this, but so far the money had not arrived. He also stated that at the time he was offered the Dakar position there was no question of his directing the course in Cairo.

On January 20, 1964, Maurice wrote to ask who was to make the final choice as to candidates for Cairo and what medical bureau would look over their records. Time was short for this, too. The answer came. The office of the director-general informed Adiseshiah that the director of IDEP decided it was up to the institute to make the final choice, as it was IDEP that was organizing the course. At the same time, Maurice had to ask for money from headquarters for excursions and visits in Egypt for the trainees. They were to visit Luxor, Karnak, the pyramids, places of interest in Cairo, and institutions relating to their work.

Overworked, without adequate help, frustrated by the apparent negligence at headquarters, Maurice wrote to the head of the Education Department to state that he wanted to stay a week in Paris, on his way to Cairo, as he had been ill. This was approved.

Then, on January 27, 1964, he was obliged to send an SOS: "Impossible to leave Dakar, no ticket, no transfer of funds. Can't make travel arrangements for trainees as cannot give instructions to TAB Cairo."[1] Bartels at headquarters cleared himself, stating in a note to the head of the department that authorization for the tickets had been given to Cooks on the twenty-fourth but the medical records had not arrived. Although the candidates had been accepted, the release of funds could only be done when all formalities were completed. It was WHO that had to give its approval, which it finally did.

Maurice came to Paris for a week, going to headquarters several times especially to make arrangements for money to be deposited in a Cairo bank from which he could draw for designated purposes. Since he was to be director and lecturer, too, he needed and meant to have local paid help. He made certain to have money for this. IDEP had sent a secretary, but other help was necessary. He left Paris for Cairo on February 8, 1964.

The course, as mentioned earlier, was organized by IDEP in collaboration with UNESCO, ILO, and the Institute of Planning of the United Arab Republic, and FAO participated. It was titled Specialized Course in Manpower and Educational Planning in Relation to Economic Development. UNESCO furnished three professors. The twenty-nine participants were from fourteen countries and of different levels of training and experience, so the degree of impact and appreciation varied. Because of the Muslim period of Ramadan, the courses, which were to begin earlier, finally began on February 18. The formal inauguration took place on the twenty-sixth with Maurice making one of the opening speeches.

After thanking the Egyptian government and all those who had helped organize the course, Maurice insisted on the need to exchange ideas and experiences, to utilize available resources and information, and to investigate thoroughly the different problems confronting planners. He stated that the problems of manpower in educational planning were of prime importance in all countries, but especially in the developing ones. He talked of the surplus of unqualified people and the shortage of desperately needed qualified manpower and how the IDEP could contribute to ease the problems. He finished by saying that he hoped the trainees would profit to the maximum not only by the course, but by what Egypt had to offer.

The course was not without risks. To bring together and keep together for twelve weeks functionaries in education of different regions of Africa, of different levels, outlooks and experiences with one common aim, to ameliorate their contribution through this special course, was a great challenge to the trainees and the lecturers. For a few, it was not profound enough. For a few, some of it was over their heads. However, after the course the trainees did concede that it had been of benefit. The more experienced admitted that the course brought home to them many problems and issues of which they had not been aware. The opportunity of getting together to discuss common problems was in itself profitable.

On April 16, 1964, Maurice sent a note to headquarters. He felt that the courses were going well as a whole. There were twenty-eight trainees. He had written to the Planning Division of the department at headquarters that it would be good if a staff member could come to Cairo to see how the course worked and to meet the students.

Maurice gave a series of twelve lectures, followed by discussions, all having to do with the role of education in economic development in Africa. They concerned the systems, the needs and problems, the organization and administration, the setting up of planning machinery, and financing. All these aspects were familiar to him. It was no hardship for him to write the lectures in French. But he gave them in English, which necessitated great care and effort. He put together a required and an optional reading list with what he had brought in the way of documentation, what IDEP and UNESCO had sent, and what the institute in Cairo made available. The lectures were printed and sent to the departments concerned, the lecturers, the trainees, and others who might be interested.

The chronological order of the program, with a few modifications, proved useful. After the reports, there were discussions. Maurice later suggested that there be, the next time, a general seminar scheduled at the end of each four-week period as a review. At first it was difficult to run the course from the organizational and material point of view, as the different collaborating agencies were geographically far apart. This concerned the payment of the grants and funds for the course as well as lecturers and technical questions: "Provision for secretarial help should be more adequate. Lecturers should be chosen in advance to have ample time for preparation. Information to governments and fellows on the requirements of the course should be much more complete. Arrangements for awarding grants for travel, for accommodations, etc., be made much earlier." (This was the way in which Maurice protested to have had to direct the course and give lectures in such short a time when he had just taken on his new responsibilities, with an added handicap that at headquarters some of the staff with which he had to work was not yet adapted to contributing efficiently to this kind of undertaking.)

However, it could be said that in spite of some unavoidable imperfections, the Cairo course (the first of its kind for African trainees) was a success and was an enriching experience for all the participants, not only the organizers, but also the lecturers and the trainees. Maurice thanked the under secretary, El-Shafie, and the director of the Planning Institute, Hamza, who had served as co-director of the course, for the collaboration and hospitality extended to him and the IDEP staff. Thanks were also due to the guest lecturers, who made an excellent contribution and worked in an atmosphere of harmonious relationships. The IDEP staff was praised.

Maurice came through the course in spite of human failures and other difficulties. Dr. A. A. El-Koussy of the Beirut center was surprised that so much was done in so short a time. R. E. Lyons of IIEP (the International Institute for Educational Planning) in Paris, who also gave some lectures, stated, after he had received the report of the course, that it was the best series of papers given up to that date. He did ask some questions, among them: "Did the trainees have enough knowledge of their home situation? Were they able to follow the high level of the lectures?" He added: "At any rate you have clearly done a first class job." The letter from Dr. Hamza showed his "appreciation for the well informed and practical approach you adopted in organizing and conducting the course. I feel fortunate to have met and worked with you."[2]

Maurice left Cairo on May 15, after everyone else, to be sure that all IDEPs and his obligations had been carried out. It was because of the contacts he made in Cairo that he let headquarters know that he preferred to have an Egyptian, P. Sammak, an expert recruited through OPEX (Operation for Executive Personnel), who had made an excellent impression, continue in Dakar with him. Maurice returned to Dakar after spending ten days in Paris to recuperate from symptoms caused by fatigue and overwork. There he plunged into the preparation of the lectures he was to give during the third semester of the nine-month IDEP course in Dakar. Some parts of the lectures he had used in Cairo were incorporated, but these lectures were far more detailed. Although Maurice, through his work in Haiti, in the Congo, and with the Emergency Program in Africa, had become familiar with the subject of planning in education for economic development, still this was the first time he was called upon to lecture in a field in which his training had been "learning by doing" and reading up on the latest developments. There were others with formal training far better informed than he was, but he did his best.

Sammak arrived in Dakar. Maurice and UNESCO were fortunate to have had him accept the post even for six months, as economists of his caliber were offered higher salaries elsewhere than those paid by UNESCO.

Maurice wrote a paper on education in Africa that he sent to headquarters. In late May, he received a letter from the head of the department of Education complimenting him on the "*good* paper." Taking advantage of this appreciation, Maurice wrote to him to thank him for his good opinion and at the same time begged him to activate the headquarters' "supporting services." Maurice needed documents, reports, address lists, and school statistics for African countries for his lectures and for the Documentation Center.

The man from the Organization for Economic Cooperation and Development in Paris, sent in a good analysis of the seminar.

He thought it had been a fair success, even though it was the first of its kind. He thought, however, that the trainees were unable to make the special effort needed to overcome their lack of experience for this kind of course. They needed to improve their work habits, adapt themselves to a regular work schedule, and profit more from staff, library, and documentation. Perhaps more study obligations should be introduced. As to the courses, he felt that they were too elevated. Only basic, general concepts, theories, definitions, approaches, techniques, and methods should be dealt with. Maurice accepted these comments as having validity, but he said that at that time "if the courses were to be given at all, candidates had to be accepted with whatever education and experience they had had. There were no others. It was hoped that they would benefit in some measure from what was offered."[3]

In June, in Dakar, Maurice was called upon to conduct two two-hour seminars on options in planning in education. Sammak was also asked to do so for university students going into their final year in the fall. These were on strategy for the development of education and problems of manpower for education in Africa. In July, Maurice gave a series of four lectures for the third term of the nine-month IDEP course on educational planning. He was quite direct in citing the hindrances delaying development and the prerequisites necessary for forward action, plus targets for meeting the present needs in education through efficient planning, probity, and dedication.

Maurice was in Paris for a month's stay from August 12 to September 13, 1964, during which time he was often at UNESCO. He hoped to improve through direct contact the collaboration with the various divisions and departments with which he had to deal. There had been annoying lapses. He also visited the new UNESCO-sponsored IIEP to contact its director, Coombs, and some of the staff, one of whom, Lyons, had been at the Cairo course and would later be in Dakar. He had sent reports to the institute as he had done for centers in Africa and headquarters.

On the invitation of the director of IIEP and the World Bank, Maurice went to Washington to attend the meeting of directors of Institutes of Economic Development held September 21–25, organized by the director of the Development Institute of the World Bank. Of greatest interest to him was the seminar on educational planning. The main paper was given by Lyons of the IIEP in Paris. Maurice was called upon to give a summary of his work and problems in Dakar. Discussion centered around the content of the courses, the need for training top echelons, new ways of fighting illiteracy, and the problem of diplomas.

The paper Maurice had written in early 1964 on education in Africa had been circulated at headquarters and had been used as reading material for the seminar and courses. It was attested as a good synthesis of the fundamental problems and a good prologue to the study of methods and techniques for planning in education. The paper was one of the areas of study in view of obtaining precise information on the state, conditions, and problems of planning in education in Africa in order to progressively put together valid teaching material for courses in planning and to assemble information that could be used for consultation services provided to governments at their demand.

The creation of the GRPE was one of the four objectives set down by the Executive Board at its fifty-eighth session, which the eleventh General Conference had unanimously approved for the Emergency Program. Another was school construction. Maurice set about to study the program of the construction of primary school classrooms in the first four-year Senegalese plan. He was also to make a study of the administration of education in Senegal, the responsibility for which was divided among four different ministries. Maurice did carry out the study on classroom construction. This study was published in August 1965. The other study could not be carried out, as he would be alone with only a secretary from January 1, 1965, on. However, with local help, he at least was able to collect the data. Perhaps those who carried on after his departure finished the study.

The study on primary school construction[4] must have reminded Maurice of his work in Haiti when, as national director of rural education, he made or had made by his staff studies for building simple one- or two-room schools and had a few schools built in rural areas, always trying to use local materials and be as economical as possible. In this study, after detailing the general objectives, the program, the national and international financing and the methods of execution, the human investment, the cost, the results, and the delays, he put down several remarks. In Senegal, there was no coordinated bureau for construction on a national or regional scale, which made for unorganized and haphazard building, without control of cost or quality. The lack of funds for the construction of proper lodgings (or any lodgings) for teachers made for high teacher turnover as well as poor teaching and absenteeism in certain regions. He suggested that a planning bureau, grouping together both education and health, be set up, an inventory of local natural resources be made, and possible revival of local fabrication of bricks, etc. (to boost the economy of the region and diminish costs of materials and long-distance hauling as well as create new small businesses), be instituted. He proposed that a pilot project be built with careful attention to costs and materials as an estimate for other such constructions. This could make for standardization and faster building. He mentioned local labor but cautioned that it could not be used unless the people had instruction or experience and were properly supervised. He linked the aspect of educational development with economic development. He finished the report stating that a four-year plan was not long enough, since it took time to make surveys, studies, and plans as well as create the infrastructure for such a vast undertaking. Maurice visited primary schools in several parts of Senegal to make certain observations as to construction, ventilation, and acoustics.

After a stay in Paris, Maurice returned to Dakar in early October to prepare for the Conference of African Planners organized by ECA and IDEP, which was to be held November 16–27, 1964. The section, meaning Maurice and Sammak, replied to a questionnaire sent out by the Educational Planning Section of headquarters for the meeting of directors of development planning that was to be held in Paris. They explained the nine-month course as well as the future action in 1964–65. Some of the salient points follow:

> As concerns the trainees, it may happen that a man from a less developed country, who has had to grapple with a variety of important educational and administrative problems and has acquired a long and successful experience at a high level may prove to be a better student than someone of a more developed country with experience in a narrow field and at a lower level, given similar professional training and equal interest and alertness. [Did Maurice remember a statement made by the head of the Department of Education at headquarters in October 1962 wherein he stated: "We need to call on the services of the most highly qualified experts of *advanced* Member States" (author's emphasis), which Maurice picked up and brought to the attention of the head of the department as showing discrimination?] Political differences do not appear to be of importance, since planning can take place under any political system. The crucial problem is the selection of mature, purposeful, competent candidates of the right kind of experience and proper level who can go back to their country to use the new acquired knowledge (follow up is difficult).

He continued to state that as to Dakar, there was much paperwork in two languages, with insufficient staff. It was a strain and a heavy burden on the director of the group. As to research, it was difficult to carry out, due again to the problem of staff. It would be of help if headquarters sent articles, reports, etc., written by UNESCO members on the subject to Dakar. There was a need to build up the documentation library. A beginning had been made, but again, the library was understaffed and the liaison with headquarters was scattered. The Division of Educational Planning could be the coordinator for this project. It was suggested that a circular be sent from headquarters to all ministries of education in Africa as well as TAB representatives, chiefs of UNESCO missions, and experts in planning to explain the broad program of educational planning to remind them of the new section in Dakar and request their collaboration.

GRPE had good contacts with IIEP, but still not with the national institutes. The fact that GRPE was connected with IDEP had its advantages and its disadvantages. Because of the recognition of the importance of educational planning, a coherent machinery needed to be set up to work in a coordinating manner with all fieldwork on an international level. Regional centers had the triple function of providing training, research, and advisory consultative services. On the national level, UNESCO sent experts at the request of member states for short and long educational planning missions. It was very important to coordinate this. The document also referred to the legal status and the financing.

As decided, the Conference of African Planners was held in November in Dakar under the auspices of ECA, Maurice and IDEP. Maurice prepared a paper for it. Sammak also prepared one. Maurice gave his paper of twenty-five pages at the opening session. It is entitled "The Planned Development of Education." In it he reiterated his deep conviction that the development of education was an essential part of economic development. The two went hand in hand. Up to that time the African school curriculum had been static, unsuited to the new demands, with emphasis on literary studies.

Maurice emphasized that

rural schools were an important feature, if not the most important, in Africa for the universal development of primary education, development in the framework of mutual dependency in various programs of development. But as only a small portion of the budget was allocated for them it was difficult to find qualified teachers. Besides, the rural population seemed indifferent. Economic and social conditions in rural areas sent the young into towns. Transformation is a global affair. The school can be part of and/or coordinated in some of the action of a concerted program to change and ameliorate life in the non-urban areas.

Maurice reaffirmed the need for a strategy, the wise use of financial and human resources, and the interdependency of school expansion and economic development:

> To be successful, the strategy must be part of a sincere and vigorous government policy. The implementation of the measures decided upon requires the setting up and operation of a competent and efficient administration. Planning to constitute a well integrated and harmonious system is indispensable. In a world of limited financial resources, with many competing needs, education must take its place in the general program of economic, social and cultural development. Educational planning should be made for each country according to the economic and social realities and goals it tries to attain.[5]

Maurice's greatest concern was the human wastage factor. To minimize this, he emphasized the importance of pragmatic planning according to needs and possibilities. For countries emerging from underdevelopment, especially in Africa, most urgent were the necessities of developing African culture and of awakening the sense of citizenship, the national consciousness as opposed to tribal loyalties. He recognized that these were added problems with which to contend besides underdevelopment, limited resources, and political ambitions. He went into detail as to the techniques and application of planning to work out a balanced, step-by-step program as part of a larger overall plan of social and economical development. (This paper has been given space as it reveals some of Maurice's constant lifelong preoccupations as concern developing nations and recognition of their special problems.)

Maurice made a trip to Accra, Ghana, and Freetown, Sierra Leone, on November 9–12, 1964, to establish personal contacts with those functionaries responsible for planning in education for future exchanges of information and documentation to obtain whatever material was available. He also wished to contact the ex-trainees of the Cairo course, three of whom were in Ghana and one in Sierra Leone. He wanted to know what effect, if any, the Cairo course had had on their work and in what way.

Maurice made this trip between the delivery of three of the four lectures he was scheduled to give before the end of 1964 for the students of the second nine-month course for economic planners, under the UNESCO-ECA, IDEP agreement. The series was titled "Education and Manpower," and the first lecture was on the planned development of education, given on

November 1, 1964. In it, as in the other lectures, he emphasized the need for a strategy of education within the larger framework of economic development. He put great stress on the lack of adaptation of the rural schools to the needs of the population in rural areas. An adapted curriculum could make for greater productivity. He then went on about the problems of organization, coordination, and implementation of plans but insisted that there is no one rigid system.

The second lecture, in December, concerned the education system as a supplier of skilled manpower. Maurice pointed out the enormous need for educated manpower in every field and at every level, public services, private industry, and agriculture. In the third lecture, "Some Crucial Problems of Education in Relation to Economic Development," he referred to the problems of priorities, administration, and adult illiteracy in its economic aspects. He went on to detail ways of going about resolving these. He felt that agriculture would still remain, for some time, the main occupation of the majority of the population in developing countries. Therefore, a consistent agricultural education program to aid the population had to be set up. As for the dropouts, specific measures were indispensable to make such young people feel included in the life of the community through youth groups and other organizations. The last lecture was given in February 1965. It was titled "A Summary of Basic Ideas Relating to Manpower Planning within the Framework of Economic Development."

The year ended with Maurice in Paris for consultations and a family reunion. While there from December 23, 1964, to January 23, 1965, he attended, at Diez Hochleitner's special request, the meeting for the directors of regional centers organized by the recently created Division of Planning in Education. At this meeting, diverse questions relating to planning in education and the programs for the training of planners and the relations with each other and with headquarters were discussed.

Maurice was happy to renew contact with Diez Hochleitner. He knew he could count on him for certain matters at headquarters. Diez Hochleitner was better qualified to help him than those in some of the other divisions of the Department of Education. He was serious and devoted. He admired Maurice for his principles, his dedication, and his sense of justice as well as his encouragement of initiative. Each appreciated and respected the other.

The Regional Group for Educational Planning, Dakar, 1965

The year 1965 would be critical for the ECA-sponsored IDEP and the GRPE sector sponsored by UNESCO. In the fall of 1964, the temporary director of IDEP, P. Vieyra, resigned. He and Maurice had gotten along very well in view of the arrangements and the problems of prerogatives. Vieyra was replaced by a newly recruited permanent director. This man appeared to be more rigid in his understanding of the roles of the two parties involved in the agreement.

Maurice made the best of a deteriorating situation, heading the GRPE and staff of experts (actually nonexistent now that Sammak had gone). Maurice did have a secretary. A documentarian had arrived who began to put together the available material for a documentation section. Maurice gave the last lecture of the second nine-month course in February. Thus ended for the time being his contribution as a lecturer. As the field was new to UNESCO, to Africa, and to Maurice, he probably learned a great deal about the subject in preparing the lectures.

While in Paris, Maurice had had talks with Diez Hochleitner and with Coombs, director of IIEP, and some of his staff concerning special courses to be held for functionaries of African educational planning sections in ministries from October 18 to December 14, 1965, in Dakar. These courses would be given conjointly with IDEP, IIEP, ILO, FAO, and GRPE. Maurice prepared the first informational note, which described the courses and the attributes of the candidates. He added that grants including lodging, travel, and indemnities would be offered, some by UNESCO. The trainees would be on leave of absence with pay. Letters were sent to governments to urge them to choose the best-qualified persons, explaining that the course would be profitable for the exchange of ideas that could lead to new thinking on planning.

By mid-March questions pertaining to the selection of the candidates came up among the African Division, the students' Exchange Division at headquarters, and Maurice as to how the course was to be conducted, what the course would contain, who was to teach, and the chronology of the program. There had been several meetings, the first when Maurice had been in Paris, then between Adiseshiah and Coombs. Maurice was to have the overall responsibility as well as give several lectures. Now it appeared that IIEP wished to have the technical responsibility for the preparation, the execution, and the evaluation of the course. Evidently, Maurice objected to this, as it made him uncertain as to his role. He let Adiseshiah know this. It was finally decided that Maurice would direct the course and IIEP could choose a staff member as deputy director. So that was settled for the time being.

Maurice asked the Bureau of Planning at headquarters to send out the first informational note on the course to the different interested governments. At the same time, he clarified the needs as to financing, personnel, translators, and secretaries. He also informed the bureau that the GRPE was uncertain as to whether it was to stay in the framework of IDEP or separate. A few days later he wrote that GRPE had separated but had no official status for the time being.

It was evident that ECA through IDEP interpreted the accords between it and UNESCO through GRPE one way, as a matter of domination and control, while the latter interpreted the association as sponsorship with an extent of autonomy and responsibility for choices of personnel and program. The differences in point of view deprived Maurice of the professional aid he needed. It came to the point that the new director of IDEP disclaimed the accords and demanded their revision.

Problems of interpretation came up also as to the roles of IIEP, IDEP, and GRPE. These were inevitable, as such partnerships were new and untried. IIEP thought that the course was to be held within the framework of IDEP, but under the responsibility of IIEP and GRPE. This, too, caused difficulties, as the director of IDEP held a different view. Maurice, through talks with the director, calmed him. It was decided that a senior staff member of IDEP would be co-director of the course with Maurice. This took time but was also settled.

From the beginning, Maurice had the responsibility of organizing the course and working out the budget. He had to be explicit with the headquarters staff, who did not realize all the work that went into a bilingual course. It was suggested (to keep down the budget) that the bilingual secretary do the translation. Maurice wrote back that a secretary was not a translator; besides, she would not even have enough time for the work for which she was hired, as there was so much to do. He also insisted that the headquarters budget estimates were too low; no money had been provided for necessary transportation of the students, as the building in which the courses were to be held was at eight kilometers from town. Not one dollar had been estimated for possible expenditures. If the course was not a success due to lack of funds or proper personnel, the blame would fall on him. Maurice must have been exasperated and overworked to have written in this vein.

Then Maurice became concerned about the teaching personnel. He took this up with the director of the Bureau of Planning at headquarters, Bousquet. Maurice especially questioned a proposed man who was good in the history of education, but was he good enough on the subject of administration and inspection? Maurice proposed that a Haitian expert in statistics, S. Mirville, now in the Congo, be permitted to come to Dakar on mission for the course. He was competent and well liked. Maurice observed that some good lecturers could be had on short-term contracts and that there were experts in Dakar of the different UN agencies who could make contributions. He needed to know how many lecturers IIEP would provide and what subjects they would treat.

Maurice wrote to several specialists at headquarters to ask them to prepare papers to be used as bases for certain courses. He begged experts in the field, with whom he had worked or of whose work he knew, to do the same. One such was Pauvert, who had worked with Maurice at headquarters on the questionnaires in 1959 and had worked with him in the Congo for a short time and who had been in Tananarive as chief expert in July 1962. Of another expert—ex-chief of mission in Bamako—Maurice asked for a study on the step-by-step reforms in Mali. He asked the chief of the Regional Center of School Construction in Khartoum to do a paper on its work.

While this was going on, Maurice had been preparing a meeting of experts to discuss problems concerning such courses. It took place May 24–28. Altogether, twenty-eight experts participated, of whom twelve were permanent. What came out of the meeting was that there were too many trainees at one time and too many not having the qualifications or experience to appreciate the courses offered. Planning in education had not yet taken root in Africa. What offices were in existence were mostly directed by foreign experts. Salaries were too low to attract qualified nationals, especially in French-speaking countries, outside of Mali. This was a grave and urgent problem. It was essential to train nationals to replace the foreign experts who did most of the work. As for the two-month course, which it was finally decided would be bilingual, it was not advanced enough for the English-speaking participants, who were, for the most part, university-level, while perhaps it was too much for the French-speaking, most of whom were on the level of primary school teachers. It was also too long for high-level functionaries and too short for profound training for the others. These reflections were harsh realities and would be a challenge for Maurice and the others who were to organize and teach the course. Other observations were made.

The director of the Planning Bureau at headquarters made a trip to Dakar in late May to discuss the various aspects of the course. He attended a meeting and met the director of IDEP. Maurice suggested that until the course was over, it might be better to let things ride while negotiations with the government for housing for GRPE could be obtained or until IDEP could be transferred. He had come to an understanding with the director of IDEP that GRPE stay on until a statute as a separate institute be worked out for it by the Senegalese government and the UNESCO director-general.

The question of budget was an irritation. Maurice wrote that he had little time to be constantly remaking it to accommodate the various sectors. The question returned as to whether it was wise to make the course bilingual. A note from Hennion, the expert in administration in the Congo, now at headquarters, said that he had considered the negative aspects of this method. It was much costlier and got in the way of direct contact between professors and the students, and thus the greatest educational value of the seminar was lost. Diez Hochleitner, now in the Planning Bureau, agreed with this. Maurice asked that the director-general decide the question. The director-general decided on the use of the two languages. Then the problem of equipment for translating came up. There was no equipment in Dakar. A portable machine was found in Paris and sent accompanied to Dakar. Maurice had the translator's cabin made locally from plans sent from headquarters, this being the cheaper way, as he discovered after inquiries.

Much of June was taken up by the correspondence for the studies and papers, for the changed and changed again outline of the course and the budget. Maurice as yet had no professional staff nor enough staff for the various services needed. Fortunately in mid-June the IIEP director, Coombs, offered to reproduce copies of reports and summaries in Paris. Maurice thanked him for this great help. At the same time, Coombs stated that he hoped to have the final course outline by June 25 so that IIEP could decide whom to send and the time it would be best for whomever to come. This Maurice did, only to receive the reply from Coombs on July 12, 1965, that the schedule would not do. It had to be remade to give a time block for IIEP staff; otherwise, much time would be wasted. It was better to do less and do it well. There were too many subjects.

Maurice tried to explain to Coombs that the course had been planned with his staff when Maurice was in Paris in January, that the outline had been discussed with the deputy director, Lyons, and that Lyons's suggestions had been followed, as well as Maurice's own past experience, as to interrelated chronology, logic, and organic relationships. The lecturers needed time to adapt to a lower level than foreseen if necessary. There was a fifty-fifty chance that the right people would come. When the syllabus had been circulated, he had received no comments. He hoped that Lyons could be spared for the entire course, as it would be an interesting experience for him. Maurice was ready to give up two of the four lecturers if this would facilitate matters. However, he felt that taking entire time blocks out of the course for IIEP alone would disorganize the relationships of the course. This problem, after some correspondence among Coombs, the director-general, Lyons, and Maurice, was solved, and the schedule was arranged. After more correspondence, it was decided that from then on the highest level of functionaries would be trained by IIEP in Paris and that the high and middle levels would be trained in Dakar.

July was taken up by letters to governments concerning candidates, resident representatives, and missions. Although invitations to governments to select candidates had gone out through the new assistant director-general, Betancourt-Mejia (Spain), as yet there were few responses. Answers did come in finally.

Then a hurdle was created by J.C. Bousquet, Chief of the Planning Division at headquarters. Maurice had earlier suggested that, as at Tananarive, the Arab states be invited. He pointed out that at the course in Cairo there had been trainees from these states as well as those south of the Sahara. He had been informed that for this course only trainees from the latter states were to be asked to participate. Now in mid-August, he was requested by Bousquet to invite Arab countries to select candidates, but they would not have fellowships. Maurice was indignant. The Division of International Exchange had sent invitations including offers of fellowships to other governments. He voiced the opinion that it was up to headquarters, either by the division aforementioned or by the BMS (Bureau of Member States), to do the inviting. The Education Department supported Maurice on this, observing that the Arab states were in Africa and invitations should have gone to them as they had for Tananarive and the Cairo program. If there was a difference, then UNESCO had to rethink its ideas concerning regions.

Before leaving for a month's stay in Paris late in August, Maurice wrote that few applications had turned up. He needed news of the candidates. He demanded urgently of Bousquet to recruit two professors and process the applications quickly.

While he was in Paris, Maurice met with Adiseshiah about the budget decided on for the statistician from the Congo, the interpreters, and the cabin for them, which would have to be air-conditioned due to its placement and small size. Money for local secretarial help was given. He was concerned what measures would have to be taken if the promised French contribution of 300,000 francs did not come through.

On September 22, Maurice returned to Dakar, where he found various matters awaiting his attention. The most important was that the course was to begin in eighteen days and as of yet the budget had not been definitely allocated. He wrote to Betancourt-Mejia that in spite of the uncertainty and the delay, he had to go through with the preparations. He knew UNESCO was awaiting the French contribution.

For the first time, a woman was proposed as a trainee. She would in January 1966 go on to IIEP in Paris for further training. She was Miss Diop of Mali, who came as a special student. As banal as it may seem today, when one considers the number of women arriving at university level now in countries in Africa, this was indeed an event.

Until the last week before the course began, Maurice was preoccupied with the lining up of the main lecturers, Mirville to come from the Congo, and Lyons of IIEP, as well as experts of other agencies who were solicited to give talks, plus the building of the cabin for the translators. The French contribution finally arrived on October 11. He also received the news that GRPE was now budgeted under the regular UNESCO program under the responsibility of the Division of Educational Planning, so that it was completely independent of IDEP. The budget permitted a staff of three professionals, an administrative assistant, a documentarian, and a secretary. However, except for the seminar, Maurice remained the sole professional. He sent an SOS to the headquarters Clearing House for needed statistics on education from African countries for his lectures.

The course began on October 18. Mirville had arrived, as did the expert from Gabon and later those from IIEP. On October 22, Maurice wrote to Betancourt-Mejia that the course was going well and the participants had formed a good group and showed interest and Lyons had returned to Paris. Maurice hoped he had carried away a good impression. To which Betancourt-Mejia replied that he was glad that all was going well. Maurice

305

managed to bring it off. In comparison with what he had done in the past, this seminar was no vast undertaking, but it was a challenge for that time and the conditions existing in the field and headquarters.

Maurice made a report after the seminar, the publication of which reached him in late May 1966, when he was already in Burundi.[6] He stated that the seminar, Annual Course in Planning in Education, was the first of a series of such courses. It was addressed exclusively to educators. It concerned itself with the problems of planning, the principles and techniques in the context of the conditions, and the needs of countries in Africa and in the framework of their economic development. It was aimed to familiarize planners with the steps to take and the essential elements to consider in the elaboration and development of educational planning and the determining of objectives and priorities. During the first two weeks of the eight-week course, the heat in the afternoon was so great that classes were held only from 8:30 to 12:45. The afternoons were given over to individual studies and pursuits. Afterward courses were given two or three times a week from 4:00–6:00 P.M. Saturdays were kept for visits. The courses were given in French and English. At the end of the course, the trainees received a certificate of attendance and diligence.

As to the trainees, thirty were accepted and twenty-nine turned up, none from Arab states. Their ages ranged from twenty-seven to fifty, indicating maturity. Thirteen had BA or BS degrees and all the others post–secondary school training. All had experience in the various fields of teaching and/or administration, with most having had functions in planning sections of the ministries of education. Such backgrounds made for better understanding of the courses offered.

As to the lecturers, Lyons returned to Dakar. He gave the most hours in lectures, with Mirville a close second, and Maurice with twenty-two. It was a really cooperative venture, with three lecturers from IDEP, four from UNESCO, three from IIEP, one each from ILO, FAO, and WHO, one from the IPN, and two from the national Ministry of Education. Most were stationed in Dakar, but one came from Dar es Salaam, Tanyanika, sent by FAO.

For his part, Maurice gave seven lectures. They came under the seven different course headings. Among the twenty-nine documents prepared for the courses and reproduced under the GRPE auspices (notice that they were no longer IDEP publications), Maurice prepared and distributed five, among them one of his earlier lectures, and his study on the construction of rural primary schools, while the three others dealt with problems of development of primary and secondary schools, especially in the rural areas.

As to the outcome of the course, after giving due thanks to all of the organizations that had participated and all the lecturers and other personnel for their collaboration, Maurice reported that the course had turned out well because the trainees were cooperative, as were all concerned. The trainees were unanimous in saying that "they had gained useful knowledge which would help them in a practical way in their work. They admitted that the courses opened their eyes to problems of education or administration and planning on which they as yet had had no time to reflect."[7] The courses were more concrete and practical than those at Cairo, stated Maurice. This was partly due to the utilization of studies made beforehand and distributed and due to the lecturers who had had practical experience in their fields and in Africa. However, Maurice recognized that the course could have been more concrete and more practical and the results more fruitful if more time had been given to GRPE, adequate personnel, and greater certainty about financing. Because of this it had been difficult to organize really practical workshops, which the students had desired. The documentation service needed improvement. It also would have been better if the lecturers had met beforehand for better coordination:

However, in spite of the unfavorable aspects, which give useful instruction for the future, the course proceeded in a regular, systematic and satisfactory manner. This was due to the competence and devotion of the teachers as well as the quality of the trainees. Most took an active part in the discussions and on several occasions were able to present problems in their countries and how they were resolved. The course also brought together French and English speaking trainees and through this contact permitted a better understanding of each others' systems. The trainees thought that it was an advantage to have the courses in two languages. The discussions brought out the sociological and political implications of educational planning. They also brought out that educational planning went beyond the specialists and involved directors of services as well as those responsible for the execution of the plans, who should familiarize themselves in various degrees with the methods and techniques of planning. There is a need to see such planning from a global point of view as one of the fundamental aspects of education itself.[8]

Maurice had written to Coombs to thank him for the lecturers, especially Lyons, and for the other services IIEP had rendered. Coombs congratulated Maurice for having been able to organize and carry out the course so well in spite of the many practical difficulties. He hoped for another opportunity to cooperate. Betancourt-Mejia also congratulated Maurice for having made the course a success: "You with your organizing abilities and devotion in sometimes difficult circumstances. My cordial wishes."[9]

Maurice was no dupe as to the limitations. The course was new for every one of those who attended. He sent the report of the course to headquarters before he left Dakar. It was just as well he did, for in the rapid move of the GRPE to new quarters it might have been lost.

Maurice's last report, a concise one on the activities of GRPE since its creation and under his directorship, is dated December 22, 1965, and carries the notation: "GRPE/1/Report/2." In it he tells of his arrival, the setting up of the bureau, his relations with IDEP, the lectures he gave in Dakar, the staff he did not have but occasionally, the course in Cairo, his trip to Washington and to Accra and Freetown in the fall of 1964, his research in school construction, the first annual seminar for educational planners and his correspondence with ex-trainees and institutions.

Maurice made several remarks of interest here. He insisted on the interdependence of the different governmental services, and pointed out that each seminar should be patterned to fit the needs of each set of trainees. The quality of the courses and their adaptation to the special needs of the trainees were important. Therefore, besides theoretical reports on the principles and techniques of planning in each country, they must take into consideration the conditions under which the plans were elaborated and, above all, executed:

In this order of ideas, the problem of administration, with its psychological and political implications, constitutes a factor of major importance in the matter of planning, which assumes in developing countries, besides technical and other aspects, a civil and moral character.

In view of the difficulties encountered when an attempt is made to modify structures, a study of the administrative set-up and functioning conditions of the administration of education may allow us to find ways to ameliorate the existing structure so as to provoke a gradual change.

Maurice left Dakar in time to be with us in Paris for the holidays. No sooner did his replacement Hennion arrive, than he was ordered off the premises by the director of IDEP with his group and given forty-eight hours to locate GRPE elsewhere. With quick telephone calls, Hennion was able to find an empty apartment, which he set up in short order. In spite of the disagreeable reception and precipitous action, Hennion stayed as head of GRPE, which later changed to BREDA,[10] for seven years. The bureau grew from four experts to twenty. It sent out teams to governments that requested its aid not only in planning, but also in school architecture and other areas of educational endeavor. Courses were instituted on different levels, one of six weeks for basic training, then one for seven or eight months. When trainees showed aptitude they were sent on to IIEP in Paris. The Special Fund and the French government supported the center at the beginning, but later certain salaries were paid by UNESCO and the grants for trainees by UNDP combined from the Special Fund and TA. BREDA is still running today.

Notes

1. UNESCO Ar. 37A(663)-56/022 07 (6) "66," cable.
2. Home Files, Hamza, Institute of Planning, Cairo, May 28, 1964.
3. Ibid., July 10, 1964.
4. Published by UNESCO for GRPE, Dakar, 1965.
5. Ibid., E/CIT. 14/CAP. 6 IDEP/ET/R/251.
6. Dartigue Files, GRPE/1/Rapport 1, December 18, 1965.
7. Ibid., *Observations générales*, p. 5.
8. Ibid.
9. UNESCO Gen. Reg. 37(6)A-06(44) "62," December 20, 1965.
10. Regional Bureau for Economic Development in Africa.

Expert in Burundi, 1966–68

The new year came in with Maurice at home in Paris and, for the first time in several years, job hunting again. He was not ready to retire, nor did he wish to return to Haiti, where the political situation would not have permitted him to make a contribution. He preferred to stay in Paris to await an opening in an educational project of UNESCO. He asked for and obtained a leave of absence without pay, to keep his final pension rights. He was almost certain he would obtain a post within six months. He was right.

As early as January 1963, Maurice had been proposed for the post of resident representative of the combined TA and Special Fund, now named the UNDP,[1] in Rwanda, which had just become independent and separated from Burundi. He was highly recommended by Adiseshiah. The post was given to one of several other candidates. In a way, this was just as well, as very soon afterwards Maurice created the GRPE in Dakar, which he directed for two years.

In January 1965, while on leave in Paris, Maurice evidently took steps to go on from Dakar to another position. He was offered one in July to Addis Ababa but felt obliged to refuse it because of the altitude. The short stays he had made there created no problem, but his doctor told him that a long sojourn could be detrimental to his health.

It may have been through Bergeaud or Bousquet that an opening came about in late March 1966 in Bujumbura, Burundi (formerly a trusteeship of Belgium), as acting director of the recently created IPN or ENS [Ecole Normale Supérieure] and principal technical adviser to the government in educational matters.

Very few people outside of Belgium, the United Nations, and its affiliates know much about Burundi. Maurice, having been with the Trusteeship Council visiting mission in 1951 and through his work at both the United Nations and UNESCO, was one of the few who did. He was aware of the special ethnic relationships and the necessity of being neutral and diplomatic concerning the barely concealed rivalries and antagonisms between the two main groups, the Watutsi, more powerful, and the Bahutu, far more numerous. The first, descendants of a Nilotic tribe that had arrived in the area 400 years before, bringing cattle to the country and forming the

310

warrior class, became the dominant group, while the Bahutu served them as herders and farmers in a complex system of duties and responsibilities. A third ethnic group, the Pygmies, much fewer in number, were given no consideration and lived in isolation. All speak the one language, Kirundi. (Incidentally, one person is called a Murundi; more than one, Barundi.)

While Maurice was chief of the African Desk, a first planning mission for education had been sent to Burundi in late 1962, preceded by Ochs's visit earlier. Another was sent after Maurice had left for Dakar to evaluate the progress accomplished by the government between the two missions and to recommend further action. As in other newly independent African countries, priorities concerned the expansion of secondary education and the training of secondary school teachers to free Burundi from its dependence on foreign teachers and administrative personnel. It was from these needs that the agreement arose between the government and UNDP, with UNESCO as the executing agent, to create an ENS. The decree had been promulgated by the old *mwami* (king) and published on September 22, 1965. The intention was that the ENS would not only train secondary school teachers, but would recycle inspectors for primary schools and, through the specialists or experts, reorient programs toward a more practical and realistic approach to the new needs of the nation.

The problem was not as acute as in several other African countries. The population was 3,350,000 persons, contained in about 10,000 square miles. At independence there were forty-eight Barundi in higher education, most in religious training institutions, with ten of them having a European *licence,* or university degree. This was a step forward, as in the report Maurice made in 1951 for the Trusteeship Council he mentioned only one. At that time a university for Bujumbura (then called Usumbura) had been projected for 1954–59. It was actually opened in 1964 by the Jesuits with a subsidy from the government. In 1967, it was still in an almost embryonic stage, for although it had several hundred students, there were few full-time professors. Most were priests teaching part-time, rotating on three-month stints among the universities of Elizabethville and Léopoldville and other Catholic universities. There were lay professors, some of whom gave courses at the new ENS as well. The library of the university contained few books and was wholly inadequate for the number of students. (This is firsthand knowledge, as I took a course at the university.) The laboratory was rudimentary. The few Barundi who had been trained abroad had graduated from a university in the Congo or at the special section of the

University of Antwerp, Belgium, set up for African students. In 1965, there were 269 Barundi studying abroad, with grants from various sources. This was indeed a great step since 1962, when the country became independent.

The university was a private Catholic institution. The ENS was a public, national, nonsectarian school. When Maurice arrived in late April 1966 there were at ENS nine full-time and seven part-time professors, furnished by the French and Belgian governments. As has been stated, some gave courses at the university. A library had been set up with donations from the French, Belgian, UK, U.S. and USSR embassies. This was also done for the laboratory. The government had agreed to provide the furnishings and the upkeep of the dormitory, dining room, and some equipment for the classrooms in the quarters loaned to house the ENS. The management of these was done by a Belgian whose ideas differed from those held by Maurice, causing some friction in their relationship later.

Maurice's first task was to contact the various personalities, authorities, and functionaries not only of ENS and the government, but also of the various affiliated and private agencies. He found several Haitians and their families among those of FAO, WHO, and UNDP. According to those who had been in the Congo for some time, Burundi was a paradise in terms of weather and security. Maurice also contacted the several officials of the various consulates and other representatives of foreign countries. The most in evidence were the French, the Belgians, and the Americans. Whatever industry or commerce there was, was in the hands of foreigners: Belgians and Greeks mostly, with a few Indians, Arabs, and British. Maurice's next step was to size up the situation of the school and take note of its needs, so he could make them known to headquarters when he returned to Paris in July.

As the country is at three degrees latitude from the Equator, it can be hot and most foreigners who could went to Europe for the summer months. Maurice spent his first days on his return to Paris going for consultations to headquarters and making arrangements for some of his personal goods to be shipped to Bujumbura, as I would accompany him on this mission. I was under the impression that it was for six months but accepted the situation as it unfolded from six months to twelve, to eighteen, then to twenty-four and finally to twenty-eight months.

While in Paris, Maurice decided to go to New York for a medical checkup. There he learned that it would be wise to have surgery. He consented and it was not until the end of September that we returned to Paris

312

and early November before we arrived in Bujumbura. The surgeons in New York urged that he get back to work as soon as possible. Starting with half-days, he gradually worked up to full days, adding evenings and weekends as he had done before.

It is certain that there must have been correspondence, knowing how much Maurice wrote. It appears that if there was, that correspondence was consumed in the fire that broke out in the UNESCO archives in the spring of 1985, which destroyed some of the three floors in one of the wings of the UNESCO building at place Fontenoy, which housed archives not yet placed in the permanent depot in the basement of the same building. A few documents from his home files and one mission report attest to his two years' work here. It is from these that his mission can be in a small measure reconstructed.

As stated, the decree for the creation of ENS for the training of secondary school teachers was announced on September 22, 1965. The training would be of three years' duration, with theory and practice, under the auspices of the minister of education and culture. The training would lead to a diploma for teaching in the first cycle of secondary school, the first two years of post-primary. When the school first opened in loaned quarters, there were admitted, as students, those who had secondary school diplomas or teachers who had had seven years' postprimary study. For the first recruits there was no age limit.

When Maurice arrived in April 1966, the old *mwami* reigned. He was deposed in July by his son, who sent him into exile and assumed the kingship. Soon after our arrival in early November, the young king was deposed by Michambero, an army colonel, through a coup d'état. He named himself president and changed Burundi from a monarchy to a republic. This also meant a change in government and ministers, whom Maurice then had to contact. (We learned about it after being stopped, as we were taking an evening stroll, by an army Jeep, one of whose occupants shouted, "Go inside! There is a curfew!" Of course we hurried home and on arriving there turned on the radio. We were later told that on that night hangings and executions had taken place. We neither knew nor heard anything.)

The UNESCO Special Fund and the government agreement had to be made over to delete references to a kingdom. This Maurice helped to do. He undertook to formulate a draft for statutes for the teachers. He advised that an administrative council be created for ENS, thus giving the school a civic personality.

Maurice sent in the first trimestrial report in late January 1967. Although ENS came into existence in 1965, Burundi only requested aid officially in January 1966. He arrived in April, but the preliminaries to the implementation of the assistance of the Special Fund to the government for ENS were carried through in November and December 1966. The formal approbation by the administrative board of UNDP did not come through until the middle of January 1967. But in anticipation of this approval, the UNDP representative authorized the recruitment of four experts, of whom the principal technical adviser was Maurice. He also authorized the acquisition of certain articles of equipment.

By the middle of December, a young Belgian specialist in French as a second language, who had been in Burundi as inspector of normal schools for primary school teachers, was recruited. His wife was also a specialist in this field. She continued her work with the government. Together they worked out a special program (although he was hired as the director of studies) for use at the different levels of the teaching of French. She produced several elementary French reading books for use in primary schools.

A bilingual (English-French) secretary arrived in early January 1967 and the librarian-documentarian the first of February. She immediately began to work on the existing library, to catalog and put in order the books and documents. The library later acquired several rare books on the history and customs of Burundi. The expert for English was also recruited but due to commitments did not arrive until the opening of school in the fall of 1967, as did the experts in educational psychology and those for math, physics, and chemistry. The program did not effectually get under way until then.

As to the equipment, Maurice addressed a list to headquarters by December 28, 1966. Among the priorities were a minibus for the students and a car for the school services, as was provided in the agreement. Maurice's counterpart had been selected by the government. He was a young graduate in philology of the University of Brussels and was given a grant to go abroad to study administration in the fall of 1967. In the meantime, he was to be initiated into his future duties by Maurice and continue as professor of French and Kirundi. However, before he could take advantage of the grant, he became the minister for foreign affairs, and he would not return to his duties as director of ENS until 1969. He did continue to give courses. In June 1967, a second-year student was selected for study abroad in library science.

Maurice, having made the first draft of the Plan of Operations, with different annexes, submitted it to the minister of education and culture in mid-January 1967. This same plan with a few modifications made at headquarters was officially presented by a functionary of UNESCO, who came for this purpose from Paris. He and Maurice submitted the plan again to the minister who, on the second encounter, accepted it, giving his accord after proposing a few minor changes in the principal points of the text.

In the agreement, the government was to turn over to the Special Fund nineteen thousand dollars as its contribution. As stated earlier, it was to help to furnish the school. It undertook the cost of a slight expansion of the quarters, a few alterations, a few book purchases, and provision in the budget for an assistant librarian.

Maurice took measures to secure periods of observation and practice teaching for the students in a few of the classes where this was not only permitted, but would be rewarding. This was a difficult undertaking, as so few of those teaching in the secondary schools could pass on enriching experiences. This was so even among the teaching staff of ENS. Maurice held several plenary sessions with the staff and some small group sessions to make for more enthusiasm and productivity. He also met with student classroom delegates and delegates of student associations.

The situation of ENS was ambiguous. Although the government had accepted the agreement, the formal protocol was not signed until December 31, 1967, and did not become operational until April 19, 1968, two years after Maurice's arrival. In the meantime, the government reduced its contribution for the functioning of the school after it had approved the budget in principle. This affected the expenditure for the live-in students and the domestic personnel, so Maurice was forced to iron out this problem with the ministries concerned. Such problems were not easy to solve until the Plan of Operations, designating on paper the responsibilities of each signatory, was signed. Knowing Maurice's meticulousness, his adherence to principles of hierarchy, and his sense of responsibility, there must have been a great deal of correspondence between him and headquarters. This must have been so, as his secretary often complained of the workload. Changes in the government also made for delays. It was only a few months before Maurice's final departure that he felt on sure ground when he requested the government's consented contribution.

At the minister's demand, Maurice prepared a new portfolio on the project for the permanent constructions for ENS. This he did without modifying either the technical presentation or the cost estimates. He changed the presentation of the whole project for easier understanding and acceptability.

From March 23 to April 1, 1967, Maurice attended the meeting of directors and administrators of UNESCO-sponsored IPNs in Africa held in Tunis. At the time there were twenty-two IPNs in Africa, three of which were in Nigeria. He was obliged to go via Paris, so he stopped off at headquarters for consultations. (I accompanied him, not wishing to stay alone in Bujumbura. We stayed at the Hilton, where dyed eggs were served with breakfast on Easter morning.) The meeting in Tunis put emphasis on the teaching of languages, taking into consideration the difficulties created by the multiplicity of languages in some African countries such as the Congo. In this respect, Burundi was more fortunate. The national language, Kirundi, had become a written idiom in the early 1900s through the work of German missionaries. It was taught as such from the first year of school. French was the official language for the government in its dealings with the outside world and the language used in conjunction with Kirundi in the late primary years and secondary schools. Often government documents were in both languages. A third language, Swahili, the lingua franca of East Africa, was used by those who had contacts in commerce. This did not affect the ENS situation. It was the natural desire of the African countries to keep alive their linguistic and cultural heritage, but they recognized the necessity of an international, vehicular language, either French or English, so welcomed innovations and better ways of teaching and learning one or both.

With the recruitment of the French expert and later the English one, the task of revising methods of teaching and introducing new ways of learning became easier for ENS. Their enthusiasm, efforts, and know-how produced results. At the primary level, a new syllabus and test were introduced in pilot projects to ameliorate the learning of French as a second language. Research had begun in 1963–64 on how French was taught and how French was learned. The results of this research produced new methods. An attempt was made to teach oral language better. One great drawback was that Kirundi was so far removed from French in construction and syntax that it was difficult for Barundi children to overcome the obstructions to understand French. It appeared that the learning of English in the secondary schools presented fewer obstacles. A survey of the existing methods was carried out, and Maurice determined to have a seminar on the subject of teaching French as a second language in the spring of 1968.

The science program also needed looking into. The Barundi before the sixties had shown little interest in science. For the most part, students came from the interior, where they and their families led pastoral lives. If they were Bahutu, they were concerned with farming or herding; if Watutsi, then in practicing the art of war or assuming the responsibilities of being proprietors of land and cattle and carrying out the various functions of the notables in their villages. They led, for the most part, sedentary lives, where modern science had little meaning. Whatever science they learned in school was mostly learned by rote and was not very well understood by most. Whatever science was taught was mostly theoretical, as there was little practical application due not only to lack of sufficiently equipped laboratories for group or individual work, but also to a lack of sufficiently trained teachers. There was no television, few magazines (and those were bought by Europeans), and few foreign newspapers. The local newspaper was rudimentary. The radio was geared to local monitored information, as few, even among the European residents, had radios powerful enough to catch news and programs from abroad.

In order to improve the teaching of science at ENS, Maurice was determined to have a properly equipped laboratory, and at great expense, due to airfreight. As it would have taken months to receive equipment sent by boat from Europe and train from Mombasa, he sent an SOS to headquarters for necessary apparatus. It was imperative in his mind to have the minimum essential elements for proper teaching and application of principles. He was willing to sacrifice part of the budget for quick delivery. He organized a seminar on the teaching of science in the spring of 1968. (The science professor at ENS remarked that the heavy equipment [due to air freight] was the most expensive he had ever used.)

On his return from Tunis in April 1967, Maurice worked on the school catalog for the year 1967–68 in collaboration with the faculty. In it he stated the reasons for the establishment of ENS. He brought out that it was a joint effort, with cooperation among the government of Burundi, the Belgian TA, the French cultural and technical aid, and UNDP, with UNESCO acting as executing agent. It was imperative to increase the number of Barundi qualified secondary school teachers for the first cycle. He then outlined the courses, with the mention of the names of the faculty members who would be teaching the courses. Among these were several Barundi. In the catalog for the first time Maurice mentioned his own background and experience in Haiti as minister of public instruction.

317

We left for annual leave to Paris and New York on August 7, 1967. The work in Burundi seemed to agree with Maurice, for the surgeon in New York thought him in fine form. As usual while he was in Paris, he had consultations at headquarters. On our return to Bujumbura at the end of September, we greeted the newly arrived expert in English and his young family. He was a Scotsman named Murdock. He had a real Scotsman's burr, which, he said, he was able to master in the classroom. Fortunately for him, as for other families of the UN affiliate agencies, including ourselves, new individual housing had opened up, which included gardens, thus giving his and other children playground space within walking distance of the ENS.

In a recent interview, Murdock briefly recounted his experience in Burundi, where he was able to remain for four or five years, thus following students from the beginning of their schooling to their graduation. He stated that he had to reteach his students English before he could go on, as their English was not only limited, but very poor. At the time there seemed no future in majoring in English. In the fall of 1967, there was only one student, a girl. (By the way, in a country of 3 million people, there were only twelve girls in the two higher-training institutions, the university and ENS. All said they had defied custom and their families to continue to study after finishing the primary school. They had persevered.) The third-year woman student thought to graduate in 1968, but Murdock found her so poorly trained that in spite of Maurice's hope of seeing the first Murundi woman graduate, he took it as a point of honor to reteach her and have her graduate in 1969, having done observation and practice teaching under his guidance in a class in the secondary school close by, which he had taken over as his own to assure proper teaching. The insistence on a high quality of English, his dynamism, and his attention to the problems of each student filtered through so that more students signed up to major in English. In 1968, there were four; in 1969, nineteen; and in 1970, thirty. The possibility of receiving a USIS grant for study at the University of California may also have been an incentive. Another aid was a new text titled *English for French-speaking Countries,* distributed by the U.S. and the UK embassies with a workbook put together in collaboration with the teachers of English in Bujumbura. Perhaps because of this learning aid, young people were better prepared to meet the challenge of mastering English and to entertain the hope of teaching it after graduation from ENS.

Two women and several young men did receive grants. One of the latter, for whom Maurice had been able to obtain one, wrote to him from

California to express his gratitude on July 5, 1968. The letter stated: "You said that I could show my thanks by working hard. I am glad to say that I have received the 'Certificate for Teaching English as a Second Language.' I hope to see you in the fall." This of course was not to be, but Murdock would be there to welcome him back.

Maurice visited secondary schools in the interior to assess for himself the quality of the teaching and the laboratory equipment, if a laboratory existed, and make contacts for possible candidates for ENS. It was always an adventure to go outside of Bujumbura. The roads for the most part were rudimentary, as there was little road upkeep. There were no garages, stores, or water or food supplies, so all eventualities had to be considered and provided for before starting out. There were periods when the roads were not safe, when it was best to go in a group of several cars. However, we made several daytime trips without mishap.

The school year began quietly. Although there was rivalry between the two institutions, ENS and the university, with rumors carried by the professors giving courses in both schools, there were no flare-ups. It is true that the university wished to incorporate ENS under its leadership, as in the Congo. The government, encouraged strongly by Maurice, had it remain a national public institution, nonsectarian, at least during the years that UNESCO was in charge of the project.

The Christmas holidays arrived. The Christmas toys did not. They arrived in June of 1968. Nor did the turkeys ordered from Nairobi arrive for Christmas. They arrived in February. They were flown in on time for Christmas; the airplane carrying them was seen and heard, since each arrival was an event, and everyone who could, enjoyed it. But the plane was not permitted to unload. So the turkeys were flown back to where they came from until the customs dispute between Burundi and Kenya was cleared up. This occurred in February, so delayed Christmas dinners were held at that time among certain foreign groups. These groups were dependent on imported meats as well as other food products not available in the local markets. (The Barundi were for the most part vegetarians, with milk and kidney beans their staples. An expert on fish was trying to introduce it into their diet.)

As soon as the festivities were over, preparations for the seminars on the teaching of French as a second language and on the teaching of science in the first cycle of the secondary school began in earnest. They were done in collaboration with the Inspection Service of the Office of Secondary

Education of the Ministry of Education and Culture. According to some statistics, only 1 percent of the population spoke fluent French, although it was introduced in the fourth year of primary school and instruction was carried on throughout the rest of the school years. More could read and write it, as it was one of the two official languages used by the government. It appeared to be a school subject to be studied, read and written, but not to be spoken.

The concentration of those who spoke French was in Bujumbura. Few spoke it outside of that city. The foreigners either learned Kirundi or resorted to interpreters. It was thought that teaching methods could be ameliorated to facilitate the learning and use of the French language. Not enough studies had been made as to how best to teach French to the Barundi, nor were all the teachers trained properly to teach it. For many of the teachers in the primary schools, either missionaries or Barundi, it was a foreign language.

The seminar held from April 4 to 6, 1968, brought together seventy-three participants, directors and inspectors of primary schools and the students of ENS. Its aim was to proceed to an exchange of views and experiences and have practical demonstrations concerning problems met with in teaching French to the Barundi. The survey had pointed out that most of the teachers of primary schools, whether missionaries or lay monitors, were non-French and used French as little as possible, so they could hardly transmit it correctly to their pupils. The missionaries, in whose hands were many of the primary schools, were given intensive six-month courses in Kirundi, so they were able to communicate in the national language. The method proposed was to begin oral French as early as the first year. Syllabi and texts, with many simple drawings, were also proposed.

Concentration on remedial work in the first cycle of secondary schools was put forward so that the student could not only speak but write in good French, as it was an indispensable tool for further studies. It was suggested that literature should be minimized if it was obvious that the oral language, grammar, and easy texts were of greater importance to a much better understanding of the French language. For this work, too, new syllabi and texts were offered. The French embassy had instituted a language laboratory to which the ENS students had access.

To all intents and purposes, Maurice felt that the seminar had been a good beginning for attacking the problem in concert. We brought back to Paris several of the papers given by the various lecturers at the meeting. He was especially impressed by the young Belgian expert and his wife and their initiatives.

The seminar on the teaching of science in the first cycle of secondary school took place at ENS on April 29 and 30. There gathered together seventy-seven participants, seventy-three of whom were directors or teachers from thirty-three secondary schools, plus four students majoring in science teaching at ENS. In 1966, the French embassy had donated several microscopes to the laboratory. Maurice had, through the UNESCO services, added other essential equipment to that already available. Therefore, simple demonstrations of practical applications of certain scientific theories could take place. The aim of the seminar was to examine ways to the better teaching of the subject "because," as Maurice said in his talk at the opening of the seminar, "of the importance of science and its technical application in economic and social development. The implications of the seminar went far beyond the limits of the immediate objectives in the national development."[2]

Diverse practical suggestions emerged for the teaching of science. It was admitted that because of the life-style of the Barundi and the little contact they had had with the world of science, they were not motivated. Moreover, their failure to really understand French prevented them from understanding much of the language of science, coupled with their having teachers who themselves either had been inadequately trained to teach or had had little practical experience and so resorted to teaching theory through textbooks. Added to these obstacles was the lack of properly equipped laboratories, even where they existed, so that it was difficult to carry out individual or group experiments. The spirit of criticism, observation, aptitude for deduction, and intellectual curiosity had not been developed for such studies.

Therefore, there was a need to arouse interest and to popularize science through magazines, movies, and clubs. It was important to reward in the form of prizes the making or inventing of any simple apparatus and to make simple equipment with locally found materials that could be copied by teachers and students. This last suggestion brought about its practical application at the seminar. Led by the science expert of ENS, the participants made several simple instruments, at low cost, out of locally bought or found components. These made the participants, the expert, and Maurice very happy. Maurice was pleased because he had always advocated this kind of

learning through doing. Not only did this application help to better understand the theory, but it also made for more manual dexterity.

Of course, certain equipment had to be bought, so there was a demonstration of a few basic laboratory instruments. Demonstrations as to upkeep
and repair were given for, in the past, what equipment had been provided
was neglected and, in the heat and the humidity, soon became unusable. This
happened in many tropical countries. One or two laboratories had been built
by the local population with the aid of the government, which supplied
building materials, and UNICEF, which supplied some of the equipment.
This had been allowed to deteriorate in several cases. There were a few
teachers who had been able to benefit from a one-month refresher course
given in Brazzaville in the Congo. Again Maurice was encouraged by the
apparent success of the seminar. The participants were enthusiastic and
expressed their satisfaction.

The next event of importance, and Maurice's last official one as acting
director of ENS and chief technical adviser in education before his definite
departure, was the granting of diplomas to the first graduates of ENS, as
teachers of the first cycle of secondary school, and the granting of certificates to the inspectors of primary schools who had taken the refresher
courses. The graduation exercises were held with pomp and ceremony in
the large, newly constructed city auditorium, filled with relatives, friends,
faculty, and government officials. The graduation was a big event. Maurice
gave a talk, as did the representative of the president of Burundi and the
minister of education and culture, to honor the first locally trained Barundi
and give out the first diplomas of ENS.

The end of Maurice's stay was taken up in orienting his UNESCO
replacement to the responsibilities of his office. We left Burundi in August.
We had enjoyed our stay in Burundi despite the drawbacks and some
inconveniences. The experience differed from what Maurice had done in
West Africa. His status here was different. The Barundi, too, were different
in their ethnic makeup and heritage.

Our stay in Burundi was a very interesting experience. The Barundi
have a different background and culture from most of the other African
peoples. Besides, the international group from the various agencies and
embassies (apart from the Russians) mingled socially, very rarely joined by
Barundi. Moreover, we were part of the group of Haitian families rendering
service to one another, the ladies of which formed a sewing group to sew
for the handicapped boys in a missionary school and a home for very young

children. (These kept us busy.) I was also able to visit several game parks and visited the spot where Stanley met Livingstone. Our two years in Burundi were very special indeed.

As to ENS, an evaluation mission from UNESCO was sent in 1971. It reported that the experts at work there were of high quality. The government had carried out its responsibilities. It was decided that the school would graduate forty teachers a year. The refresher courses for inspectors of primary schools would be stopped, as enough of them had taken refresher courses. In 1971, there were 143 students registered and 110 teachers sent in for in-service training.

Soon after this report, another came out in the newspapers, that of the massacres, first of a number of Watutsi by Bahutu, and then mass murder of Bahutu by Watutsi. It is difficult to know how many trained ENS teachers disappeared. Many hopes of the first efforts of ENS went "by the board" with this bloodletting.

This mission was to be Maurice's last as part of UNESCO staff. As early as March 1968, René Maheu, the director-general, sent Maurice a cordial letter expressing his gratitude for the competence and devotion Maurice had shown in serving UNESCO. He wished Maurice personal satisfaction in whatever he undertook to do. So ended twelve years of an enriching experience.

Notes

1. United Nations Development Program.
2. Dartigue Files, ENS/Sem.S/68 Report.

The Last Missions—the Final Years

The years 1969, 1970, and 1971 gave Maurice more opportunities for professional service. Missions of short duration were offered him. His pension rights were taken care of. He was able to continue with the UNESCO medical scheme as an associate member. He was recruited for the missions as a consultant, such as he had been instrumental in recruiting while he was at UNESCO. His experience and status were taken into consideration, so he was well remunerated.

Maurice's first such mission came about in the fall of 1969. It was for the purpose of evaluating the teaching of English and French in the teacher training colleges of West Africa that had been set up by UNESCO with Special Fund support. He was one of a mission of three. The others were a French inspector of schools in France and an American. They visited a school in each of the following countries: one in Freetown, Sierra Leone; then an ENS in Abidjan, Ivory Coast; the University College of Cape Coast, Ghana; the ENS in Bamako, Mali; and finally the ENS in Yaoundé, Cameroon.

Some of the mission's conclusions, cited in the report published in April 1970, were that these institutions had proven to be vitally useful, since all of these countries desperately needed certified secondary school teachers of languages, and that their purpose went beyond just turning out a given number of teachers in a specified time but were pilot institutions "operating as effective agents for renovating the secondary educational system."

They went on to suggest several practices for more effective management and organization in view of more effective teaching. They mentioned the need for teachers trained in linguistics and the need for greater ease in a language before entering into the study of literature with an "encyclopedic approach" in the first foreign language. The same could be applied to the second language, with a first year of intensive courses, preferably audiovisual, and daily laboratory. There was need for more training in methodology, a varied category of books for the libraries with trained librarians in attendance, better maintenance of language laboratories, research centers dealing with problems of language learning and teaching, and then evaluation of the different sectors of the projects. They suggested in-service training and refresher courses for teachers. Finally, the mission maintained that contact between these schools and other institutions, as well as with UNESCO, was vital. They thought UNESCO should have a special staff member assigned as coordinator and liaison officer.[1]

Maurice's last mission for UNESCO was to Equatorial Guinea, now Guinea Bissau, a former Spanish colony, which became independent in 1968. The dates were from June 27 to July 21, 1971. He was again one of three members. The mission was to study the actual role and potential of the UNESCO missions already there and to analyze the actual system of education (structure, program, methods). It was to make an inventory of immediate and long-term needs, especially as to training and in-service training of teachers. It was to collaborate with the proper ministers on the preparation of a request for aid from UNDP, to create a center for the development of education. Finally, it was to study a system of grants with UNICEF for further training of nationals to replace the foreign personnel of the proposed project.

Equatorial Guinea was a very poor country about the size of Haiti, ten thousand square miles. There was a great difference in population numbers, Equatorial Guinea having 300 thousand people while Haiti at the time numbered 4 million. As soon as it became independent, Equatorial Guinea requested and obtained membership in both the United Nations and UNESCO and probably in other organizations. It also demanded immediate aid. UNESCOPAS provided twenty-six foreign secondary school teachers in the first year.

Marceau Louis, a Haitian who had been in the Congo, was now in Equatorial Guinea as an expert in planning in education attached to the minister of education. He was of great help to the mission for contacts with the various officials and personalities. On its first day, the mission met with the education minister, who admitted the precarious position in which the education system found itself and expressed his thanks to UNESCO for its concrete and substantial aid. He praised the UNESCOPAS teachers and their spirit of cooperation. On the mission's second visit the project of the Educational Center and the financial implications and responsibilities of the participating partners were discussed. The minister was reassured when he learned that the funds accorded by UNDP were a gift.

The mission learned through conversations with experts that there was no economic plan and that the most elemental services had to be taught, such as the work of telephone operators and electricians. There was not one dentist in the whole country. The mission suggested a WHO-sponsored dentist and an oculist, as there would be enough work among the families of all the international agencies. The services would be paid for by them.

The mission visited several schools at which they noticed that sanitation was either nonexistent or very primitive. There were three high schools in the entire country, two of which were in the capital. The programs were outdated Spanish ones. The method of teaching was traditional, with Latin and Greek on the program. The laboratory in one school had been turned into a classroom, since the school, built for 800 students, now housed 2,300. For the most part only science theory was taught. There were too many students in each class. The teachers taught thirty hours a week or more.

At least 60 percent of the primary school teachers, Guineans, had no pedagogical qualifications and very little general cultural background. The situation of the schools was pitiful, with no material for teaching, overcrowding, and poor teaching because of lack of teachers or poor training. The major problems that the mission reported were (a) the need to adapt programs and methods to the new realities of the independent state; (b) the training of a teaching body; and (c) the preparation and production of manuals and other teaching materials. This for the primary schools.

As for the secondary schools, of the 173 teachers, 77 were foreigners; only 11 of the remaining 96 were qualified. There were 5,000 students, 30 percent of whom were girls in three schools. Eighty-five percent of the students were in the first cycle of the secondary school. This indicated many dropouts before the final years were reached. Books, what there were, came from Spain, as did the program and the subjects for the examinations as well as the correction juries. All this, the mission felt, was completely out of focus for the feeling of the Guineans as a people of an independent, autonomous nation.

Discussions were held with the UNESCOPAS teachers. The conditions stated above did not encourage them to take a determinant role in improving the program or giving support to the young Guinean teachers. They had been able to demonstrate through their methods how to ameliorate the teaching. One or two did give help for organizing better the administration of their school, especially one who, besides his teaching load of math and physics, was also director of studies. He was later proposed as director of the future Education Development Center. The UNESCOPAS teachers suggested they be given the upper secondary grades, where there were fewer students, so they could give time to program and aid for the nationals in pedagogical matters. The mission was in accord.

After discussions with the minister and others, the mission worked on the preparation for the request by the Guinean government for the UNDP project. The two financial points would have to be decided upon by the president of the country, who was in the midst of celebrating the first anniversary of independence. The mission went on in the expectation that the hesitations would be cleared away once the president understood the roles of the various parties and the little financial disbursement needed from the government. It felt that without the development center, Guinea could not hope to face the problem of cadres, teachers, programs, etc., to efface the vestiges of dependency. In conclusion, the mission stated that for the primary schools UNICEF could help by offering cars for the transport of inspectors for primary school inspection; and that with the help of secondary school teachers and qualified instructors in-service training or short courses could be held for primary teachers. Especially urgent was the improvement of the sanitation facilities.

In the report concerning secondary schools the mission stated that if more classes were to open to meet the demand, more teachers would have to be recruited or students sent back to the provinces and classes opened there. However, this was not a good solution. The experienced teachers should have fewer class hours so as to give time to aid the newly trained young teachers, make reports, and prepare work and do research. Classes were too overcrowded for good teaching. The UNESCOPAS teachers must be maintained for at least another year. The report recommended adding four more of these teachers to ensure more areas of better teaching. There was need for an expert for the technical training school to reorganize the program and the workshop in collaboration with other colleagues of that specialty.

The report concluded that if UNDP approved the project, then the acting director chosen by UNESCO should not be inferior to the thirteen experts proposed in the request and that the recruitment for such a person be begun to ensure his presence before the center opened by at least two months. It also stipulated that an international secretary was necessary for the first years. If so, the salary indicated in the project had to be upped.

So the mission in the few weeks it was in Equatorial Guinea sized up the situation and made its recommendations, not that it thought they were the best, but under the circumstances such as could be followed through. It helped prepare the proposal of the government's request for aid of UNDP for the establishment of an Educational Development Center. The actual draft was written in Dakar with the help of GRPE and Hennion. Maurice returned directly to Paris from this last mission for UNESCO.[2] (He was fortunate to have been received and aided by Marceau Louis and his wife. He came back to Paris looking very well.)

Moorhead State College

Although in 1970 no missions were forthcoming from UNESCO, Maurice and I did a teaching stint of five weeks in the summer courses being given at Moorhead State College in Moorhead, Minnesota, U.S. It came about through the visit in Paris in the spring of 1970 of a former colleague at UNESCO, H. Abraham, who had been chief of the Division of Higher Education and on retirement, had accepted a teaching post at the college. The college had received monies to recruit for the summer courses professionals with interesting backgrounds and experience. Abraham had already brought in Dr. Kim of Korea, working in UNESCO, to do a course on his way for home leave every other year. Abraham therefore thought that both we and the college would profit from our experience. Consequently, we found ourselves professors for the five weeks in this Teachers' College in June 1970.

Maurice had been in the area before as guest of the Department of the Interior for Indian Affairs, when he visited Pine Ridge, an Indian reservation, in April 1941, but he had not visited beyond the reservation. Through the kindness of the director of the Department of Education, we were taken to see the source of the Mississippi, its headwaters (a small creek starting from a small lake), the Badlands of North Dakota, and the forests. We had to spend most of our time, however, outside the classes studying, writing, or in the library to be ahead of our students, as our assignments were changed from those first given to us. Each gave two courses, he for administrators and directors of primary schools, I for primary school teachers. As the first classes were held at 7:30 A.M., it was a challenge to keep the students awake. Most were teachers and directors profiting from the facility given them to take the courses for an increase in salary, better status, and latest knowledge of educational trends and interests or "modes."

We returned to Paris, via Washington, where we were guests for the last time of the Hulsizers and where we had a reunion with several exiled Haitians and Mercer Cook.

It was in the early months of 1972 that we decided to return to Haiti for a few weeks. "Papa Doc," François Duvalier, the president since the fall of 1957, died in 1971, having at his deathbed made his son, Jean-Claude, familiarly called Baby Doc, president for life. Maurice had not been back since the winter of 1957, first because he was too busy with the work he had to do at UNESCO and later because the disturbances and the political climate were not conducive to trips there. As the months went by under the new presidency, a more normal way of living developed. People no longer feared for their lives. We reasoned that we could return to decide whether to go back definitely to resettle there.

Maurice and I picked up the strains of life there immediately and felt at home. But due to a fall and the recurrence of the malady that was later to end his life, we realized that Maurice needed better medical care than Haiti could provide. The decision was made to stay on in Paris, as we were well established there and he was more comfortable as to language, culture, and prevailing social attitudes there than in the U.S. We returned to Haiti every winter for a month or more, with a stop-off in New York to see our son and for medical and social purposes, until the last winter of Maurice's life, when travel was out of the question. We went to Spain often until 1976, as we had thought to retire there, and to Switzerland, where we had friends.

During the years between 1971 and 1983 in Paris, Maurice received the visits of Haitians and others with whom he had had contacts in his profession, mostly those going to or returning from Africa or interested in its problems. A few asked for advice or aid in procuring employment in UNESCO. For these he did what he could, going to headquarters to knock on doors and see people.

On his trips to Haiti, Maurice visited projects and listened to those who came to see him, both Haitians and foreigners. He was very careful to stay clear of specific problems, stating that he could only refer to his experience in Africa and had not followed Haitian educational matters closely since 1959 so was not in a position to give advice for current particular problems. He had become a "sage" and was treated as such, especially by some of those who had been on his staff or in education back in the 1930s and 1940s.

The question arises as to the reasons why Maurice kept the UNESCO correspondence and did not write an account of his contribution. He had also kept copies of his published reports, bulletins, surveys, etc. in Haiti.

329

Yet, neither for the one nor the other did he manifest a strong desire to write. The correspondence of his four years as minister of public instruction, agriculture, and labor came to light only in the winter of 1978. By that time he was mentally and physically too tired. He was happy to see it and watch the arranging of it in proper order but made no mention of using it for a book.

Another question arises as to whether UNESCO used to the full the capacities of this pioneer in education from a third world country, or did political considerations take precedence both at the United Nations and at UNESCO?

Maurice died quietly on July 9, 1983, after a few months' rapid decline but without real suffering. He had not written about his career. This he left for others to do.

Notes

1. Dartigue Files, ED/WS/75, Paris, April 22, 1970.
2. UNESCO Mission to Equatorial Guinea, Home Files, June 27–September 21, 1971.

Maurice Dartigue Through the Eyes of His Peers

... I wish from this circumstance to render public homage to Monsieur Maurice Dartigue who, since 1941 with patriotism and courage is bringing about to the satisfaction of our government the reforms in the domain of education that were so necessary. ...

—Speech given in October 1945 in Cape Haitian
Elie Lescot, president of Haiti

... I cannot hide my great pride in the brilliant promotion of Maurice who at this moment, is organizing public instruction in the Congo. It is neither favoritism nor powerful support which has served him. He has been served by his high competence and seriousness. It is not the promotion of a former collaborator, nor that of a dear friend that makes me so joyful. The principal reason for my joy and pride is to see designated a Haitian for this important work. ...

—Elie Lescot, former president of Haiti
March 1961, in a private letter

... During this period, Dartigue has been mainly responsible for studies relating to educational conditions in NSGTs although he also did research in labor problems. He was responsible for the drafting of the labor section in the paper on social relations submitted to the committee in 1952. He was responsible for the drafting of papers on compulsory education and education of women in NSGTs and cooperated in the preparation of some of the reports covering the other aspects of educational conditions. The educational studies were of particular importance in 1953 owing to the working programme of the committee. In addition, he was responsible for the final presentation of some of the volumes of the "Green Book." All these functions he

331

carried out with high competence. He could be depended upon for accuracy, sound judgment and resourcefulness.

—Ralphe Bunche, Under Secretary-General,
UN Trusteeship Department,
October 1953

. . . It was a great privilege and opportunity to work with Maurice Dartigue for almost four years. He was an outstanding good educator, manager, and a leader with vision. He was also a dear colleague and became a true friend. . . . He inspired the work of the Division as a born leader. Through the day-to-day work he taught me about the spirit, the goals and the working methods of UNESCO. In his amiable way he effectively exercised as nobody else I have known . . . a real teamwork spirit as another major mark of his always generous personality devoted to the ideals of international cooperation.

—Ricardo Diez Hochleitner,
Club de Rome (a think tank)

Glossary of Acronyms

AID: Agency for International Development
IBE: International Bureau of Education
BIRD: International Bank for Reconstruction and Development
BMS: Bureau of Member States
BOC: Bureau of Control
BREDA:: Regional Bureau of Educational Development in Africa
ECA: Economic Council for Africa
TAC: Technical Assistance for the Congo
ECOSOC: Economic and Social Council of the UN
EPTA: Enlarged Program for Technical Assistance
FAO: Food and Agriculture Organization
GRPE: Regional Group for Educational Planning
ICA: International Cooperation Administration
IDEP: Institute of Planning for Economic Development
IIEP: International Institute for Planning in Education
ILO: International Labor Organization
INEAC: National Institute for Agricultural Studies in Africa
IRSAC: Institute for Scientific Research in Central Africa
LAMP: Latin American Major Project
OAS: Organization of American States
OECD: Organization for Economic Cooperation and Development
OPEX: Operation for Executive Personnel
PADS: Program Activities Details
PER: Bureau of Personnel
RIO: Relations with International Organizations
SF: Special Fund
SHADA: Haitian American Society for Agricultural Development
SNPA-ER: Service National de la Production Agricole et l'Education Rurale
TA: Technical Assistance
UNCO or UNOC: UN Operations in the Congo
UNDP: UN Development Program
UNESCOPAS: UNESCO Operational Assistance
UNTA: UN Technical Assistance
WHO: World Health Organization

Bibliography

A few works and Bulletins written by Maurice Dartigue or in collaboration with others or under his guidance.

Bull. No. 1   Rapport Annuel SNPA et ER (Service National de la Production Agricole et l'Enseignement Rural—Division de l'Enseignement Rural)

Bull. No. 5   Rapport Annuel 1932–33 SNPA et ER l'Enseignement Rural

(no number)   Rapport Annuel 1933–1934   "   "

Bull. No. 8   L'Oeuvre d'Education Rural du Gouvernement du Président Vincent (1936). Imp. de l'Etat SNPA. M. Dartigue

Bull. No. 10   Rapport Annuel 1934–35 SNPA et ER l'Enseignement Rural

Bull. No. 11   "   "   1935–36 "   "   "   "

Bull. No. 13   "Conditions Rurales en Haiti." Quelques données basées en partie sur l'étude de 884 familles par M. Dartigue, 1938 Imp. de l'Etat SNPA

Bull. No. 14   "L'Enseignement en Haiti" (1804–1938) M. Dartigue 1938—SNPA

Bull. No. 15   Rapport Annuel SNPA et ER 1936–37 et 1937–38 l'Enseignement Rural

Bull. No. 17   Rapport Annuel SNPA et ER 1938–39 l'Enseignement Rural

Bull. No. 27   Rapport Annuel SNPA et ER 1939–40

Bull. No. 31   Rapport Annuel SNPA et ER 1940–41, 1941–42 Imp. de l'Etat

Bull. No. 33   Rapport Annuel SNPA et ER 1942–43, Imp. de l'Etat

Bull. No. 34   Département de l'Agriculture et de Travail SNPA et ER. Programme des Courses à l'Ecole Nat. de l'Agriculture 1944, Imp. de l'Etat

Bull. No. 36   Rapport Annuel SNPA et ER. 1943–44, Imp. de l'Etat

Dept. de l'Instruction Publique—The Decree for the Reorganization of the Urban Education Administration—General Interior Rules and Regulations 1942

Secrétaire d'Etat de l'Instruction Publique—Survey of Urban Primary School Situation 1941 Imp. de l'Etat

Departement de l'Instruction Publique—General Direction of Urban Education—The Results of the First Year of the Reform of Urban Education Sept. 1, 1941–Sept. 30, 1942 Imp. de l'Etat

Department of Public Instruction—General Direction of Urban Education, The

Results of the Second Year of the Reforms in Urban Education, 1944, Imp. de l'Etat, 1942–43

Bull. Tables and Statistical Graphics of Urban Education, Department of Public Instr. 1942–43 Imp. de l'Etat

Bull. The Preparation of Cadres by the Government of President Elie Lescot, Department of Public Instruction, Sept. 1942, Imp. de l'Etat

Bull. The Program of the Preparation of Cadres Continues. Third Bulletin on the Preparation of Cadres of Public Instruction, 1944

Bull. Summer Courses for Secondary School Teachers—1943. Department of Public Instruction—Council of the University of Haiti

Bull. No. 20—Guide for the Evaluation of Employees of SNPA and ER. 1942

Bull. No. 5—Resumé of the Report on the Situation of Commercial Instruction—Dir. Gen. of Urban Education. 1943

Department of Public Instruction Gen. Dir. of Urban Education. The Results of the Third Year of the Reform in Urban Education, 1943–44, Imp. de l'Etat 1945

Short Books

Dartigue, Maurice and Liautaud, André "Geographie Locale" Imp.—Deschamps Port-au-Prince, Haiti, 1931

Dartigue, Maurice "Les Problèmes de la Communauté." Imp. de l'Etat, Port-au-Prince, Haiti, 1930

Dartigue's Plans for Legislation for Labor and Insurance in Haiti by Taddée Poznanski, Prof. Laval U—for the Administrative Council of Social Insurance Funds, Haiti, Dept. of Labor, Imp. Henri Deschamps—The Fund Created by the Decree of May 15, 1943

Recommendations Concerning the Elaboration of Legislation for Labor by David Blelloch—BII Montreal for the Council of the State Fund of Social Insurance in Haiti, Imp. Henri Deschamps, 1944

Nota bene

Much of Maurice Dartigue's correspondence as minister in Haiti and photocopies of his short books and bulletins are in the Schomburg Research Center for Black Culture in NYC, including the French correspondence with SHADA (Société Haitiano-Américaine pour le Developpement de l'Agriculture). The English one is in the Manuscript Division of the Archives of the Library of Congress. The UNESCO correspondence is in the UNESCO archives.

United Nations—Non Self-Governing Territories

team work	Summaries of Information transmitted to the Secretary-General, Lake Success, N.Y. 1947
team work	Information transmitted to the Secretary-General for the year 1951, Vol. II, N.Y. 1952
1952	Resumés of Information transmitted for the year 1951, ST/TRI/SER.A/6/Add.1 Fev. 1952
1951-Alone	Report on the Trust Territory of Ruanda-Urundi Together with the Relevant Resolution of the Trusteeshp Coun. Official Records: 11th Session (June 3–July 24, 1952)
1952	Supplement No. 2 (T/1031) N.Y. 1952
Alone	Special Study on the Educational Situation in the Non Self-Governing Territories UN ST/TRI/SER.A/11 Analysis of the information transmitted
1956	(1954–56) 1956 VI.B.2

Sources of Information, UNESCO Archives, UNESCO before August 1960

(Unpublished)

Registry files
REG 372(8) MPOI pts I–IV Latin America Major Project

371.214 AO 22 Pts I–IV International Advisory Committee on Curriculum Revision

37(6)A64/20 Emergency Programme Africa Educational Needs

37(6)A06(?) "60" TA First meeting ministers of Education in Tropical Africa— Emergency Programme Africa

37(6)A64/20/57 Emergency Programme Africa 1959, 60 Pt I

(Published)

10th General Conference:	10C/28 1, 2 add. 10C/3

11th General
Conference: 11C/5 PRG/20, 11C/DR/40
              11C/36, 11C/PRG/14
Executive
Board
Meetings: 48EX/3 Pg 7, 48EX/5 Pg 6 (4) 48EX/9
              48EX/8 Pg 38: Apercu d'un Projet majeur relatif au developpement
              de l'éducation de Base en Afrique
              55EX/2, 55EX/2, EX/9 add I
              Report on TA
              Transfer of funds for Tr. Africa
              55EX/1 pt 4.1, 4.2
              56EX12 item 1.42, 56EX/14
              Report on Conference and Directives
              57EX/11 pg 3—Int. Coop. with newly independent countries.
              Mostly on Congo
Dottrens R. The Primary School Curr. UNESCO 1962
Pittsburg R. UNESCO in Action in ED. 1963
Thomas Jean UNESCO Gallimard 1962

Congo-Zaire Emergency Programme

United Nations, New York (Published)

General Assembly Fall 1960
October 17, 1960 D. Hammarskjöld—statement of UN operations in the Congo
  before the General Assembly
December 7, 1960 "Extract from statement on ONUC before Security Council"
UN Year Book. ONUC Education 1961
8th Edition L'ONU pour Tous—service de l'Information Questions politiques et
  de Securité. Questions Relatives à l'Afrique Le Congo. pages 200–217
UNESCO Archives
11th General Conference—Paris November 14, 1960 to December 13, 1960
  UNESCO 11 C/34 The Congo
12th General Conference—Paris November 14, 1962 to December 12, 1962 12 C/3
  Pt. II ED Reso. 1.26—Aid 17.1.2 para 104 to 122
Executive Board Sessions
57EX/22 Paris November 4, 1960, Annex I, II, III, IV,V,VI,VII,VIII.

59EX/7 Paris July 4, 1961 point 7.1.5
60EX/10 add Paris November 27, 1961
61EX/5 Paris April 16, 1961 point 4.2.2
65EX/4 Paris March 29, 1963 point 4.2.3
66EX/20 Paris August 16, 1964 point 4.2.3
67EX/4(I)Paris April 23, 1964 point 3.3.3
67EX/PX/DR/10 (II) Paris June 1, 1964
70EX/26 Paris March 25, 1965 Annex I and II point 5.2.8
71EX/4 Paris August 2, 1965 pt 3.4 annex I–IX (21 pages)
71EX/4 add Paris October 8, 1965

New York Times Archives (Ben Franklin Lib.—US Embassy, Paris) 1960: July 26,28; August 15,27,29; September 3,5,6,8,11,13,15,16,18,20,24,27,29; October 14,18,22,28; November 3,7,14,21,22,29.

1961: February 14,16; March 22; May 2,21; June 16, 21, 22. This reporting goes as events occur in the Congo.

UNESCO Press Releases—No. August 12, 1960, August 16, 1960 (2147) October 2, 1961 (1456) November 30, 1960 (2169) December 4, 1961, December 5, 1962, March 29, 1962

American Foreign Relations (Harper. Ben. Franklin Lib. Paris)

Congo 1960: July 14, 20; September 16

Congo 1961: US in World Affairs—Harper Council on Relations

(Unpublished)

Central Registry Files

37(675)A64-66 Pt I July 24, 1960 through Pt VI December 31, 1966
37(675)A64-187 Pt I and II 186
37(675)AG4/06 196 Special File on Reports many missing
37(675)A64-138, 373, 371, 101, 136
37(6)A64/20/57 Pts I and II

Reports by Chiefs of Mission (CPX/REP)

REG X 07.21 (675) 1960–77 (not open to me)

BMS/4/ Memo 85 November 13, 1961 (Just learned some will be in the Archives in a month under names of countries)

Experts CPX, BMS—Reports by Experts in the Congo among others L. Bourand, S. Chiappano, R. Hennion, A. Desenclos, R. Lemoine, M. Louis, S. Mirville, J. Deheyn, P. Perrot (many others missing)

Maurice Dartigue's Personal Files Given to UNESCO Archives which are not all in Central Registry Files

Dartigue's Home Files

UN **Archives** Park Ave. at 25th St. NYC.
DAG I/22.1 Box 63
DAG I/22.1 Box 56
DAG I/22.1 Box 25

UNESCO Archives (Unpublished)

Gen. Registry files 37 (6) (44) "62" TA (meet Paris March 23–30, 62) 37.214 (6)
    A06 (691) "62" TA (meet Tananarive 7/62 Prog. Reform Sec. Ed.) 37.(6) A06
    (666.8) "64" TA (meet Higher Ed. Tananarive 9/62)
ED 50.i/59.426 Mission Report West Africa May 11, 1959
ED 47/916/60.134 Mission Report Nigeria June 29, 1960
Registry file No. 37(6)A64/20/Pts I and II
37(6)A64(63)"60" TA (meet AA 60)
37A56/022(663)07(-6)"66"
ODG Files 4–7 Memos—Adiseshiah—Inter Office Notes
Central Registry Files
37(6) A64/20/57 Planification missions
371.214(6) A06(691) "62" TA meet Tananarive July 1962
371.124.8(689) Supply of Teachers
37(6)A06(63) "60" TA. Paris meet, 1962
37(6) (666.8) "64" Meet Tananarive Higher Ed.
371.124.8(675.571), (676.1), (675), (675.572), (667.3), (698.2)
GRPE, IDEP, IIEP Dakar, Senegal
37A56/022 (663) 07 (-6) "66"
Mission Report December 22, 1965
Burundi—Dartigue Home Files and UNESCO Records
Reports on mission 1966–67, 1967–68
Reports of Seminars held April 1968
Short Missions to West Africa Home Files
Report, mission to Five Countries
West Africa October 1–25, 1965
Report, mission to Equatorial Guinée June 27–July 21, 1971

Sources of Information on the UNESCO Emergency Programme for Tropical Africa

Unesco Archives (Published)

Executive Board Sessions—First the D.G's report
48EX/3, 49EX, Pg 7, 48EX/5 Pg 6(4), 48EX/9, 48EX/8 Pg 38: Apercu d'un projet
    majeur relatif au development de l'Education de Base en Afrique
51 EX item Doc T 1429, 1433, 1442
54EX/1 pt. 4.1, 4.2
55EX/32 D.G's Report EX/9 Add 1:TA
56EX/12—item 1.42(d), 56EX/14. budget
57EX/22 Congo, 57EX/11 Int. Coop. with newly independent countries
58EX/9 Emergency Prog for Africa, 58EX/DEC 15 Coop SF
59EX/4 59EX/5, 59EX/DEC. Prog 7.1.2, 7.1.3
60EX/8 Emergency Prog, Add I, 60EX/4, 60EX/14
61EX/4 Add 4, 61EX/5 (Congo)
62EX/4.21, 62EX/11
63EX/2, annex II and III, 63EX/5, Special Fund
64EX/2
65EX/2, 65EX/3
66EX/4, 66EX/DEC/Prog 422
General Conferences
10th session 10C/3, 10C/28 (1,2) 2811 add, Res. 8.62
11th session 11C/PRG 14, pt 7.1.1 (Report AA) 11C/52
12th session 12C/PRG 17, 12C/PRG 32
12C/3, 12C/PRG, inf/7

Meyer, Hans. *Les Barundi*. Oho Spaner Leipzig, 1916
Traduction Resumé—S.P. Chretien (Prof. Agrégé)
Zuure, Bern, Dr. "L'ame du Murundi." Gabriel Beauchesne et ses Fils MCMXXXII
    Ed. à Paris 117 rue de Rennes.
Notes et Études Documentaires No. 3364 *Le Burundi* La Doc. Francaise Sec. Gen.
    du Gouvt. 29-21 Quai Voltaire 75007 Paris
Newspapers
Le Monde. May 13, 27–29, June 3, 6, 1972
Le Soir. June 2, 5, 1972
La Croix. July 14, 15, 1972

Some Collateral Readings That Apply

Beyly, Joseph T. *Congo Crisis*. Grand Rapids, MI: Zondervan Pub. House, 1966.

Bouvier, Paule. *L'Ascension du Congo Belge à l'Independence*. Brussels: Editions Inst. de Soc. Univ. Libre de Bruxelles, 1965.

Bunche, Ralph. *UN Operations in the Congo*. New York: Columbia U. Press, 1965.

Chomée, Jules. *L'Ascension de Mobutu*. F. Maspero Cahiers Libres (Paris).

Cordier, Andrew. *The Quest for Peace*. New York: Columbia U. Press, 1965.

Cornevin Robert. *L'Intervention de l'ONU au Congo* 1960-64 Mouton (Bib Mouffetard-Contrescarpe: Rue Mouffetard, Paris).

———. 1960–64 *Histoire du Congo-Leo*. Kinshasa Berger et Lerrant 1963–1970 Paris.

CRISP *Du Congo au Zaire* 1960–1980 sous la dir. Vanderlinder: 35 rue du Congres Bruxelles.

CRISP *Congo 1959–1967* Realisé sous le Dir. Gerard Libois.

Dayal, Rajeshwar. *Mission for Hammarskjöld: The Congo Crisis*. Princeton, N.J.: Princeton U. Press, 1976.

Dinant, G. *L'ONU en Face de la Crise Congolaise*. Editions de Remargues Congolaise, 1962.

Diallo, Djeme. *Problemes de l'Ed. et de Pedagogie en Afrique Francophone.*

Ekiva, M. *Perspectives de l'Enseign. au Congo* No. 36 CADECEC No. 36 2eme tri. Kinshasa.

———. *Reforme de l'Enseign. Secondaire Leo 1961*. Ministere de l'Ed. Nationale Doc Ed/41/11, July 31, 1962.

Fehrenback, T. R. The UN. *This Kind of Peace*. New York: David McKay Inc., 1966.

Fullerton, Gary. *UNESCO 1964* "UNESCO Au Congo."

Gendebien. *L'Intervention des N.U. au Congo 1960–1964*. Mouton: Hess Press, 1967.

Hoskyno, Catharine. *The Congo Since Independence*. Oxford: Oxford U. Press, 1965.

Kimpesa, M. M. *L'Operation de l'UNESCO au Congo 1960–1964*. These de Doctorat—Fac. de Psych. et des Science de l'Ed. U. de Geneve 1983—Un Zairois.

Kita, Pierre. *Quelques Aspects de l'Inadaptation de l'Enseignment au Congo Kinshasa*. Memoire pour l'Obtention du Dip. Prat. des Hautes Etudes U. de Paris, 1972.

Langenhave, F. van *Le Congo et les Probs. de la Decolonisation*. Bruxelles, 1961.

Livamba, R. *L'Assistance Civile des N.U. au Zaire* 1971. Hautes Etudes Internationales U. de Paris.

M'Bokolo, Elikea. *La Formation de la Bourgeoisie Zairoise* 1945–1980. Centre d'Etudes Africaines U. de Paris, 1981.

Merlier, Michel. *Le Congo de la Colonisation a l'Independence.* Cahier Libres F. Maspera No. 32, 33, 1962.

Ohaegbulam, Festus. *The Congo Crisis.* Dissertation, Graduate School of Int. Studies, U. of Denver, December 1967.

Tournaire, Helene. *Le Livre Noir du Congo* Perrin. Paris: Bib. Mouffetard-Contrescarpe, 1963.

United Nations. *L'ONU au Congo—Quelques Fait Essentiels.* UN, February, 1963.

————. *The Blue Helmets—A Review of UN Peacekeeping Operations.* UN Department of Public Information, 1985.

Urquhart, Brian. *Hammarskjöld.* New York: Harper Colophon Books, 1972.

Verhaegen, Benoit. Les Dossier de CRISP. *Congo: 1961.*

Young, C. *Introd. à la Politique Congo.* CRISP, 1965.

Ziegler, Jean. *Le Contre-Revolution en Afrique.* Payot Etudes et Documents, 1963.

Zaire: A Country Study, 1978. (UNESCO Library) Area Handbook Series Foreign A.S. The Am. U. Washington DC. pages 44–55 Congo 1960–1965.

Index of Names

UN and UNESCO

346